Ch. 10 — elim quality problem
Ch. 11 ↓ cost while retain + ↑
Ch. 12 ↑ customers expectation

? Improvent toucli— check list (new guide p. 185 :)

THE IMPROVEMENT GUIDE

A Practical Approach to Enhancing Organizational Performance

Gerald J. Langley, Kevin M. Nolan,
Thomas W. Nolan, Clifford L. Norman,
and Lloyd P. Provost

JOSSEY-BASS
A Wiley Imprint
www.josseybass.com

Published by Jossey-Bass
A Wiley Imprint
989 Market Street, San Francisco, CA 94103-1741   www.josseybass.com

Jossey-Bass books and products are available through most bookstores. To contact Jossey-Bass directly call our Customer Care Department within the U.S. at 800-956-7739, outside the U.S. at 317-572-3986, or fax 317-572-4002.

Jossey-Bass also publishes its books in a variety of electronic formats. Some content that appears in print may not be available in electronic books.

Interior design by Gary Head

Library of Congress Cataloging-in-Publication Data

The improvement guide: a practical approach to enhancing organizational performance /
Langley, Gerald J. . . . [et. al.]
        p.   cm.—(The Jossey-Bass business and management series)
    Includes bibliographical references and index.
    ISBN 0-7879-0257-8
    1. Organizational effectiveness. 2. Organizational change. 3. Quality control.
I. Langley, Gerald J. II. Series: Jossey-Bass business and management series.
HD58.9.I467 1996
658.4'063—dc20   96-16014

Printed in the United States of America
FIRST EDITION
HB Printing   20 19 18 17 16 15 14

The Jossey-Bass
Business & Management Series

Contents

List of Exhibits

List of Tables

List of Figures

Preface

This book is for people who want to make improvements—or more specifically, those who realize that making effective changes in how businesses are run is a matter of survival. Change is occurring so rapidly in our society today that we have no choice but to embrace this change and make it work in our favor. We all have a choice to make: to accept passively the changes that are thrown at us, or to use our resources to create our own changes that result in improvement. This book should be viewed as a survival guide for people who realize the importance improvement plays in keeping an enterprise viable. It is our hope that the ideas and methods presented in this book will guide you in increasing the rate and effectiveness of your improvement efforts.

As statisticians involved in improvement since the early 1980s, we have seen many tools, methods, and techniques presented as the one best way to achieve results. Many of these approaches indeed have merit. The overall effect, however, has lacked integration. Results have been mixed. In this book we hope to provide a fundamental approach to improvement that promotes integrated improvement activities that deliver more substantial results in less time.

Since the dawn of the twentieth century, a science of improvement has emerged. The intellectual foundation for this science was recognized by W. Edwards Deming and articulated in his "System of Profound Knowledge." Practical, pragmatic examples of the application of this science have been seen in industries throughout the world. Dramatic results have been obtained. However, this science has been applied in only a small fraction of the circumstances in which it is applicable. The purpose of this book is to describe a system of improvement based on this science that will increase substantially the number of successful applications.

We researched this book for ten years by studying the needs of people who were attempting to make improvements in quality and productivity in many diverse settings. These settings were in the United States and abroad and included manufacturing plants (for computers, food, and pharmaceuticals), hospitals, clinics, trucking firms, construction companies, law offices, government agencies, landscape architecture and maintenance firms, schools, and industry associations. As we observed or participated in these improvement efforts, we asked ourselves what methods would help increase the effectiveness and results of these efforts.

Given this context, we eagerly absorbed, enhanced when we were able, and integrated a variety of methods and approaches. In the United States, many of these approaches were introduced with much fanfare and in a way that implied that the method replaced what had come before. For example, in the early 1980s, the emphasis was on continuous improvement of processes throughout the organization. The idea was that everyone should have a chance to improve their work. This was a positive approach. The emphasis had two weaknesses, however: major subsystems—in particular, business subsystems—were not improved in a holistic manner, and the changes that were made were relatively small and produced only incremental improvement. When reengineering (major innovation in large subsystems) was introduced, it addressed those weaknesses. However, it came to be seen as replacing the incremental approach to improving process rather than as supplementing it. Our approach integrates these ideas, and other worthwhile approaches, into a complete system.

The foundation of this system is a framework that we call the *Model for Improvement*. The model is based on three fundamental questions:

1. What are we trying to accomplish?
2. How will we know that a change is an improvement?
3. What changes can we make that will result in improvement?

The questions define the endpoint. Any effort to improve something should result in answers to these questions. The answers could be obtained in a variety of ways depending on the complexity of the situation and the inclinations of those doing the work. We designed the model to be flexible and comprehensive, because we observed some of the inhibiting aspects of the rigid, step-by-step approaches to improvement that have been in use.

Another aspect of our approach that makes this book different from others is our focus on change. Much of the book is concerned with developing, testing, and implementing changes. We recognized some time ago the fundamental relationship between improvement and change. By this we mean specific, identifiable changes, not broad or vague organizational or cultural change. The rate and extent of improvement is directly related to the nature of the changes that are developed and implemented. It is through this focus on developing substantive change that the art of improvement is combined with the science. Developing changes that by definition are new requires a creative effort.

To assist people in making changes, we have suggested a variety of methods based on the concepts contained in the resource guide at the end of the book (which includes two to four real-life examples of each concept). Examples of change concepts include smoothing the flow of work, scheduling into multiple processes rather than one, and building in consequences to foster accountability. This catalogue of change concepts and the real-life examples are a major contribution to the science and art of improvement. The list allows beginners to have at their disposal the concepts of change that would, up to this point, have been found only in the heads of some of the world's most experienced practitioners in improvement.

Structure of the Book

The book is organized into three parts and the resource guide mentioned above. Part One introduces the Model for Improvement and some of the basic skills needed to use the model. The reader need not have any prior experience with formal improvement methods to be able to read and understand the material in this section. Those with some experience in improvement methods should find these chapters a good review and will appreciate the simplicity and flexibility of the model. Although the book as a whole is aimed at people who desire to make improvements in businesses or other work settings, Part One is written in such a way that applications to other aspects of life will be evident.

Part Two of the book addresses the core of the science and art of improvement: developing, testing, and implementing changes. This section delves more deeply into the business applications of improvement and at a more advanced level than Part One.

Part Three discusses the implications for leaders of the science and art of improvement. An approach is described for leading and managing an organization using the methods described in Parts One and Two. Part Three also focuses on the business applications of improvement. Change is organized using three categories of improvement: eliminating quality problems, reducing costs while maintaining or improving quality, and expanding the expectations of customers with new products and services.

As discussed, the resource guide contains a rich collection of ideas for improvement and examples of their application. To develop the resource guide, we reviewed hundreds of improvements in which we were involved or with which we were familiar. For each improvement, we identified the specific change and the basic concept behind the change. For example, a hospital organized services around the needs of patients. By combining on the same unit patients who had similar needs, they were able to locate on the unit the most frequently used diagnostic testing facilities. This eliminated the work and delays associated with transporting the patient to a central testing area. The change was organizing patients and equipment by health care needs. The more general concept underlying the change was to "move steps in the process closer together."

To make the book more readable, we chose not to break up the text with footnotes or reference indicators. Instead, the source notes are placed in a single location at the back of the book, and page numbers are provided to indicate to what pages of the text each note applies. In addition, we often include explanations to help place the reference material in context.

How to Read the Book

A relative novice to formal improvement methods could improve his or her abilities to make effective changes by a combination of reading and application of the methods. The reader could start with Part One and begin applying the model to some aspect of work or personal life. Another approach would be to read Part One and some parts of the resource guide to gather some ideas about the types of changes that others have found useful. As the reader's skill increases or encounters particular problems, he or she may want to read specific sections of Parts Two or Three.

The more experienced reader could quickly read Part One as a review and as an introduction to the Model for Improvement, which provides the framework for the methods discussed in the book. Even readers experienced in improvement will find in Part Two new ideas and approaches to making improvements. Those skilled in improvement will no doubt find in the resource guide many of the ideas that they have applied in their efforts to make improvements. Nevertheless, we believe that they will be intrigued by the comprehensive list of change concepts and examples. We hope that this collection will motivate readers to add to the list and customize it to their own industries or professions.

Leaders in organizations are advised to read Parts One and Two and then Chapter Thirteen to understand how the science and art of improvement can best be used to benefit an entire organization. The remaining chapters of Part Three will provide leaders with three approaches to improvement that can be used to focus the improvement efforts in the organization.

Throughout the book we have attempted to include substantive content that describes the essence of what improvement is about and how to accomplish it. We have also strived to make the reading pleasant and interesting by including many stories and examples to illustrate the concepts. So, we hope that a substantial portion of people will read the entire book.

This book is intended primarily for use in business situations. In Parts Two and Three, the examples and stories used to illustrate the methods are mainly from the world of business. However, the examples in Part One are a mixture of both business and individual experience. They show the breadth of possible application of the methods.

Acknowledgments

Many people have helped us with this work or inspired new ideas. We wish to acknowledge our friend and colleague Ronald Moen for his significant contributions to the Model for Improvement. Noriaki Kano first introduced us to the ideas that led to the three categories of improvement covered in Chapters Ten, Eleven, and Twelve. Edward DeBono's work on methods for creativity provoked some new ideas that eventually led to the list of change concepts. We were also influenced by Brian Joiner's book *Fourth Generation Management* to use stories and examples to convey substantive concepts and methods.

Our clients have shown the applicability of the ideas and methods described in this book. They are the ones who kept us grounded, who helped us take a pragmatic approach to improvement. Their willingness to test new methods contributed greatly to the material in this book. They learned and we learned. In addition, the following reviewers of the manuscript provided us with many ideas for improving the book: Ross Carn, Jed Doyle, Paddy Meskell, A. Keith Smith, and Ed Sweeney.

Ultimately, it was W. Edwards Deming who ten years ago inspired us to write this book and then gave us the theoretical foundation for it with his development of the System of Profound Knowledge. To him we owe our deepest debt and to his memory we dedicate this book.

Finally, we heartily express our appreciation to our families for their sacrifices that allowed us time to do our research and to write the many drafts of the book.

May 1996

Gerald J. Langley
Cameron Park, California

Kevin Nolan
Silver Spring, Maryland

Thomas Nolan
Silver Spring, Maryland

Clifford Norman
Austin, Texas

Lloyd Provost
Austin, Texas

The Authors

Gerald J. Langley is a statistician and consultant to a variety of industries in the methods of improvement. He earned his B.S. degree (1973) in mathematics at the University of Texas at Austin, and his M.S. degree (1975) in statistics at North Carolina State University. He became a principle of Associates in Process Improvement (API) in 1985. Before joining API, he worked at Hewlett Packard Corporation as a statistician and manager.

Langley's main focus in both his consulting work and his research is helping organizations make improvements more rapidly and effectively. His expertise with data and computers plays a key role in this work. He has published articles on sampling and survey design, modeling, and fundamental improvement methods.

Langley has been the keynote speaker at numerous conferences and seminars, where his talks have ranged from technical applications in statistics to the more general area of accelerating improvement. He has also contributed his time to the improvement efforts of several educational organizations, both at the state level and with individual schools.

Kevin M. Nolan is a statistician and consultant with Associates in Process Improvement. He earned his B.S. degree (1970) in mechanical engineering from the Catholic University of America, and his M.S. degrees in measurement (1979) and statistics (1989), both from the University of Maryland.

Over the past ten years, Nolan has focused on developing methods and assisting organizations to accelerate their rate of improvement in quality and productivity. He has worked with manufacturing, service, and healthcare organizations. A requested speaker at numerous conferences and seminars, he has also published several articles on improvement.

Thomas W. Nolan is a statistician, author, and consultant. He earned his B.A. degree (1969) in mathematics from Catholic University and his Ph.D. degree (1986) in statistics from George Washington University. He cofounded Associates in Process Improvement in 1984. Before founding API he worked at Radian Corporation and the U.S. Department of Agriculture.

He has assisted organizations in improving quality and productivity in many different industries including healthcare, manufacturing, trucking, and professional services in the United States, Canada, and Europe. Among his clients is a recent winner of the prestigious Malcolm Baldridge National Quality Award. He is the coauthor of a book on statistical methods for improvement, *Improving Quality Through Planned Experimentation* (1991). His recent interests include the use of multi-organization collaboration for improvement, and he is currently chairing a collaborative project with twenty-three healthcare organizations to significantly reduce delays in their systems. Nolan is frequently requested to deliver keynote addresses and write articles on the science of improvement and its implications for leaders.

Clifford L. Norman has a B.S. degree (1975) in police science and business administration from California State University at Los Angeles. He has more than fifteen years of experience in manufacturing and quality with Norris Industries, McDonnell Douglas, and Halliburton. He has extensive experience in implementing the quality process since 1979. In 1989, Norman joined Associates in Process Improvement after working as a consultant and developing statistical process control products and consulting services for Philip Crosby Associates. He has spent the last ten years consulting with domestic and international clients in a variety of industries. Norman's work focuses on top management's involvement in leading the change process to integrate improvement into their business strategy. He is also a Certified Quality Engineer and a member of the American Society of Quality Control.

Lloyd P. Provost has a B.S. degree (1970) in statistics from the University of Tennessee and an M.S. degree (1976) in statistics from the University of Florida. He is a cofounder of Associates in Process Improvement. Provost has consulted with clients worldwide in a variety of industries. His consulting experience includes planning, management systems, planned experimentation, measurement, data analysis, and other methods for improvement. He is coauthor of *Improving Quality Through Planned Experimentation* (1991), and has authored several papers relating to quality and measurement.

The Science and Art of Improvement

Due to the interest that a growing number of children were showing in Little League baseball, a group of parents started a league for children eight to ten years old. A dilemma arose when in the first set of organized games no one got any hits—not one. Parents exhorted the children to try harder, to keep their eye on the ball, or to throw the ball over the plate, but to no avail. Most of the youngsters could not pitch the ball successfully from the mound to home plate. Most often the ball hit the dirt before it got to the plate. However, two teams had players who were big for their age and could pitch quite well. None of the batters could hit their powerful pitches. What to do?

Someone suggested moving the pitching mound closer to home plate. This did indeed help some of the smaller pitchers get the ball to the plate, and some hits did occur. The two teams with the strong pitchers, however, were now unbeatable. Their pitches now came so fast that the coaches were concerned about safety and considered banning players over a certain height and weight.

Another suggestion was to set up the ball on a stand directly over home plate. This did help. The players now had more hits. But many kids complained that without pitching, it was not really baseball. The organizing parents felt at a loss to find a solution that would be viewed as successful by everyone.

Finally, one of the mothers who knew very little about baseball asked the question, "Why can't an adult do the pitching?" Some were shocked at this suggestion. Before she could explain, objections and counterarguments came in a steady flow. "You cannot have anyone but team players on the field!" "The adult might be pulling for one team or the other and intentionally or unintentionally pitch too fast to the opposing team." "We could get an umpire to decide if the adult was pitching fairly."

Finally, the mother who had made the suggestions was able to continue. "Let the coach of the team that is up to bat pitch." The coach would have an incentive to pitch as easily as possible to the players so that they would have the best chance to get a hit. In addition, the coach would not need an umpire to call balls and strikes. Each child was given three swings or six pitches, whichever came first. The nonbatting team would still have a player fielding hits from the pitcher's mound.

Although many of the parents were still skeptical, two teams conducted a test at a practice game the next week. Everyone saw the logic in the change. The adult pitcher knew what an appropriate pitch was for each child's age and could physically produce the pitch almost every time. The children had a lot of fun playing baseball, and so did a few of the parents.

How can you make changes that will lead you in a new direction? In this case, the change desired was in a baseball game, so the eight- to ten-year-old kids could get hits. The science of improvement is actually based on making informed and intelligent change. All improvement will require change, but not all change will result in improvement. A primary aim of the science of improvement is to increase the chance that a change will actually result in sustained improvement from the viewpoint of those affected by the change. Because of the central role of change in improvement, it is useful to contemplate what is meant by change and how it comes about.

People use the word "change" all the time, but it can mean many different things. We change our clothes. We change a tire on our car when we have a flat and the oil in the engine when it is dirty. We change the light bulb after it burns out. All of these changes are really reactions to things wearing out or breaking, reactions to problems. It is important to react to special situations when they happen, but this is not usually a source of improvement.

The baseball story illustrates some common reactions to problems. The parents' first reaction was to simply *exhort the children to do better.* They hoped for improvement without real change. Somehow, the situation would just get better on its own. One can easily imagine the undesirable consequences had they continued this behavior. Bad situations left unchanged usually do not stay the same; they get worse.

The first change—moving the pitching mound closer to the batter in order to help the unskilled pitchers—resulted in an unwanted side effect: the good pitchers were even more overpowering than they had been. The reaction was to *consider passing a restrictive rule* (players who were too big would not be allowed to play). The change was thus an improvement for some but a loss for others. The change failed to account for the diversity of those affected by the change.

When it was suggested that an adult do the pitching, concerns of fairness were expressed. To take care of the flaws in the change, *a check or inspection* was suggested: let the umpire decide if the adult was being fair.

Despite these reactions, an idea was finally developed and tested that resulted in a very successful and fun baseball season. The characteristics of this development illustrate some of the more useful ways of making improvements:

- The change was innovative; it *fundamentally changed the system for the better.* It did not adversely affect any other part of the game.

- The idea was *tested first on a small scale* at a practice game to increase the degree of belief among the participants that the change would be an improvement.

- The change *did not require undue restrictions* on who could play, nor did it add any requirements for an umpire (inspector or regulator) to keep the game fair.

- The system was *self-regulating* in that the coach had an incentive to pitch in a way that enabled his players to hit the ball easily; it did not add additional complexity to the game.

This book is primarily concerned with improvements in business and other work settings, not leisure activities such as baseball. The objective embraced by many organizations can be stated succinctly: *make changes that result in improvement from the viewpoint of the customer.* In nonbusiness settings, "customer" could be replaced with "beneficiary," "organization's purpose," "family," or "individual." What is so difficult about accomplishing this objective? Why the need for this book, and others about improvement? Some of the difficulties that arise in putting this objective into practice include:

- *Taking the time to meet the objective*—time that may currently be devoted to carrying out the day-to-day business and solving pressing problems.

- *Thinking of a change that anyone would predict would be an improvement.* When trying to develop a change, people often have difficulty imagining how tasks could be done or results be accomplished differently from the way things are currently done.

- *Overcoming resistance to change.* Even when an innovative change is suggested and shows promise, it is difficult to get others to try the change and adapt themselves to the new situation.

- *Recognizing when a change is an improvement.* The goal of this book is not change for the sake of change. The goal is improvement. No matter how long you ponder a change and plan for its implementation, you cannot be absolutely sure that improvement will result. Changes must be tested, preferably on a small scale, and even well-designed tests do not guarantee certainty.

- *Satisfying diverse or changing viewpoints.* Different customers may have varying viewpoints about what constitutes an improvement. Customers are free to change their minds whenever they choose. What is desirable today may be undesirable tomorrow because of advances in competitors' products or services.

The reader could no doubt add to this list, and despair at the thought of trying to make significant progress. While these difficulties are real, they can be overcome. Helping people surmount these difficulties is a primary focus of the science and art of improvement.

Why Take the Initiative?

Why should you bother with making changes? Why not simply deal with problems as they arise and try to maintain the status quo? The theme of this book is making changes that (1) would not have happened unless someone had taken the initiative, and (2) will have a significant long-term positive impact. Change is happening all around us, in all aspects of our lives. Information is moving faster than ever. The skills needed to earn a living are rapidly changing. Many of the concerns that were important in our lives and businesses ten years ago have been replaced with new concerns. What are our choices, in light of all this change?

In business, there is only one choice: change faster and more effectively than your competitors, or you are gone. As the American automobile industry found out in the seventies and eighties, being the biggest on the block does not ensure success. Japanese auto manufacturers developed better cars more quickly than Detroit thought possible. The "big three" U.S. automakers (Ford, Chrysler, and General Motors) had to learn how to make improvements. They are still learning.

Diane had worked for the state government's department of education for ten years. She was comfortable with her job of managing the records for school district certification. One day she was told that the department was going to switch to a paperless record system within two months. Other departments had been experimenting with the change for several years and the decision had been made to implement the paperless system in all departments. She had heard from Justin, a friend who worked at the department of motor vehicles, about the difficulty of learning the new computer systems. She was worried.

Ultimately, the answer to the question "Why change?" is "You do not have any choice." Change is going to happen. The choice you have is to let the change happen to you—to react—or to be more proactive—to decide to make a change in some aspect of your business, your community, or your private life. Once you have made this decision, the methods and skills described in this book will help make your efforts more successful.

Successful change is enjoyable. This book presents a framework and a simple yet powerful set of methods for making tangible changes that result in improvement. Once methods are learned and practice has shown results, it is hard to go back to a more passive approach to change. Purposefully setting out to make an improvement and then seeing it happen and produce the results you hoped for is extremely rewarding. You may find that you want to get others involved, and you may wonder at their apparent resistance. Have patience with them. Teach them the science and art of improvement.

The Science of Improvement

What we mean when we use the term "science" in the phrase "the science of improvement" is *knowledge of general truths or the operation of general laws, especially that obtained and tested through the scientific method*. Obviously, to create improvement you need knowledge relevant to the particular problem at hand. This may be knowledge of medicine, of law, of engineering, of finance, or simply of how things are currently done. The science of improvement is concerned with how knowledge of specific subject matter is applied in diverse situations. How are improvements made in hospitals, in grocery stores, in manufacturing plants, in insurance companies, in churches, or in communities? Is each application so specific that only specialized knowledge and expertise can be useful?

W. Edwards Deming made an important contribution to the science of improvement by recognizing the elements of knowledge that underpin improvements over a wide spectrum of applications. He gave this body of knowledge the foreboding name "a System of Profound Knowledge." "Profound" denotes the deep insight that this knowledge provided into how to make changes that will result in improvement in a variety of settings. "System" denotes the emphasis on the *interaction* of the components rather than on the components themselves. According to Deming, these components are appreciation of a system, understanding of variation, theory of knowledge, and psychology.

Appreciation of a system. Because most important products, services, or outcomes result from a complex system of interaction among people, procedures, and equipment, it is vital to understand the properties of such systems. Appreciation of a system helps us to understand the interdependencies and interrelationships among all components of a system and thus increases the accuracy of our predictions about the impact of changes throughout the system.

Understanding of variation. Systems constantly exhibit variation. We are forced to make decisions in our lives based on our interpretation of this variation. Is my child's school improving? Does this month's change in sales mean we are losing market share? Do the two medication errors this month in our hospital indicate an undesirable trend? Was the improved performance this week the result of the change we made or just luck? The ability to answer these questions and others like them is inseparable from making improvements.

Theory of knowledge. In the context of improvement, a change is a prediction—if the change is made, improvement will result. This prediction is made and a plan must be developed from it, even though no one can foretell the future. The more knowledge one has about how the particular system under consideration functions or could function, the better the prediction and the greater the likelihood that the change will result in improvement. Comparing the predictions to the results is a key source of learning. Skillfully building knowledge by making changes and observing or measuring the results is the foundation of the science of improvement.

Psychology. Knowledge of psychology helps us to understand people, how they interact with each other and with a system. It helps us to predict how people will react to a specific change, why they resist change, and how to overcome this resistance. People are different from one another; they have different preferences, aspirations, motivations, and learning styles. Most changes that are aimed at improvement will have to recognize these differences and account for them.

Each of these four components has a rich intellectual history and great contributors. However, any one component on its own will not provide the depth of insight necessary for building a true science of improvement. The focus on the interaction of the components as a system of knowledge is one of Deming's lasting contributions.

At this point the reader may be concerned that being skillful at improvement means studying these four areas in depth. Some people may desire to do so, but it is not necessary. The methods described in this book are based on this system of knowledge. However, one can use the methods without knowing the theory behind them, just as one can drive a car without knowing how or why it moves. According to Deming, "One need not be eminent in any part of profound knowledge in order to understand it and to apply it."

Some practical, pragmatic approaches to the improvement of quality and productivity that rely heavily on the elements of knowledge in Deming's framework have been developed in Japanese and American industry and in other countries throughout the world. Kauro Ishikawa, Joseph Juran, and Deming have been instrumental in documenting these approaches since the 1950s.

The theory underlying the science of improvement is interesting in itself. But improvement comes from action: from *developing, testing,* and *implementing* changes. These basic components of improvement are dealt with in detail in this book. A brief introduction to the issues that will be addressed is provided here.

Developing a Change

Some common approaches to developing changes that are well-intentioned but misguided include making changes only in response to problems, developing changes that are "more of the same," and trying to develop the perfect change. The old saying, "If it ain't broke, don't fix it," is not a recipe for improvement. In a dynamic world, making changes only in reaction to problems leads to decline. To counteract or take advantage of forces in the market or changes in society, individuals and organizations must continually look for different and better ways to accomplish their goals. Organizations that are averse to change are often slow to recognize a problem, and may not recognize it until it is too late. Their inclination to avoid change, and their lack of practice in making real change, can cause them to deny the need for change even as a crisis approaches.

Many people who are unskilled in improvement react to the need for change by advocating "more of the same": more people, more time, more money, or more equipment. If crime increases, build more prisons. If sales decline, spend more on advertising. If profits decrease, work longer hours. If test scores decline, lengthen the school year. While recognizing that increased effort or time may be appropriate in some situations, "more of the same" is very limited as a long term strategy for improvement.

An inhibitor of *real* change is the search for the *perfect* change. It is believed that continued analysis and debate will eventually find it. The job will then be to implement the perfect change with a sufficiently well-thought-out plan. Since unanticipated side effects are always possible and objections to any change can usually be articulated, the search for perfection can continue endlessly. One result of this approach is an attempt to make very broad changes by relying on planning rather than on testing the proposed changes. Another possible result is a reduction in the magnitude of the change because of fear of unanticipated side effects. It appears that large organizations, both private and public, are particularly susceptible to this pitfall.

Alternatives exist to these three approaches to developing changes. This book emphasizes the development of changes that fundamentally alter the system to achieve better performance. The changes can be developed in one of two ways: (1) by examining the current system using, pictures, flow diagrams, or data, and based on learning and common understanding, identifying possible changes to aspects of the current system—in other words, by redesigning an existing system; or (2) by inventing a new idea, without recourse to the way things are presently done—that is, by designing a new system. Obviously, technology may play a part. Both of these approaches to developing change are discussed extensively in this book.

Testing a Change

One reason for advocating "If it ain't broke, don't fix it" is that changes can make matters worse. What sounds like an improvement in the conference room may turn out in practice not to be an improvement. Systems often have delays built into them, so a change may even appear to be an improvement at first but result in serious negative consequences some time later.

The approach to improvement described in this book is based on trial and learning. Develop a change, find a way to test it on a small scale to minimize risks, and observe how the system reacts to the change over time. The change may be fine as is, or it may need to be modified or discarded. Whatever the outcome, something will be learned and the next test or trial will be better informed than the previous one. The pursuit of improvement relies on cycles of learning.

For some people, testing a change implies a large exhaustive study of the type that might be conducted in a research and development facility or at a university. While such large experiments certainly are one means of testing a change, this book will usually refer to less sophisticated approaches. In many organizations, changes and decisions are made without any reflection on the result. Our objective is to improve that situation. We provide methods for people to make a change on a small scale and to study the result of that change using data acquired in the course of their daily work. The data may be as unsophisticated as collecting subjective impressions of people affected by the change at a meeting a month after the test has begun.

Some people fear that emphasizing testing will slow progress and provide people with a means to resist change. If a test fails—that is, if it is determined that the change will not result in improvement—people should learn from it and develop the next change from a higher level of knowledge. Testing is not meant to facilitate a decision about whether to keep the current system as it is, but rather to promote continuous change and improvement in the system.

Implementing a Change

It is not enough simply to show in a test that a change is an improvement. The change must be fully integrated into the system. This takes some planning, and usually some additional learning. It is easy at this stage to assume that implementation is simply a matter of planning and careful execution of the physical change itself.

People who were not part of developing the change must accept it and help to sustain it. A balance must be struck between dictating the change and delaying progress until a full consensus has been reached. Some people will resist any change. It is difficult to know whether the objections are reasonable and the specific change must be adjusted or whether the objections are emotional and the process of change must be addressed.

This book supplies some methods to help with implementing changes so that they are sustainable. The methods will address both the physical and emotional aspects of change.

The Art of Improvement

More than two hundred years ago, German poet and dramatist Goethe suggested that humans are possessed of two spirits, the logical and the artistic. It is only in the second half of the twentieth century that the physical explanation for this duality of human thinking has been documented. It has been found that the two halves of the brain are different in the types of thinking activities that each supports. The left half of the brain is the source of logical processing. It provides us with the abilities to count, to construct and use grammar, and to form logical conclusions. It provides us with our languages; the very text you are reading is being processed by the left half of your brain. The right half of the brain has been shown to be the source of the ability to see the big picture, to recognize a piece of music from one or two notes, to write and enjoy poetry, and to visualize new ideas. The right half has been referred to as the artistic side of the brain.

The science of improvement, as outlined earlier in this chapter, is based on a logical approach to improvement. However, for improvement to be most effective, both aspects of the brain must be tapped. The art of improvement is a vital part of being successful at improvement. As mentioned earlier, improvement implies change. Change implies a newness, a creative aspect. The right half of the brain is where these kinds of strengths live.

The question, then, is how can people purposefully activate the artistic, creative (right) side of the brain? Although everyone is familiar with the obvious, traditional forms of art, such as music, poetry, painting, and so on, the creative methods presented in this book are more focused on generating new ideas for change. For example, one of the many methods described in Chapter Five is "challenging the boundaries" within which a change must be made. The method directs the user to simply list a number of the boundaries influencing their improvement effort, and then to challenge them by asking, "What if that boundary was not a boundary?" This illogical process of saying a boundary is not a boundary blocks the left (logical) half of the brain and allows the creative (right) half to dominate. When this is done, new ideas for change are often generated.

Ultimately, it is not that one of the two approaches (science or art) is more important than the other in improvement efforts. It is the integration of the two skills, the use of the whole brain, that leads to continuous, rapid, substantive improvement. The three modes of thinking described in Chapter Five and the methods for utilizing them provide some guidance for this integration. Chapter Twelve also explores methods for provoking the artistic, creative side of people. Finally, the change concepts in the resource guide at the end of the book provide a direct method for integrating the logical and creative sides of thinking.

Conclusion

As this introduction has shown, changes that have a significant long-term positive impact occur only if someone takes the initiative. Someone has to stand up and say, "Lets make this better." But there are risks involved any time a change is made. Things could get worse. The rest of this book expands and provides the details of the science and art of improvement. It describes the emerging methodology previously introduced, which guides improvement efforts in such a way as to lower the risk and improve the results.

INTRODUCTION TO IMPROVEMENT

The chapters in this section introduce the Model for Improvement (Chapter One) and some of the basic skills needed to use the model (Chapter Two). The model provides a framework that is easy to employ and that can be applied in many diverse situations; examples of such applications are provided in Chapter Three.

The reader need not have any prior experience with formal improvement methods to be able to read and understand this part of the book. Those readers who have some experience with improvement methods should find Part One to be a good review and will appreciate the simplicity and flexibility of the model. While the methods presented in the book are aimed at readers who desire to make improvements in business settings, applications to other aspects of life are evident in this section and are certainly encouraged by the authors.

CHAPTER 1

A Model for Improvement

Most people at one time or another have thought about trying to do something better. It might have been at home or at work, in recreation or business, for friends or customers. Thinking about doing something better is often easy—actually making a change usually is not. What is the best way to approach trying to make a change that results in improvement?

Throughout history, people have used trial and error as an approach to improvement. This approach is often defined as making a change and then seeing if anyone complains, or if something stops working because of the change. The trial-and-error approach, which can be carried out with various degrees of sophistication, has sometimes been criticized as jumping to solutions without sufficient study both before and after the trial. In response to this criticism, some people have turned to extensive study of the problem before a change or trial is attempted. This approach can lead to paralysis. Focusing on the key principles of change and improvement should allow us to take advantage of the best of these two approaches. The three questions introduced in the following section provide a framework for this balance. Use of these questions will allow people to turn their thoughts about improvement into successful actions.

Fundamental Questions for Achieving Improvement

Improvement comes from the application of knowledge—of medicine, engineering, teaching, driving a truck, or simply the way some activity is currently done. Generally, the more complete the appropriate knowledge, the better the improvements will be when the knowledge is applied to making changes. Any approach to improvement, therefore, must be based on building and applying knowledge. This view leads to a set of fundamental questions, the answers to which form the basis of improvement:

- What are we trying to accomplish?

- How will we know that a change is an improvement?

- What changes can we make that will result in improvement?

For ease of reference, these three questions will at times be referred to as the first, second, and third improvement questions. In practice, the questions can be answered in any order.

These questions provide a framework for a "trial-and-learning" approach. The word "trial" suggests that a change is going to be tested. The term "learning" implies that criteria have been identified that will be used to study and learn from the trial. Focusing on the questions accelerates the building of knowledge by emphasizing a framework for learning, the use of data, and the design of effective tests or trials. This approach stresses learning by testing changes on a small scale rather than by studying the problem before any changes are attempted.

Although the chapters in Part One focus on using these questions to guide improvement efforts, it is worth pointing out that many people have also found these questions useful in performing their day-to-day work. For example, managers often give their employees assignments that are not clearly defined. The manager assumes that the employee understands the aim and the expected results. Giving or receiving assignments by providing answers or partial answers to the three questions would improve managerial processes.

The following example will help clarify the application of the three questions.

The Parkside diner has been in business at the same location for ten years. During this period the diner has built a reputation for good food and service. Recently, however, customers have been complaining that they are spending more than one third of their lunch break waiting to order and get their food. Since the diner thrives on customers who have only thirty to forty-five minutes to eat, both its reputation and business would suffer if something was not done.

The owners of the diner decided to do something about the long lines that were occurring every day. Their answer to the first improvement question—*What are we trying to accomplish?*—was that they wanted to make changes in how they prepared for and ran their lunch business so that their customers would receive better service.

The key idea in answering the first question is to provide an aim for the improvement effort that will guide and keep the effort focused. The use of data, especially data related to what customers think is important, is often useful to make sure the aim is focused in the right area. A common pitfall is to spend too much time trying to get the perfect answer. A good rule of thumb is to keep the answer short and concise.

After discussions with their employees, several important facts came to light:

- Customers were waiting in line for up to fifteen minutes.
- Tables usually were available.
- Many of their customers were regulars.
- People taking the orders and preparing the food were getting in one another's way.

To measure the improvement that might result from any change they made, they decided to collect data during lunch on:

- The number of customers in line
- The number of empty tables
- The time it takes each customer to get served

Criteria or measures need to be identified to answer the second improvement question: *How will we know that a change is an improvement?* If they made a change and these measures got better over time, they would then conclude that the change led to improvement. The effectiveness of the effort to improve depends in part on the ability to measure these criteria. Having data available for determining the impact of the changes will enhance the learning. Both the owners and the employees of the diner will be able to sustain improvements through common understanding.

The diner's owners and employees spent some time one afternoon attempting to answer the third improvement question—*What changes can we make that will result in improvement?*—specifically, what changes could they could make that would improve the service to their customers at lunchtime. They developed changes that they believed would have an impact on the criteria they had come up with earlier. Some of the changes suggested were:

- Change the menu
- Move to a new location
- Change the layout of serving, dining, and food preparation areas
- Have regular customers phone in their orders ahead of time
- Add another cash register
- Have regular customers fax in their orders ahead of time

Once the list of possible changes had been developed, the owners of the diner needed to develop a plan to test a change. The plan included collecting information on customers waiting in line, the number of tables available, and how long it takes a customer to get served.

Testing is done to evaluate the impact of a change and to learn about different alternatives. The goal is to increase the ability to predict the impact that one or more changes would have if they were implemented. The plan for the test should cover who will do what, when, and where.

The PDSA Cycle

Testing a change is not always easy. Things may happen that were not planned. The change may not impact the measures. There may be unwanted side effects. To help people develop tests and implement changes, we suggest the use of the PDSA (Plan, Do, Study, Act) Cycle as the framework for an efficient trial-and-learning methodology (see Figure 1.1). The cycle begins with a plan and ends with action based on the learning gained from the Plan, Do, and Study phases of the cycle.

The use of the word "study" in the third phase of the cycle emphasizes that the purpose of this phase is to build new knowledge. It is not enough to determine that a change resulted in improvement during a particular test. As you build your knowledge, you will need to be able to predict whether a change will result in improvement under the different conditions you will face in the future.

Using the PDSA Cycle

The owners of the diner decided to test a change but to limit their change to one that would cost less than $500. The following discussion shows what they accomplished within each phase of the cycle.

The Plan Phase The owners predicted that changes that would allow them to prepare orders ahead of time would reduce waiting during lunchtime. The changes that they settled on were:

- Provide a way for customers to fax their orders in ahead of time (rent a fax machine for one month).
- Construct a preparation table for fax orders in the kitchen, where there was ample room.
- Devote one of the two cash registers to handling faxed orders.

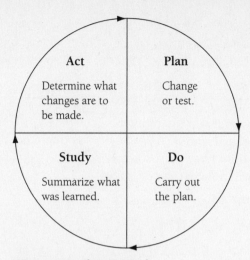

Figure 1.1. *The PDSA Cycle.*

Since it would take a few weeks to get the phone line and the fax machine and to inform customers of the new way to place orders, the owners decided to use this time to collect data on the important measures. Both the length of the line and the number of empty tables would be measured every fifteen minutes during the lunch hour by one of the owners. In addition, when the fifteen-minute line check was done, the owner would note the last person in line and measure the time until that person got served.

The Do Phase The data collection was continued for three weeks after the change was made. Some problems with keeping track of the recorded numbers were eliminated once a form to record the data was created and put on a clipboard by the front cash register.

The Study Phase Several improvements were detected. Time spent waiting in line went from fourteen minutes before the change to an average of five minutes after the change. To visualize the impact of the change, they plotted the time spent waiting in line before and after the change (see Figure 1.2). The line length was cut to a peak average of twelve people. The number of empty tables decreased slightly.

The Act Phase After a meeting with all employees to discuss the results of the test, the owners decided to:

- Purchase the fax machine they had rented.
- Prepare phone orders at the preparation table constructed in the kitchen for the faxed orders.
- Use both cash registers to handle walk-in and faxed orders.

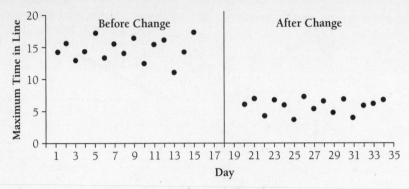

Figure 1.2. *Plot of Time in Line Before and After Change.*

The owners of the diner could use additional cycles to refine or monitor the above changes or to test other changes. This approach is in contrast to using one cycle to attempt to accomplish everything. The use of multiple cycles for sequential testing and implementation reduces risk as the change process progresses from hunches, theories, and ideas to actual changes that result in improvement. The concept of multiple cycles is depicted in Figure 1.3. Remember, not every idea for change will result in improvement. Try to test changes on a small scale whenever possible in order to minimize the negative consequences of a failed test. The owners of the diner realized that much can be learned from testing a change on a small scale, regardless of whether the change results in improvement.

Implementing the Changes

The owners of the diner used a second cycle to implement the changes that were successful during the first test. Implementing a change means incorporating it into the day-to-day activities of a process or service or into the next version of a product. If attention is not paid to implementation, the improvements that were seen when the change was tested can dissipate over time.

The Plan Phase To make the fax ordering part of the day-to-day operations of the diner, the owners decided to document the faxed-order process and then train all their employees in it. In addition to the owners, two employees were trained on the use and maintenance of the fax machine. The owners also decided to continue monitoring the three types of data: time in line, number of empty tables, and number of people in line. They felt, however, that monitoring once a day during the peak rush hour (beginning at

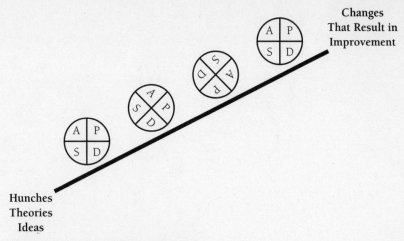

Figure 1.3. *Use of Multiple PDSA Cycles.*

11:45 A.M.) would provide them with enough information to insure that the improvement was holding. In addition, they wanted to track the number of faxes they received each day.

The Do Phase It took the owners longer than they had planned to document the order faxing process and to get everyone trained. Also, they found that about one day per week they failed to collect their data. The purchased fax machine had no problems. The number of faxes received each day increased steadily for about four weeks and then leveled off.

The Study Phase The improvements to customer service continued. The faxed orders increased to about one third of all orders. All of the employees became comfortable with the process of handling faxed orders.

The Act Phase The owners concluded that the implementation was successful. They decided to keep monitoring the three customer service measures.

The Model for Improvement

Combined, the three questions and the PDSA Cycle form the basis of the Model for Improvement (see Figure 1.4). The model is an improvement framework that is both widely applicable and easy to learn and use.

The diner example demonstrated the application of the model. The focus on

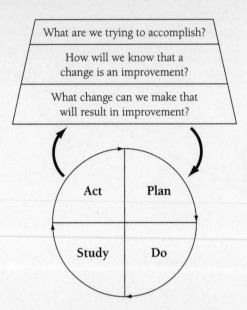

Figure 1.4. *The Model for Improvement.*

the three questions and the cycle allows for the application of the model to be as simple or as sophisticated as necessary. Efforts may differ based on the complexity of the product or process to be improved; in terms of whether the effort is focused on a new design or on a redesign; based on the depth of knowledge possessed by those people closest to the process or product; or because of the number of people involved in the improvement effort.

Because of these differences, application of the improvement model will vary in terms of the formality of the approach. A more formal approach might increase the amount of documentation of the process, the complexity of the tools used, the amount of time spent, the amount of measurement, the amount of group interaction, and so on. Figure 1.5 shows eight different improvement activities on a scale of the formality of approach that may be required. They range from an individual improving a hobby to a national effort to redesign a national system such as Medicare. Part Two of this book (Chapters Four through Eight) discusses how the application of the model can accommodate these diverse activities.

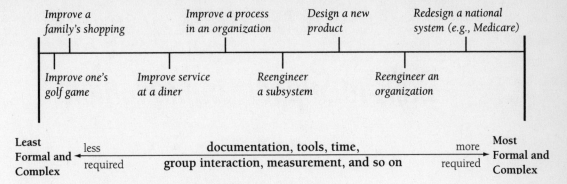

Figure 1.5. *Scale of Formality of Approach for Improvement Efforts.*

Conclusion

Improvement comes from the application of knowledge. This chapter has introduced the Model for Improvement, which provides a framework for individuals and groups to gain and apply knowledge to the improvement of a wide variety of endeavors. The next chapter discusses five areas of knowledge that will increase the ability to make changes that result in improvement.

CHAPTER 2

Skills to Support Improvement

Many people would like to increase their effectiveness and efficiency in making changes that result in improvements. They can do this by becoming more skilled at answering, or helping others to answer, the three fundamental questions for improvement introduced in Chapter One. In addition to increasing their knowledge of the activity or thing they want to improve, what should people be learning to help themselves become more skillful at answering these questions and making improvements?

People have found that after becoming comfortable with the basic form of the Model for Improvement, a study of the following five areas expands their ability to make improvements:

1. *Using data:* What is it? Why do we use it? How do we use it to learn? What information is contained in the patterns of variation in data? Where does variation come from? How can we use this information to guide actions for improvement?
2. *Developing a change:* What is change? Where do ideas for change come from? What should one consider when trying to develop change aimed at a long-term positive impact? How will the change affect other people and areas?
3. *Testing a change:* Can we be sure that the change we have developed will result in improvement? How can we test the change? Will the test allow us to predict improvement once the change has been implemented?
4. *Implementing a change:* It is not enough to know that a change would be an improvement. What are the barriers to making a change permanent? What is the role of the PDSA Cycle in implementation? How can resistance to a change be reduced?
5. *Working with people:* How do we obtain the cooperation necessary to make and sustain improvements? How do people manage change? What motivates people to make improvements?

Using Data

To make effective changes we have to be observant. We have to look around our world and notice what is happening before the change and what is different after the change. The use of data plays an important role in moving from the trial-and-error approach described at the beginning of Chapter One to a trial-and-learning approach. The collection and analysis of data are important when a cycle is needed to answer any of the three fundamental questions in the Model for Improvement, and they are important any time a cycle is used to test or implement a change.

Observation is an important source of learning while trying to improve. There are, however, some weaknesses associated with relying only on observation. Our minds filter observations. Often we observe only what we want or expect to observe. Also, our present observations are affected by our past observations, especially those in the immediate past. For example, a temperature of fifty degrees Fahrenheit will feel warm if the previous week's temperatures were in the twenties, and quite cold if the temperatures were in the eighties. The use of data helps overcome these and other weaknesses of using observation alone.

When the word "data" is mentioned, most people immediately begin to think about computers, engineering, statistics, and other highly technical disciplines. If you take a minute, however, to think about activities that you are regularly involved in, you will see that the collection and use of data are common to everyone. For example, in most sporting activities (such as bowling and golf), the collection of data is quite extensive. Each of these activities has its own special data collection form (a score card) that is recognized and used by hundreds of thousands of people. Our children bring us data on how their education is going (report cards and test scores). Our banks send us data on our financial status. Some people track the gas mileage of their cars, or their weight. And most people keep data on income and expenses, which they in turn summarize and give to the Internal Revenue Service.

Data may be defined as the documentation of an observation or a measurement. Examples of data include a video recording of your daughter's basketball game, an entry in a personal journal, the numbers written in the register of your checkbook, a record of how much you weigh each Monday, or a log of the gas mileage of your car. How many times have you written a shopping list, a check, or used a credit card? You were involved in the creation and collection of data.

The Power of Data

When data are collected, something happens: the act of collecting data can cause change to occur. If you want to reduce the occurrence of a problem, such as the number of interruptions you experience or the amount of time it takes to

Things that went wrong	How many times
Interruption	XXX
Computer lockup	XXXXXXXXXXX
Did not know answer	XX
Entered wrong data	XXXX
Deleted record too soon	X
Phone disconnected	XXXXXXX
Angry customer	XX

Note: Computer lockup happens while trying to access other files.

Figure 2.1. *Data Collected to Help Employees Understand Problems with New Job.*

respond to a phone call, just start to measure or record observations. This action alone may trigger the desired reductions. The act of measurement itself can often move things toward the results you want.

Focusing on data can also help you begin to recognize when useful information is being generated and when it is not. For example, when a supervisor at the state's department of motor vehicles asked a relatively new employee how his job was going, the employee replied, "Fine." When the supervisor asked him about his workload, he replied, "Fine." When she asked him if he was getting used to the computer system, he said it was going (you guessed it) "fine." The supervisor wanted to know whether the employee wanted or needed help in any aspect of his job, but the response she got from him provided her with no useful information. She decided to help the employee collect some data.

Together they constructed a form to collect and display the data. The chart shown in Figure 2.1 is the result of one week of data collection. It is easy to see that the chart gave the employee a way to discern problems that occurred while he was doing his job. Both the employee and supervisor could see that the computer system was causing the employee many problems. Being able to distinguish "accessing other files" from other computer activities allowed them to know where improvement was needed.

Learning from Data

In the diner example in Chapter One, the owners collected data on the amount of time that customers had to wait in line during the lunch rush hour. To understand the impact of the change they had made, they plotted the data over time (see Figure 1.2). Another example is the use of data collection to help a child improve his or her study habits.

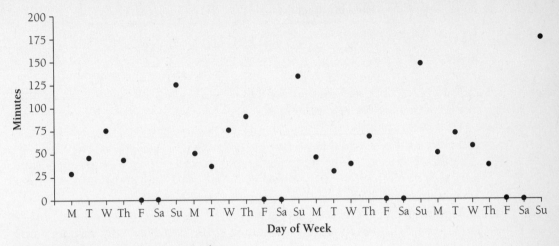

Figure 2.2. *Minutes per Day Spent Studying.*

Sharyn recorded the time she spent on homework each day for a month. She could see from a chart of her time spent studying that the reason she always complained on Sunday night about all the homework she had to do was that she did no studying on Friday and Saturday. Sharyn decided to find an hour to study on Friday (right after school) or early Saturday morning. After making this change, Sharyn no longer had to spend two hours or more studying on Sunday night.

Figure 2.2 shows the data that Sharyn collected. Plotting data over time maximizes the learning from any data you collect and allows the information to unfold as it happens and eventually display a pattern. It is hoped that the pattern will show improvement, as Figure 1.2 does for the diner, or an opportunity for improvement, as Figure 2.2 does for Sharyn.

Data can also be collected on what people think and how they feel about something. You could ask people to simply respond to a simple question, such as "Is this format for the newsletter easier to read than the normal one?" It is also very easy to have people rank things. You could give them each a list of items and ask them to place a one beside the item they think is most important, a two beside the next most important item, and so on. You could also ask people to rate a new procedure or piece of equipment on its ease of use according to the following scale: poor, fair, good, very good, excellent. These methods can be used to measure people's reactions to changes.

Understanding Variation in Data

There is variation in all aspects of life. Household expenses, stress level, weight, time spent traveling to work, and a car's gas mileage will vary over time. There are also variations among people. The ability to perform a task, intelligence, method of learning, and perception of quality all vary from person to person, as well as over time for each individual.

There is variation among institutions. Profit margins vary from company to company in the same industry, and from quarter to quarter for an individual company. Test scores differ for students in different schools. Community crime rates vary from month to month. Success rates for the same operation vary from hospital to hospital and over time for individual hospitals.

People are constantly having to make decisions based in part on their interpretations of the variation they encounter. Is it time to have the car tuned up? Is my child's school work improving? Is crime increasing in my community? In the early twentieth century, Walter Shewhart developed the concept that variation should be viewed in one of two ways: either as variation that indicates something has changed or as random variation that is similar to variation that has occurred in the past and does not indicate that a change has occurred. Decisions should be based on the nature of the variation.

Bill had been on his new diet for two weeks, but the scale said he weighed two more pounds than he had the day before. Bill knew it would take a while to lose weight, but he didn't think he should be gaining weight. He decided to give up on his diet.

Figure 2.3 is a chart on which Bill's weight, taken every morning for one month is plotted. Notice that although the weights vary, their variation appears to be predictable within a range of 164 to 168. Although Bill was not yet losing weight, the chart indicates that he was not gaining weight either. If Bill had used such a chart, he might have decided to stick to his diet.

A key idea behind Shewhart's concepts is that one should not react automatically to each observation. Data should be plotted over time. This approach allows one to observe the patterns in the data and understand when a change has occurred.

The administrators of the hospital were worried. The total number of patient beds being used was down. Some of the administrators said it had been going down for a while, others thought the drop was more recent. But the real arguments started when they discussed why it was down and what they were going to do about it. Would it continue to go down? They decided to plot patient bed use for the previous five years (see Figure

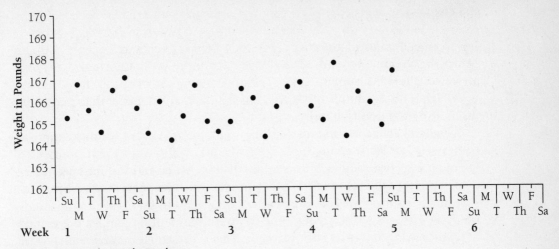

Figure 2.3. *Daily Weight Readings.*

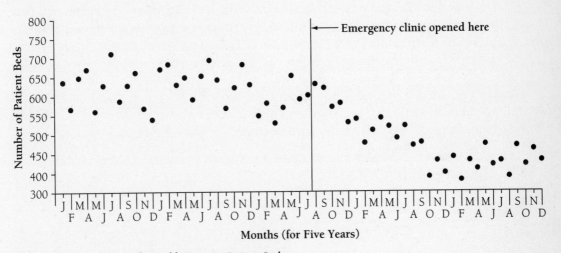

Figure 2.4. *Five Years of Monthly Data on Patient Beds.*

2.4). The variation revealed on the chart indicated that the biggest drop had occurred two years before, at about the time that a group of local physicians had started an emergency clinic.

The hospital administrators were able to determine when a change occurred by viewing the patterns in the data over time. If data are available from both before and after a planned change, a plot of data over time can be used to see if the change caused the level of improvement that was predicted. In the diner example in Chapter One, for example, the amount of time customers spent in line averaged fourteen minutes and varied between ten and eighteen minutes before the changes were introduced (see Figure 1.2). After the change, the variation was altered. The new average was five minutes and the new high and low were eight and two minutes. This increased the owners' belief that using a fax machine would lead to improvement.

Shewhart's concept of variation is important for answering the third improvement question: What changes can we make that will result in improvement? If the common, everyday variation in the data is disturbed by some specific circumstance, as shown in Figure 2.4, improvements can be developed by understanding what these special causes are. If the variation that is seen is all simply random within a predictable range, more fundamental changes are usually needed to bring about an improvement. This is the situation now faced by the owners of the diner.

Often, plotting the data over time is enough to pinpoint when the variation is no longer following a predictable pattern. The chart may show an isolated observation or two that are outside the normal variation, or it might show a new trend. The data plotted in Figure 2.5 were taken by a young man who was trying to learn to deal with his asthma. The readings were made to test for lung capacity using a Wright Peak Flow Meter. The man took readings twice a day for ten days and then one reading per day thereafter. On the thirty-first reading, it was obvious that his lung capacity was reduced. He started his medication on that day. Collecting and plotting the data helped this young man reduce the frequency and severity of his asthma attacks by allowing him to react quickly to special circumstances.

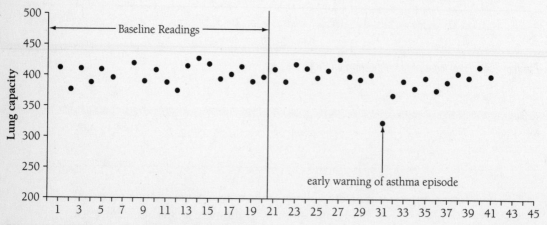

Figure 2.5. *Data on Asthma Patient's Lung Capacity.*

Developing a Change

When confronted with the need for change, the first response is usually to attempt a previously tried change. More of the same (more money, more people, more checking-up and inspection, more equipment, more rules, and so on) is a common response. The improvement, if any, that results from this type of response usually is costly and does not last long. Another problem response is to get all tied up in trying to define the perfect change. This approach usually leads to nothing being done. People become so busy developing the perfect change that they do not have time to develop and test some good ones.

In the diner example, the change chosen—using the fax machine to take orders—was outside the normal way of doing things. The owners could have responded to their need to improve by hiring more employees and/or by moving to a larger location. This would have cost more than the change they came up with, and it may very well have hurt rather than helped the service to their customers.

What we have found is that most change that results in long-term effective improvement comes from one of the following sources:

- An understanding of processes and systems of work

- Creative thinking (looking for a change outside the normal approach)

- The appropriate use of new or existing technology

We discuss here the first two approaches to change; all three approaches will be presented in more depth in Chapter Five.

Understanding Processes and Systems of Work

A law firm was concerned that many of the new talented lawyers that they hired each year did not perform up to their potential. Some of these new lawyers even left the firm in the first year or two. After interviewing a variety of young attorneys at the firm as well as some who had left, it became apparent that the orientation of new lawyers to the firm was haphazard and chaotic. Everyone interviewed related some horrible anecdotes. It was obvious to the partners who did the interviews that the firm did not have a standard way to bring new lawyers into the firm. They decided that they needed to design a process of orientation and stick to it regardless of the time pressures they were under.

A basic understanding of systems provides a new way to look at the world. Systems are everywhere—in our families, our neighborhoods, and our workplaces.

One of the first ideas to grasp about systems is the concept that all work is a *process*. Driving to work, cutting the lawn, paying bills, and shopping for food are all processes that everyone performs in daily life. The concept of a process provides a structure for making improvements in any situation.

A process is a set of causes and conditions that repeatedly come together in a series of steps to transfer inputs into outcomes. By thinking about daily activities (work, play, tasks, and so on) as processes, we gain a perspective for making improvements. All processes have inputs, all processes have steps, all processes have outcomes. Inputs, steps, and outcomes provide tangible elements that can be measured, on which data can be collected, and around which changes can be developed and tested. For an individual or organization that is just beginning to develop skills of improvement, creating standard processes to replace chaotic activity is an important source of improvement. An example of a process is obtaining a blood analysis for a patient at a hospital, illustrated in Figure 2.6.

As people advance in their skills at making improvements, they realize that bigger improvements can be made by putting processes in the context of the *system* in which it is embedded. Then, changes to the bigger system can be developed. A system is an interdependent group of items, people, or processes with a common purpose. Driving to work is a process. Getting a family out of bed, fed, dressed, and transported to work and school is a system. The process of obtaining a blood analysis for a patient, is part of the bigger system of providing health care for a patient in a hospital.

To develop effective changes, people need to understand the nature of the relationships among the processes that make up the activity they are trying to improve. In a system, not only the parts but the relationships among the parts become opportunities for improvement. These relationships or interdependen-

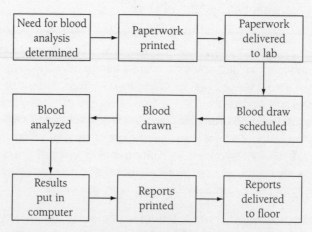

Figure 2.6. *The Process for Obtaining a Blood Analysis.*

cies can prevent the results of various improvement efforts from joining together in a straightforward way. In a system, everything affects everything else. Someone may make a change in his or her area that results in improvement there, but the same change could harm the overall system. From the customer's viewpoint, things could be worse than before.

An interesting example of thinking about systems is the debate over the minimum wage. Most people support the common purpose of improving the pay of people at the lowest end of the wage scale. Some advocate increasing the minimum wage to be paid to anyone holding a job. Others argue that such an increase would actually hurt a large number of people because companies would eliminate jobs rather than pay the higher wage.

When fundamental changes are developed, the purpose, structure, and interdependencies within the system must be considered. An appreciation of the interdependencies within a system also verifies the need to test changes on a small scale.

Creative Thinking

A group of nurses and physicians wanted to reduce the time and cost associated with patients recovering from hip replacement surgery. They were asked to consider doing some of the hip replacement steps in a different order. The team first listed and then rearranged the steps in the current process. This led to developing a change to begin some of the rehabilitation before the operation (prehabilitation). The result was improvement in many aspects of the hip replacement process. The surgery itself went better because the patient's body was in better shape (due to the prehabilitation therapy). Consequently, the patients recovered quicker, saving them both time and agony.

Before the idea of changing the order of steps in the hip replacement process was introduced to the nurses and physicians, they had assumed the order was fixed. They assumed that rehabilitation always comes *after* surgery. The challenge to those who want to develop changes that result in improvement is to think outside the normal pattern.

Where do people find new thought patterns? Where do new ideas come from? There is more than one approach to developing new ideas, but we have found the following methods to be useful in a wide variety of situations:

1. *Challenge the boundaries.* People can be limited in their thinking by the boundaries they impose in a particular situation. To challenge these boundaries, begin by listing the boundaries within which a change must occur. Many times the boundaries define the current system or how people view it. Real changes to the system are often outside of the original constraints. Once the boundaries are

listed, think about how they can be expanded or even eliminated. Sometimes this method leads to ideas that need to be further explored before they can become useful or be discarded. Other times, testable ideas for change are the direct result.

During a discussion among the employees and the owners of the diner, someone said that one boundary was that the person taking the orders had to match the speed of the people preparing the orders. When this boundary was challenged, people started to think of other ways that orders could be taken. The idea of a faxed order evolved from that discussion.

---

2. *Rearrange the order of the steps.* List the activities involved in the process or system in order and then move them around. Seeing the steps in a different order—for example, rearranging the steps in the hip replacement process—can provoke ideas for change that the regular order prevents. This idea is really a subset of the first idea since the order in which things are done is a boundary. It is worth mentioning separately, however, because it is so simple to do and often produces significant improvement.

3. *Look for ways to smooth the flow of activities.* Fluctuations in flow cause a ripple effect in all other aspects of the system. When the flow is smoothed out, things can get done in a more predictable way. For example, the owners of the diner could have looked for ways to smooth the flow of customers. Perhaps they could have enticed some customers to an early lunch at a special price. Late lunchers could have been given free tea or soda with their meal. The result would have been more customers spread out more evenly across the lunch period.

4. *Evaluate the purpose.* Challenge why you are doing something. Take a close, hard look at the reason behind the activities on which you are focusing. This approach often produces ideas for change such as eliminating steps that are not vital to the purpose. Often, when people have been involved in an activity for a long time, steps and material have been added to the process or system that were perhaps needed at one time but are no longer necessary.

A woman was teaching her daughter to cook a pot roast. She taught her to cut off the ends of the roast before putting it in the pot and cooking it. The young girl, not knowing any better, questioned her mother as to the reason for cutting the ends off. The mother answered that it allows the cooking to draw out the flavor of the roast better. But the young girl's question started her wondering about the real reason. She eventually called up her ninety-three-year-old grandmother to ask about the source of this family tradition. The grandmother explained that back when she was young they owned only one small pot and they always had to cut off the ends of the roast to make it fit.

5. *Visualize the ideal.* Describing aspects of the situation in an ideal state can generate new ideas for change. The phrase "Wouldn't it be nice if . . . " is an example of a visualization that can start the formation of ideas.

An organization was experiencing long delays in responding to the many requests for its brochures. The requests could arrive through many different departments, and each department would generate forms documenting the requests. The forms were then passed around (or buried in someone's in-basket) before reaching the distribution center. A team formed to improve the process asked themselves, "Wouldn't it be nice if no forms were needed?" This question helped them to focus on the use of the computer networking system to allow anyone to forward requests for brochures directly to distribution without the need for any paperwork.

6. *Remove "the current way of doing things" as an option.* New ideas for change are needed if the current system is not an alternative. Begin by understanding the current system. Then declare that part or all of the current way of doing things can no longer be used. Let people explore the possible alternatives.

Everyone believed that George kept the place running. Each morning, George would get the manufacturing schedule and go from station to station to make sure everything was in place to accomplish the day's goals. If a packaging line was down, George would rearrange the schedule to keep everybody busy. It was hectic, but it seemed to work—except when George was sick, taking one of his five weeks of vacation, or just in a bad mood. Efforts by the plant manager to get the production department to improve the scheduling process had met with opposition. People were afraid to disrupt this fragile situation. So, the plant manager announced that starting in three weeks George would no longer be involved in scheduling. People immediately began to develop a new way of scheduling that required increased cooperation among the planning, production, and quality assurance departments.

When ideas for change are being developed, it is important that everyone involved put forth a creative effort. Time should be devoted to thinking of changes that are not the standard solution.

Mark was very frustrated about the way the meeting was going. He wanted to reach agreement on some ideas for change that could be used to improve responsiveness in a critical area. He had even tried some new creativity methods that had been suggested to him. However, every time an idea was suggested, Kathy would offer some reason why it would not work. Then John would become highly emotional and express some strong feelings about the impact of the change. At least Lisa was attempting to be optimistic about the different ideas, but it still did not seem that any progress was being made.

Mark was experiencing the many different ways that people think. The people on a team devoted to developing changes should understand that there will be time to express critical and emotional thinking once the ideas for change are further developed. The development of change is explored in great depth in Chapters Five, Ten, Eleven, and Twelve.

Testing a Change

How many times have we all been involved with a change that turned out to make things worse instead of better? How can we avoid this kind of catastrophe if we are busy making changes with the hope of improvement? Once a change has been developed, the answer to the question *What changes can we make that will result in improvement?* should be further explored by testing the change. Testing is a way of putting the change into effect on a temporary basis and learning about its potential impact. Testing helps to predict whether a change will be an improvement. The PDSA Cycle provides the framework for testing a change.

The idea of testing a change does not seem to come naturally. People tend to want to solve all their problems with one change, and they try to implement the whole change with one plan. Being successful at testing changes requires a very different approach. A test should be designed so that as little time, money, and risk as possible are invested while at the same time almost as much is learned from the test as would be learned from a full-scale implementation of the change.

Janet needed to find out how the parents of her students would react to a change that required the parents to help out at the school for a certain amount of time each month. Many of the teachers and the administrator wanted to write a letter to the parents simply informing them of the new requirements. Janet convinced them to first test the change instead. One parent from each grade was invited to attend a meeting at which the school's plan would be presented. The parents felt uncomfortable with the required aspects of the plan, but they had many good ideas for generating parent involvement with the school. Some of these ideas were tested and successfully implemented in later cycles.

Testing a change often makes people nervous about the results. Sometimes the results of the test turn out opposite from what was predicted, but the learning that comes from the test is significant. Unfortunately, many see this result as a failure. Those people who are good at testing changes consider it a normal occurrence to have the results of a test be different from what was predicted. The success of a test lies in what is learned from it, no matter how it turns out. The focus is on the learning, and on the belief that the learning will eventually lead to a successful change.

When a change is tested with multiple PDSA Cycles, and as each cycle brings the change a little closer to being a permanent part of how things are done, the ability to predict the results of the test gets better. When it becomes possible to predict the results, it is time to consider making the change permanent. As was pointed out in the sections on data and variation, plotting data over time is extremely helpful in predicting how things will turn out.

Another factor to consider when testing a change is that circumstances will be different in the future. In other words, even though the test worked well, it is possible that next month the change may not work.

Ryan wanted to speed up his process of delivering newspapers every morning. He decided to test the idea of reversing the order of his deliveries. Even though this meant starting at the farthest point from his house, it made it possible for him to pick up more papers from a central location as he needed them. He did this for a week. The results were that it took him twenty fewer minutes each day. Two weeks later, when the rainy season started, he saw the flaw in his change. His new route did not provide him with a way to keep his central supply of papers protected from the wind and rain.

The key principles for testing a change are:

- Keep your tests as small-scale as you can and rely on multiple cycles to achieve your overall aim.

The owners of the diner rented a fax machine for one month to test their change. After the one-month test showed improvement, they bought the machine. Subsequent cycles at the diner were used to refine and monitor the use of fax ordering and to test other changes, such as phone orders, deliveries, and so on.

- Include conditions in your test that will affect your change in the future, and collect data over time to measure the impact of your change under differing conditions.

It was by collecting data on the amount of time customers spent waiting in line that the owners of the diner were able to see the improvement that resulted from their change, despite varying conditions. Continued monitoring of the impact of fax ordering in future cycles will allow the owners of the diner to learn about the impact of other conditions. They should use their knowledge of the lunch business to predict how the use of the fax ordering system might change from summer to winter, or how the rainy season might impact the number of fax orders.

A large body of knowledge is available on planning and performing tests. It is not necessary to run sophisticated experiments to test changes. However, using the principles described earlier will speed up the rate of improvement. Chapter Six explores in greater depth the concepts and methods for testing a change.

Implementing a Change

Because of a change in the county tax laws, the clerks in the tax processor's office were given a new way to verify tax status and to calculate changes in taxes owed. Six months after telling the clerks about the new procedure, Bernie, the supervisor, discovered that about one third of the tax bills being processed were being verified and calculated using the old method. Why had this happened? What could Bernie have done six months earlier to prevent the clerks from slipping back to the old procedure?

Implementing a change means making it a permanent part of how things are done. Implementation differs from testing in several important ways. First, testing a change is not permanent. There is no need to create a support structure (training, documentation, standardization, and so on) for the change beyond the testing period. To implement a change, support processes have to be implemented at the same time. Second, while the results of a change that is being tested are uncertain, it is wise to implement only a change that you are very sure will result in improvement. Third, since a test is usually conducted on a small scale, fewer people will be involved in the test than in the implementation of the change. This means that the resistance to the change will likely be much larger with the implementation than with the test. Successful implementation requires activities to address and minimize the resistance.

Depending on the situation, change can be implemented in a number of ways. In very simple cases, it is just a matter of doing it. Implementation could be as simple as following a flow diagram for a new process. Nevertheless, the PDSA Cycle should be used to study the impact of even apparently simple changes to ensure that the predicted results are achieved. The effect of the change on the people involved should also be considered. The implementation cycle helps to ensure that the predicted results are achieved and the change is irreversible.

If the change is not simple, it can be implemented parallel with the present way of doing things to lower the risk. The implementation can also be accomplished in phases, which will require multiple PDSA Cycles.

After developing and testing a change that you are convinced will result in improvement, you of course want the other people affected by the change to accept it. The reaction of other people to the change can range from total commitment to open hostility (strong resistance). The following guidelines help to reduce resistance to change:

- Begin by letting people know why a change is needed. This should be done as soon as the aim question—*What are we trying to accomplish?*—has been answered.

- Continue to inform everyone who will be affected by the change of the progress being made during the development and testing of the change.

- Give specific information on how the change will affect people.

- Get input from others on how to make the implementation successful.

Once improvements have been implemented, consistent ways of doing the work usually need to be created. This could involve establishing standard ways of performing work activities, training, documentation, and measurement to ensure that the change becomes the normal way things are done. Some change in the system is usually required to ensure that the change is maintained and the desired improvement realized. Many people make improvements only to discover later that things have somehow returned to the old level or that some new problem has been created. More detailed methods for insuring the success of implementation are presented in Chapter Seven.

Working with People

A team of physicians, nurses, and staff of a large multispecialty clinic had developed a system to drastically reduce the amount of time that physicians were behind schedule in seeing patients in the office. They had tested the system in one area of the clinic and verified that it worked. They spread the word around the clinic about the new system. One month later they were discouraged that the system had not been adopted by any part of the clinic except the one involved in the original test.

People play an important role in almost all improvements. Most improvement efforts involve an informal or formal team of people. Therefore, basic skills of listening, resolving conflicts, and running effective meetings are necessary. Simple things, like having an agenda for any meeting that might be necessary, can speed the improvement effort and result in more effective changes. The three improvement questions and the PDSA Cycle provide a very useful structure for running any meeting, formal or informal. Using a common approach to improvement, such as the Model for Improvement presented in Chapter One (see Figure 1.4), is very beneficial to any group of people who are working together in an improvement effort. Using the model is a skill, and like any skill the more a group of people use it together, the better they get at using it. Using a common approach develops a shared language and understanding that speeds up the whole process.

Developing a better understanding of differences in people and how they are motivated will greatly increase your ability to cooperate with them to develop and implement effective changes. The importance of skills for relating to people can be better understood by considering the three fundamental questions. The questions are focused on making a change. Most changes require people to do something different. The success of a change often depends on the decisions and support of all the people involved.

In some cases, a person or group of people will need to take a loss or give up some control as part of the change. People must be willing to cooperate for the benefit of the customer or the organization as a whole. A group of people exhibit cooperation when they work together toward a common purpose. An organization that focuses on the customer rather than inward on itself will more easily be able to agree on a common purpose. The Model for Improvement stresses the need for this common purpose through the question, *What are we trying to accomplish?* Different parts of the organization may be trying to accomplish different things, however, so not everyone will be as interested in your improvement effort as you are.

Successful implementation of change is greatly enhanced by the realization that different people have different concerns when faced with developing a change. These concerns can be elicited and recognized by including multiple measures when answering the question, *How will we know that a change is an improvement?* Including a measure that relates to people's concerns and interests allows people to be more cooperative and creative in answering the question, *What changes can we make that will result in improvement?*

Psychology provides understanding about what makes people resist or accept change. Two things that can cause people to embrace change are discomfort with the current situation and/or an exciting picture of a possible better way. Just as important, psychology provides ways to reduce people's fear of actually making changes. One way is to remind people that they can test changes on a small scale. It is often psychologically difficult for people to develop fundamental changes because of the risk involved. Testing changes on a small scale minimizes risk and thereby helps alleviate people's fears. (Chapters Seven and Thirteen address in detail the people issues that arise when making improvements.)

Conclusion

This chapter has introduced five skills that will enhance the effectiveness of anyone interested in applying the Model for Improvement: using data, developing a change, testing a change, implementing a change, and working with people. Each of these skills is expanded upon in Parts Two and Three of this book.

Examples of Improvement Efforts

This chapter presents five examples of the use of the Model for Improvement. The skills and areas of knowledge discussed in Chapter Two are illustrated in varying degrees in the examples. These stories are not meant to portray "perfect" applications of the methods presented in Chapters One and Two; rather, they are meant to convey realistic first attempts to use them. The first, third, and fourth examples are from business settings, the second example describes a personal improvement, and the fifth example narrates a teacher's effort to improve a biology class.

Example 1: Improving the Morning Meeting

The owner of a construction company was frustrated by the difficulties experienced by the managers and site supervisors at their daily morning meeting. The owner would start the meeting by asking if there were issues and problems that needed to be addressed. Also discussed at the meeting was the scheduling of materials and labor for the company's various projects, as well as other topics.

There never seemed to be enough time to discuss all the important issues. Often, arguments would occur and tempers would flare. When this happened, the rest of the meeting would be devoted to resolving the issue and smoothing ruffled feathers. The meetings would often run past the scheduled one and a half hours. The company had almost doubled its business in the previous year, but the frustrating morning meetings were beginning to visibly hurt the quality of the company's work.

The owner introduced the idea of improving their morning meetings to his management team. He asked the three improvement questions and obtained the following answers:

1. *What are we trying to accomplish?* Everyone agreed to investigate ways to make their daily meeting shorter and more effective.

2. *How will we know that a change is an improvement?* They picked the length of time of each meeting and the number of items or topics covered as measures of improvement.
3. *What changes can we make that will result in improvement?* A group of attendees at the morning meeting brainstormed a list of changes that they thought would result in improvement:

> Have fewer people at the meetings
> Meet less often
> Make and use an agenda
> Give assignments to prepare for the meeting
> Quit having the meetings
> Limit the meeting time for each issue
> Make decisions by voting
> End the meeting at 8:00, no matter what
> Have the owner be more of a dictator during the meeting
> Keep notes of the meeting
> Limit the issues to critical ones (with minor issues to be worked out in smaller groups)

The owner was originally upset by several of the ideas for change. He felt that a few of them might be destructive. Then he realized that he could use the suggestion "quit having the meetings" as provocation to himself and others to start thinking about improvement.

In a conversation with the purchasing manager after work that day, the owner suddenly saw a path to follow. The purchasing manager was talking about the process for ordering all their construction materials and equipment. He was describing changes that the purchasing staff had made to their process. The owner realized that there was no process for preparing and running the daily management meeting. They just let things happen as they might. Compared to the process of ordering materials, their meetings were chaos. The owner wondered why the activities for ordering materials should be so clear and understood while the way a critical meeting was run was such a mess. He saw that many of the ideas suggested to improve the meeting could fit together to form a standard process.

Cycle 1

Plan. The owner and two of his managers spent a Saturday morning designing a management meeting process. They incorporated several of the change ideas into the process, including setting an agenda, having fewer meetings (Monday, Wednesday, and Friday), making assignments before the meeting, submitting topics the day before the meeting to be included in the agenda, and assigning roles during the meeting (someone to take notes, someone to keep time, and so on). They thought that this new process would cut the weekly meeting time in half. They decided to document the new process and give it out to all the other managers and supervisors for comment.

Do. It took more than a week to get comments back from everyone.

Study. Everyone was worried about the assignments before the meetings and having to submit agenda topics the day before. Most of the managers and supervisors felt that the day before they would not know what the critical issues would be. Some were also concerned about being asked to fill a role, such as notekeeper.

Act. The owner felt that the managers' concerns were due to fear of the unknown rather than any real reason, so he decided to go ahead with the change.

Cycle 2

Plan. The owner made the following announcement at the morning meeting on Friday: "Beginning on Monday the new process will go into effect. If you do not submit an agenda topic today, it will not be covered in the meeting on Monday. Joe will take notes at the meeting, Mary will keep us on our time schedule, and I will put together the agenda late this afternoon." Everyone predicted a short meeting.

Do. Only one topic was submitted that Friday, so the agenda the owner wrote had only two items: resolve scheduling problems for the construction site at the college, and figure out why only one agenda topic was turned in.

The meeting was indeed short. The scheduling problem took twenty minutes, but the discussion about submitting agenda topics was even shorter. People said they had issues they would like to have on the agenda but were unsure of the format for submitting them. (Several people said they felt stupid giving the owner some scribbled notes on the back of a napkin, but was that OK?) Everyone agreed to use a form that Joe volunteered to design.

Study. The meeting was short, but for the wrong reason. Issues that should have been discussed were not because people were not comfortable and familiar with the new process. The owner saw that other pieces of the process would have to be defined and people would need some time to get used to it.

Act. Joe designed a standard, simple form for submitting topics, which was used in preparation for the Wednesday meeting. Everyone was to submit at least one topic, even if it was not critical.

Cycle 3

Plan. The owner would gather the submitted topics from everyone and construct an agenda on Tuesday afternoon. Everyone would get a copy of the agenda to use to prepare for the meeting. Again, Joe volunteered to keep notes and Mary agreed to keep track of time. Since everyone had been asked to estimate the amount of time for their topic, the owner used these estimates to set the timing for the agenda.

Do. The meeting went well. It lasted three hours. All fifteen topics on the agenda were covered, most in less time than planned. Only one topic was not finished in its allotted time. The group decided to finish it on Friday as per the process.

Study. One of the reasons the meeting went well was that knowing ahead of time what the topics would be allowed people to study and bring information that was helpful to resolving the issue. Everyone agreed that this element alone made the new process worthwhile. They had never been able to resolve more than five issues at any one meeting before. In this meeting, fourteen issues were resolved and one was to be continued.

Act. Everyone was ready to commit to keeping the meeting process. They would continue to refine the process, as appropriate.

Discussion of Example 1

The three improvement questions helped the owner to focus his management team on improving their morning meetings.

Use of data. Although the management team did specify two measures they would track to measure the impact of any change they would try, initially they did not look at the data over time. Later, when they plotted meeting time and number of topics covered, it was easy to see the improvement. Figure 3.1 shows the effect of the change and the pattern that developed after the change. The three weekly meetings lasted, on average, about one hour and twenty minutes and covered an average of 6.8 topics. They did not look into the reasons for the variations in the length of time of the meetings or in the number of topics covered. They could also have used a five-point scale ranging from poor to excellent to evaluate each meeting.

Developing a change. The brainstorming session alone did not produce the new idea for change. They did successfully avoid just adding more of the same (more time, more people, and so on). Further thought about change was stimulated by use of the provocative suggestion "quit having the meeting." It was only when the owner was outside his normal area of concern that he had the insight for a change. The breakthrough was his realizing that the morning meeting was a process. Improvement was achieved by designing and standardizing the meeting process.

Testing a change. The owner and his management team used multiple cycles to test the change. Their testing was very small scale in cycle 1. They simply asked the meeting participants to visualize using the process and to comment on it. Cycle 2 could have been on a smaller scale. They could have applied the

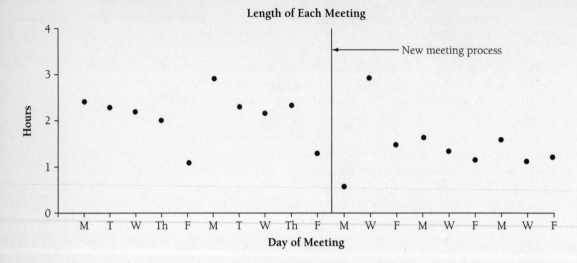

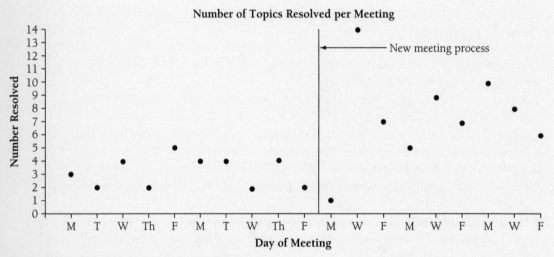

Figure 3.1. *Data on Morning Management Meetings.*

new meeting process to a shorter meeting with fewer people. The problem with submitting topics would have surfaced and the Monday morning meeting would have been more productive. The risk, however, was relatively low. Once there was a lack of topics on the agenda, the problem was addressed immediately.

Implementing a change. The three cycles all dealt with testing a change. The owner will need to run at least one more cycle to implement the change. The implementation cycle will have to address ways to make the morning meeting process permanent. How will notes be taken and who will take them? What process can be put in place to see that the time limits are kept?

Working with people. Working with others was a key issue in this improvement effort. How could the owner have created more cooperation? Is he still going to have trouble getting some of his managers and supervisors to participate in some of the roles in the meetings (notetaker, timekeeper, and so on)? Although the owner asked everyone to comment on the new process, if he had gotten other meeting participants involved in designing it, support and participation would have been stronger.

Example 2: Improving One's Golf Game

A middle-aged man (we will call him Charlie) decided that his workaholic lifestyle was not good for his health. Charlie wanted to take up a hobby that would provide ample opportunity for exercise but not be too strenuous. After considering a number of possibilities, he settled on golf as the perfect hobby/exercise. Since he had played golf twenty years earlier in high school, he would not have to learn a new sport.

Through a friend, Charlie met some men who played golf every Saturday morning. He told them that the last time he had played he had shot in the upper 80s but that had been a while ago. The men said that they shot between 85 and 95 and that he would fit right in. So, it was agreed that Charlie would join the Saturday group. The first Saturday that Charlie played he shot 130. He was horrified by how poorly he had played and decided to improve his golf game.

Charlie answered the three improvement questions as follows:

1. *What am I trying to accomplish?* Charlie wanted to play golf well enough to fit in with the Saturday group. He wanted to improve his game to get his scores in the low to mid 90s.
2. *How will I know that a change is an improvement?* Charlie's primary concern was the number of strokes it would take him to sink a golf ball in eighteen holes.
3. *What changes can I make that will result in improvement?* Charlie decided that the old clubs he had not played with in nearly fifteen years were the root of his problem. He decided to buy a new set of clubs.

Cycle 1

Plan. On Friday night, Charlie would shop for golf clubs and use them on Saturday.

Do. Charlie went to the local discount golf store and purchased a new set of clubs on Friday evening. With his new clubs in hand he met the Saturday morning group at the course and proceeded to play worse than the week before. Charlie had a truly frustrating, miserable day.

Study. Charlie was ready to quit. Not only had he shot 138 but he had just spent $600 on a set of clubs that had certainly not helped his game! Charlie had forgotten to practice one of the key principles of effective cycles: to test the change on a small scale. He could have done this by renting a set of newer-style clubs or even borrowing a set from his brother.

Act. Charlie knew that he had to try something on a smaller scale in his next cycle.

Cycle 2

Plan. Charlie made a list of several actions he could take that would possibly result in improving his golf game. Some of them were taking lessons, going to the driving range, watching videotapes, and playing at the smaller "par-three" course. Charlie was now so focused on the concept of small scale that he used only that criteria for his next plan. He decided to go to the driving range two nights per week.

Do. The driving range practice helped Charlie gain some consistency in his swing. He noticed that he flubbed (mishit) fewer balls on his second night at the range. He played with his Saturday group and discovered that he had a pretty severe tendency to hit the ball far to the right of the target, the familiar "slice" of the novice.

Study. Charlie shot 118. He was not flubbing the ball nearly as often but he was still unable to keep the ball in the fairway. His small-scale action had resulted in improvement of his score.

Act. Charlie decided to continue his practice at the driving range, but he felt he needed to do more to be able to play comfortably with the Saturday golf group.

Cycle 3

Plan. Charlie decided to take one golf lesson. He arranged to take it early in the week so that he could practice what he learned at that week's driving range practices.

Do. The lesson focused on the fundamentals. Charlie found that he grasped the fundamentals almost as if he were remembering them from fifteen years before. The practice at the range was more comfortable than it had been the week before. On Saturday, Charlie shot 105.

Study. The lesson combined with Charlie's weekly driving range practice had really helped to improve his score.

Act. Charlie decided to take another lesson and to continue his driving range practice.

Charlie ended up taking three more lessons, thereby going through three more cycles. After the total of four lessons, his score was in the mid 90s. Charlie stopped the lessons and cut back to one practice session per week. As can be seen in the plot of his scores in Figure 3.2, he has maintained his low to mid 90s score ever since.

Discussion of Example 2

Although Charlie did use the structure provided by the three questions, he did not use the principle of testing on a small scale in his first cycle. Because of this, he will never know if he could have accomplished his aim without spending $600 for new clubs.

Use of data. Charlie did collect data with each of his cycles. The plot of the results of twenty games (see Figure 3.2) shows the impact of his cycles and that a predictable pattern developed after his four lessons. Even after the lessons Charlie's golf scores vary, but within a predictable range. Charlie is able to see that when he shoots a 96 it does not mean he has lost the improvement in his game. Training and practice of the same type after the system is stable probably will not result in further improvement.

Developing a change. At the beginning, Charlie thought he knew what the problem was: his old clubs. He did not think about the processes involved in playing golf. He did not spend any time exploring other changes that would result in improvement of these processes. For example, it did not at first occur to him to take lessons because he had taken many lessons when he was younger. After the first cycle, Charlie did think about some other changes he could make.

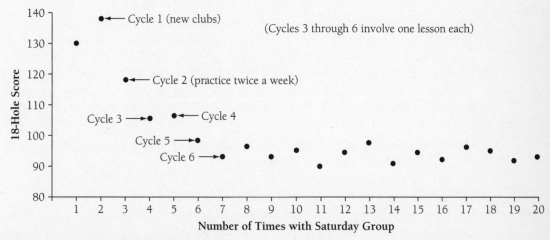

Figure 3.2. *Charlie's Saturday Golf Scores.*

Testing a change. In his first cycle, Charlie completely forgot about one of the key principles for testing a change: test on a small scale. Even if he had still felt that new clubs would be the best change, he should have borrowed or rented the new clubs. Charlie might also have thought about testing his change on different courses, under varying conditions.

Implementing a change. In improvement efforts as simple as this, implementation boils down to collecting some data to make sure that the improved results are maintained. What will happen when Charlie plays at a different course? What if he plays with a different group of people?

Working with people. Since the changes Charlie made really affected only his game, cooperation with others was not a key issue in Charlie's improvement efforts.

Example 3: A Taxi Driver Improves His Business

John, a taxi driver, wanted to increase his business. He had a daughter who was about to enter college, and for John to be able to pay for it he would have to increase his income by $600 per month. He knew that other cab drivers were able to earn that much more than he was.

As a taxi driver, John spent less than 50 percent of his on-duty time actually transporting paying fares. The best spots to pick up fares usually had long lines, so much of the time was spent waiting for a fare. He drove an average of nine hours a day, five days a week. Picking up fares at the large international airport produced about half of his income.

John did not want to make a change that would simply be more work, such as to work six days per week. He had done so for several years in the middle of a recession. He remembered the stress that a fifty-five- to sixty-hour work week had caused him and his family. He also remembered that working the sixth day had not increased his income by 20 percent as he had thought it would. He remembered being tired often and missing fares that he would have gotten if he had been more alert.

When he asked himself the three improvement questions, John came up with the following answers:

1. *What am I trying to accomplish?* John wanted to increase his monthly income by at least $600 without decreasing service to his customers.
2. *How will I know that a change is an improvement?* With any change he might try, the key measure of improvement was, of course, income from fares.
3. *What changes can I make that will result in improvement?* John talked with other drivers about ways to increase his fare-related income. Most of their ideas seemed like simply more work or more distasteful work. While talk-

ing, however, to an old friend who was now in the limousine business, John got an idea. His friend had installed a cellular phone in his limousine several months before and talked about how it let him speak directly with his customers in a more timely manner.

Cycle 1

Plan. John decided to rent a cellular phone for a month to see if he could reduce the amount of time that his cab was idle. He wrote his phone number on his business cards. He planned to give these out to passengers he picked up at the airport or train station and tell them to call him directly a few hours before they needed to return.

Do. At first, John only gave his card and sales pitch to people who were visiting his city (thinking they would be most likely to remember the service). After a few days, however, someone who lived in the city struck up a conversation about the cellular phone and ended up asking for a card. After that, John gave the card (and pitch) to all his customers who would listen. Although he found himself at the airport more often, during his trial month he often was not waiting in the taxi line.

Study. Although he had not tracked the number of return trips to the airport before getting his phone, he was sure that the forty-seven return trips during his test month were at least double what he had had before. In general, he was busier with fares more often than he used to be during his nine-hour workdays. His income for the month, after paying $100 in phone costs, was $740 more than his average for the previous year.

Act. John could see that by giving the customer easier access to him, his use of the cellular phone was going to be a permanent way of doing business. He decided to implement the changes by purchasing a cellular phone and having nicer cards printed with more information, such as his hours and a ten-word description of the direct contact services.

Discussion of Example 3

John had no trouble using the three fundamental questions for improvement. The questions supported his need to increase his earnings. Having gotten an idea for a change from a friend, the PDSA cycle provided him with a simple, effective way to test the idea.

Use of data. John collected data on his earnings from fares and the number of return trips to the airport. However, he did not look at these data over time; he simply compared averages from his one-month test to previous averages. A simple plot of earnings per day over the one-month period may have revealed a pattern over time that indicated some special reason for the increase other than the new phone. For example, if almost all the increase in income was from one week when a large convention was in town, a plot over time would have shown it.

Developing a change. John knew that he did not want to try a change that simply meant spending more time at work. He wanted a change that would not only increase his income but would just as likely make his job more enjoyable (by decreasing the time he spent waiting for fares). The phone allowed him to better integrate his services with his customer's systems. This idea for change came from outside the normal way taxis are operated. It came from someone in a related yet different business. John also took advantage of a new technology.

Testing a change. John applied the principle of testing on a small scale. He rented the cellular phone, wrote his cellular number on existing business cards, and set a one-month time frame for the test. To help determine whether the change was an improvement, John compared his income during the month he used the phone to his average income per month for the year before. This comparison would have been more useful if he had plotted the data on income over time.

Implementing a change. John has not yet addressed any implementation issues. What are the barriers that he might run into over the next six months?

Working with people. The main aspect of interacting with people that John had to worry about was getting the cooperation of customers in calling him when they needed transportation. To help with this effort, he developed a business card and a short sales pitch for the idea.

Example 4: Improving Service in a Dental Office

Beth, a dentist, wanted to improve the service to her customers. She had a good reputation for quality of work; she was known for taking great care and time to see that the work was done right. She had two full-time and two part-time assistants, as well as two office administrators (one worked halftime). The two part-time assistants mainly did teeth cleaning, while the full-time assistants helped Beth with dental procedures other than cleaning. Beth was thinking about expanding and selling a partnership to another dentist.

Beth answered the three improvement questions as followed:

1. *What am I trying to accomplish?* Beth decided that if she could increase her patient base by 15 to 20 percent it would justify bringing a second dentist into the practice.
2. *How will I know that a change is an improvement?* Beth felt that the most important measure of her business was the number of people who consistently came to her office for their dental care. She had records of the number of patients she had seen since she started her practice. Because of her

good reputation, many of her patients had been coming exclusively to her for the ten years she had been in business.

3. *What changes can I make that will result in improvement?* Beth was not sure how to answer this question. She felt that the answer was probably in bringing in the latest technologies, but she was worried that this answer could come from her thinking and technical training rather than from what might be best for her patients (existing and potential). She decided that to be able to answer this question well she would need to talk to patients and ask them this question.

Cycle 1

Plan. Beth chose six names from her list of patients. She made sure that the six patients represented both long-time and newer patients. The plan was to meet individually with each patient outside of the dental office and ask them each three questions:

1. When you have chosen a dentist in the past (not just my office) what were the main things you looked for?
2. What are some aspects of the services you have received from me and my office that would make you recommend or not recommend my services to friends or relatives?
3. What are some improvements you would like to see in the service you receive from my office?

Do. It took Beth three weeks to complete the six interviews. It turned out that two of the six patients were seeing another dentist. Beth realized that she did not have a good way to track the number of patients who had changed to another dentist. One of the patients that had quit coming to her talked about many reasons: convenience of location, less expensive, a bad experience during a cleaning, and so on. The other ex-patient said very plainly that after two very painful cleanings she had said, "No more!" All six of the patients interviewed shared their ideas about what makes a good dental visit.

Study. Beth had not been aware of two important issues: (1) her patients were not as loyal as she had thought, and (2) her patients were having problems with the teeth cleanings they received at her office. Beth also learned that the patients were not very concerned about new technology. They assumed that she would take care of that. They were more concerned about things that increased their anxiety and comfort before and during a dental visit.

Act. Beth decided to make some changes that would specifically affect how teeth were cleaned in her office. She had hired all four of her assistants and she knew that the ones who did the cleaning were as well qualified as the other two. So, the answer was not in blaming the two assistants who did the cleaning, which would have been easy to do.

Cycle 2

Plan. Beth discussed the results of her first cycle with her assistants. Although the assistants were not comfortable at first with the whole discussion, Beth kept pointing out that the reason they were working on this was to improve their service to the patients and that all five of them would benefit from a larger, more loyal patient base. "If patients enjoy their dental visits more, our work will be much easier," she told them. The assistants all had to agree with this and eventually got excited about their own involvement in the changes. They all agreed that the following changes would make the teeth cleaning process less of a pain for patients:

- Rotate assistants (between working with Beth and doing the cleaning)

- Standardize the cleaning process

- Get patients involved in the cleaning (such as have patients do their own flossing at cleaning with supervision and use it as an opportunity to teach proper flossing)

- Use gentler cleaning tools (especially those that come in contact with the patients gums)

These changes would be developed and tested for two weeks. Also in the plan was to ask patients to rate the cleaning experience relative to past cleanings.

Do. It took more than two weeks to develop the new process. Beth and her staff seemed to have more fun at work as a result of all the interaction among them in making sure the plan was carried out.

Study. The forty-six patients who had cleanings during the two-week test also enjoyed the new process of getting their teeth cleaned, although three patients did not want to do their own flossing. The data from the rating the patients gave the cleanings clearly showed that they experienced less pain and anxiety. Figure 3.3 shows the average rating for each day.

The rotation of assistants between assisting Beth and doing the cleanings had a few problems related to scheduling and technical experience. Beth saw that she would have to set aside some time for training.

Act. The new process was implemented, with the exception that patients were given the option of flossing themselves or having it done by the assistant. Beth asked the office administrator to work on the scheduling problems.

Discussion of Example 4

Beth was initially ready to follow her first idea about bringing new technology into her practice. This would have cost a considerable amount of money and

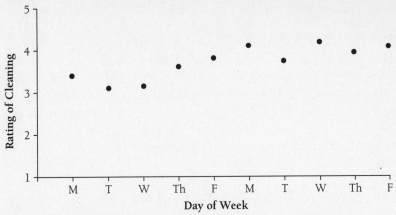

Rating: 1 = much worse; 2 = worse; 3 = same; 4 = better; 5 = much better

Figure 3.3. *Dental Patients Rate New Procedures.*

may not have helped with patient satisfaction at all. The framework of the three questions and the learning experience of the first cycle opened a new direction for her improvement efforts.

Use of data. Beth collected data during each of her cycles, including the responses to the six interviews and the comments and ratings the forty-six patients gave the cleaning process. She also had data on her patient base. Variation in the cleaning process was a source of trouble. The variation was reduced by establishing a standard process. The chart of the ratings the patients gave the new cleaning process (Figure 3.3) shows that it took two or three days to get the process working well. Beth and the four assistants all learned and helped each other learn during those first three days. After that, the process seemed to be established, as shown in the chart.

Developing a change. This example, like the others, shows that it takes a different approach to come up with ideas that are not just more of what has been done in the past (for Beth, that would have been spending money on the latest technology), to develop a change that is new. Beth asked patients for input. Their feedback helped her to realize that she needed to develop a standard process for cleaning that would result in improvement from the viewpoint of her patients.

Testing a change. The two cycles were both small scale yet they involved enough patients to explore a range of conditions. The cycle to test the change was run over a short period with a limited number of patients. The scale of the test could have been made even smaller, if the assistants had first tried the new procedure on themselves or on a small select group of customers.

Implementing a change. Beth learned in cycle 2 that training was needed. She also learned that to implement the changes she would need a process for scheduling her assistants. These and other maintenance problems would be addressed in an implementation cycle.

Working with people. It was necessary for the five people working together on this improvement effort to support each other in many aspects of their work; scheduling, skills, knowledge, and so on. They needed to cooperate to agree on a standard process. Each of the assistants had to change some aspect of his or her approach to cleaning to conform to the standard process. At the beginning, Beth was able to use the aim of the effort to keep everyone focused and cooperating. Once they all felt ownership of the changes, cooperation grew.

Example 5: Improving Methods for Teaching Biology

A teacher of a college-level introductory biology course was interested in improving the methods she used in teaching the course. In particular, she identified the module on cellular respiration and protein synthesis as difficult for the students, especially those who were not majoring in science. As a result of this difficulty their interest was low, which had a negative effect on their enjoyment of the entire course. Grades for the test on this module averaged about sixty-five out of a hundred. In addition, students' interests and abilities in science in general varied widely, which presented difficulties for all the science teachers.

The teacher decided to focus on this topic first and then to use what she learned to improve her teaching of other topics in the course. She used the Model for Improvement to guide her efforts.

1. *What am I trying to accomplish?* The teacher wanted to improve the teaching of cellular respiration and protein synthesis in the introductory science course. She particularly wanted the improvements to help those going into health professions to use the knowledge from this module to understand the results of interventions they would make. She also wanted the improvements to help nonbiology majors understand and appreciate the world around them.
2. *How will I know that a change is an improvement?* The primary measures that the teacher used to know whether the changes were improvements were test scores and observations of the students during class (questions, enthusiasm, posture, and so on).
3. *What changes can I make that will result in improvement?* Two cycles were run to test improvements, one for each of two semesters.

Cycle 1

Plan. The teacher's review of the lesson plan for the module indicated that the students may have been overwhelmed with detailed information on the subject before they had a grasp of the basic concepts. She therefore rearranged the lesson plan to improve the progression of topics. She developed a simplified handout to highlight the module's major points. She tested the new approach during the next semester.

Do. The plan was carried out. Early in the semester the teacher distributed the handout she had developed for students to follow during lectures. The handout was simplified by using drawings for clarification. Throughout the semester the teacher noted other topics that could benefit from an approach similar to the one being tested.

Study. The teacher observed some improvement in interest in the topic and about a ten-point increase in the average test score (see Figure 3.4). Nevertheless, she was still not satisfied with the teaching of the topic.

Act. The teacher decided to keep the changes made to the lesson plan and incorporate some new ideas for the next semester.

Cycle 2

Plan. The teacher retained the changes made to the lesson plan during the previous cycle and added some other changes, including more time introducing the significance of the material and establishing the context for the subject matter. She also informally incorporated the learning from cycle 1 into other topics in the course besides cellular respiration.

Do. The plan was carried out. The teacher observed that students displayed a substantial interest in the topic relative to their interest in other classes. She discerned no obvious difference in the makeup of the class relative to other semesters.

Study. Student interest in the topic increased from the previous semester and the average grade for the test on the module was eighty. The teacher changed the

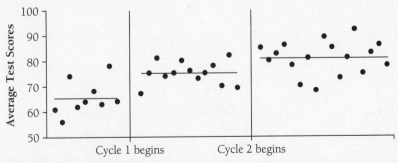

• Groups of four students

Figure 3.4. *Average Test Scores for Students Studying Cellular Respiration and Protein Synthesis.*

specific questions on the test each semester, but the different versions were believed to be of comparable difficulty. Figure 3.4 illustrates that an improvement in test scores resulted from cycle 2.

Act. The teacher decided to retain the changes made to the lesson plan and discuss them with other biology teachers. She hoped to get the other teachers to incorporate what she had learned into more of the biology curriculum. She also decided to continue her cycles and build on the improvements she had made.

Discussion of Example 5

Although the teacher essentially had worked by herself to improve the biology class, she decided to share her learning and improvement ideas with other teachers. While working with the other teachers she can still use the three improvement questions as a framework.

Use of data. The teacher relied on the traditional test scores as data. She did take note, however, of other kinds of data, such as the interest of the students, their participation, and so on. She tracked this data over time. Although students' test scores varied quite a bit, the impact of the changes the teacher made is clear.

Developing a change. The teacher made changes to the order in which topics were presented. Rearranging the order of the way something is currently being done is a good way to provoke ideas for change. Often, quite simple changes result in significant improvement.

Testing a change. Both of the cycles were small in scale (one semester each) and yet they produced results that are obvious improvements. Because the makeup of the class during the semesters in which she tested was similar to the makeup of the class in other semesters, the teacher believed that the improvement she observed was due to the changes she had made.

Implementing a change. The implementation issues are simple because the teacher is doing this improvement work on her own. Implementation problems such as resistance and maintaining the change will become more complex when she expands her efforts to include other teachers.

Working with people. The need for cooperation will be great when other teachers get involved.

Conclusion

The examples presented in this chapter are meant to show that the three questions, the PDSA Cycle, and the skills to support improvement (use of data, developing, testing, and implementing a change, and working with people) are easy to use and practical for everyday applications. Once you understand how these methods are meant to work, your next step is to utilize them to make your own changes that will result in improvement. This is where the real learning and the fun begins. The second part of the book explores in more depth all of the ideas and methods presented in the first part, and adds some new ones. As you gain experience in making improvements, the chapters in Part Two will prove more and more useful.

METHODS FOR IMPROVEMENT

Part One of this book presented the Model for Improvement, some basic skills associated with effective use of the model, and five examples of improvement efforts. The improvement efforts explored thus far have been of relatively low complexity. The chapters in Part Two explore the use of the Model for Improvement across a range of complexity. Chapter Four expands on the skills of using data and understanding variation introduced in Chapter Two. Chapters Five, Six, and Seven provide more sophisticated methods for performing the basic work of improvement—developing, testing, and implementing changes. Chapter Eight presents three case studies that illustrate the use of the model in some detail. The material presented in Part Two will deepen your understanding of the science and art of improvement and its varied applications.

CHAPTER 4

Using the Model for Improvement

Change and improvement are never easy. Even an apparently simple system becomes much more complex when change is contemplated or introduced. This chapter will use the two parts of the Model for Improvement presented in Part One (see Figure 1.4)—the three fundamental questions and the PDSA Cycle— to guide the reader in expanding the use of the model to more complex applications than those discussed in Part One. Figure 1.5 illustrated the wide variety of settings and levels of complexity in which this very simple framework can be used to guide improvement efforts. Mastering the methods for working on complex projects presented in this chapter will increase your ability to make improvements in some of the less-complex settings described in Part One.

What Are We Trying to Accomplish?

When the owners of the diner described in Chapter One decided to improve the lunch service, they were able to discuss and agree on the aim of the project over a cup of coffee. They might even have been able in this short period of time to come up with some ideas for changes. This was possible because so few people were involved in the effort, those initiating the effort were also doing the work, the system was relatively simple, and unintended consequences were easily identified.

As the scope of an improvement effort increases, the system becomes large or complex, more people become involved in or affected by the work of improvement, those initiating the effort may not be doing the work, and unintended consequences of the changes may be difficult to identify or anticipate. For these reasons, it is recommended that the answer to the question of what is to be accomplished be written down. This written statement of aim is sometimes referred to as a *charter*. The written document can be discussed and circulated for comment to a variety of people who have a stake in the work or the outcome of the project.

Charters can take many forms, but a charter that contains a general description of aim and some guidance for carrying out the work has proved useful, especially for projects that were initiated by someone other than those who are working on the project. The charter should explain in broad terms what is to be accomplished and why. The guidance section of the charter should include information that helps an individual or team begin to answer the fundamental questions about the improvement effort. Information that might be included are such things as suggestions for measures, aspects of the system on which to focus initially, boundaries within which the changes are to be developed, and recommendations for possible changes. If specific results are expected from the improvement effort, they should be included in the charter. Exhibit 4.1 contains examples of charters. Some additional examples are included in the case studies in Chapter Eight. The sample charters in Exhibit 4.1 address two issues that arise when setting the aim of an improvement initiative: the use of numerical goals and the removal of the current system as an alternative. Both of these issues will be addressed in Chapter Thirteen, but they are worthy of brief consideration in this chapter.

Use of Numerical Goals

Advice about the use of numerical goals in setting an aim for an improvement project ranges from "never use them" to "always provide one and let other people figure out how to achieve it." This book's authors recognize the abuses associated with numerical goals, including falsifying figures, unfairly holding people accountable for results that they are incapable of achieving, and achieving the goal at the expense of other parts of the system. We do not believe, however, that these instances of poor practice or abuse should preclude the use of numerical goals in ways that are beneficial.

We also recognize that some hardy souls need only the challenge of a numerical goal to find ways to actually improve the system. The existence of these few individuals does not justify the wholesale use of numerical goals without associated methods for achieving them. Our experience indicates that a middle ground between these two extremes is achievable and useful.

Numerical goals can be a convenient way to communicate expectations. Are small incremental improvements expected or are large breakthrough changes necessary? If the numerical goal is used well, it not only communicates the expectation; it also communicates the support that will be provided. Large changes to big systems usually require investment of time and sometimes capital.

Individuals and teams rarely will significantly exceed their own expectations of what is possible. Those providing the goal must convince the team that the goal is feasible. Means of doing this include:

Example 1: Medication System in a Hospital

General Description: Redesign the medication system to reduce errors, improve customer satisfaction, support care, and reduce costs.

Guidance:

1. A multitude of relatively small improvement projects have been completed on various processes in the medication system, resulting in some improvement, but the fragmented nature of the efforts prevented the optimization of the system as a whole. This project should address the system as a whole.

2. The system includes all processes inside the hospital relating to the use of medications, but it also extends outside the hospital to impact the continuum of care—for example, the patient's primary-care physician.

3. The project should obtain significant results in reduction of errors, increase in customer satisfaction, and reduction of cost. Preliminary analysis of the opportunities for improvement indicates that at least a 50 percent reduction in errors and a 15 percent reduction in cost are achievable.

Example 2: Computer Support

General Description: Improve the process for supporting computer hardware and software needs in the organization. Emphasis should be placed on improved response time of software and response to customers' requests.

Guidance:

1. An expected result is a documented process for support of hardware and software needs.

2. Some important measures of performance are:
   - Response time to requests for software support
   - Down time
   - Response time to customers with software needs

Exhibit 4.1. Examples of Charters.

- Observing other organizations that have accomplished similar goals

- Providing some basic concepts or ideas that, if pursued, could feasibly result in achieving the goal

- Drawing out ideas from participants themselves by asking questions like "What would it take to get a 50 percent reduction in time to ship an order?"

- Showing data on current faults of the system and computing the performance levels of the system if these faults were eliminated

Removing the Current System as an Alternative

Change is difficult. The current system pulls innovative changes toward more familiar ground like a giant magnet. What begins as a large change often results

3. Some boundaries for the activities are:
   - Existing and new software should be addressed.
   - The different hardware configurations of all customers should be accommodated.
   - Initial focus should be on the software supporting the organization's primary products.

Example 3: Budget for Capital Expenditures

General Description: Redesign the system for budgeting capital expenditures so that the system better supports the business initiatives of the company.

Guidance:

1. The expected result of this project is a system that:
   - Is responsive to the strategic needs of the business units, manufacturing, and research.
   - Deals effectively with the distribution of limited capital so that customers of the process feel that the distribution has occurred in an objective manner.
   - Minimizes the time needed to operate the process.
   - Minimizes the difference between the capital budgeted and the amount actually spent, except under unanticipated changes in the business environment.

2. The boundaries for the project are:
   - The capital planning system to be improved will have as an input an upper limit of expenditure defined by the CEO. The team is not asked to address the process of defining this upper limit.
   - The team will work on the mechanical part of approving appropriation requests for individual projects.
   - The current system is in need of significant redesign; the team should not be constrained by existing procedures.

in only a small adjustment. Frequently, it is implicitly or explicitly assumed that if changes resulting in improvement cannot be developed, then remaining with the current system is an option. This is comforting to participants, but it inhibits improvement.

The charter can be used to prevent this assumption from being made by including the following:

- A statement of fact, such as, "Remaining at the current level of twenty-one days is not an alternative if the custom business is to remain viable."

- A numerical goal that clearly is not attainable with small changes to the current system.

- Some ideas for changes to be pursued if no better alternative is developed.

- Logical consequences that follow from failure to make the improvements, such as discontinuing the product or service.

- A statement that takes part of the present system away, such as, "Computer Services will delete the old version of the accounting package from all computers on the tenth of the month."

How Will We Know That a Change Is an Improvement?

An effective answer to this question provides the foundation for the learning that is fundamental to effective improvement. Changes to large and small business, government, or social systems are frequently made without thoughtfully answering this question. Consequently, valuable opportunities to learn and to accelerate improvement are lost.

In simple systems it is often easy to discern that a change is an improvement by informally observing the system. In more complex systems, measurements or other types of data are almost always necessary to answer this question. For example, measures of improvement in redesigning a hospital's medication system might be customer satisfaction, medication error rate, timeliness of administration, and costs associated with the system; measures for reducing labor costs in the lab might be hours of overtime, costs for temporaries, turnaround time, and accuracy; and measures for developing a new flooring tile might be whether it holds a shine, its ease of installation, its durability, and its visual attractiveness. Some guidelines for developing such measures are:

1. Make sure that the interests of the customer of the product or process are strongly represented in the list of measures.

A company that makes garage door openers had to decide what their customers would call good quality. They knew from their 800-number survey that ease of installation was one of the measures of quality. They constructed a simple three-question form for their customers to fill out about the experience they had had during installation. They put the three questions on the back of the warranty registration card. As the company made changes to make the installation easier, they expected the responses to the three questions to show improvement.

---

2. It is useful to look at data collected both before and after a change; however, this is not always necessary, or possible. Often, looking at data collected after a change is enough to justify calling the change an improvement.

Sally was quite happy. The chart of the number of errors showed that they were producing consistently fewer than ten errors per week in statements sent to customers. From their weekly meetings the previous year she knew that they used to produce more than fifteen errors per day. Although she did not know precisely the effect of the changes that were made, she was confident that it was substantial. The data that had been collected since the latest changes would serve as the baseline against which to assess changes in the future.

3. In many situations, the data needed to measure the impact of a change will not be available for a long time. When this is the case, select a surrogate or intermediate measure that is related to the measure(s) you most want to impact.

The leaders of a large health care organization wanted to make some changes that would result in the reduced occurrence of lung cancer. They decided to start a clinic for helping people to stop smoking. Obviously, what they wanted was to see the rate of lung cancer go down. It would take many years, however, for this result to be detectable. They decided to focus on an intermediate measure, one that could be measured immediately, one that they strongly believed is related to a reduction in lung cancer. They decided to measure the success rate of people trying to quit smoking (specifically, the percentage of people that went through the workshops who were still not smoking six months after the program).

4. Multiple measures are almost always required, in order to provide a balance among competing interests and to help to assure that the system as a whole is improved. Try to keep the list to six or fewer measures—certainly fewer than ten. Strive to develop a list that is useful and manageable, not perfect.

A state's secondary education system was interested in increasing the scores that its high school students achieved on the Scholastic Aptitude Test, necessary for admission to most colleges. Some people were concerned that some high schools would achieve the aim by discouraging the poorer-performing students from taking the test and thus hurting their chances of going to college. To accommodate this concern, the percentage of students taking the exam was included in the list of measures.

Levels of Measurement

Item 3 of the previous list described intermediate measures. Intermediate measures are actually part of a hierarchy of measurement. To facilitate learning while improving a complex system, the use of different levels of measurement is particularly helpful. In simple systems, two to four cycles may be all that are needed to accomplish the aim. In complex systems, many more cycles will usually be needed. The need for multiple cycles raises two questions: (1) How can we learn from each cycle if it takes many cycles to achieve the results we want? and (2) How can we assure that the cycles will actually combine to provide real improvement at the system level? These questions can be answered by responding to the question, *How will we know that a change is an improvement?* at several levels. These are (1) global or outcome measures, (2) intermediate measures, and (3) process measures.

Global Measures   Global measures are measures of the big system under study. They relate directly to the aim of the project. Improvement in these measures signifies accomplishment of the aim.

To support one of the initiatives in its strategic plan—to improve quality and reduce cost— a computer manufacturing company chartered a team to change how suppliers of components are brought into the new-product process. Jed, the project leader, chose five measures relating to quality and cost of the computer.

Global measures facilitate learning from a sequence of cycles by providing evidence that the sequence of changes are actually having an impact at the system level.

Intermediate Measures   An intermediate measure is related to the global measure, but improvement in the intermediate measure is not sufficient to ensure the accomplishment of the aim. Intermediate measures could be thought of as indicators of progress.

Jed realized that it would take a year or more to see improvements in the measures of quality and cost of the computer. He chose the average number of vendors per component as one of several intermediate measures to help guide the learning as they worked through the project. Having fewer vendors was not the aim of the project. However, the company believed strongly that reducing the number of vendors was a prerequisite for close cooperation on improvement efforts.

Intermediate measures are chosen by making a rational argument—supported by research, experience, or common sense—that improvements in the intermediate measures will eventually lead to improvements in the global measures and accomplishment of the aim of the project.

Process Measures In large systems, the global and intermediate measures most often assess the impact of several cycles. Process measures, usually associated with a specific cycle, are often used to determine if the cycle was carried out as planned.

As part of the new working relationship with suppliers, key technical people from the supplier companies were invited to participate in the design of the components for the computer. In the past, the suppliers were given little say about the design of the components, even though they had potentially valuable expertise. Jed and the team decided to run a cycle to test the theory that suppliers could contribute to the design of components. One of the process measures they used was the number of suggestions from suppliers that were actually included in the design of the components.

Unambiguously classifying global, intermediate, and process measures is not the aim of this discussion. The important lesson is that a variety of measures will be needed to guide the learning and action as a project progresses, especially for improvement of complex systems. Some data should be collected and plotted over time for the life of the project, and others will be used only for a short time as part of a PDSA cycle.

What Changes Can We Make That Will Result in Improvement?

Answering this question requires developing possible changes. For relatively simple systems, a list of changes may be developed and tested almost immediately. For larger, more complex systems, or for any efforts that require fundamental design or redesign, it is advantageous to answer the question in two parts. First, provide some broad concepts for the system design, sometimes referred to as *concept design*. Second, provide more detail on the actual changes that will be made to the components of the system.

A teaching hospital associated with a leading medical school was concerned about the performance of the system of ordering, distributing, and administering medications to patients. Hospital management was also concerned that patients were having problems obtaining or properly using the medications once they left the hospital.

A multitude of relatively small improvement projects had been completed on various processes in the medication system over the preceding five years. This had resulted in some improvement, but the fragmented nature of the efforts prevented the optimization of the system as a whole. Management decided to charter a project to address the system as a whole. Their aim is presented in Example 1 in Exhibit 4.1. To decide whether the changes were improvements, they used a patient survey, measures of error rates, timeliness of administration of medications, and costs associated with the system.

A small core group of nurses, physicians, and pharmacists were responsible for providing a concept design to guide the overall project. Some of the major design concepts for accomplishing the aim were:

1. Patient service
   a. Standardize patient education regarding medications.
   b. Provide multilingual medication information.
   c. Follow-up on problematic cases after discharge from hospital.
   d. Provide information on where hard-to-obtain medications can be found in the community.
2. Clinical decision support: Many choices of medication are available for the complex problems experienced by the varied patients treated in this hospital. It is difficult for physicians to keep abreast of the existing choices and the latest developments in medication. Support physician decisions concerning medication by providing electronic information systems and by making pharmacists available to them for consultation.
3. Timely administration of medications
   a. Keep frequently used medications on the unit rather than in the pharmacy. Investigate the use of automated dispensing systems (similar to ATM machines at banks).
   b. For medications that must be ordered from the pharmacy, consider using fax and pneumatic tube system.
   c. For appropriate drugs, the pharmacy should carry some inventory to be dispensed when ordered rather than having to produce a dose of the drug from each order.
4. Standardization
   a. Provide the same information about a medication in the same format to patients and clinicians on all units.
   b. Standardize times to administer drugs to patients.
   c. Standardize procedures for restricted drugs.
5. Error proofing
   a. Minimize the transcription of medication orders by providing on-line ordering systems.
   b. Use industrial error-proofing methods to reduce errors during the production of medications.
   c. Streamline and optimize inspection.
6. Optimize the mix of pharmacy tasks.
   a. Increase efficiency by centralizing and streamlining production.

b. Take advantage of efficiencies to provide unit-based consulting.

c. Establish cooperative relationships with community pharmacists.

With some guidance from the hospital leadership, the core group chartered thirteen teams to build on the concept design. The teams developed and tested changes to components of the system that were consistent with the spirit of the concept design.

Chapter Five provides methods for developing changes. In addition, Chapters Ten, Eleven, and Twelve address developing changes for particular business goals.

The Plan–Do–Study–Act Cycle

The PDSA Cycle is the primary means for turning the ideas into action and for connecting action to learning. Using the cycle effectively takes some discipline and effort. Figure 4.1 provides some detail on what should be considered in each phase of the cycle.

Jed and his team planned a cycle to evaluate the participation of supplier experts during the early concept design phase for a new computer. This cycle was part of their project to increase the quality and lower the cost of their computers and associated products through better supplier relations. In theory, the idea of including suppliers in the design phase was appealing. However, it did take more work, it made the meeting arrangements more complex, and it required additional time for technical people from the suppliers. The team wanted to learn about the return on this investment.

The plan for the cycle was to invite suppliers to three upcoming design meetings. Each meeting was concerned with a different product, so only one or two people would be at all three of the meetings. In some cases, more than one supplier for the same component would be at a meeting. The team was interested in seeing the effect of having competitors at the same meeting. Two members of the team were assigned to attend all three meetings to observe and record their observations. In particular they were to record (1) attendance from the suppliers and their level of technical expertise, (2) ideas that came from the suppliers and that would be pursued in the design, and (3) the willingness of suppliers to perform further investigative work after the meeting. In addition, a survey questionnaire would be sent to each person who attended the meeting to get their general impressions of the meeting and the usefulness of including suppliers at this phase in the design of a new product.

The data for the three meetings would be studied at a meeting of the improvement team. Based on the results, they would take some action, such as changing the criteria

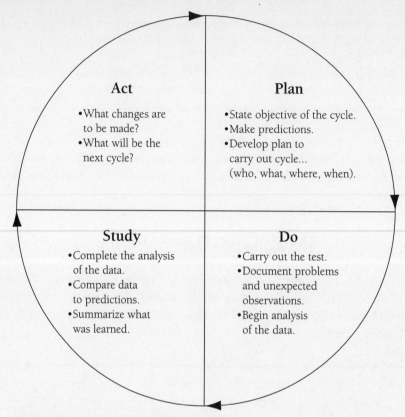

Figure 4.1. *Elements of the PDSA Cycle.*

for who gets invited, structuring the meetings differently, changing the timing for when to invite the suppliers, or continuing the meetings in the same format.

Jed and his team thoughtfully planned a cycle to learn from the three meetings. They did not just invite some suppliers to see how it would work. They realized that since only a few people would attend all three meetings, some important information would be lost, and if they simply asked the participants to comment on the meetings, much of the detail would be lost. Neutral observers were used to collect the data. The team also set aside some time to reflect on the results by studying the data from the three meetings. They planned to take action based on what they learned.

Contrast what Jed and his team did with a more-familiar scenario: have the meetings; hear some anecdotes about how the meetings went during a weekly staff meeting; decide whether to keep inviting suppliers, based on the most compelling anecdote, and regardless of the decision, neglect to set up a process to carry out the decision. Although in this scenario action occurred, it should not be considered a cycle.

To be considered a PDSA Cycle, the following aspects of the activity should be easily identifiable:

1. The activity was planned, including a plan for collecting the data.
2. The plan was attempted.
3. Time was set aside to analyze the data and study the results.
4. Action was rationally based on what was learned.

Not all improvements require cycles; some just happen. However, most purposeful improvements will require answers to the three fundamental questions. Purposeful improvements in large or complex systems will almost always require one or more cycles. Exhibit 4.2 is a worksheet that has proved useful for establishing a degree of discipline and thoughtfulness in carrying out a cycle. Filling out a worksheet for each cycle is a convenient way of documenting the project.

The PDSA Cycle is a vehicle for learning and action. The three most common ways for using the cycle as part of an improvement effort are:

1. To build knowledge to help answer any one of the three questions
2. To test a change
3. To implement a change

The next sections clarify the use of the cycle as an aid to answering the three questions. (The use of the cycle to test a change is discussed in Chapter Six, and the use of the cycle for implementing a change is discussed in Chapter Seven.)

Using the Cycle to Build Knowledge

The PDSA Cycle is used when current knowledge or readily available background information are not sufficient to answer one or more of the three questions. The primary use of data in answering the question *What are we trying to accomplish?* is to determine why a particular aim should be chosen from among the many alternative initiatives. The data might be warranty claims, responses to a customer survey, an analysis of defects or complaints, plots of measurements over time, or documented comments from employees.

Several workers had complained to the plant manager that the glass bottles they had to use were "nothing but junk." They pointed out that they had to throw away hundreds of pounds of glass every day. By examining the reject records and by plotting the weight of rejected glass daily for three weeks, the operations manager was able to show the workers that the quality of the glass was better than they had expected. Once they began

---

PDSA Cycle

Cycle #_____   Date begun_____

Date finished_____

Plan

Describe the following: objective of the cycle, questions and predictions, and details (who, what, when, where; include data to be collected).

Do

Carry out the plan and document problems and unexpected observations.

Study

Complete the analysis of the data.

Compare the data to your predictions and summarize the learning.

Act

What changes are to be made?

What will happen in the next cycle?

Exhibit 4.2. *Worksheet for Documenting a PDSA Cycle.*

to collect other data on rejects, they found that the items rejected most frequently were the packing containers.

The following example illustrates the use of a cycle to set the aim for an improvement effort.

A manufacturer of a garage door opener established an 800 telephone number to assist customers. As an input to their quality planning process, management planned a cycle to collect and analyze data from the calls to the 800 number according to the following procedure:

1. A summary of each call was logged for one week.
2. The calls were classified into six categories (installation, warranty, parts, new model, billing, and cosmetics).
3. The data were then collected for three more weeks by using a worksheet to record the time of each call and the category into which it could be classified. Space was provided for summaries of calls that did not fall into any of the six categories (other).
4. The analysis of the data was used as input to planning for improvement.

Figure 4.2 contains a Pareto chart (graphs that illustrate the relative frequency of occurrence of an activity) for calls for assistance received on the 800 number. Two aims were adopted as a result of analyzing the data presented in the figure: (1) to improve the ease of garage door installation and use of accompanying instructions, and (2) to make warranty information more understandable.

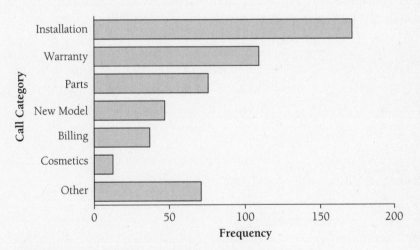

Figure 4.2. *Pareto Analysis of Calls from Customers.*

A cycle can also be used to answer the question, *How will we know that a change is an improvement?* A cycle might be run to determine a balanced set of measures. The cycle could consist of a survey of customers or interviews with a sample of people who have a stake in the system. Other cycles that might be completed to help answer this question include:

- Collecting baseline data on the performance of the system

- Testing the feasibility of using a new measurement device, such as a new color-measuring instrument

- Testing the clarity of survey questions

- Assessing the ability of workers to routinely collect data

- Testing the accuracy of a lab result

One way to answer the question, *What changes can we make that will result in improvement?* is to use existing knowledge or some creative activity, as discussed in Chapter Five. When the knowledge or ideas for specific changes are not available, one or more cycles can be used to build the knowledge necessary to develop the changes.

The following example illustrates the use of a PDSA Cycle to build knowledge to develop a change.

The management of a rapid rail transportation system in a large metropolitan area designed a cycle to help set priorities for improvement. The cycle included soliciting suggestions from riders of the subway as to how the system could be improved. More than eighteen hundred replies were received. The replies were analyzed in a variety of ways. One analysis took into account the relative merits of the suggestions by qualitatively choosing a subset of the suggestions for testing. The output of the analysis was simply a list of changes to be tested:

- Pay telephones on station platforms
- Better lighting in the stations
- More directional signs
- Farecard vending machines that accept $10 and $20 bills
- A twenty-four-hour telephone assistance line for riders
- Mailboxes at station entrances
- Use of credit cards to buy farecards
- Transit system information on display near the convention center
- Selling the family/tourist pass at all stations
- Indicators showing the color of the next scheduled train (by track)

Detailed design of the tests was then accomplished in subsequent cycles by small teams.

One caution: Make sure that when a cycle is run in order to build knowledge that the knowledge gained is subsequently translated into action. Do not forget the A in PDSA. In each of the examples just provided, immediate action was taken based on what was learned.

Using the Cycle Sequentially

The Model for Improvement is based on a trial-and-learning approach to improvement. The PDSA Cycle is the vehicle for learning and for transforming that learning into action. In general, increased frequency and number of cycles results in increased improvement. We strongly advocate the rapid testing of changes on a small scale and the subsequent use of other cycles to scale-up the changes. In our experience, spending more time in the conference room trying to perfect the change before testing is not an effective way to make improvements. Too many uncertainties will exist. (This concept was discussed in Chapter One and illustrated in Figure 1.3.)

Although the use of small-scale, rapid cycles runs counter to intuition, it is an effective approach for the design or redesign of large or complex systems. The bigger the system is, the more uncertainties there will be and the less likely it will be that conference-room analysis will uncover them. A criticism of this approach is that for large systems all of these small cycles will not be coordinated and therefore will not result in real change to the system. This potential weakness is overcome by using a concept design (discussed earlier in this chapter) to set the context for all the smaller cycles. (Note: small cycle refers to the size of the test or the scope of the implementation. The change being tested could be very innovative and a significant departure from current practice—a very large change.) The concept design is refined and more detail is added as cycles for testing components of the design are completed.

For the redesign of large systems it is usually effective to run simultaneous sequences of cycles.

Dave ran one of three major businesses within a manufacturing company. Dave, Ruth, Ellen, and Todd were working to fundamentally redesign the system for their custom products. The charter for their effort was the following:

General description: Reduce the time to get custom sampling tubes for air pollution monitoring from twenty-one days to fewer than seven days.

Guidance:
1. Surveys and discussions with customers indicate that providing customer orders within seven days would make our product extremely attractive to them. Customers who are making their own custom tubes would be willing to buy from us rather than make the tubes themselves if that type of reliable service were available.

2. The initial focus should be on custom products, but the team should also communicate changes that could benefit the system for standard products.
3. Remaining at the current level of twenty-one days is not an alternative if the custom business is to remain viable.

Within a year they were able to accomplish the charter, and business increased 30 percent. To accomplish their aim, they had to make improvements simultaneously in several areas: increase manufacturing efficiency, improve scheduling, streamline quality assurance, and redesign the price-quoting system. Each of these areas of focus included sequences of PDSA Cycles, as illustrated in Figure 4.3.

People frequently comment that the simultaneous approach to running cycles prevents one from knowing which changes actually produced the result. Some considerations when addressing this concern are:

1. Sometimes, even when the changes are improvements at the local process level and are not impacting the global measures, a simple cost-benefit analysis results in the changes being implemented.
2. Often, no one change or sequence of changes is responsible for the overall improvement. The newly redesigned system as a whole is producing the increased performance. Thus, investigations into what the one important change might be are often futile.
3. For situations in which the changes are expensive or it is desirable for other reasons to implement only those changes that effect overall system performance, various methods of testing are available. Changes can be "turned on and off" one at a time to see if the performance degrades. More sophisticated

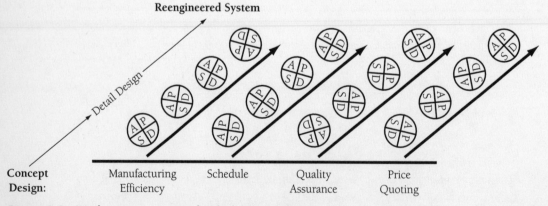

Figure 4.3. *Simultaneous Sequences of Multiple PDSA Cycles.*

experiments can be designed so that the effect of more than one change at a time can be evaluated. (Such experiments are briefly described in Chapter Six.)

Using Data in a Cycle

The use of data in a cycle to facilitate learning and action is an important aspect of the approach presented in this book.

Sally was a midlevel manager in a large corporation. Her department was responsible for the processing of hundreds of complex forms every day. To improve the performance of her group, Sally purchased new high-speed computers and new software. She was quite sure that these changes had resulted in improvement of the department's performance. Some of the clerks complained that the new programs were too hard to use, but others talked about how fast the new computers were "once you learned the new system." Sally's boss argued that errors were still being made and that her department's work was backed up worse than before they had "invested all that money."

The problem Sally faced could have been greatly reduced if her plan for the change (new computers and new software) had included the use of data collection and analysis. Data could have been used to answer the fundamental question, *How will we know that a change is an improvement?* Instead, Sally relied on observation, memory, and feelings to judge the success of the changes being implemented in her department. But people will always disagree on what they have observed. Human beings filter the information they get from their observations. In fact, what people "observe" is strongly affected by other recent observations. For example, salespeople often show a customer an expensive item first so that the cost of the item the customer originally asked about will seem less expensive. The consideration of data both reduces the impact of subjectivity and brings independence to the analysis.

For the purposes of this discussion of improvement efforts, data may be defined as *documented observations or measurements*. Observations play an important role in change efforts. The only difference between observations and data is that data are thoughtfully documented. The documentation can take the form of activities recorded on videotape or in a photograph; ideas and feelings written in a diary; and words, letters, or numbers written on paper or in an electronic file. Documentation of observations and measurements provides a more balanced and objective view of the behavior of the systems you are trying to improve.

Most people think of data as numbers that result from measurement of such factors as time, cost, or length—elements of the physical world. The idea of data is often associated with the physical sciences. People engaged in improvement efforts, however, are also interested in data about personal behavior and experience.

Data about personal experience can be obtained indirectly by recorded observation (written or visual) or by counting the frequency of certain behaviors. Some examples of observations of behavior that could be recorded and analyzed are being tardy or absent, making repeat purchases, volunteering answers in a seminar, searching for a salesperson in a store, signaling for service in a restaurant, paying attention to a product displayed in a store, volunteering for a task, and committing unsafe acts. These observations can be quantified by using classifications or counts of the observed behavior during some fixed period of observation.

Data about personal experience can also be obtained directly by asking people about their feelings or by asking them to record their feelings at specified or random times. So-called "attitude surveys" are another example of obtaining this type of data. In efforts to determine whether changes to products are improvements, aesthetic characteristics would fall into the category of personal experience.

Ranking or rating scales can be used to obtain data on personal experience. Figure 4.4 contains three such rating scales. The following are some examples of questions and statements that could be used with the scales:

Examples of Questions Used with the Poor-Excellent Scale
- How would you rate your health in the last four weeks?

- How would you rate the courtesy shown to you during your stay at this hotel?

- How would you rate the landscaping around this building?

- How would you rate the relationship you have with our project manager?

Examples of Questions Used with the Worse-Better Scale
- How would you rate your overall health now compared to four weeks ago?

- How would you rate the new process for taking orders compared to the old one?

- How would you rate the appearance of floor tile A compared to tile B?

- How would you rate the new sick-leave policy versus the old one?

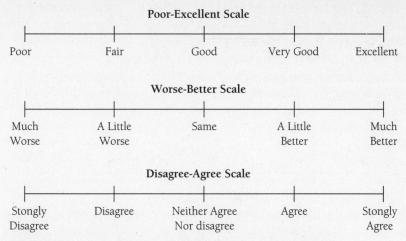

Figure 4.4. *Simple Scales for Turning Personal Experience into Data.*

Examples of Statements Used with the Agree-Disagree Scale
- Our attorneys exhibit the highest integrity.

- Our instructions for assembly of the bookcase are easy to follow.

- It is easy to find what you are looking for in our catalogue.

- Conscientious efforts were made to relieve your anxiety during your stay in the hospital.

The response to the question can be put anywhere on the scale. It need not be limited to the five discrete labels. The scales are provided to establish a basic level of measurement for almost any application. These scales, along with common measurements of such factors as time and cost, will allow those who are trying to improve quality in service or administrative applications to use continuous data as readily as their manufacturing counterparts.

Some Suggestions for the Proper Collection of Data Data are usually collected as part of the PDSA Cycle. The object of the cycle may be to build knowledge or to test or implement a change. The following are some suggestions for the proper collection of data:

1. *Explicitly state the questions to be answered by the data.* Data are collected to facilitate learning. The data collection will be most efficient if the questions to be answered by the data are stated ahead of time. This is why part of the planning phase of a cycle includes identifying the questions to be answered by the data to be collected in the cycle. Deciding how the data will later be analyzed (perhaps by sketching some "dummy" tables and graphs that will be used to present the results of the analysis) provides those planning the cycle with a way to check that they are collecting the data necessary to answer the pertinent questions.

2. *Use sampling to collect the data.* It is often better to study a sample rather than all available items. For example, rather than using a simple check sheet to record every call to an 800 number, analyze every twentieth call in more detail. Much can be learned from small samples, especially if they are collected over time. Sampling reduces both the cost and the workload. Reducing the burden of collecting a large amount of data also enables people to do a better job of measuring and studying the items selected. Studying a sample therefore often provides better information than studying all of the items that are available.

3. *Design and test a form for collecting the data.* Using a form that has been carefully designed and tested to collect the data will make the collection process easier and reduce the opportunity for error. The form should contain the necessary instructions for collecting the data and definitions of terms.

4. *Train those who will collect the data and give them understandable instructions.* In most cases the collection of data to aid improvement efforts calls for some new tasks for those collecting the data. Do not assume that people will know how to do the necessary tasks. Provide training that includes the reasons for collecting the data and the importance of the data. The specific process of measurement or recording should be reviewed and practiced.

5. *Record what went wrong during the data collection.* The data will be collected during the Do phase of the PDSA Cycle. Every collection of data will have some problems, some things that did not go as planned. Be sure to include in the instructions to those collecting the data that they record these occurrences and not hide them. The people analyzing the data must then assess the impact of these unexpected occurrences on the conclusions drawn from the data.

The Display and Analysis of Data Of the many ways to analyze data, visual displays provide a particularly useful form of analysis. Figure 4.5 contains examples of five basic types of data displays: a run chart, which plots observations over time; a histogram, which plots observations to show their distribution; an ordered bar chart known as a Pareto diagram, which illustrates relative frequency of occurrence; a scatter diagram, which plots observations to show the relationship between two sets of data; and a map, which plots data across locations.

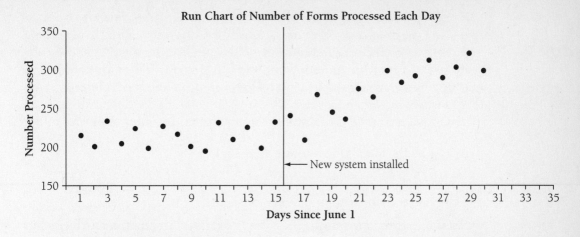

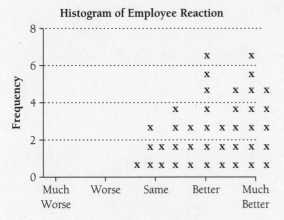

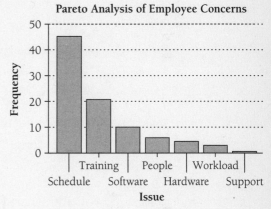

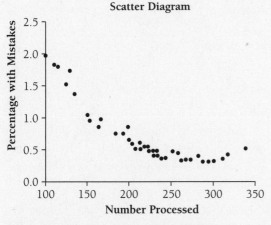

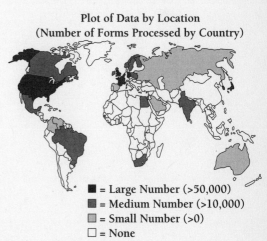

Figure 4.5. *Various Types of Data Displays.*

As noted earlier, good data analysis begins with clarifying what question is being asked of the data. Are you trying to predict future performance, determine the extent of a problem, find out where you should focus your efforts, or determine a relationship? The question you want to answer will not only guide you to the appropriate data to collect but will also guide you to the appropriate type of data display.

Graphs that are useful for learning, communication, and improvement should:

- Show all the data (at least in the first analysis)

- Separate sources of variation

- Emphasize comparisons and relationships

- Minimize text, markings, colors, and so on that are not directly related to the data

- Label data to provide enough explanation for self-interpretation

- Be simple enough for the appropriate people to learn from quickly

- Avoid fancy embellishments such as huge splashy fonts, art deco backgrounds, or 3-D displays (unless, of course, the data is three-dimensional)

Of all the displays in Figure 4.5, the plot of data over time plays the central role when making improvements. Change is a prerequisite for improvement, and people experience change as a time-related phenomenon. Often, the answer to the question, *How will we know that a change is an improvement?* is that one or more measures will either increase or decrease over time. By plotting data over time, patterns that indicate improvement can be discerned.

One of the pioneers in the use of time plots for purposes of improvement was Walter Shewhart. His work dates back to the 1920s. When plotting data over time Shewhart observed two situations. In some cases the patterns in the data were predictable. (See the time plot before the new system was installed in Figure 4.5.) Shewhart theorized that this predictability indicated that the system was stable and that only a fundamental change to the system would alter the pattern. In other cases, the pattern of variation over time was not predictable from historical patterns. The system was unstable. To Shewhart this indicated the presence of specific circumstances that should be identifiable (such as the installation of a new system). Based on these observations, Shewhart used statistical theory to develop a means of understanding variation in systems based on patterns of variation over time. His method is based on the following definitions:

Common causes: those causes that are inherently part of the process (or system) over time. They affect everyone working in the process, and affect all outcomes.

Special causes: those causes that are not part of the process (or system) all the time or do not affect everyone, but arise because of specific circumstances.

A process that has only common causes affecting the outcomes is called a *stable* process, or one that is in a state of *statistical control.* In a stable process, the cause system of the variation remains essentially constant over time. This does not mean that there is no variation in the outcomes of the process, that the variation is small, or that the outcomes meet the requirements. It only implies that the variation is predictable within statistically established limits. In practice, this indicates that a fundamental change to the system is needed for improvement.

A process whose outcomes are affected by both common causes and special causes is called an *unstable* process. An unstable process is not necessarily one with large variation. Rather, the magnitude of the variation from one period to the next is unpredictable. If special causes can be identified and removed, the process becomes stable. Its performance becomes predictable. In practical terms this implies that improvement can occur by identifying the special causes and taking appropriate action, which often means much less change than for a stable system. Once a change is made, plotting data over time helps to determine whether the change is an improvement.

In addition to providing the basic concepts, Shewhart also encouraged the plotting of data over time, and developed the control chart method for determining whether variation in a system is dominated by common or special causes. Although there are many situations in which the statistical formality of control charts is useful, often it is adequate to rely on run charts, or simple plots over time (see Figure 4.5). Statistically minded readers are encouraged to learn and apply Shewhart control charts.

Conclusion

This chapter has expanded on the options presented in Part One of the book by discussing ways to apply the Model for Improvement to large and complex systems. Concepts introduced were the use of a written charter to state aims and provide guidance for achieving them; the use of various levels of measurement; the idea of using a concept design and a sequence of cycles to guide fundamental system design or redesign; the value of using simultaneous sequences; and the effective use of data.

Developing a Change

As noted earlier, improvement requires change, but not every change is an improvement. So, where do changes that result in improvement come from? Sometimes people are just lucky. For instance, a change in the business environment may open up new opportunities for a company. Unfortunately, organizations cannot count on luck. So, opportunities for change need to be pursued in a purposeful way.

Fred had managed the distribution department for eight months. When he first started the job, he sat down with some of the people in the department to get an understanding of how things were going. What he heard gave him a headache! Orders were not being filled promptly, and many were returned because of mistakes. Fred hoped that things would get better, but eight months later, similar things were still happening.

Fred needs to begin to pursue purposeful change. When people make changes, they are usually trying to improve the quality of their work or lives. For a change to have this kind of impact, it will involve altering an existing activity or product, or developing something new. In business terms, this is called the design or redesign of a process, product, or service.

All change should be thought of from the standpoint of those who will benefit from the change. When people make changes in their lives, the people who benefit are themselves, their families, and their friends. When changes are made in an organization, the focus should be on benefits to the customer. When answering the fundamental questions, the customer's voice should stand out. Fred heard the customer's voice loud and clear, through complaints about the time it took to ship orders and the number of errors that were made. Fred will learn that complaints are perhaps the least desirable way to hear the customer's voice.

The Model for Improvement introduced in Chapter One and further explored in Chapter Four provides the framework for making effective change. The three fundamental questions and the PDSA cycle all play a role in making a change that results in improvement. Sometimes, when confronted with the third question, *What changes can we make that will result in improvement?* the answer is obvious. The knowledge to support a specific change has existed for some time, but the conditions, resources, or inclination needed to make the change happen have not existed. Many times, however, a change that will result in improvement is not obvious. In such cases, people have a tendency to resort to some common and often ineffective ways of developing change.

Some Problems in Developing Changes

Once Fred decided that something had to be done, he set up a meeting with Susan, the vice president. Fred requested that an additional person be hired to work in the distribution department, or at the very least, that the current people be allowed to work overtime. Susan was somewhat skeptical about this approach, since an additional person had been hired a little more than a year ago. She asked Fred about some of the other things he had tried in order to improve the timeliness of shipments. Fred said that he had tried weekly pep talks to encourage people to work faster. He had even gone as far as trying to enforce daily work quotas. Nothing was working. Susan would not agree to hiring another person. She suggested that Fred try having the people inspect one another's work to reduce the number of errors made.

Both Fred and Susan employed some common, ineffective approaches to improvement. They resorted to doing more of the same—more people, more money, more time, more exhortations. Susan also suggested adding inspection. Although such changes are commonly used, none of them will alter the basic way work is accomplished in the distribution department. They may result in some improvement in the short term, but they will also probably add expense and complexity to the system.

There are some situations in which a desired improvement may be achieved by applying more of the same (such as adding heat or warm clothing to combat cold). In many other situations, however, this type of solution does not achieve the improvement desired because it leaves the structure of the system unchanged. Such a solution can often contribute to the problem, or actually become the problem. Some examples are:

- Trouble with meeting customer requirements: add more resources (more money, more time, more people).

- Trouble with a product: introduce or add more inspection.

- Trouble with variation in a process: make more adjustments.

- Trouble with adherence to procedures: add more procedures or define them more rigorously.

- Trouble with discipline: add more restrictions.

It is also common for people to look for perfection when they are developing a change, a tendency known as the *utopia syndrome*. This syndrome causes them to suffer a sort of paralysis of action. Part of the motivation of looking for the perfect change is fear of failure. To make a change is to take a risk. The change might not result in improvement; in fact, a change might actually make things worse. As long as people are busy working on perfection, they will not have time for testing new ideas. The fact that doing nothing may be a bigger risk is little consolation. To support the development and testing of change, people must be willing to embrace the unexpected (things not working out as planned) as an opportunity for learning. (Many of the ideas and techniques described in this chapter and in Chapter Six are meant to provide the reader with an approach that minimizes the risk of making a change.)

First- and Second-Order Change

Developing a change that is a significant improvement from the viewpoint of the customer is not always easy. It requires that a fundamental change be made to the system. The change need not be expensive or time consuming; it just needs to involve design or redesign of the process, product, or service.

In developing changes, it is useful to distinguish between changes that are needed to keep the organization running day-to-day (first-order changes) and changes that are needed to create a new system (second-order changes).

First-Order Changes

First-order changes are required to maintain the system at its current level of performance. The following are some aspects of first-order change:

- They are often made routinely, to solve problems or react to a special circumstance.

- They often result in putting the system back to where it was some time before.

- Sometimes they take the form of a trade-off among competing interests or characteristics (such as increasing quality but also increasing costs, reducing errors but also reducing volume).

- Their impact is usually felt immediately or in the near future.

When dealing with problems, there is often a need to make first-order change. A customer may not receive a shipment when they expected it because a truck broke down; a physician may be called away on an emergency, affecting the waiting time of scheduled patients; or a bad raw material may result in a faulty product. In each of these cases, there is a need to make changes to remove the immediate problem and bring the performance of the system back to where it had been. Special circumstances could also affect costs. Materials may run out, resulting in a company having to pay retail prices; waste could be increased by a faulty machine; or a pipe could break, causing excessively high water bills.

When Fred looked more closely at the work being done in the distribution department, he noticed that the postal meter broke down quite often. This added to the delays in fulfilling orders. Fred brought this problem to the attention of the company that provided the meter. They promised to get a repairman there quicker the next time the meter was out of order.

Second-Order Changes

Making first-order changes is important. If the postage meter were not repaired quickly when it broke down, customers would experience long delays. First-order changes should not, however, be confused with second-order changes, which prevent problems from occurring. After a first-order change has been made, customers will perceive that an immediate problem has been solved. After a second-order change has been made, customers should perceive that an improvement has been made.

Second-order changes are required to improve the system beyond historical levels. The following are some aspects of second-order change:

- They result from design or redesign of some aspect of the system.

- They are necessary for the improvement of a system that is not plagued by problems.

- They fundamentally alter how the system works and what people do.

- They often result in improvement of several measures simultaneously (such as quality and cost, or time-to-ship and errors).

- Their impact is felt far into the future.

Fred was happy that the supplier of the postal meter was being more responsive when the machine broke down. He was not happy that he did not see a significant impact on service to customers. So, he decided to have discussions about improvement with the people who worked in the distribution department. After a few meetings, they agreed that there were many times during the year when their workload surged because of special offerings. If they could only find out about these specials earlier they could begin to prepare them for shipment during their slow work periods. The people were sure that this would reduce the time to fulfill requests, and that it would also reduce the number of errors. They used a couple of PDSA Cycles to test this change. The result was a reduction in the average time to fulfill requests and in the number of orders that were returned because of errors. What made the group even happier was that the improvement was often mentioned by customers on the company's monthly survey. The people in the department were so encouraged that they began to think about other changes they could make to improve performance.

A second-order change can be made by redesigning part of the current system or by designing an entirely new one. When redesigning a system, it is important to consider whether the system is even needed. Eliminating part or all of a system is one possible second-order change. The important notion is not the size of the change but the impact the change has. Big improvements can often be realized by making small changes directed at the right places in the system.

Fred's group decided to focus on the system of order fulfillment for large orders (see Figure 5.1). Two departments played a major role in the system. The customer service department took the orders and printed the picking tickets. Fred's distribution department then pulled the items, packaged them, and loaded them onto a truck.

After the picking tickets were printed in customer service, someone walked the tickets down to distribution twice a day. This resulted in alternating periods of light and heavy workloads. If the heavy period was in the afternoon, shipments often were not completed that day. Operation of this system resulted in only about 40 percent of orders being shipped on the same day they were received. To improve upon this performance, Fred's group worked with customer service to make two small but significant changes. The first change was to move the customer service printer into the distribution department. The

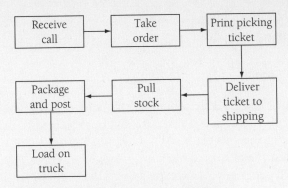

Figure 5.1 *The System of Order Fulfillment.*

picking tickets could then be printed in distribution every hour. The second change was to move the final time a truck left from the distribution department from 4:00 P.M. to 5:00 P.M. These two small changes resulted in same-day shipments being made more than 85 percent of the time. The group is now considering whether certain orders can be entered by customers directly into a computer in the distribution department, which could result in a fundamentally "reengineered" system.

Making second-order change has now become the focus of the people in the distribution department. It is their aim to continuously improve the system. They must keep in mind, however, that once second-order changes are made, unanticipated problems could occur. It is important to make the first-order changes required to remove any immediate problems until the appropriate second-order changes can be developed to eliminate them.

Fred noticed that once in a while the picking tickets would pile up in the printer. When he asked his group what was going on, they said that sometimes they forgot that the picking tickets were no longer being delivered to them by customer service. Fred wrote himself a reminder to get the picking tickets from the printer. He could not be there all the time, however. He realized that he needed to get his group together again to develop a way to assure that the picking tickets would be picked up every hour.

Developing Second-Order Change

Some approaches to developing second-order changes are:

1. Critical thinking about the current system
2. Using technology

3. Creative thinking
4. Using change concepts

Critical Thinking About the Current System

Sometimes it just takes a little time to develop good ideas for change, by reflecting on the system (perhaps with the use of a flowchart) and using already-existing knowledge of the subject matter. Talking about or documenting the way a process is currently performed or how a product works or is used might be sufficient to identify changes. This is the approach Fred took with his group in the distribution department. Reflection on what is wrong with a system can be enhanced with knowledge of some principles of good system design (which will be introduced in the discussion on change concepts later in this chapter).

Figure 5.2 contains an example of a flowchart that was created by a group working in a blood plasma donation center. Their aim was to improve the process by which new donors were selected. Once the group had spent some time reviewing the flowchart, it became obvious to them that some things were wrong with the current process. The fact that donors could be rejected at three different steps in the process added complexity. Some simple changes were made that had the physician and phlebotomist working more as a team, which resulted in more plasma being collected and increased customer satisfaction. The changes made are shown in the flowchart contained in Figure 5.3. (This example is discussed further in Chapter Eight.)

To assist in critical thinking, data can be collected and analyzed to build knowledge about the current system. The collection and analysis of data contributes significantly to identifying problems and their causes so that changes

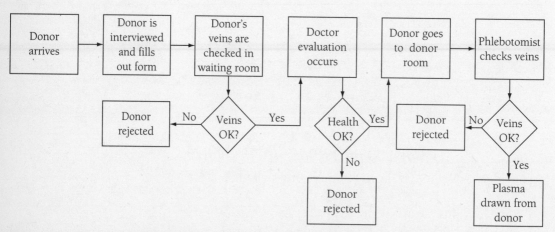

Figure 5.2. *Flowchart of Original Process of Selecting New Plasma Donors.*

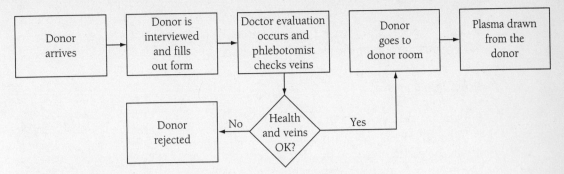

Figure 5.3. *Flowchart of Redesigned Process of Selecting New Plasma Donors.*

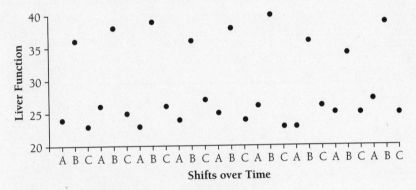

Figure 5.4. *Blood Measurements from One Source.*

can be developed. These changes can then be tested in later cycles. An example of collecting data in a rapid rail transportation system to help develop a change was included in Chapter Four. Another example follows.

The nurses at a Midwest hospital felt that certain blood serum measures made by the hospital's laboratory were unreliable. They decided to run a cycle to better understand the nature of the variation in the blood measurements. They sent the lab a sample of blood from one large stored bottle once every shift for two weeks. The data obtained was plotted on a run chart (see Figure 5.4). The nurses learned from the plot that the B shift consistently produced higher results than the A or C shifts. Based on this knowledge they determined that any change made to reduce the variation in blood testing should be related to the differences in shifts.

More sophisticated approaches to data analysis (such as planned experimentation, regression analysis, time series analysis, or simulations) are available. When appropriate, these methods can be used to assist in developing changes.

Using Technology

For the purposes of this discussion, technology will be defined as the practical application of science, including equipment, materials, information systems, and methods. Technology can be used to generate second order-change. For instance, Fred's group in distribution might try a change that uses automation to pick and package orders. If approached correctly, new technologies offer organizations the opportunity for making big improvements by just applying what others have developed. However, large amounts of money and time are often necessary to make a technology-related change happen, especially in a capital-intensive industry such as manufacturing. In some situations, the change may not even result in improvement.

A transportation company introduced a computerized reservation and routing system. The system left thousands of potential passengers unable to get through on the phone and thousands of actual passengers stranded in terminals. Ridership and the companies stock price plummeted.

This company is not alone when it comes to the introduction of new technology. Between 1985 and 1995, companies invested more than a trillion dollars in new information systems alone. These systems have created opportunities to solve quality problems, reduce costs, and develop new products and services. Some would question, however, whether they have resulted in all of the improvements desired. By considering methods for improvement when acquiring and using new technology, the likelihood increases that the technology will result in an improvement.

To take advantage of new technology, processes for recognizing relevant technological breakthroughs should be in place within the organization, along with processes for bringing beneficial technology into the organization. In some situations, an organization might also consider getting involved during the early stages of the development of the new technology. This might be done by establishing partnerships with other organizations or by allowing the developers to test the technology in one's own organization.

The identification of new technology will begin to answer the third fundamental question of the Model for Improvement (*What changes can we make that will result in improvement?*) The other two questions of the model (*What are we trying to accomplish?* and *How will we know that a change is an improvement?*) should also be answered. This will mitigate the acquisition of technology for technology's sake.

Organizations must determine ways to test the new technology on a small scale, which should help reduce the risk involved in bringing it into the organization. Renting or leasing new equipment, having a supplier provide a few lots of a new material, and using new medicines on laboratory animals rather than on people are examples of ways to test new technology.

Just as (or possibly even more than) any other change, the use of new technology will face resistance and other problems. Some people will find it difficult to change to using the new technology. When computers are introduced, some people feel more comfortable using the more familiar typewriters and file cabinets. Often, the appropriate training is not provided. Sometimes when it is provided, people find ways to avoid it. To lessen these problems, management must have a plan to help people make the transition to the use of the new technology. The guidelines for implementing a change discussed in Chapter Seven should prove useful when integrating technology-related changes into a system.

Following are some cautions for making changes that include technology:

1. Do not automate a bad system.

A professional association processed more than two hundred requests for materials each week. Most of the requests were initiated by a form that appeared monthly in the association's journal. In an attempt to reduce the long delays in responding to these requests, a scanner was purchased that allowed the form to be read directly into the association's computer system. Unfortunately, this did not speed up the process very much. The same information was still missing from or incorrect on the form.

It appears that the association is attempting to automate a bad system. This just allows errors to be made faster. In this case, the use of technology was a high-cost change that did not result in improvement. Improvement could have been made through simple redesign of the system. Changes such as mistake proofing and simplification of the form, minimization of the number of hand-offs, and standardization of the system should be considered. Cycles might be run to redesign the system first before a change involving automation is developed and tested.

2. Try to reserve technological solutions for improving stable systems rather than fixing special causes.

The variability of the semifinished product coming from a particular operation in a large manufacturing facility was so great that the product was difficult to process at further operations. This resulted in large scrap and rework costs. To reduce the variability, the plant manager proposed to the division vice president that they purchase a new piece of equipment. Although the new equipment was expensive and more costly to maintain, the plant manager felt that the savings in scrap, rework, and other costs would offset most of this extra cost.

Before a change involving technology is developed, it should be understood whether special causes affect the variability in the system. If the above system was studied by the people in the plant, they might discover that special circumstances were the source of much of the variation. Special circumstances might include changes in lots of raw material, substitute operators, or changes in operating conditions. Although the new equipment could mitigate the effect of these special causes, a more cost-effective change might be possible. Once the special causes have been identified and removed, if further reduction in variation is needed, then a more fundamental change will be required. Only then should the use of new technology be considered.

3. Direct changes that involve technology at a bottleneck.

A hospital invested in a new computer system to speed up the paperwork required for admissions. New patients could now be processed in half the time. They were not in their rooms any faster, however, because they still had to wait until a room was available.

A bottleneck within an organization is any juncture where the demand for a resource is greater than its availability. Since the throughput of the system is dictated by the capacity at the bottleneck, changes should be directed at increasing the flow through that resource. Using technology to increase capacity in areas that are not bottlenecks will not result in increasing the throughput of the system. It will just result in greater waiting times at the bottleneck. The hospital used new technology to increase patient flow through admissions. This did not decrease the total time for patients to get to their rooms because the discharging of patients was the bottleneck in the system.

4. A technology that is unreliable is worse than none at all.

John was very happy to have a new garage door opener to ease his way in and out of his garage. Shortly after it was installed, however, it failed to open the garage door when John was trying to leave for work. Unfortunately, this made him late for a very important meeting.

Once a change involving technology is implemented, people rely on the performance of that new technology. The new technology should therefore be thoroughly tested so there is no doubt about its reliability. In John's case, the improvement realized by the installation of the garage door opener was lost by his bad experience.

Creative Thinking

In its simplest form, creativity is the inventing of a new idea. Where does the new idea come from? How does one go about getting some more creative ideas? The way the human mind works is very well-suited for producing new ideas—for being creative. This means that creativity is not something that a few gifted people possess, but rather a capacity that everyone possesses. How can people begin to unleash that capacity?

The nature of the mind that makes it a bountiful source of creativity is also the force that hinders creativity. A way to think of the mind is as a self-organizing information system. As perceptions and experiences occur, the mind attempts to find meaning and order. This organizing process uses existing thought patterns to judge the meaning of the new experiences. Using existing thought patterns severely restricts the options for change that people consider. It is one of the primary reasons that individuals or groups who are not skilled in improvement usually produce ideas for improvement that are "more of the same."

The normal thought patterns that occur in a particular situation have a logic that has been sharpened over time (Figure 5.5). Since a new idea does not yet have an acquired pattern of logic to support it, it can easily be defeated by the more well-developed logic of the existing thought patterns. Thus, a promising new idea can be squelched before it has had a chance to be refined into a change that would result in improvement.

One can easily imagine the logical objections that arose from others at the distribution department's meeting when someone first suggested preparing shipments in advance. If Fred as the supervisor had not supported the idea, would these objections have been overridden? An important breakthrough in creativity is often produced by recognizing and utilizing different modes of thinking. Recognizing the different modes is especially helpful in group or team settings.

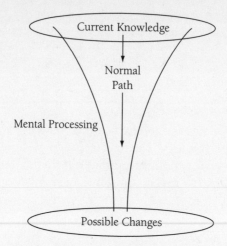

Figure 5.5. *Normal Thought Process.*

The three modes of thinking that are usually present when changes are being developed are:

- *Creative thinking,* which results in new ideas and possibilities

- *Logical positive thinking,* which is concerned with how to make a new idea work

- *Logical negative (critical) thinking,* which is focused on finding faulty logic in the new idea

All three modes are important and play a role in developing changes that result in improvement. Without creative thinking, some incremental improvement may result, but often there is only "more of the same." Without logical positive thinking, good concepts for change will not result in practical, workable changes to the system. Critical thinking is needed to surface problems. As discussed earlier, critical thinking is useful when reviewing the current system. It is also particularly useful during the design of a test for a change. What could be the negative effects of the change? How can the change be tested on conditions that would give these potential negative effects a chance to occur? Logical positive thinking will help to develop ways to overcome these difficulties.

These three modes of thinking must be recognized and managed by teams that are developing changes. It is usually better for a group to engage in one type of thinking at a time. When new ideas for change are being developed, creative and logical positive thinking should be used. This allows logical thinking to enhance creative thinking rather than stifle it.

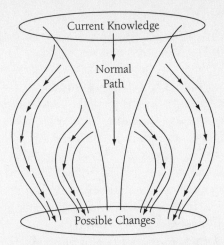

Figure 5.6. *Provoking New Thought Patterns.*

How can these three modes of thinking be used to develop creative, second-order changes? Methods for improving creative thinking have their foundation in provoking new thought patterns that lead to new ideas for change. (Figure 5.6 illustrates this concept.) Without new thought patterns, a very limited set of potential changes will be produced. Provoking new thought patterns opens up a limitless variety of changes that can result in dramatic improvement. Following are some general methods for provoking new thought patterns:

1. *Take time.* This is the simplest method. Spend perhaps even just five or ten minutes to expressly do some creative thinking.

2. *Be in the right place at the right time.* A story claims that Isaac Newton was provoked into thinking about gravity by an apple falling on his head as he sat under a tree. Spending time observing customers or taking the role of a customer can allow a person to be in the right place when serendipitous events occur that provoke new ideas.

3. *Challenge the boundaries within which the change can be developed.* People are often limited in developing changes by implicit or explicit boundaries. To challenge these boundaries, begin by listing them. Then eliminate or expand the boundaries. One of the boundaries listed by a group working on improving service in an office cafeteria was that the food was always paid for after it was selected. When the team challenged this boundary, the use of prepaid meal tickets or a set-price buffet were suggested as possible changes.

4. *Attack the solution.* Many times the changes that are suggested are "more of the same" and are a result of current thought patterns. Make a list of the suggested changes and identify what they have in common. As in challenging the boundaries, attack the common themes as hindrances to new ideas. Look for a change that does not possess this commonality. A group working on improving

efficiencies in their order fulfillment process examined previous changes that had been made. Although some of the changes were successful, all of them were focused on reducing paperwork and handoffs within the organization. A review of these solutions resulted in someone suggesting that customers enter their orders directly into a computer in the distribution area.

5. *Use "unrealistic" goals.* When the current way things are done is clearly inadequate to meet the goal, ask the question, What would it take to _____ ? (Fill in the blank with a seemingly unrealistic goal). This will help people to abandon the current way of thinking.

6. *Focus on the need.* For any particular product or service, articulate what the need is that the product or service matches, and then similar to attacking the solution, discard the current products and services as options. There will be many ways to match the need with new products and services. For example, a landscaping company provided the service of mowing lawns. After they articulated that keeping the grass short and neat was the need for this service, they began to experiment with regulators that slowed the growth of the grass. This almost eliminated the service of mowing.

When new thought patterns are provoked, new ideas for change should result. These ideas can often be brought to life through some form of expression, such as giving an example, drawing a picture, storytelling, or acting them out. Ideas are slippery things and the skill of representation tends to stabilize them, allowing them to be studied and improved upon. Representation also provides a way to share the idea with others.

After Tony drew a picture of the new handles he had been talking about, everyone was able to see why it would help with lifting the large pots. Mary added some detail to the picture and they took it down to engineering to see if they could install the handles on one pot.

Using Change Concepts

If a concept is a general notion that is carried out with a more specific idea, what is meant by "change concept"? A change concept is a general notion or approach that has been found to be useful in developing specific ideas for change that result in improvement. When Fred and the group in the distribution department began to consider changes that would improve service, they took time to think critically about how work was being accomplished. This did result in some improvements. Suppose, however, that to provoke new ideas Fred was able to apply already existing concepts for change to his situation. He would have been able to start with a concept such as "smooth the work flow." Then, to develop a specific change, this concept could have been combined with the knowledge of how the distribution department worked. Starting with such a concept helps people to accelerate the quality and the quantity of new ideas.

Included in the appendix are seventy "change concepts" that are at the heart of changes that result in improvement. Many of them are based on the elements of W. Edwards Deming's System of Profound Knowledge, discussed in the introduction: appreciation of a system, understanding variation, theory of knowledge, and psychology. Others have been collected over time by this book's authors. Regardless of the origin of the concepts, it is their usefulness to improvement that makes them valuable. Using change concepts will provoke new ways of thinking about the problem at hand.

Fred and his group in the distribution department were having difficulty developing additional ideas for change to further improve the flow of work. A friend who was familiar with Fred's dilemma passed on to him a book. In the appendix, Fred found concepts that could be used to develop ideas for change. In fact, there was a group of concepts that dealt directly with improving work flow. Fred was very excited about sharing these concepts with his group. He felt the concepts would help to generate some specific ideas for change.

At the next meeting, Fred explained to the group members what he was going to do and asked them to think positively while changes were being suggested. He started by presenting the change concept "minimize handoffs." Immediately Mike said that they did have a tendency to hand off a particular job, from picking to packing to postage. There would be fewer holdups if one person could both pick and package the order. Others nodded in agreement and offered some other suggestions. Fred was starting to feel good about this approach. He tried another concept: "smooth the work flow." Karen said that they had smoothed the flow by starting to prepare orders earlier. She wondered why they had not been given this concept before they had spent so much time trying to come up with that idea.

Next, Fred tried "do tasks in parallel." John jumped up and almost screamed, "Let's get the paperwork going at the same time we are preparing the order." Everyone laughed because John was usually not that animated, but they all agreed with his idea. Fred was very happy about how the meeting was progressing. They had begun to develop a number of good ideas for changes, and he still had more change concepts left. The possibilities for improvement now seemed almost endless.

Fred employed a good approach for using the change concepts. He first picked a general grouping, "improve work flow," that characterized the improvements he was trying to make. Then he used some of the change concepts from that grouping to provoke specific ideas for change. Fred's approach is not the only way that the change concepts can be used, however. A specific idea for a change might be generated first (such as the idea of having one person both pick and package the order), then people could be asked what the general notion is that is being applied to generate that idea, which should lead to the change concept "minimize handoffs." New ideas can then be generated from that change concept (for example, that one person could complete all the steps in distribution to fill an order, or that customers could input their orders directly into a computer system). Other change concepts in the general grouping "improve work flow" might be explored to generate other ideas for changes.

A change concept is not specific enough to use directly. Concepts such as "smooth the work flow" and "minimize handoffs" must be applied to specific situations and then turned into ideas for change. The two ways suggested here for using the change concepts are similar; they are based on the skill of going back and forth between the general (change concepts) and the specific (ideas). The examples provided in the appendix demonstrate the use of this skill. It is an important one to practice when using the change concepts. Some others ways of using them are as follows:

- Select a change concept at random and see what ideas are provoked.

- Study the appendix to learn all the different change concepts and some ideas for their use. Rely on this knowledge when faced with a particular situation.

- Copy the specific ideas in the examples included for each change concept in the appendix if they apply directly to your situation.

Chapters Ten, Eleven, and Twelve include further discussion on the use of change concepts.

Change concepts can be used to stimulate both critical and creative thinking. The change concepts in categories such as "improve work flow," "focus on variation," and "mistake proofing" contain principles of good system design. If you are reflecting on what is wrong with your current system, having in mind some of the change concepts should increase the quality and quantity of the changes you develop. Creative thinking can be stimulated if certain change concepts are selected (perhaps even at random) and used as provocations.

Many of the change concepts in the appendix might be familiar to you already. There might also be other concepts that you would add. The change concepts listed are not meant to be original nor complete. The important thing is that the list can serve as an easy reference and that other concepts can be added to it. The rate of improvement will accelerate as people not only use the change concepts but also develop and document new ones. Some of the new concepts may prove more useful in a particular field, such as in health care or education. One way to discover change concepts is to study the improvements that have been made in your organization and ask:

1. What was the specific change that was made?
2. What was the idea used for the change?
3. Where (who) did the idea come from?
4. Which of the change concepts could generate that idea?
5. Can the idea be generalized for other situations?
6. Would a new concept be useful for describing this idea for change?

Fred kept a list of the ideas for change that were developed using the change concepts. The list was very impressive. Although the group believed that all the changes had potential, they also realized that the changes needed to be tested to determine if they actually would result in improvement. So, they prioritized the different changes, considering such things as the predicted impact, the cost, and the ease of testing and implementation. The group was excited, but Fred was worried. He had never thought about testing a change before. When he referred to the book *The Improvement Guide,* there it was: Chapter Six, "Testing a Change." He began to read it.

Conclusion

What change can we make that will lead to improvement? The first step in answering this question is to develop an idea for a possible change. The idea can come from critical thinking about the current system, from technology, from creative thinking, or from using the change concepts in the resource guide at the end of this book. The next step is to test the idea.

CHAPTER 6

Testing a Change

Chapter Five discussed methods for answering the question, *What changes can we make that will result in improvement?* This chapter is concerned with determining whether the changes developed are really improvements. This is done by testing the changes using the PDSA Cycle.

Tim was a supervisor in a lab. He had recently become aware of a new procedure that could be used to measure the amount of a key ingredient in a product. Another lab that used this procedure reported improvements in accuracy and time to complete the test, and attributed it to the fact that the new procedure eliminated a lot of complexity. Tim decided to test the new procedure in his lab.

Tim thought that the change had some promise. He made a wise decision when he decided to test the new procedures rather than just implement them. When making improvements, it is important to distinguish between testing and implementing. Testing is used to evaluate one or more changes. Implementing means making a change part of the day-to-day operations for a process or service or incorporating it into the next version of a product. An important practical consequence of testing before implementing is that some tests are expected to fail, and we can learn from those failures. That is why testing on a small scale to build knowledge while minimizing risk is so important. Once a change is implemented, we should expect very few failures. (Implementation of a change is discussed in Chapter Seven.)

Tim is interested in learning whether the new procedure will be an improvement in his lab when used by different technicians for different batches. He needs to make a prediction whether the change will result in improvement once it is implemented. The use of good methods to test the new procedure will increase Tim's ability to make that prediction.

Change as a Prediction

A prediction is a statement of how a system, process, or product is expected to perform. Implicit in every change is a prediction that the change will result in future improvement. Will a new teaching approach be successful in all classes in upcoming years? Will a new computer system result in faster and more accurate order processing? Will a new surgical procedure, when used routinely, result in shorter rehabilitation time for a variety of patients? A prediction of the impact of a change puts one in a better position to learn as the change is tested.

A prediction is made in response to a question. Tim asked, "Will the new procedure result in improvement in the lab?" A prediction is usually stated in terms of the particular measures or outcomes that the change is attempting to affect. Tim predicted that the change would improve the accuracy of the procedure by approximately 10 percent and cut the time to perform the procedure in half. A prediction should also include the reasoning or theory on which the prediction is based. Tim based his prediction on the theory that the new procedure reduced the complexity of the test. He could articulate the details of his theory to those in the lab. Tim was confident in his prediction because there was evidence available from a similar lab to support it.

A government agency was concerned about the low rate of immunizations (shots for measles, polio, and so on) among children. The agency proposed a change that consisted of the agency buying the available vaccine and distributing it free of charge to physicians. Their prediction was that this would substantially increase the rate of immunization among children. The prediction was based on the theory that the high cost of shots is the reason people do not have their children immunized.

Just as Tim did, the government agency made a prediction about a change. In making any prediction, one has some "degree of belief" (high, medium, or low) that the prediction is a good one. The concept of degree of belief provides a way to assess the depth of one's knowledge about whether a change will result in improvement in the future. One's degree of belief in a prediction depends on two considerations: (1) the extent to which the prediction can be supported by evidence, and (2) the similarity between the conditions under which the evidence was obtained and the conditions to which the prediction applies.

Is the cause of the low immunization rate the cost of the vaccine, as the agency suggests? Perhaps it is something else, such as lack of knowledge that the shots are important, neglect, or complacency because no one gets certain diseases anymore. What is the evidence to support the theory that cost is the issue? Do poor people have lower immunization rates? What about poor people who have the shots paid for by a government program, by an employer-supplied insurance plan, or by an HMO? Data consisting of evidence related to the prediction will help answer these questions.

Degree of belief will be high, medium, or low depending in part on how much the evidence supports the prediction. If the degree of belief is low, it does not mean that the change should be abandoned or not tested. However, a low degree of belief is a reason for caution. The test should be kept small and the risks low. Implementing the change on a large scale when the degree of belief is low may not be prudent.

Suppose the government agency decides to run a test of the free vaccine to gather more evidence on the merits of the change. This test could be made more informative by including people from all parts of society—such as people who have no family doctor and those who do—and by conducting the test in different regions of the country. The range of conditions that should be included in the test or tests are those to which the prediction will apply. Someone with knowledge of the area under consideration must decide those conditions.

Satisfactory prediction of the results of tests conducted over a wide range of conditions increases the degree of belief that the change will result in improvement. Test results that do not agree with predictions may be cause to rethink the theory that is the basis of the prediction. This reassessment will allow for the formulation of new theories to help in the development of other changes. The PDSA Cycle should be used as the framework to carry out such tests.

Using the PDSA Cycle to Test a Change

The four phases of the PDSA Cycle—planning the details of the test and making predictions about the outcomes (the Plan phase), conducting the test and collecting data (the Do phase), comparing the predictions to the results of the test (the Study phase), and taking action based on the new knowledge (the Act phase)—were discussed in Chapters One and Four. Figure 6.1 summarizes what should be considered in each phase of the cycle when testing a change. Developing a good plan for a test is critical to its success. Exhibit 6.1 contains a form that can be used to develop a plan.

The plan begins with a statement of the specific objective of the cycle. Cycles to test a change will have varying objectives depending on the current degree of belief.

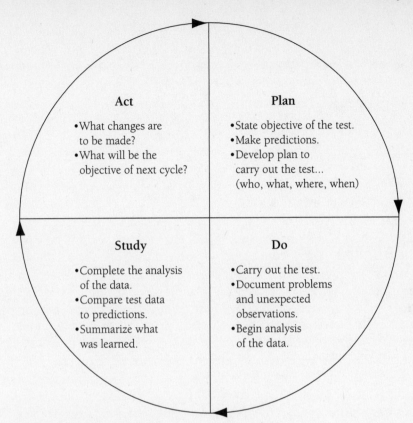

Figure 6.1. *Using the PDSA Cycle to Test a Change.*

The following are some possible objectives of cycles:

- To increase the degree of belief that the change will result in an improvement

- To decide which of several proposed changes will lead to the desired improvement

- To evaluate how much improvement can be expected if the change is made

- To decide whether the proposed change will work in the actual environment of interest

- To decide which combinations of changes will have the desired effects on the important measures of quality

- To evaluate costs, social impact, and side effects from a proposed change

1. Objective of the test:

2. Change being tested:

3. Questions and predictions:

4. Key background information:

5. Measure(s):

6. Design of the test:

   Scale of the test and the risks involved:

   Type of study:

   Method of data analysis:

   How a range of conditions will be included:

   Randomization:

   Who, when, and where:

Exhibit 6.1. *Form for Planning a Test.*

Mike was the manager of production planning. He spent four months redesigning all aspects of the scheduling process. When he explained the process to his planners, they were not happy with such a large change to their normal procedures. When the planners tried to use the new process to schedule production the next month, there were numerous problems. Mike quickly switched back to the old scheduling process.

Mike made a common but often disastrous mistake in his attempt to improve scheduling: he developed the "perfect" change and then implemented it. What seems exactly right after many hours of planning and analysis around the conference table may collapse under the stress of everyday reality. Remember, change is a prediction. Rough prototypes of the change or some of its components should be tested in PDSA cycles as soon as possible. Instead of redesigning the entire scheduling process over four months, Mike could have begun with a rough concept of the new system. He then could have used multiple cycles over the four months to test and improve the components. In this case and in most others, using multiple cycles to increase one's knowledge of a change will accelerate the rate of improvement.

The use of multiple cycles allows knowledge to be increased as a change progresses from testing to implementation. It allows risk to be minimized. As degree of belief that the change will be successful is increased, the scale of the test can be increased.

Suppose a change is developed in a manufacturing process. In the first cycle, people with knowledge of the subject might review it. Then, in the second cycle, it could be tried in a pilot plant. In the next cycle, the change might be tested on one line in the production area. The change might then be revised and tested in a fourth cycle. If the learning from the first four cycles increases to a high level the degree of belief that the change will result in improvement, all or part of the change could then be implemented full-scale in production. The collection and analysis of data in each of these cycles is essential to the learning process.

Based on the results of a test, a change or some part of a change could be implemented as is, or it could be modified and retested, or it could be abandoned. Figure 6.2 illustrates changes in degree of belief as a team or individual uses cycles to go from the development of a change to testing and implementing it.

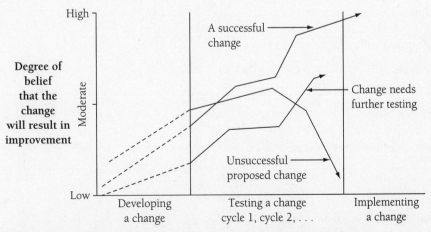

Figure 6.2. *Moving from Developing to Testing to Implementing a Change.*

Types of Studies

Several different types of studies can be used within a PDSA cycle to test a change. They range from simple, informal tests to comprehensive, complex experiments. The individual or team involved in testing a change should select a level of formality and complexity relevant to their situation. In this section, two types of studies—the before-and-after test, and the simultaneous comparison of two or more alternatives—are introduced. These studies are widely applicable and occupy the midrange of formality and complexity. The examples in this section show that the methods for the analysis of data are almost exclusively graphical. The aim of graphical methods is to visually display the impact of a change on the data being collected. Run charts and histograms are commonly used because of their simplicity. Using graphical methods also has the side benefit of allowing everyone involved with planning the test to be involved in the analysis.

Before-and-After Test

A common and very useful way to test a change is to make the change and compare the circumstances after the change to the circumstances before the change. The collection of data before the change provides the historical experience that is the basis of the comparison. A before-and-after test was used in the example of the diner in Chapter One.

Figure 6.3 presents a run chart that was used to analyze the results of a test conducted by a group of physicians. The test was designed to determine whether

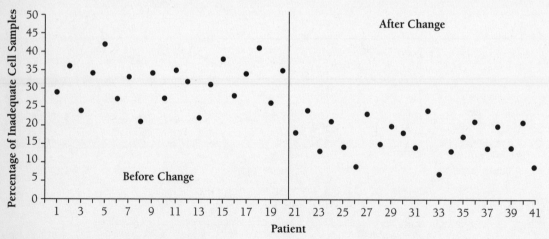

Figure 6.3. *Data from a Before-and-After Test.*

a new instrument to obtain cell samples from patients would be an improvement over the existing instrument. One of the measures of quality that was used in the evaluation was the percentage of inadequate samples. An inadequate sample was one that did not contain enough cells to proceed with the diagnostic test. Data were obtained on the percentage of inadequate samples before and after the use of the new instrument. Collecting data over time makes it possible to see whether patterns indicating improvement coincide with the time of the change. In the run chart in Figure 6.3, the reduction in inadequate samples coincides with the use of the new instrument.

Since the basis of comparison in a before-and-after test is historical experience, the test is vulnerable to misinterpretation if a special cause unrelated to the change occurs at or about the same time that the change is made. Perhaps a seminar was given on a new way to use the old instrument while the new instrument was being introduced. It is up to those conducting the test to make the judgement that the effect seen is due to the change being tested. There is a rational basis for this judgement if there are no obvious external events and the system has been stable in the past. In the example just presented, the physicians believed that the improvement in the percentage of inadequate samples was the result of the new instrument. They decided to plan another cycle to test the use of the instrument under a wider range of conditions.

The data collected during a before-and-after test is susceptible to another special cause, one that is difficult to detect: the effect of conducting the test in the first place, sometimes known as the Hawthorne or Sentinel effect. During the test, the people involved may be more careful or diligent in their work. This may be the cause of the improvement rather than the change being tested. This difficulty can be mitigated by testing over time so that the initial novelty of the test wears off. Also, if it is possible and ethical, people might not be informed that they are part of a test. Open communication, however, is often the better alternative. If the Hawthorne effect is suspected, the data collected during the test can be used to provide feedback to people. This feedback allows them to change what they are doing so that the improvement seen during the test can be sustained.

In the example illustrated in Figure 6.3, it was possible to collect a sequence of data during the test. In some situations, it might be practical to collect data only once before and once after the change. For example, scores on a pretest and posttest might be used to evaluate the effect of new audiovisual materials in a history class, or a group of patients undergoing rehabilitation might be asked to evaluate the amount of pain they are feeling before and after a new exercise program. In this case, displaying on a histogram the data collected prior to and after a test is a useful way to do the analysis.

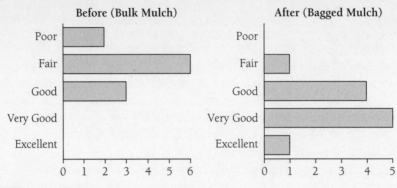

Figure 6.4. *Data on the Use of Mulch.*

A landscape maintenance organization purchased mulch in bulk quantities. The mulch was delivered to a central location. It was used around trees, shrubs, and flower beds at various sites. Bulk purchasing was the cheapest way to buy the mulch, but it resulted in waste and cleanup problems. A team was formed to consider alternative ways to purchase and use mulch. After some research, they decided to test the use of mulch supplied in bags.

Customers at the different sites were asked to rate the appearance of the mulch on a scale ranging from poor to excellent, both before the test of bagged mulch and after the bagged mulch was used. The responses before and after the change were compared on a histogram (Figure 6.4). Data on the cost of mulch during the test was kept by the purchasing department and compared to past expenditures.

After reviewing the data, the team concluded that appearance was improved with the use of bagged mulch. The members of the crews did not feel that any change other than the use of bagged mulch delivered to the site resulted in the improvement shown. Purchasing reported that the cost for mulch was only slightly higher when the bagged mulch was used. Considering ease of application and delivery, the total cost to the system was considered to be less. The degree of belief of the team was high that the use of bagged mulch was an improvement. Purchasing was asked to arrange with the supplier to provide the mulch required. The team decided to track any problems encountered during the implementation of this change.

The rating question used in this example could have been "Regarding appearance, how would you rate the bagged mulch versus the bulk mulch?" and a "much worse" to "much better" scale (such as that introduced in Figure 4.4) could have been used. Data would then need to be collected only after the change.

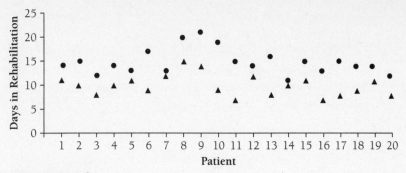

Figure 6.5. *Data Collected on Rehabilitation Time.*

Simultaneous Comparisons

In a simultaneous comparison test (commonly called a paired comparison study), two or more alternatives are compared at the same time, in the same space, or under other similar conditions. When one of the alternatives is the current system, the test is often called a simultaneous comparison with a control. By comparing alternatives in such a way, the effect of external events on the different alternatives can be studied during the test. A simultaneous comparison test can therefore help to rule out alternate explanations for the improvement.

Figure 6.5 shows the data a physician, Dr. Smith, collected on rehabilitation time. The data were collected during a simultaneous comparison test of a new rehabilitation procedure. Based on previous research, Dr. Smith's degree of belief was high that the new procedure would result in improvement. It was also her belief that if it turned out that the new procedure was not an improvement, the risks involved were not high. She advised the patients and received their consent to include them in the test of the new procedure.

The run chart juxtaposes the data that resulted when the current rehabilitation method was used on a group of patients with the data obtained from patients using the new method. Both sets of data were collected over the same four-month period. The run chart reveals the impact of the change and the effect of an external event on both the current and the new method. The external event that caused a higher rehabilitation time for both procedures (although the new procedure was still lower) was identified as the presence of a new physical therapist. This therapist conducted the rehabilitation for a short time when the regular therapist was on vacation. The results of this test increased Dr. Smith's degree of belief that the new method was an improvement over the old.

Randomization

After reviewing the run charts on rehabilitation time, one might question whether the two groups differ not because of the procedure used but because of some preexisting difference (such as the age of the patients). Dr. Smith overcame this possible alternate explanation for the results of the test by using random assignment.

Random assignment is the use of a device such as a table of random numbers to assign the change being tested to the people or things selected for the test. In this example, an equal number of people were assigned to each procedure using a table of random numbers matched to the list of patients participating in the study—odd numbers for the old procedure and even numbers for the new procedure. If random assignment is used, it is assumed that the groups do not differ systematically before the test.

In some situations, a check can be done on the random assignment by collecting data on the groups before the change is tested. The differences in the groups can then be evaluated before the change.

Planned Grouping

Based on the results of her test, Dr. Smith believed that the new rehabilitation procedure did have an impact on rehabilitation time. She was now interested in learning whether the procedure would prove successful when used by different therapists, in different hospitals, and with young and old patients. She decided to run another cycle to consider a wide range of conditions in her test. She planned to set up two groups with extreme conditions to determine whether the new procedure would result in improvement in both groups. She selected two hospitals, one small and one large; two therapists, one with two years of experience and one with ten; and two sets of patients, one under thirty years of age and one sixty years of age and older.

Dr. Smith was using *planned grouping*, in which important conditions are held constant within each of two or more groups but varied between the groups. The use of planned grouping allows for a wide range of conditions to be included in a test in a systematic way. The two groups Dr. Smith planned were:

Group 1	*Group 2*
Small hospital	Large hospital
Therapist with two years of experience	Therapist with ten years of experience
Old patients	Young patients

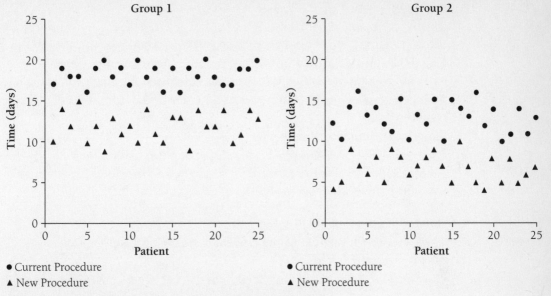

Figure 6.6. *Simultaneous Comparison Test Using Planned Grouping.*

In her test, Dr. Smith purposely set up two groups that had very different conditions. If the new procedure resulted in improvement in both groups, her degree of belief would be high that the change would result in improvement in the future. To conduct the test, she ran a simultaneous comparison study in both groups. Once the patients were selected for a particular group, they were randomly assigned to receive the new or old procedure. The results of the test are shown in Figure 6.6.

The run chart shows that the new procedure resulted in improvement in both groups. Although the rehabilitation time was generally higher in group 1, the new procedure still resulted in shorter times. Dr. Smith's degree of belief was increased that the new procedure would result in improvement under the different conditions to which it would be applied.

The possibility exists that the change will show improvement in some planned groups but not in others. If this results, the next cycles should be used to study the relationship between the change being tested and the different conditions in the groups.

Choosing a Study

The before-and-after test and the simultaneous comparison can be used in many situations. Following are some things to consider when deciding which type of study to use:

Consider a before-and-after test when:

1. The data that are available or that can be collected before the change are sufficient to form the basis of comparison.
2. There is a minimal threat of misinterpretation of the results because some external event is present on or about the same time the change is made.
3. Data will continue to be collected over a long period of time after the change has been made.
4. Large improvements are expected.
5. Groups needed for a simultaneous comparison test cannot be isolated—for example, when a group of mechanics assigned to use an old maintenance procedure prefer the new procedure and begin to use it.

Consider a simultaneous comparison when:

1. Two or more alternatives to the current system (for example, two new suppliers) are being tested.
2. Only one alternative is being tested but external events pose a threat to the interpretation of the results. A control group (a group using the current system) should be used along with the alternative group being tested.
3. There is a desire to include a wide range of conditions in a test during one cycle. This is possible by using planned grouping.

Tests in Which More Than One Change is Made

It is possible to test more than one change at the same time by using a type of test called a *factorial experiment*. A factorial experiment provides an alternative to testing one change at a time. It allows for the study of the impact of different combinations of changes. For example, a factorial experiment could detect that some combination of temperature and pressure has the optimal effect on an important characteristic of a product. Also, a teacher might want to test having students working in teams versus a standard lecture format and at the same time test the impact of class size. Perhaps, the team approach will result in improvement only when the class size is small. Although factorial experiments are beyond the scope of this chapter, many books are available for further study.

Evaluation of the Evidence

The prediction that a change will result in improvement is based on the knowledge of the people making the change and the evidence or data that is collected during the test. In some cases, the evidence is very strong. In the examples in the last section, the impacts of the changes were obvious. The data indicated that the changes had the desired effect. That is, the patterns in the data after the changes could not be explained by the patterns before the changes. These results made it easy to move toward implementation of the changes. In some situations, the evidence will not be as strong. Does this mean the change should be abandoned?

Since he had become the manager of the production area, Jim had used a run chart to plot data on yield for a key product. He had seen large variation and very little improvement in the data over the previous few years. Jim was confident that the changes developed recently would improve yield. While these changes were being tested, data was collected and plotted on the existing chart (Figure 6.7).

Whether the data from a test is analyzed using a run chart, a histogram, or some other method, experts in the subject under consideration must evaluate the data and determine the actions that should be taken. That the evidence is not strong does not necessarily mean that the change should be abandoned. This decision depends on the development stage of the change and the prediction of the results.

In the initial cycles, knowledge may be built about problems or side effects of the change. The prediction might be that the change will not result in improvement until these problems or side effects are removed. At this point, people should become advocates of the change. The initial cycles should result in the change being revised and improved. Indications of improvement should be seen

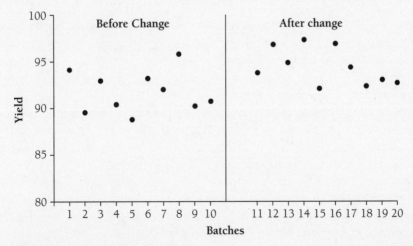

Figure 6.7. *Data Collected on Yield.*

in the next cycles while the change is being refined. In the final cycles, the change should be critically evaluated, and strong evidence of improvement using graphical methods should be acquired.

In a few cases, the prediction might be that the impact of the change will be small compared to the large variation in the system, but even a small improvement will be beneficial. This might be true with yield improvements for expensive raw materials or with the reduction of serious side effects of a drug. A decision might be made to continue the change to determine whether the improvements seen can be sustained over time. In such cases, a statistician might be consulted to help plan the cycle and evaluate the evidence.

Principles for Testing a Change

The ideas discussed in the previous section, on maximizing learning and minimizing the negative side effects during a test, can be summarized in two basic principles that should be considered in the plan phase of a cycle to test a change:

1. Build knowledge sequentially.
    Test on a small scale.
    Use multiple cycles.
2. Increase the ability to predict from the results of the test.
    Collect data over time during the test.
    Test over a wide range of conditions.

Principle 1: Build Knowledge Sequentially

Because not all changes result in improvement, those responsible for developing the change should continually be looking for ways of reducing the risks of the test while maximizing the learning.

Test on a Small Scale The scale of the test should be decided according to (1) the degree of belief that the change will result in improvement, and (2) the risks from a failed test. As shown in Table 6.1, very small-scale tests are needed when the consequences of failure will be major and the degree of belief in success is low. Consequences might include severe negative impact on customers, financial loss, or injuries. The use of expensive new technology, introduction of a new service, or the test of a new medical procedure would fall into this category. When risks are high, it is always wise to have a contingency plan developed that describes the actions needed in case the test fails.

If the consequences of a failed test are major but one's degree of belief in suc-

Table 6.1. *Deciding the Scale of a Test.*

	DEGREE OF BELIEF IN SUCCESS	
CONSEQUENCES OF FAILED TEST	LOW	HIGH
Minor	Medium-scale tests	One cycle to implement the change
Major	Very small-scale tests	Small- to medium-scale test

cess is high, then small- to medium-scale tests should be considered. The test of a medical procedure or a drug shown elsewhere to be an improvement would fall into this category. The test is directed at learning about the use of the procedure or drug in a new environment.

Consequences are often minor when tests are run that affect processes or systems that are internal to the organization—that is, when the tests do not have a direct impact on the organization's customers. Examples might be mail delivery or the storage of inventory. In these cases, tests can be done on a larger scale.

If small-scale tests are appropriate, one way to design such a test is to simulate the change in some way.

Consideration was being given to installing a pneumatic tube system to carry sample parts between two areas in a large organization. Before the installation, the supervisor in one of the areas decided to run a test to determine the utilization of such a system. For a week she wore a beeper. If anyone wanted to send parts, they would beep her and she would hand carry them to the other area.

By simulating the pneumatic tube system and measuring utilization, the supervisor was in a better position to make a decision about whether to implement this change. Modeling a change on a computer or role playing are two other ways to simulate a change. Often, some imagination is all that is needed.

Besides simulating the change, some other ways to design a small-scale test are:

- Have others who have some knowledge about the change review and comment on its feasibility.

- Test the new product or the new process on the members of the team that developed the change before introducing it to others.

- Incorporate redundancy in the test by making the change side-by-side with the existing process or product (a simultaneous comparison test).

- Conduct the test in only one facility or office in the organization, or with only one customer.

- Conduct the test over a short period.

- Test the change on a small group of volunteers.

Testing a change on a small scale is an important way of reducing people's fears of making a change. When small-scale tests are not considered, people procrastinate. They try to develop the perfect change because of the potential consequences of a failed test. This approach might be particularly prevalent in some big corporations or government agencies where any change to programs or policies is usually scrutinized. When planning a cycle to test a change, much thought should be given to developing ways of building knowledge through small-scale tests.

Use Multiple Cycles Testing on a small scale leads to the use of multiple cycles to build knowledge sequentially. Attempting to get all the answers concerning a change from one large cycle should be avoided. Besides the negative effect such a large change might have on normal operations, the people the change affects will have more difficulty committing to the change. Some initial cycles might be used to decide whether the change is workable under the best conditions. This will also increase people's interest and willingness to buy into the change.

Based on what is learned from any cycle, a change might be:

- Implemented as is

- Abandoned

- Increased in scope

- Modified

- Tested under different conditions

In the last three situations listed, additional cycles for testing the change are needed. As the degree of belief in the success of the change is increased, the scale of the test can be increased with less risk. (See Figure 4.3 for an illustration of how the repeated use of the cycle can be used to build knowledge.)

A company that manufactures tiles for floors and ceilings was experiencing some difficulties with the accuracy of their inventory records. A computerized material control system (MCS) was used to keep track of the amount of inventory on hand. Actual physical counts to verify the computerized records were made frequently by a variety of people. Discrepancies were often found between the MCS and the physical counts. Adjustments made to reconcile the discrepancies seemed to make the problem worse. The situation was having an effect on the schedule for manufacturing. A team was therefore formed to make improvements to the process of monitoring inventory. The team had great success in increasing inventory accuracy by using numerous cycles to test and implement changes. The objectives of some initial cycles were as follows:

Cycle 1   Test changes to standardize procedures for the physical counts for residential tile.

Cycle 2   Test the revised counting procedures (based on the learning from cycle 1) for physical counts for residential tile.

Cycle 3   Implement the new counting procedures for the physical counts for residential tile.

Cycle 4   Test the new counting procedures for other products.

Cycle 5   Implement the new counting procedures for other products.

Cycle 6   Collect data to determine the impact of adjustments to the MCS, based on physical counts of the inventory of residential tile.

Cycle 7   Test the use of a control chart to determine when adjustments to the MCS for residential tile should be made.

Cycle 8   Implement the use of control charts to determine when adjustments to the MCS should be made for all products.

Principle 2: Increase the Ability to Predict from the Results of the Test

Collect Data Over Time The measures of a product or process will always be affected by common causes of variation that are unrelated to the change being tested. Therefore, viewing the patterns in the data over time is critical to determining the effect of the change. After a change, data must be analyzed to decide whether the system is stable; a prediction about future performance can then be made.

Figure 6.3 contained a run chart of the data collected on the percentage of inadequate samples obtained during the testing of a new instrument used in a medical procedure. Variation is evident before the change, but also evident is the impact of the change on the data. It is possible to see the impact because a sequence of data was collected and plotted on the run chart both before and after the change. After the change to the medical procedure, the percent of inadequate samples stabilized at an average of approximately 15 percent. Unless some other change in the system occurs, one would expect this same level of performance in the future. When collecting a sequence of data over time is not possible, histograms should be used to analyze data from a test (see Figure 6.4 for an example of a histogram).

In most tests of change, conditions during the test are a more important consideration than sample size (the number of items tested). A change may have the predicted effect in the short term, but most tests also have the aim of determining whether the effect will persist in the future. Since conditions will naturally change over time, more information is usually obtained from a sample selected over a long period than from a larger sample collected over a short period. (One cycle or several cycles might be used to provide an appropriate period.) The time required to increase degree of belief that the change will result in improvement and that the improvement will persist is a matter of judgement.

The importance of time in determining if a change is an improvement sets a context for determining sample size for the test. The sample size needs to be adequate to detect patterns that indicate improvement. Some rules of thumb for determining the number of plotted points necessary to detect patterns on a run chart are:

Number of Points	*Situation*
Fewer than 10	Expensive tests, expensive prototypes, or long periods between available data points; large effects anticipated.
15 to 50	Usually sufficient to discern patterns indicating improvements that are moderate or large.
50 to 100	The effect of the change is expected to be small relative to the variation in the system.
More than 100	The change is intended to affect a rare event.

Usually, fifteen to twenty-five plotted points will be sufficient to recognize patterns indicating improvement. Sometimes as many as fifty points might be necessary if no historical data are available to establish a baseline before the change is made. From fifty to one hundred points would be necessary only when the effect of the change is anticipated to be small relative to the variation in the system. Examples are situations when the variation in the measurements themselves are large or when the variations among people—students, patients, or customers—can mask the effect of the change. More than one hundred points might be needed if the change was intended to affect a rare event, such as the side effect of a new drug or a serious but rarely occurring defect. In cases such as these, it might be wise to consult a statistician to help in the design of the test.

In certain situations it is not practical to collect fifteen or more points during the testing of a change. Prototypes might be very expensive, such as prototypes of a new automobile engine, or the cost of conducting the test might be high. Possibly the data is financial in nature and only available on a monthly basis. In cases such as these, it may be that some data is better than none. However, if only small amounts of data are available, their worth can be enhanced by including a wide variety of conditions in the test.

Test Under a Wide Range of Conditions Making a change in order to improve a process, system, or product involves making a prediction. The prediction is that the change will be beneficial in the long run. It is important to recognize that conditions in the future will be different from the conditions of the test. Circumstances will arise that were unforeseen or not present at the time of the test. Is the change still an improvement under these new conditions? The degree of belief in the results is increased as the same conclusions are drawn for a variety of test conditions (different times, materials, environmental conditions, types of people, and so on). Dr. Smith increased her degree of belief that the new rehabilitation procedure was an improvement by testing the procedure under different conditions. She tested the procedure in different hospitals, with patients of different ages, and with physicians who had different levels of experience.

Too often, tests of changes are not conducted over a broad range of conditions. Some reasons given for limiting the conditions include limited resources, time constraints, difficulty in analysis of the data, lack of knowledge of how to efficiently include different conditions, and the existence of too many possible conditions to consider. Following are some simple ways of dealing with these reasons:

1. *Collecting data over time.* Many conditions change over time. So, one way to include a range of conditions is to incorporate into the study a period during which conditions are expected to change significantly. If a sequence of data collected after a change exhibits a predictable pattern that shows improvement, one's degree of belief that the improvement will be sustained in the future will be increased. Dr. Smith used the new rehabilitation procedure on twenty patients over a four-month period. Except for the one special cause that was identified, the data collected on the new procedure exhibited a predictable pattern with an average of about nine days (see Figure 6.5).

2. *Using planned grouping.* Another way to include a range of conditions in a test is to use planned grouping. Planned grouping allows for different conditions to be brought into the test in a systematic way. Dr. Smith was able to conduct the test of the new procedure under different conditions but still do a simple analysis of the results, because the analysis was done within two planned groups in which the conditions were uniform.

3. *Using judgement samples.* The selection of people or things to be included in the test provides an opportunity to consider a wide range of conditions. A random selection of units is rarely preferred to a selection made by a subject matter expert. This selection is called a judgement sample. Dr. Smith selected the patients for her test from those who were either under thirty years of age or over sixty. She judged that age could have an impact on the results of the test. This judgement sample assured her that both young and old people would be included.

Conclusion

Running cycles to test proposed changes logically follows from developing changes. What happens to the changes that the testing indicates will result in improvement? The next chapter discusses the implementation of these changes.

CHAPTER 7

Implementing a Change

Sally Hudson, a second-shift nurse, had a great idea for increasing quality and reducing the cost associated with documenting patient information in the medical records. She tested the idea on her floor during the second shift, and everyone she worked with agreed that it worked great. Sally sent a note about the idea to the shift supervisor. She encouraged everyone to start using the idea. But nothing happened! The other nurses continued to enter the data using the old procedure.

Why is it so hard to implement change? During the early phases of developing and testing changes, the existing system remains in place. While these early investigative stages may arouse people's interest, the fact remains that nothing has yet been permanently altered. When the development and testing of changes are finished, it is time to implement what was learned. To many people, this implementation would appear to be a matter of simply "installing" what was developed and tested. If implementation does not involve people, then the physical, emotional, and logical challenges that hinder most planned changes may not be an issue. However, most changes in an organization have a social component. The social challenges that usually accompany the implementation of a change can surprise the sponsors of the improvement effort.

The PDSA cycle provides the structure for both testing and implementing change. Besides the similarities between testing and implementation (making predictions, collecting data, and documenting things that go wrong) that result from use of the cycle, there are also important differences. When a change is tested, it is often "implemented" on a limited scale to study the effects of the change in comparison to the predictions. When a change is implemented, it could be considered a test of whether the change will be an improvement on a large-scale, permanent basis. The following are some differences between testing and implementation:

Testing
- The change made during testing is not permanent and therefore does not need supporting processes to maintain it beyond a brief period.

- The opportunities for learning from testing are expected to be significant, including learning from mistakes. Some percentage of tests—perhaps, 25 to 50 percent—are expected to result in no improvement, to "fail," but to result in substantial learning nevertheless.

- The number of people affected by a test is usually smaller than the number that would be affected if the change was implemented full-scale. Thus, the resistance to a test of a change is often relatively low.

Implementing a Change
- The implemented change is expected to become part of the routine operation of the system. Therefore, supporting processes to maintain the newly redesigned system will usually need to be designed or redesigned. Supporting processes include feedback and measurement systems, job descriptions, procedures, new employee training, and so on.

- Because learning can occur anytime action is taken, implementation should be carried out as part of a cycle. However, assuming that testing has been effective, only a small percentage of implementations are expected to result in no improvement.

- The increased scope of a change that accompanies moving from testing to implementation is usually accompanied by increased resistance to the change.

- Implementation cycles generally require more time than testing cycles.

Implementing change can be very challenging to many organizations, especially when the scope of the change is broad. This chapter focuses on the implementation of changes that involve some complexity, as opposed to simple changes, which can be made with little interdependence on other processes, people, procedures, or other structures. Simple changes can be implemented with little formality, and the steps for implementing them are usually readily apparent to the person or persons making the change. For example, improving food-shopping procedures might involve simply posting a shopping list on the refrigerator. To implement complex changes, however, it is generally useful, if not necessary, to develop a formal plan involving procedures and training.

The following ideas have been found to be important in implementing complex changes effectively:

- Managing implementation as a series of cycles

- Recognizing and addressing the social aspects of implementing a change

- Providing support for the change to maintain the improvements after the change is implemented

Implementation as a Series of Cycles

For some changes, the people involved do not even have to be told about the change in order to implement it. For example, a computer service department added additional memory chips to all of the computers in the office over the weekend. On Monday, all of the employees noticed that their applications performed much faster. This change resulted in an increase in the productivity of the office.

For more-complex changes, however, multiple cycles are required for implementation. For example, changing the type of wrapper on a food item to make it environmentally safe may be viewed as simple as changing the material. However, when the implications of the change are viewed from the production, legal, and customer perspectives, the change becomes relatively complex. Changing the food wrapper may take months and several cycles.

Customers of a grocery store chain complained for several months about chicken packages that leaked. Gertrude, the manager of the butcher department, decided to contact the vice president of sales for the Chicken King Company to voice her dissatisfaction with the leaking packages. The vice president, Dave, was concerned, but he informed Gertrude that he was sure that this was an isolated problem, that perhaps the packages were being stacked improperly by the personnel in Gertrude's department. He further informed Gertrude that she was the only customer who had lodged a complaint. Gertrude let Dave know about other stores in her company that had had the same problem. She suggested that if Chicken King was interested in keeping the company account, Dave should be in her store the next day to see the problem firsthand.

Dave did make a visit to the grocery store and learned about the leaking package situation from the viewpoint of the customer. Gertrude also told Dave that her customers generally preferred the competition's shrink-wrapped package to Chicken King's simple plastic wrap. The visit resulted in Chicken King conducting research on the technology that would be needed to use the shrink-wrap. A series of cycles were conducted to develop and test changes in equipment and materials. Chicken King was now ready to implement changes across its eight plants. The plan for the first implementation cycle is contained in Exhibit 7.1.

Objective: Implement the new shrink-wrap equipment and process at the Gainesville plant.

Questions:
1. Will the equipment operate as effectively as under test conditions?
2. Will the new process be easy for our operators and maintenance personnel to learn?
3. What difficulties will we experience with the implementation?

Predictions:
1. Yes. The tests were conducted under similar plant conditions at Oscar Equipment Co., and all the equipment being used is manufactured by Oscar.
2. No. The new equipment is computer controlled. Many of our people will require training in the use and maintenance of this complex equipment.
3. The computer equipment will add some complexity. The acceptance of new set-up methods by maintenance will add some challenges. The equipment looks sufficiently different that the operators may find it difficult to learn at first. Training will be essential to this effort. This plant was selected because of its ability to embrace change.

Who: Hank Duval's people will carry out the implementation at the Gainesville plant. The shrink wrap and equipment suppliers will be available if needed.
What: New equipment installation, shrink wrap material, and necessary training.
When: Training will begin in October 1992. Equipment will be installed in November.
Where: Chicken King plant in Gainesville

Exhibit 7.1. *Plan for the Implementation Cycle for the Gainesville Plant.*

Depending on the complexity and the risks involved, implementation can be conducted in a number of ways. Three approaches will be considered here:

1. The "Just do it" (or "cold turkey") approach
2. The parallel approach, which implements the change while the old system is still in place
3. The sequential approach, by time and location

The "Just Do It!" Approach

Many times, implementing a simple change is simply a matter of doing it—for example, following a flow diagram for a new process. Nevertheless, the PDSA

Cycle should be used to study the impact of even apparently simple changes to ensure that the predicted results are achieved. The effect of the change on the people involved should also be considered.

If the situation is a little more risky, then testing on a small scale may be important. After a successful test on a relatively low-risk change, implementation can then be accomplished by running one more cycle. The implementation cycle helps to ensure that the predicted results are achieved and that the changes will be made so as to be irreversible.

If unforeseen negative consequences occur, the "Just do it!" approach will maximize their negative impact. If the change is complex and the system is large, one of two types of a phased-in approaches should be considered.

The Parallel Approach

A manufacturing organization historically had maintained control of its schedule and inventory with a manual system of documentation, a schedule, expediters, and a "war room" to control work in the shop. A computer system for materials management had been purchased and tested and was ready for final implementation. While some of the work was already being completed with the aid of computers, the change to complete automation of the paperwork tracking system represented a major change for the business. To ensure that orders were not delayed or missed, the new system was installed while the manual system was used for backup in the event of a failure during the implementation cycle.

Sometimes changes must be phased in by operating them parallel to the existing system. Business cannot just stop during implementation. Changes must be accomplished while the business is running so that customers will be satisfied while the changes are being implemented. Implementing complex changes while trying to satisfy normal business demands has been compared to changing the fan belt on a car while the motor is running. Planning and phasing in the changes parallel with the existing system should reduce some of the risks. This type of implementation will take a bit longer than the "Just do it!" approach, but it is usually less risky. If changes are planned and implemented properly, then the implementation will produce the expected results.

The Sequential Approach

The third approach is to implement the change sequentially over time or by location—progressing gradually in terms of the *completeness* and the *coverage* of the change. For example, a change could have five major components that must occur within an organization with ten locations. Implementation could begin by implementing one of the components across the entire organization, so that 20 percent of the change would be completed with 100 percent coverage of the organization. Alternatively, the entire change could be implemented at one location, producing 10 percent coverage. Obviously, many other combinations of completeness and coverage could be devised. Cycles should be planned to carry out the appropriate strategy. After the first few cycles, coverage may not be 100 percent and the change may not be complete, but there is also not the risk of 100 percent failure. As the implementation process progresses, it can be improved as learning occurs.

When determining which sequential strategy to use, consider the following:

1. *The path of least resistance.* What strategy will use the skills and capabilities of the people involved, consider the environment (other changes that are going on and the support that exists for the change), and minimize geographical issues?
2. *The impact.* What strategy will result in the biggest improvements early in the implementation process?
3. *The potential learning.* What strategy will permit the most learning as the change is implemented? The knowledge obtained can then be used in the next phase or location.
4. *Resources.* What strategy will allow for the best scheduling and use of available resources?
5. *Interdependence.* What strategy will focus on implementing the entire change at one location? Such a strategy should be used if the change cannot work without all of its components.

Cycles should be planned for carrying out the appropriate strategy. After the first few cycles, coverage and completeness may not be 100 percent, but there will be no associated risk of 100 percent failure. As learning continues, the implementation can be improved.

When planning cycles to implement a change, consideration should be given to whether the change is being repeated (same change on the same scale in more places) or expanded (same change on an increased scale). When a change is repeated, there is little additional impact on the system. An example would be a new nursing task that is successfully tested on one unit in a hospital. During implementation, the new task can simply be carried out in a similar fashion on all units. Achieving 100 percent coverage of such a change should not be difficult. However, when the scale of the change is expanded during implementation, additional cycles may be needed in order to ascertain the additional impact on the system. For example, a new menu could be successfully tested on one unit in a hospital, but before the new menu can be used on all units, systems to support the preparation and delivery of the new food items on an increased scale may need to be determined. Achieving 100 percent coverage of such a change is not as easy as when the change is simply repeated.

An Example of Sequential Implementation Focused on Coverage For organizations with multiple locations it is not prudent, cost-effective, or physically possible to implement changes completely and throughout the system at one time. A safer way to proceed is to implement by region, state, location, store, restaurant, plant, and so on.

Chicken King completed testing various types of plastic wraps and bags. The plastic shrink-wrap had been the preferred package from the viewpoint of the consumer. In addition, the grocery store chain preferred the shrink-wrap for storage and stacking purposes. The new wrap required each plant to have new equipment controlled by computer technology. The Oscar Equipment Company was selected as the supplier of the equipment. This change meant that the operators and maintenance personnel in the eight plants needed to be trained to use the new equipment. Chicken King decided to phase in the implementation across its eight plants.

What would be a good strategy for implementing this change? Chicken King's strategy featured the following ideas:

- The implementation was organized as eight cycles, each focusing on a particular location.

- One hundred percent completeness of the change would be achieved after the first cycle, but only 12 percent coverage. It would take all eight cycles to achieve 100 percent coverage of the change.

- All components of the change would be made in each cycle: installation, training, and initiation of production.

- The location of the initial cycle was chosen to maximize the probability of success.

- The cycles incorporated learning from one location into the implementation at the next location. The schedule anticipated that the implementation would go much quicker during the later cycles.

- Responsibility for managing the cycle was assigned to the production manager at each plant.

Exhibit 7.1 describes the plan for implementing the change at the first plant. Table 7.1 shows the schedule for implementation in all eight plants.

Table 7.1. Implementation Schedule for New Packing Equipment for Eight Chicken King Plants.

CYCLE	PLANT	COMPONENT 1: TRAINING	COMPONENT 2: INSTALLATION OF EQUIPMENT	BEGIN PRODUCTION
1	Gainesville	October, 1992	November, 1992	December, 1992
2	Athens	November, 1992	January, 1993	February, 1993
3	Anniston	January, 1993	February, 1993	February, 1993
4	Daleville	March, 1993	April, 1993	April, 1993
5	Forrest City	May, 1993	June, 1993	July, 1993
6	Meridian	July, 1993	July, 1993	August, 1993
7	Leesville	August, 1993	August, 1993	August, 1993
8	Mansfield	September, 1993	September, 1993	September, 1993

Table 7.2. Implementation Schedule for Change at a Distribution Company.

CYCLE	LOCATION STORES	COMPONENT 1: INSTALL NEW ORDER SYSTEM	COMPONENT 2: SUPPORT TRAINING	COMPONENT 3: CUSTOMER MEETING	COMPONENT 4: INSTALL EDT CAPABILITY
1	Both		September, 1993		
2	Galena	October, 1993			
3	Braxton	November, 1993			
4	Both			January, 1994	
5	Galena				February, 1994
6	Braxton				April, 1994

An Example of Sequential Implementation Focused on Completeness Table 7.2 shows the schedule for the implementation of a change at a distribution company with two locations. The schedule called for the use of six cycles, and each cycle was focused on one of the four components of the change.

The first cycle addressed training, the second component of the change. It was convenient to schedule personnel from both locations to attend the same training sessions. After cycle 1 was finished, 100 percent coverage of the change was achieved, but that coverage was only 25 percent complete. Cycles 2 and 3 focused on installation of the equipment at each site, the first component of the change. The same company installed the system at both locations, but the work was organized as two separate cycles so that learnings from cycle 2 could be incorporated into cycle 3. Cycle 4 addressed the third component of the change: communication with customers. Since many customers ordered from both locations, one cycle was planned for this aspect of the implementation. The installation of the fourth component, the electronic data transfer (EDT) capability, was done in cycles 5 and 6, after each location had time to get comfortable with the new ordering system. EDT would permit the electronic transfer of orders and billing between the stores and their customers, which should result in more accurate orders, quicker payment, and less cost for the stores and their customers.

The distribution company planned the six implementation cycles with predicted results in two key measurements: (1) the percentage of customer orders satisfied on the first pass would increase, and (2) the average number of days outstanding for accounts receivable would decrease. The run charts in Figure 7.1 show that the predicted results were achieved during the final phase of implementation. A dip in the percentage of orders completed on first pass during the first month of implementation reveals a special cause, which was the result of the people learning the new system. The learning curve improved as people became better trained, and the predicted level of 80 percent was surpassed by an even better performance of 84 percent. In addition, the introduction of EDT decreased the average number of collection days from forty to twenty-two. The

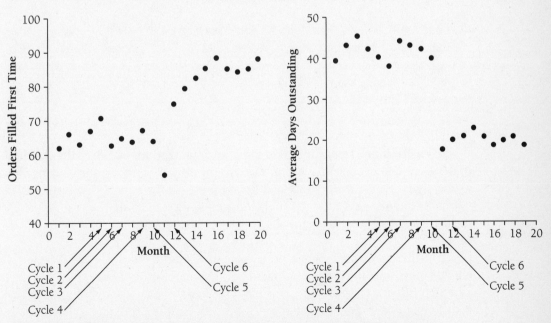

Figure 7.1. *Key Measures for Implementation Effectiveness at a Distribution Company.*

implementation team had predicted an improvement of twenty days. Both run charts indicate a positive change to the system, and the team concluded that the changes were in fact delivering the predicted results.

The best strategy for implementation of a change will depend on the particular circumstances. A study of the scope, complexity, and risks associated with the change should drive the implementation plan. Sometimes, however, even with a good plan the implementation efforts still do not go as intended.

The Social Consequences of Change

Hank Duval, manager of Chicken King's Gainesville plant was anxious as he drove into the plant and parked. He was eager to see the results of the new packing equipment and materials on the productivity of the line. What he saw as he entered the packing area was nothing short of chaos. Rooster, the maintenance mechanic, was arguing with Alice, the production supervisor. Rooster was trying to explain to Alice the new setup procedure required for the recently installed equipment. Alice explained, "I want to see the results that the testing from headquarters predicted. I'm not interested in the intricacies of the new equipment. I want to see the line rate that was promised by the Oscar Equipment Company. Rooster, if you need help in understanding this equipment, then get the equipment supplier in here to help us learn the setup procedure in a real-time environment."

Rooster knew that Alice was right. He had attended the training at Oscar headquarters and hated to ask those smart aleck "Nintendo-trained" equipment engineers for help. After all, he had been a setup man for twenty-two years. Those engineers had intimidated him with their "computerese lingo." Now he would have to ask for their help. He would rather submit to a public flogging.

Successful implementation of change in organizations requires that leaders understand that change involves more than the tangible and technical changes—a new product, a new procedure, a different form—if the expected improvements in quality and/or costs are to be attained (see Figure 7.2). Once the required technical change has been determined, the desire is to implement it immediately to capture the predicted economic benefits. Often, however, the lack of social acceptance of the change precludes the expected economic benefit. The impact of change on people must be anticipated and planned for.

The problems that the Chicken King Company was experiencing were the result of people undergoing change on the job. People need time to learn about changes, to understand precisely how the change is going to affect them. They

Figure 7.2. *Tangible and Social Change for Improvement.*

need to understand *why* the changes are being made, and they need to receive the necessary training to make the change a success.

Implementation of tangible change creates some predictable consequences for many situations. Most improvements will actually add difficulties immediately after implementation. Patience and perseverance are needed to stick to an improved method until it succeeds. Most improvements would vanish without a trace if they had to show success on the first trial.

Initial Results of Implementation

A simple experiment can be used to show the initial impact of a change that involves people doing something differently. An individual is asked to write his or her name as fast as possible ten times. Each time the name is written, the time is recorded. Then a change is introduced into this simple process. The person is told to write only every other letter in their name; the theory is that this change will reduce his or her work by 50 percent. The results shown in Figure 7.3 demonstrate the impact on the person of writing 50 percent fewer letters. The

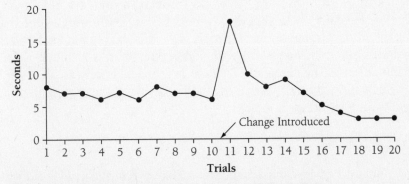

Figure 7.3. *Results of Experiment with Change in Writing a Name.*

time more than tripled on the first cycle after the change, and it took five more cycles for the change to produce the expected level of performance. While this example is simple, it demonstrates the familiar learning curve that usually accompanies tangible changes in the work environment. People who are implementing change need to plan for this potential result. Many changes have been needlessly cancelled or tampered with based on the results of the first or second trial.

Rooster was asking questions of Stan, an Oscar Equipment engineer. The prescribed setup procedure that had caused delays during the first stage of implementation was Rooster's major concern. The setup was to take less than twenty minutes, but it had taken an hour and a half. Rooster explained, "We would never have gotten the machine running if we hadn't overridden the computer." Stan asked why the computer was overridden. Rooster became very uncomfortable with Stan's question and finally said, "I really don't understand the use of the computer as it relates to the setup procedure for the equipment." Rooster thought to himself, "There, I've admitted I don't understand. If Stan gets smart with me, I'm leaving." Stan said, "No problem, let's review the setup procedure on your next setup." Rooster thought to himself, "All this worrying about the computer . . . all I had to do was ask. My pride got in the way of my learning."

Three months after implementing the new wrapping equipment, the Gainesville plant was the most productive plant in the Chicken King Company. Hank Duval had carried the day with some dedicated people. The new Oscar equipment and shrink-wrap material was being praised by Dave. Alice was being congratulated on her very productive line. Rooster and the other folks had received training on the use of the computer and had even suggested improvements to Stan at Oscar. Most important of all, Gertrude, the customer at the grocery store, was very pleased with the new package. Hank Duval was asked to make a presentation at the next plant managers' meeting on how to manage an effective implementation of a change.

The learning from the first cycle was utilized in the very next cycle: the glitches and mistakes that were discovered at Gainesville were avoided at the Athens plant. As implementation progressed, the learning at each plant was incorporated into each successive plan, making the process go much easier. The implementation of the change to a new type of packaging was successful—at last. The management at Chicken King did not abandon the change after the initial results, but stayed the course.

Reactions to Change

After a company has developed and tested a change that it is convinced will lead to improvement, it will want people to accept the implementation of the change.

It is only natural, however, that people will seek to maintain control of their environment. Some sort of reaction should be expected when a change is announced. This is the stage at which the leaders of the change must explain the *why* and *how* of the change. Properly addressing concerns and questions helps people commit to the change. The behavior of the people affected by the change might range from open resistance to commitment, depending on how the change is communicated and what the circumstances are surrounding the change (that is, the degree and relevance of the change, the current situation in the organization, the credibility of management, the way changes were handled in the past, the style of leadership, and the organization's culture). The following behaviors may be observed:

Resistance: responding with emotions or behaviors meant to impede change that is perceived as threatening

Apathy: feeling or showing little or no interest in the change

Compliance: publicly acting in accord while privately disagreeing with the change

Conformance: changing behavior as a result of real or imagined group pressure

Commitment: becoming bound emotionally and/or intellectually to the change

People have a need to understand the physical implications of the change (How much smaller will my new office be?), the logical implications (Why is this change necessary?), and the emotional aspect of the change (How do I feel about this change?). The leaders of the change should not view people's initial reactions as resistance; however, if these reactions are not properly dealt with, they can develop into full-blown resistance.

Mitigating Resistance to Change

The following techniques and methods can be used to mitigate any resistance to change. The social impacts observed during the testing cycles should prepare the leaders of the change for the future implementation. After all, if resistance is experienced during testing, which is temporary change, what will the situation be like when the change is implemented permanently? Change leaders can begin to temper the resistance long before the time comes to implement the change by:

- Beginning the explanation of why a change is needed as soon as the organization agrees on the aim for an improvement effort

- Continuing the communication through visual displays, newsletter articles, and so on, as the changes are being developed and tested

- Publicizing the various people in the organization who are involved in developing and testing the change

- Publicizing the positive results of tests of the change

Whether a change will be repeated or expanded during a sequential implementation could have an impact on the resistance that may surface. During an expansion, the change must be pervasive; it would not be logical for only one part of an organization to implement the change. Consider the example given earlier of the use of a new menu in a hospital. Once a decision has been made to implement the new menu throughout the hospital, it would be difficult for certain units to continually resist its use and have a separate menu. However, when a change is simply repeated, it may be possible for some elements within an organization to implement while other elements do not. Resisters to a change could prevail without having a major impact on the other parts of the system. Nevertheless, an organizational decision must be made on how continued resistance will be addressed.

Why would some units resist implementing a successful change? This behavior is sometimes related to the NIH (not invented here) factor, which is commonly referred to in business when people who are being asked to implement a change did not have a hand in developing and testing that change. The identification of this factor supports a commonly held belief about people everywhere—that *people have a tendency to support what they help to create.* Keeping this idea in mind can help those who must implement change to ensure that resistance is mitigated.

Using the Purpose Statement to Communicate Change Many organizations have a written statement of *values, principles, or tenets.* These statements describe the behaviors that are expected and necessary to carry out the organization's purpose. How can these statements be used to minimize resistance to change? When a change in structure is being proposed, the "why" of the change should be explained in terms of the organization's values, principles, or tenets. If the change is consistent with these statements, then the logic of the change will be understood and accepted. If the change violates these values or tenets, then the people may have a very difficult time adapting to the new structure. The people leading the change will have to explain why the new behaviors are needed.

A project management organization had recently introduced the idea of self-managed teams into its engineering group. The managers had attended a seminar on the value of self-managed teams. Afterwards, they had organized the department using a self-management concept. One level of engineering management had been eliminated, and the position of chief engineer had been turned into that of team leader. This change created much resistance on the part of the newly appointed team leaders and several engineers. The managers were shocked at the response. After all, the engineering management personnel who were affected were relocated in other management positions throughout the organization. In most cases, these moves had been requested by many of those who had been relocated. As the engineering director stated, "Why are we getting all this hassle?"

During a meeting to discuss the reorganization, the human resources (HR) manager, who had been invited to the meeting, began reading the "Engineering Role Statement" that was on the wall of the conference room. One of the phrases in the role statement was that the "system will encourage people to be innovative, self-directed, and proactive in their pursuit of good engineering practice."

The HR manager asked how the role statement (which had been written five years earlier) was used in the introduction of the new organization. The answer: It was not considered. The managers decided to meet with the individual groups of engineers to explain the "why" of the change and to show how the new organization supported the role statement of engineering. This was accomplished over the next two months with much dialogue among the teams and engineering management. The result: there was no more open resistance to the change, and the dialogue produced several good ideas for a better reorganization. The managers were able to avoid resistance and actually started the process of commitment to the change.

Guidelines for Getting Commitment to Change The following guidelines have proved useful in helping people minimize resistance to change and get the desired commitment of those affected by the change:

1. Provide information on why the change is being made:
    Empathize with the anxiety created by the change (but do not expect to eliminate it).
    Show how the change supports the purpose of the organization.
    Put the change in historical perspective.
    Link the change to the outside customer.
    Reframe the change as an exciting opportunity, not something being forced on people.
    Provide a special hot line for recording questions and comments during implementation.
2. Provide specific information on how the change will affect people:
    Use the results from the testing cycles to share visual displays of data and test results.
    Be prepared to discuss questions, requests for clarification, or ideas about the change.
    Study rational objections to the change and be prepared to address them.

Include in presentations representatives from the organization who actually carried out the tests or implementation.

3. Get consensus on solutions, resources, and other necessary support to implement the change:

Decide on a plan of action with defined milestones and dates.

Ask leaders and key people in all parts of the organization to publicly show their support.

Express confidence in the ability of those who must carry out the change.

4. Publicize the change:

Use symbolism (stories, analogies, pictures, staged events).

Summarize all key points and agreements as they are made.

Show appreciation for the efforts of everyone who was involved in the development and testing of the change.

Take advantage of significant events (record sales, loss of a big customer) and tie the implementation of the change to these events.

Following these guidelines will help organizations to overcome most people's resistance to change. But what if some resistance continues? Obviously, it cannot be allowed to go on forever.

What If the Resistance Cannot Be Mitigated? If the resistance continues in the face of the facts, then the sponsor, or possibly a higher-level manager, must deal with the resistance by direct measures. In this unhappy situation, the resister or resisters should be confronted as candidly as possible. Typically, this means that management will state expectations and provide incentives or spell out what the consequences will be if certain behaviors are not demonstrated. The following story of implementing a change in a zoo illustrates how difficult making a change can be. As you read the story, consider how the workers were involved in implementing the change. What would you have done differently if you had been leading the change?

After one of its elephant keepers was accidentally stepped on and instantly killed, the San Diego Zoo decided to change the way its elephants were trained and handled. Experts in the use of behavior modification with animals were brought in to work with the elephant keepers. None of the experts had any experience with elephants. The purpose of the change was to improve safety for the keepers, to improve the methods used to discipline the elephants, and to provide better access to veterinary care for the elephants.

Gary Priest, head of the Department of Animal-Behavior Management at the Zoological Society of San Diego reported that at first the keepers accepted the work with the elephants as "an amusing diversion not to be taken too seriously. But as we began to see results, we discovered that to propose significant change is to invite ridicule." Priest had discovered what many people learn as they try to make changes.

The method that the elephant keepers were currently using to train and discipline the elephants had been in use for thousands of years. It was based on the elephants' social behavior of being led by the dominant cow of the elephant herd. This cow was usually the oldest and most experienced of the herd. Challenges to the authority of this dominant cow were met with swift retaliation. The elephants understood this hierarchy of control and it was on this hierarchy that the ancient training methods were based. The elephants were taught to be subordinate to the trainer as they would be to the lead elephant. Priest reported, "The elephants' unquestioned acceptance of the pecking order was a matter of life and death for the trainer. Unfortunately, elephants do sometimes challenge the pecking order . . . often with disastrous results."

The proposed changes differed from the traditional method in a number of ways:

1. Trainers would no longer go into the elephants' enclosure.
2. There would be a protective barrier between the trainer and the elephant.
3. The elephant would present various body parts on command in exchange for a reward.
4. No physical discipline of the elephants would be permitted.
5. Training would rely only on positive reinforcement and "voluntary" cooperation from the elephant.

This strategy of training was predicted to work because the elephant is a very social animal and appears to enjoy interaction with the human trainers and keepers. Within a few days, the elephants had discovered the connection between their behavior and the reward of a carrot or apple. The elephant with the worse behavior, Chico, was chosen for the first cycle. Within six months of using the new method, Chico would voluntarily submit to a pedicure on all four of his feet. He had not had a pedicure for ten years under the old method, even though infections from the foot are the leading cause of death for elephants in captivity.

Although the new method of control proved successful with Chico and the other elephants, the keepers still insisted that "the new system wouldn't work, that it was stupid, and they [the animal behaviorist and management] were being unrealistic." Priest observed the keepers stubbornly trying to prove the new methods would not work, rather than practicing the new system of training. After exhausting various positive reinforcement methods to entice the keepers to voluntarily change their approach, management was left with no alternative but to step in and make the new method a contingent of employment. Priest reported, "It was especially ironic to me that we had abandoned a discipline-oriented, negative training system with our elephants only to adopt it with our employees."

The new parameters were enforced using twelve-week review periods. The first review identified multiple incidents of keepers not operating within the new training parameters, and it was a negative experience for everyone involved in the review. However, as each review was conducted, incremental improvements were noted. Each new improvement and behavior conformance created an opportunity for management to recognize and reinforce the new behavior. After one year, all keepers were using the new training methods, and the elephants were performing beyond expectations. "The atmosphere during the review was transformed from bristling hostility to informal, relaxed and open discussion of the program, its direction, and the keepers' participation in it." Now, positive reinforcement plays an important role in managing and maintaining the program.

The elephants accepted the change much more easily than the workers in the zoo. The shift in attitude that took a few months for the elephants did not take place in the workers until after more than two years. This story illustrates how resistance was formed in a group and how the zoo management had to resort to some rather harsh measures to implement a change.

What can we learn from the zoo story? Change is an uphill battle, no matter who is leading it. In this case, "outsiders" were brought in to teach some new methods to a group of keepers who were practicing methods that had been used successfully for a thousand years, and these experts did not have prior experience with elephants. Perceiving these "experts" as coming in to correct things would in itself have created a movement toward resistance to the change. How were the new keepers informed of the change? Did they get a chance to help with the experiment? The involvement of the keepers in testing and implementing the change should have been critical. People have a tendency to support what they help create.

If the zoo's management had used some of the guidelines given earlier, they may have had a chance to mitigate the resistance. Involvement of the keepers in testing the change, using some of their ideas from experience with the elephants, and explaining the "why" of the new methods may have resulted in much earlier commitment to the change. Because these issues were not addressed appropriately, resistance developed, resulting in the need for incentives, negative twelve-week reviews, and threats of job loss.

What choices do change leaders have when they have not done a good job in their testing and initial implementation cycles of preparing individuals for change? The options include:

- Modifying the planned change to compensate for the resistance.

- Using incentives.

- Using logical consequences.

- Demanding conformance as an expectation of continued employment.

These management practices are not necessarily positive or desirable. In most cases, they will produce a negative environment. However, when a change is not properly managed, such practices often become necessary. Some of the change concepts in the appendix address these situations (see number 29, "take care of basics"; number 35, "share risks"; number 30, "reduce demotivating aspects of pay system"; and number 36, "emphasize natural and logical consequences").

Maintenance of Change

Dave picked up the receiver of his ringing telephone. It was Gertrude. "Dave, the ink from the new package is flaking off the plastic wrap." Dave asked, "Gertrude, what plant did this shipment come from?" Gertrude responded, "From Duval's plant at Gainesville." Dave thanked Gertrude for the information and called Hank Duval immediately.

Everything had gone so well for several months. All the plants were now on-line with the new equipment and shrink-wrap packaging. The grocery store chains were happy, and more importantly, their customers preferred the new package to that of the competition. However, now a whole shipment of chicken had been rejected.

Hank Duval answered the phone on the second ring. Dave asked Hank if he knew of the problem. Hank said that he had just been made aware of the problem by one of the store managers of a grocery chain from Texas. Dave was now concerned that the problem was not localized. A meeting was called for the next morning with the plant people, the plastic-wrap supplier, and Dave in Gainesville.

Dave was on his way back to the Atlanta airport and was reflecting on the meeting with Hank, Stan from Oscar, and Irene from the Kelvin Plastics Company. It was frightening for Dave to realize how a decision by a purchasing agent at Kelvin could cause so much trouble. After Dave had opened the meeting, Irene had explained what she had discovered the night before in preparing for the meeting, "I am sorry to report that the problem with the flaking of the printed labels on the shrink-wrap lies in our court, at Kelvin. One of our purchasing people managed to get a better price on some ink. This ink worked fine with the other package, but not with the new film composition. This detail was missed by our people. I am very sorry for.this situation, and we are prepared to pay for the losses to Chicken King, their customers, and whatever corrective action is necessary."

Dave and the rest of the team were impressed with Irene's straightforward approach. Everyone started to work together to correct the situation. Hank raised the question that was now bothering Dave, "How will we document and control changes throughout this system to prevent losses of this nature in the future?"

Once improvements are implemented, practices need to be established to ensure that the change becomes the normal way the business is run. Holding the gains usually requires some change in the system to ensure that the change is maintained. Many organizations make improvements on the job only to discover later that the improved performance has degraded to the old level or some new problem has been encountered. Some of the practices that help make improvements permanent in an organization are standardization, documentation, measurement, and training. Periodic self-audits can be useful in determining whether these practices are being followed.

Standardization

A hospital's records showed much variation among patients in recovery time from knee operations. The hospital's average costs for this particular operation were higher than in other health care systems. A team of doctors and therapists worked with the administration to develop a standard process for patients who have a knee joint replaced. After implementing the new process, recovery times were more consistent and the hospital's costs were in line with other systems. Two years later, however, costs had crept back up and a variety of procedures were again being used. What happened to the improvement that had been made?

As in many organizations, the hospital attempted standardization of critical aspects of recovery therapy only to have it change back to the way it had always been. Standardization is the method of establishing specific recognized policies and practices that act as a model or guidelines for a process. The actual documented policies, materials, methods, equipment, and training are usually called "standards" or "best practices." Organizations that effectively use standards exhibit many of the following conditions:

- Management requires the use of standards, especially to document improvement efforts.

- Different employees and shifts utilize the same standards and expect similar results.

- Employee training focuses on the documented standards for materials, methods, and equipment. Critical elements and impact on internal and external customers are discussed.

- Employees document and compare results to the standard when solving problems.

- Standards are regularly updated and changed based on new knowledge about better methods. To avoid suboptimization, conditions that get similar results are reviewed for least cost and best results for the overall system.

- Employees share information with co-workers and managers in ongoing efforts to improve.

- Variability in the outcomes of processes is reduced, resulting in more predictability.

Documentation

An organization in the international construction industry recently reengineered its ten major subsystems. When the task was finished, they had ten volumes of materials describing the new processes. Several million dollars had been expended in gathering information, benchmarking other companies, testing, purchasing software, and finally, implementing the system. Much learning had occurred and many changes in policies, structures, and procedures had been implemented. The one thing that was visible after all the effort was the ten volumes of documentation.

One person observed, "If we don't have a process to update our process books, pretty soon we will have ten process books that are no longer useful. We would then risk losing all of the investment we have made in these major improvements."

Documenting a change after the implementation cycle is most important, but more often than not, it is the least-appreciated task. The term "documentation" has a bureaucratic ring to it and usually means "more paper"—and more paper means more work: filing it, maintaining it, and so on. Unfortunately, many changes are only as good as their documentation. Organizations depend on the documentation for education and training during the implementation of the change, for consistency from one group to another, for understanding a method or process, for a common definition of the change, for instructions, and so on. For many changes, the documentation represents the "deliverable." It is what the organization bought with all its efforts and resources aimed at gathering data, testing, and implementing cycles. The final product is sometimes a simple document defining the change.

Once people are trained and best practices are established, how is a system to be created by which changes are communicated and the new system is properly documented and improved into the future? Maintaining a system depends on the complexity of the organization (size, number of locations, number of products and services, and so on). Understanding the system and how a proposed change will be maintained in that system should be part of the implementation plan. This approach should apply to all changes. Even small changes can sometimes cause big effects, some desirable and some very undesirable.

The following points should be considered in developing a system to maintain changes implemented in the organization:

- A process should be developed to capture all important changes in the organization:

  In deciding if the change needs to be documented, consider if the change will have a small (localized) or large (interdependent) effect on the system.

  Who has the authority to implement a change? What will their responsibility be in seeing that the change is properly implemented and documented?

- How will the change be communicated to those affected inside or outside the defined system?

  How will improvements and learning be shared with interested people in other departments, divisions of the same company, suppliers, and customers?

  Will training and education be required to implement the change?

- What will the process be for updating flow diagrams, best practices, measurements, and other important process or product information?

  Information technology offers the opportunity to provide real-time updates to documentation of procedures to all parts of the organization.

Measurement

Good documentation of a process does not mean that the process is always performed as documented. Visible measurement of the process is a good way to ensure that the changes that were implemented are in fact being carried out.

Measurement provides a source of learning during implementation and a method of maintenance after implementation. Some of the measurements developed and used in testing and implementation cycles should be considered for permanent use after implementation. Viewing measurements over time allows an organization to determine whether it is continuing to get the desired results and whether those results can be predicted to continue in the future. Is there a need to update the process, make changes, and so on?

Training

Some form of training is usually required to implement a change. If the change to be implemented is a simple extension of the work currently being performed, then a one-time discussion of the change with the workers affected may be all the training required. Such training could be done on the job or by reviewing the new standards at a meeting.

If the change is complex (for example, if it involves the use of new technology), then extensive, formal classroom training may be required to implement the change. The type of change that is being proposed, who will be asked to implement the change, and the skill level and work experience of the target group are all considerations in how much training gets done.

People are motivated to learn when they perceive a need or reason to learn something new and when they believe that training will satisfy this need. Leaders of the change effort must again be ready to explain the "why" of the change. Also, the timing of the training is essential. If it is given too early, people will stall on the learning curve due to nonapplication. If it is given too late, people will be rushed, force fed, and ill-prepared.

Training should be designed to aid the employee in successfully making the change in the use of equipment, materials and/or methods. Expected results should focus on increasing the knowledge and skills of the worker while being sensitive to the social implications of the change. Adult learners appreciate being involved in the training through practice, hands-on exercises, and coaching. How the trainers convey their understanding of and enthusiasm for the change is also important. They act as ambassadors and advocates for the change.

Exhibit 7.2 provides a checklist that can be used for review whenever a change is being implemented, to ensure that predicted results are evaluated, that there is sufficient communication with the people affected by the implementation, and that the necessary training and documentation are completed to implement the change.

A Case Study in Implementing Change: What Happened to the Metric System?

A good example to study to learn about the difficulties of implementing a change is the intention of the United States to change from the English system of measurement to the metric system.

During the 1970s, many people heard about the impending conversion of business and industry from the inch-pound system to the metric system. In the 1990s, the metric system is not the preferred system of measurement in the United States, and we have been left with two measurement systems. What happened?

The metric system has a long history in the United States that dates back to 1790.

Description of change:
Implementation dates: from _____ to _____.

Number of cycles for implementation:

Predicted impact of change on key measures:

	Measure	Current level of performance	Predicted level after change
1.			
2.			
3.			

Processes affected by the change:

	Process affected	Process owner	People affected	Change in standards?	Predicted acceptance
1.					
2.					
3.					
4.					

Documentation of change:
Materials/forms defined?
Procedure defined?
Equipment defined?
Change request procedure?
Changes in job descriptions or role statements?

Impact on training:
Training procedure defined for implementation?
Training resources allocated?
Training schedule?
New-employee training procedure?

Measurements required:
New measurements defined?
Measurement procedures defined?
Measurement responsibilities defined?
Measurement review schedule and responsibilities?
Analysis of data?

Exhibit 7.2. *Implementation Checklist.*

During that year, Thomas Jefferson recommended a measurement system based on "multiples of ten." In the same year, a French commission had developed the metric system, and by 1795, the French government had made the metric system compulsory for France. Jefferson deeply admired French culture and technology, so one could assume that his recommendation was influenced by the French system.

By 1821, Secretary of State John Quincy Adams recommended the metric system to Congress. It took Congress until 1866 to pass the Kassen act, which "legalized" the voluntary use of the metric system in the United States. During 1878, the United States signs the "Treaty of the Meter" with sixteen other nations. After the Senate ratified the treaty and President Hayes signed it into law, the Federal bureaucracy worked to kill it. The Treasury Department formally adopting the Troy Pound as the standard for coins. By 1893, the Congress proposed a dual system of metric and inch-pound measurements.

From the end of the nineteenth century and well into the twentieth, the metric system continued to be adopted around the world as the preferred system of weights and measures. By the end of the twentieth century, the advantages of the metric system are apparent to most governments around the world: its use enhances the ability to compete in worldwide markets, it is easier to teach the metric system, and two systems of measure are no longer economical for most businesses.

The pressure from other nations to adopt the metric system culminated with Congress passing the Metric Study Act in 1968. The study resulted in the Metric Conversion Act of 1975. It established a Metric Board and made the use of the metric system "voluntary." The act made it clear that the government is not allowed to break legs or otherwise force people to go metric. The idea was to use reason. By 1982, the Metric Board was found to be lacking in its efforts to convert the United States to the metric system and was eliminated.

Why did the implementation of the metric system fail? Social barriers are at fault:

- The culture of the United States is emersed in the inch-pound system.
- Every adult and child has been educated in the more-complicated system and there is resistance to learning a new system.
- It is perceived that business, education, and industry costs will increase without corresponding benefits.
- There is no real leadership on the issue from the federal government. Adoption of the system remains voluntary.

In 1988, Congress amended the Metric Conversion Act and, in the Omnibus Trade and Competitiveness Act, made the metric system the "preferred system of weights and measures for United States trade and commerce." In 1991, President Bush issued an executive order requiring the use of the metric system by the federal bureaucracy. Congress amended the Fair Packaging and Labeling Act to require both metric and inch-pound units on most consumer-item package labels. Only time will tell if this last round of changes will be accepted by the American culture. The implementation of this change has already taken 170 years!

What lessons can be learned from this effort?

1. When given a choice between two systems, one of which they understand, people will use what they know.
2. If you want to truly make a change, you must present an expectation and put in place a structure to effect the change. The metric system has been voluntary in the United States since the 1878 Treaty of the Meter, but there have not been very many volunteers. In France, where the metric system is standard, its use was made compulsory in 1795.
3. People need information in order to change. They need to be helped to understand the costs of the present system, of having to maintain two sets of standards. This cost is passed on to the consumer and contributes to the challenge of competing with products abroad.

Conclusion

Implementing change can be very challenging to many organizations, especially when the scope of the change is broad. This chapter focused on the implementation of changes that involve some complexity. It emphasized the importance of managing implementation as a series of cycles like those used to test the changes; recognizing and addressing the social aspects of implementing change; and maintaining the changes after implementation so as to "hold" the improvements. The next chapter presents several case studies in which people have used the Model for Improvement and its methods for developing, testing, and implementing changes.

Case Studies of
Improvement Efforts

The case studies discussed in this chapter demonstrate a more structured approach than the examples described in Chapter Three, but they are still guided by the Model for Improvement. The three improvement efforts are from health care, manufacturing/construction, and education. The specific areas covered are:

1. Improving the process of screening blood donors (health care)
2. Reengineering the process of acquiring new business (manufacturing/construction)
3. Improving a Ph.D. program (education)

Each case study begins with a short introduction, followed by a description of the work done within the framework of the Model for Improvement. The emphasis in each case study is on the changes that were developed, tested, and implemented using a variety of the methods and tools for improvement that were discussed in Chapters Four through Seven. Some of the case studies do not include all of the PDSA Cycles that were used to accomplish the aim, but they do include most of the key ones. The studies use various formats to document the cycles. Each case study concludes with a section that summarizes what can be learned from the study about the concepts and methods that were used to make the improvements. The studies are meant to reinforce the concepts, methods, and other examples presented in the book, and to enhance the reader's ability to make improvements.

Case Study 1: Improving the Process of Collecting Blood Plasma

The primary business of a certain organization was the collection of blood plasma. The plasma collected was supplied to another organization that used it in the manufacture of drugs used to treat patients suffering from such things as shock, burns, and hemophilia.

The organization consisted of eight centers for plasma collection. At these centers, a phlebotomist would extract blood from the donor, removing twenty-five to thirty ounces of liquid plasma. The key considerations were that every blood donor should be treated safely with a minimum of tissue trauma and that the amount of blood collected should be maximized. People with unsuitable veins caused by far the largest problems in collecting a sufficient amount of plasma, resulting in what is known as a partial. Once an attempt was made to venipuncture a donor, the person was paid even if only a partial resulted.

Data on complaints were collected at the eight centers. This data indicated that most of the complaints were coming from new donors. Waiting time and problems with the extraction of blood were the major complaints. A team was formed at one of the centers to explore how to eliminate the quality problems in the process of collecting blood plasma. The focus was on the reduction of partials.

What are we trying to accomplish? The following is the charter developed by the team:

General Description

Improve the process of collecting blood plasma to reduce the number of partials.

Guidance

- Consider donor safety and the amount of blood plasma collected from each donor to be important measures of quality.
- Reduce the number of partials by at least 50 percent.
- Consider how new donors are screened.
- Consider the interactions among the phlebotomist, the physicians, and other staff members.
- Share the team's findings with other sites.

How will we know that a change is an improvement? The measures of quality for the process of collecting blood plasma would be the number of partials, the amount of patient discomfort, and the time spent in the donation center.

What changes can we make that will result in improvement? Some prospective donors were in the center for more than an hour before they saw the phlebotomist. The phlebotomist often felt pressure to at least make an attempt to draw blood, which could result in a partial, and in an increased number of resticks, which are a large source of customer complaints. To achieve the goal of a 50 percent reduction in partials, it was necessary to focus on the process of selecting new donors. A flowchart of this process to the point of venipuncture was developed (see Figure 8.1). Contacts with other centers determined that

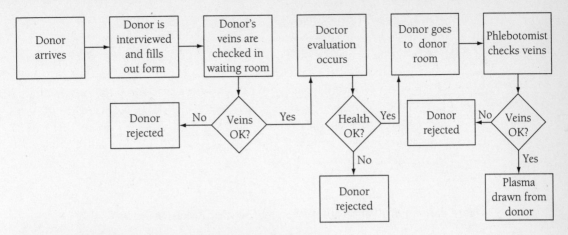

Figure 8.1. *Flowchart of Process of Selecting New Blood Donors.*

most of the centers had a similar process.

Some additional information came to light when the flowchart was reviewed:

- The current process allowed as many as sixteen people to evaluate new donors for suitable veins. There was great variability in their decisions.

- A medical evaluation by a physician was conducted on all new donors. There was often a wait to see the physician.

- The procedure for a venipuncture was very precise. The number of years of experience of the phlebotomist was believed to be very important in accomplishing the procedure successfully.

Based on their documentation of the process and the use of change concepts from the category "improve work flow," the team developed some changes. The new flowchart is shown in Figure 8.2. The biggest change was getting the physician, the phlebotomist, and other personnel at the center to work together. A group of experienced phlebotomists was also selected to do the vein inspection using documented procedures. These phlebotomists wore pagers so they could respond quickly. The team used cycles to test and implement the changes.

The team used the worksheet for documenting a cycle (see Exhibit 4.2) to come up with the following testing plans.

Cycle 1

Plan
Objective: To test changes to the process of selecting blood donors.

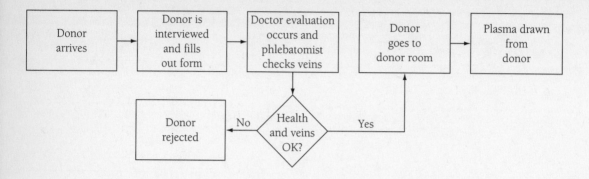

Figure 8.2. *Flowchart of Redesigned Process of Selecting New Blood Donors.*

Questions and predictions:

1. Will the changes to the procedures for checking new donors for suitable veins reduce the number of partials?
   Prediction: Yes, the changes should almost eliminate partials because most partials result when venipuncture is attempted on people with unsuitable veins. The occurrence of such attempts should decrease because the changes will allow the physician, the phlebotomist, and other personnel at the center to work together to evaluate patients' suitability.
2. Will the changes to the procedures for checking new donors for suitable veins decrease the number of customer complaints?
   Prediction: Yes, the amount of patient discomfort and the waiting time will be reduced.

Who, What, Where, When:

1. The phlebotomist, physicians, and staff will use the new flowchart.
2. People who work in the center will be asked to attend a meeting on June 13 to discuss and comment on the changes.
3. The new process will be used beginning the week of June 20.
4. The team will collect data on the number of partials and the number of customer complaints. This data will be plotted weekly on a run chart. Historical data are available. A before and after test will be used.
5. The test will be run for three months.

Do

The data collected is shown on the attached run charts (Figures 8.3 and 8.4). No problems were encountered when the data was being collected.

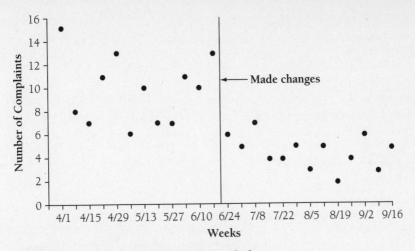

Figure 8.3. *Customer Complaints Before and After.*

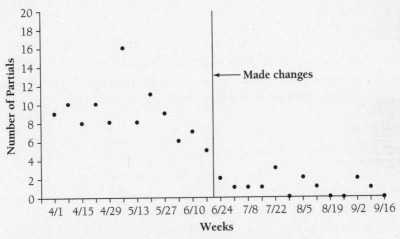

Figure 8.4. *Partials Collected Using New Donor Selection Process.*

Study
As predicted, the run charts indicate that the tested changes resulted in fewer partials and fewer customer complaints. Partials were reduced by more than 50 percent.

Act
- The new flowchart will be made part of the policies and procedures book.

- The experienced phlebotomists will document the best practices for a venipuncture. They will develop a checklist. These procedures will become the basis for current training and the training of new employees.

- To monitor the process, data on number of partials and customer complaints will continue to be collected and will be plotted on a run chart for analysis. The phlebotomists will collect and plot the data on partials and the office manager will collect and plot the data on complaints.

- In the next Cycle, the process will be tested at another center. The remaining centers will be informed of the progress of the tests.

Cycle 2

The objective of this cycle was to test the new process of selecting donors at Center 2. This center was selected because it had one of the highest numbers of customer complaints. Information on the new process, the training, and the results of the test were supplied by Center 1. The phlebotomists at Center 2 made some minor changes to the best practices for venipuncture. These changes were agreed upon by the phlebotomists at Center 1. The test at Center 2 was run over a three-month period.

It took more than a month for customer complaints and the number of partials to begin to decline. For the last six weeks of the test, the results were similar to those achieved at Center 1. It was therefore decided to implement the new process at all the centers in the next cycle.

Cycle 3

The objective of this cycle was to implement the change at the remaining six centers to achieve 100 percent coverage. Information on the new process, the training, and the results of the two tests were supplied to all the centers. The two centers that tested the new process were available to answer any questions that arose. Some of the centers made changes to the new process to better suit their situations. Results were favorable in all centers. Each center will continue to collect data on number of partials and customer complaints and will plot the data on a run chart for analysis.

Learnings

1. *Consideration should be given to developing changes that remove complexity from the process or system.* Complexity is often added when changes are developed that are "more of the same" (more people, more money, more steps, more inspection, and so on). These types of changes should be avoided. When complexity does exist, changes should be developed that simplify the process or system. In this case study, the team constructed a flowchart of the existing process

of selecting new donors. A review of the flowchart indicated that there were three stages in the process where a potential donor could be rejected. It was obvious that this complexity in the process did not benefit the donors. A change was developed so that the complete evaluation of the donor could be performed during one stage of the process.

2. *Improvement often results if all the people involved consider themselves part of the same system.* This change concept is focused on getting people who interact to cooperate with one another. In the original process of selecting blood donors, the physician, the phlebotomist, and other personnel at the center considered their work in isolation and focused only on their part of the process. A change was developed that brought them together in one stage of the process in order to optimize patient care.

3. *If inspection is used, it should be done before the bottleneck.* The capacity of a system is determined by the capacity at the bottleneck. Therefore, the bottleneck resource should never be used to work on anything that will be rejected later in the process. The bottleneck in this process was the medical evaluation done by the physician. In the original process, some donors were rejected after this evaluation was done. Having the phlebotomist check the donor's veins prior to the medical evaluation allowed donors to be rejected before reaching the bottleneck.

4. *Test changes on a small scale and build knowledge sequentially.* It is necessary to reduce the risk of a change that does not result in improvement. If possible, a change should not be tried first in full scale implementation. Knowledge about the change should be built in a sequence of small-scale tests. The organization described in this case study has eight centers where blood plasma is collected. The new process for selecting donors was tested at two of the centers in the first two cycles. Information on the tests and the results were then sent to the other centers for their consideration.

5. *Collecting data over time is a way to include a wide range of conditions in a test.* In this before-and-after test, data was collected for three months after the changes were made. This allowed for a variety of donors and a variety of conditions within the center to be present during the test. The data indicated that the changes resulted in improvement under these different conditions. This increased the team's degree of belief that the improvements would continue once the changes were implemented.

6. *Cycles should be used to implement successful changes.* It is not enough that improvement is shown during the test of a change. Improvement must be maintained over time, when a team is no longer specifically focusing on the activity. To do this, the change must be implemented. The changes that are successful in one area of an organization should be spread to other areas. In this case study, documentation, training, and monitoring of the changes were carried out during the implementation cycle.

Case Study 2: Reengineering the Process of Acquiring Business

A company involved in the design and manufacture of cooling towers decided to redesign the process they used to acquire new business. Cooling towers are used in the chemical industry to change the temperature of liquids during the manufacturing process. The process for acquiring business is the first step in the core of this design and manufacturing business. It begins with an inquiry or a request for proposal (RFP) by a customer, and it ends with the award or loss of a contract. The company had a good reputation in the marketplace, but their top management believed that significant improvement could be made in customer service and the reduction of costs by improving the business-acquisition process.

As part of the proposal to build a cooling tower, the company provides a preliminary design, an estimate of costs, and a schedule. The biggest improvement in the company would be for the design, estimates, and schedules developed to acquire the business to be used to do the work. Responding to a proposal could be seen as the beginning of the contract work. As it stands, all the work that is accomplished to get the contract is later needlessly redone by different departments before the cooling tower is constructed (see Figure 8.5). This system results in it taking an average of four thousand hours to construct a cooling tower; it takes more than a year to complete a project from the time an RFP is received.

This organization also reengineered other major systems, and many of these reengineered systems contributed greatly to the success of the effort to improve the business acquisition process. Because the business-acquisition process contributed most to the overall improvement, this case study highlights that part of the redesign effort. The case study begins with the charter prepared by the management team in early 1994. The changes developed and tested by the project team to accomplish the charter were implemented at many locations by January of 1995.

	→ System →		
	Precontract	**Contract Work Begins**		
Process	Business Acquisition	Engineering Manufacturing Construction	
Current Use of Process	Estimating Scheduling Designing Proposing	Reestimating Rescheduling Redesigning	Reestimating Rescheduling Building

Figure 8.5. *Current System for Acquiring Business and Beginning Construction of Cooling Towers.*

What are we trying to accomplish? The following is the charter developed for this effort:

General Description

Design and implement a business-acquisition process that will secure profitable new business. The work accomplished in acquiring business should be in a form that can be used after the business is obtained.

Guidance

Expected results:
1. Standardization of the business acquisition process for all locations.
2. Less downstream waste in time and money re-doing work done during acquisition.
3. Reduction of the cycle time from the time an RFP is received until completion of the project.

Boundaries:
1. This process will focus on standard components for cooling towers, but what is learned will be applied to nonstandard work where possible.
2. Testing and implementation will be in selected locations first.
3. This process will not address the acquisition of new companies or management of contract changes.
4. This process must integrate with other redesigned systems (management information systems, procurement, engineering design).
5. Additional resources needed by the team should be coordinated with the management team sponsor.

How will we know if a change was an improvement? The current process of acquiring business has an average success rate of 18 percent on projects that are bid. The time to respond to an RFP is currently averaging about ten days per inquiry (see Figure 8.6).

What changes can we make that will result in improvement?

- As shown in Figure 8.5, the current system can create up to three estimates for the same job during the life of the project. This duplication of effort was created because of the lack of communication and the low level of trust in information coming from another department. The use of multiple estimates creates costly work for the employees and confusion for the customer.

- The contract work begins at the end of the business-acquisition process. The business acquisition process varies from office to office. People who are transferred have to be trained in the new office's procedures and methods.

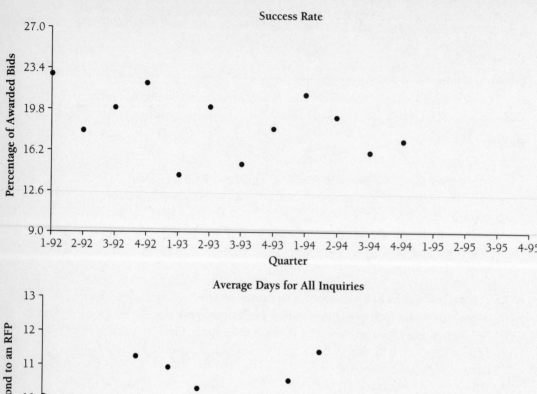

Figure 8.6. *Current Measures of Business Acquisition Success Rate and Days to Respond to an RFP.*

- Knowledge of engineering, purchasing, manufacturing, and construction is critical during the acquisition process.

- Figure 8.7 shows in detail the business acquisition process that is now used at some locations within the company. Notice the complexity introduced in the process because of the multiple reviews that are required by different departments.

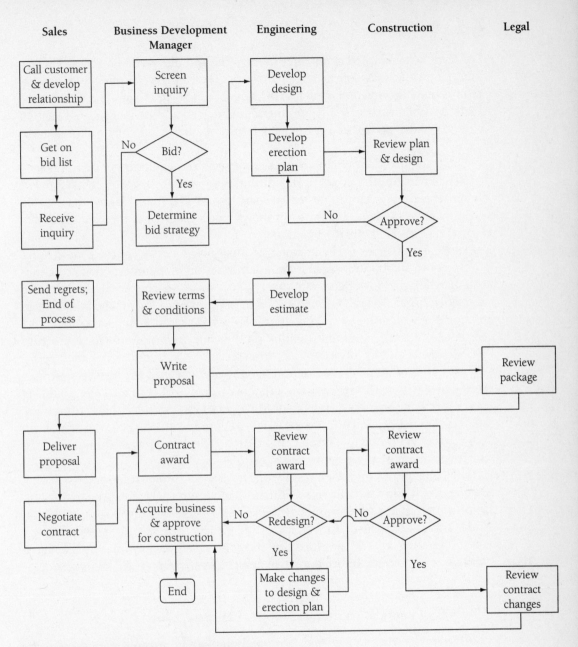

Figure 8.7. *Current Business-Acquisition Process.*

After some initial information was gathered from sales managers, contracting managers, and estimators, the team decided to benchmark some other organizations on best practices in the acquisition of business.

Cycle 1

The team benchmarked companies in the same and different industries. The key learning was: *It is possible to develop the design, schedule, and estimates for the proposal and use them with a minimum of change throughout the project.* This will be made possible by the use of computer-aided design and by focusing on custom products with standardized components. Information technology will play a critical role.

The team also defined a two-phase approach to developing a plan. Phase 1 was the creation of a concept design for the process. Based on this concept design, the team developed, tested on a small scale, and implemented the detailed system design in Phase 2. Figure 8.8 shows a flow diagram of the concept design for the process of acquiring business.

The major changes to the business acquisition process were the project summary report, the inquiry screen, and the formation of a contract team to eliminate handoffs and foster cooperation. The success of the concept design was also dependent upon several redesign efforts in other parts of the organization. These processes enabled the new acquisition process to accomplish its aim. Table 8.1 contains some additional information on the concept design for the new acquisition process and for the enabling processes.

Just as important as the reduction in complexity was to the business acquisition process was the impact the changes to this process and the enabling processes were predicted to have on the overall system once the contract was started. Figure 8.9 compares the current system to the proposed new system from the precontract phase to contract completion. The new process should result in no downstream work on estimates, schedules, or designs.

The concept design relies heavily on the project information database. This database will allow for the use of the project summary report prepared in the acquisition process (precontract award phase) to generate the design, schedule, and estimates to be used for the life of the project. The detailed system design for the database will be developed by the contracting and estimating managers with support from the information technology department (IT). The project database will:

- Accept information from the project summary report

- Provide a specific plan for the execution of an entire contract

- Document the utilization of standard components for design to minimize costs

- Contain specific design information that can be used to develop standard designs for projects

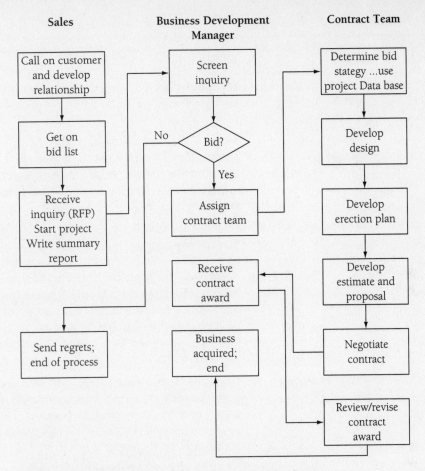

Figure 8.8. *Concept Design of the Business Acquisition Process.*

The next cycle was designed to assess the feasibility of the new project database.

Cycle 2

Plan
Objective: Assess the feasibility of using the project database in the business acquisition process.

Questions and Predictions:

1. Will the use of the project database during the precontract award phase simplify the business acquisition process and reduce work during the contract phase?

Table 8.1. *Concept Design of the New Acquisition Process and Other Enabling Processes.*

FUNCTION AND PROCESS TYPE	CONCEPT	PURPOSE
Engineering Enabler Process	Use of standardized components for the cooling towers	Reduce engineering time to zero after work is awarded. Other downstream work previously duplicated on many projects can also be eliminated.
Procurement Enabler Process	Purchasing standard components	Purchased components identified by standard designs are ordered at the time of contract award. Suppliers and costs are predetermined from the standard design. Eliminates need to seek suppliers. Reduces lead time of 16 weeks to less than five weeks once the contract is awarded.
Management Information System System-Enabler Process	Use of project information database	The project information database will be fully integrated into the corporate information system. It will be used in designing, monitoring, and tracking construction projects. It will contain many items (e.g., scope of work, financial impact, contracting issues, details on site work) that needed to define a project from the start of the award to the final on-site construction of the cooling tower. The database can be used to define a project because of the use of standardized components design.
Sales Acquisition Process	Use of project summary report	Contains the information about a project gathered during the pre-contract award phase. Input of this information into the project information database will result in the necessary design, schedules, and estimates for the project. This is because of the use of standardized components. The designs, schedules and estimates will then be used during the actual contract work. This will reduce rework on estimates *after* the contract is awarded. Predicted: This should eliminate an average of five weeks from the overall schedule once the contract is awarded and reduce the amount of time it currently takes to respond to an RFP.
Sales Acquisition Process	Use of a contract team	The contract team concept will eliminate the travel of documents and information between departments within the organization. Travel of documents and approvals has historically taken 4-6 weeks. Information technology will also enable us to reduce waiting time spent in approvals and changes with suppliers and customers significantly.
Sales Acquisition Process	Use of an inquiry screen	The new process will include a step to screen the inquiry. This will help to eliminate high risk work. The screen will allow for identification of premium opportunities ensuring that the selling effort is concentrated in the right place.

	Precontract	Contract Work Begins		
Process	Business Acquisition	Engineering	Manufacturing	Construction
Current Use of Process	Estimating Scheduling Designing Proposal	Reestimating Rescheduling Redesigning		Reestimating Rescheduling Building
Concept of New Process	Estimating Scheduling Designing Proposal			Building

Systems

Figure 8.9. *Comparison of Current System and New System.*

Prediction: Yes, the tools are available to develop such a database. The database will contain information about the use of standard components. The use of the database by the contract team will allow for the development of estimates, schedules, and designs during the precontract phase that can be used for the life of the project.

Who, What, Where, When:

1. Other team members from construction, engineering, manufacturing, and sales will review the detailed system design of the database for completeness.
2. Missing information will be discussed and added to the final database.

Do
The team met and assembled all needed information. This information was then put into a prototype database and given to the other team members for review.

Study
All of the team members had additions to the initial screen but they believed that the project database could be used as described in the concept design. For the company to effectively utilize the information to reduce costs, support from IT will be critical to the implementation of the new process at all locations.

Act
Based on the results of this cycle, the team feels confident that with IT support the goals of capturing all relevant information and reducing downstream

work will be accomplished. It was determined that the use of the database would be tested at three sites on real projects. In the next two cycles, the project database will be tested in the following locations with the noted products and customers:

Location	Product	Customer
Mobile, Alabama	Cooling Tower Type I	Allied (Cycle 3)
El Monte, California	Cooling Tower Type II	City (Cycle 4)
Texas City, Texas	Cooling Tower Type I	Chem TEX Industries (Cycle 4)

Cycle 3

Now that the project database was operational, the objective of this cycle was to test and further develop the new business acquisition process, including the project database, on a project in Mobile. The test in Mobile was very productive. The contract team functioned well. One weakness uncovered in the test was that the project database was not user-friendly to the test group. It was very apparent that a significant learning curve was involved. The Mobile group felt that with additional practice, the project database would be better than the present system, even without full IT support. This site would move toward implementation of the new business acquisition process and the use of the project database.

For the next test, the team decided to provide more up-front training on the use of the project database. A comprehensive set of instructions was prepared.

Cycle 4

Tests were run at the El Monte and Texas City locations. The training and instructions resulted in greater ease of use of the project database. These changes produced very positive results. The team's confidence in the new business acquisition process and in its applicability over a range of customers, including the government sector, was increased. Both of these sites will implement the new business acquisition process. The team feels that implementation of the changes should precede at other locations to achieve 100 percent coverage.

Cycle 5

The objective of this cycle was to implement the new business acquisition process in six different locations. Results were monitored throughout 1995. After some initial learning, the success rate for acquiring business averaged 35 percent throughout the organization beginning in the second quarter. The time needed to respond to an RFP averaged five days from June to December (see Figure 8.10).

Long-Term Results

The original charter included the need for less downstream waste of time and money in engineering and construction. The new business acquisition process eliminated the causes for creating multiple estimates for both engineering and construction. Time savings allowed engineering more time to respond to customer changes. In construction, the savings were concrete. Figure 8.11 shows

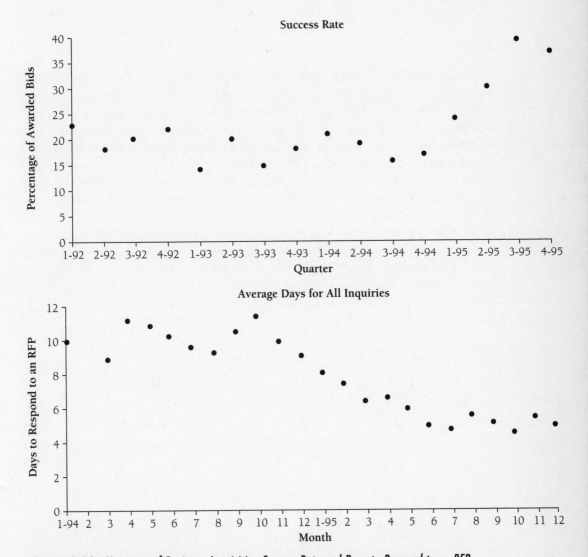

Figure 8.10. *Measures of Business Acquisition Success Rate and Days to Respond to an RFP After Implementation of New System.*

that the average number of hours to construct a tower in the field was reduced from 4,000 to 3,500. (This data was collected from projects started in the third quarter.) The high number of hours for project 16 was due to the project turning from a standard into a nonstandard project. The acquisition process was now more discriminating on the work that was selected to bid. The success rate stabilized at about 35 percent. This also reduced costs in engineering and construction. In addition to the savings in these areas, several support areas reduced overtime hours and other costs associated with responding to every inquiry received.

Learnings

1. *In large redesign efforts (reengineering), it is useful to create a concept design and then a detailed system design.* Multiple PDSA cycles are then used to test the components of the detailed design and the entire system. In this case study, the team benchmarked other companies in the first cycle to gather information to create a concept design. This concept then guided the development of the detailed system design. The principle of testing on a small scale at selected locations was used. This approach is appropriate for the design or redesign of large systems that include multiple processes and products. The Model for Improvement provided the structure for this effort.

2. *When improving large systems, several simultaneous redesign efforts are necessary.* In most improvement activities, multiple cycles are needed to test and implement changes. When improvement efforts are focused on a large system, multiple cycles to test and implement change will be going on in several areas

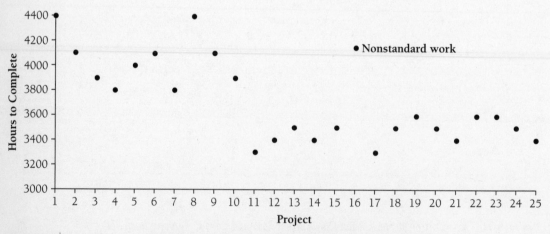

Figure 8.11. *Construction Performance on Towers After Implementation of New System.*

at once. In this case study, improvements in the use of standardized components and in purchasing and the development of the project database and project summary report required multiple consecutive cycles focused on different areas.

3. *The change concept of standardization can be a key to improvement.* The customers in this case study were impressed not only with the quality of the cooling towers they received but also with the turnaround time of documents and the reduced time to complete the project. This enhanced service was due to the standardization provided by the project database.

4. *Breaking down barriers between departments, cooperation, and team work can result in short-term and long-term benefits.* The use of the contract team in this case was critical to the reduction in the costs of the overall project while at the same time improving overall service to the customer. The contract team minimized the waiting time for approvals, and increased communication and response time both inside the organization and to suppliers and customers.

5. *Structure and methods are required to nurture teams and cooperation.* The creation of the contract team was a structural change to how the business operated; it provided a systems view of the organization and caused the people in the processes to behave differently than they did in their "organizational boxes." People not only understood their role on the contract team, but also understood their role in the "system" and the impact their work had on the final customer. The project database provided a method for people to communicate the status of a project from inquiry to final completion. This method enhanced communication throughout the system.

Case Study 3: Improving a Ph.D. Program

Customer research at a university revealed that there was some concern on the part of faculty, alumni, and students about the Ph.D. programs. The major concern was the time it took to receive the degree, which they felt was a major cause of high attrition rates. The academic dean put together a team consisting of herself and seven faculty members. The faculty members were chosen to cover a variety of academic disciplines.

What are we trying to accomplish? The following is the charter developed by the team:

General Description

Improve the Ph.D. programs in the College of Arts and Sciences

Guidance

Consider the quality of the research work, the time to complete the degree, and the attrition rates as important measures of quality.

Findings from this team should be shared with other schools in the university.

How would we know that a change is an improvement? The following measures would be used to assess the quality of changes to the Ph.D. program:

- Quality of the research

- Attrition rates

- Time-to-degree

- Total credit hours (all students in the program/number of degrees conferred)

What changes can we make that will result in improvement? The team summarized their experiences and their knowledge of the processes in the Ph.D. programs, interviewed students from their own university and faculty members from their own and other universities, performed a literature search, and analyzed some historical data on attrition rates and time-to-completion of the degree. From this material they compiled a summary of some relevant information:

- Students who relied on their own financing had substantially higher attrition rates and longer time-to-degree than those who received financial aid.

- Completion rates tended to be somewhat higher for teaching assistantships than for fellowships.

- Most students had no specific plan for working on and completing their dissertation.

- Inability to get advice from the faculty was frequently mentioned as a serious problem. There was large variation in the amount and quality of the contact between student and faculty adviser.

- Significant amounts of attrition were found before and after "all but dissertation" status.

- Better completion rates were found in smaller programs than in larger ones.

- The time between the end of course work and the start of work on a dissertation topic was a critical time for many students.

- Quality of research and time-to-degree could both be improved simultaneously.

Based on this information, the team developed some ideas for changes in the Ph.D. programs.

- More structure in the programs would be helpful.

- The serial nature of course work and then dissertation work can be improved upon.

- A better balance could be achieved between independent research on the part of the student and advice and encouragement by the adviser.

Cycle 1

Plan
Objective: To test an approach to helping students choose a dissertation topic during the first two years of the program.

Questions and predictions:

1. Will students be able to select topics for research during their first two years in the Ph.D. program?
   Prediction: There may be some difficulty during the first year due to the lack of appropriate knowledge.
2. Will the new approach have an effect on the measures of quality?
   Prediction: Yes, beginning the selection of a research topic earlier should have a positive effect on the measures of quality.

Who, What, Where, When:

- Four of the team members agreed to test an approach to helping students choose a dissertation topic and begin the literature search during their first two years of the program. Each professor was assigned three students.

- The test would be conducted for the next three years.

- The professors would record their observations of the ability of students to choose topics at this early stage and of the ease of the students' transition from course work to dissertation research.

- The professors involved in the test would also be surveyed as to their prediction of the impact of this approach on the four measures of quality.

Do
- Although the ability to select topics during the first year seemed to help the students begin to focus, it was not a good approach.

- One student involved in the test dropped out to accept a full-time job.

Study
- Students were able to choose topics for their dissertations. The professors observed that most of the choices were made in the second year in the program.

- All of the students in the test were able to begin working on their dissertation very shortly after their course work was completed.

- There was almost universal agreement by the professors that the new approach would have an effect on the measures of quality. (Figure 8.12 provides data on the students involved in the test, including the professors' opinions about the students' prospects.)

- Giving students the ability to select topics for their dissertation in the first two years will have a positive effect on the Ph.D. program.

Act
- As a result of the professors' predictions about the impact the changes would have on the measures of quality, all of the Ph.D. programs were to be changed to allow for the selection of dissertation topics in the first two years.

	Time to choose topic	Number of changes to topic	Delay in starting after course work completed	Early indication of quality of research	Likelihood to complete degree
Professor A					
Student 1	1¼ years	0	1 month	H	H
Student 2	1½ years	1	3 months	M	M
Student 3	1 year	1	0 months	H	H
Professor B					
Student 1	1¾ years	0	2 months	H	H
Student 2	1 year	1	0 months	H	H
Student 3	1¼ years	0	0 months	M	H
Professor C					
Student 1	1¾ years	2	3 months	C	M
Student 2	1½ years	0	2 months	H	H
Professor D					
Student 1	2 years	2	2 months	M	H
Student 2	1 year	0	1 month	H	H
Student 3	1¼ years	1	0 months	C	M

H = high   M = medium   C = cannot judge

Figure 8.12. *Data from Ph.D. Program Improvement Effort.*

- Permission was granted to allow the students to earn dissertation credits earlier than usual.

- The decision was made to test additional structure for the new approach in the next cycle.

Cycle 2
Three of the team members agreed to test additional structure in two areas. One test consisted of a requirement that the student and the adviser develop a plan for conducting the research and finishing the dissertation. The plan would include an agreement on the frequency of interaction between student and adviser, and deadlines for the noncreative aspects of the work. The second part of the structure included a workshop for students conducting research or writing their dissertation. The professors participating in the test would collect data on the usefulness of the plan and on the ability of the students to develop and follow the plan. Data on the benefits of the workshop would be obtained from the students and the professors. The results of the test would determine what if any additional structure would be included in the redesigned process. The redesigned process would be evaluated over time using the four measures of quality.

Learnings

1. *Significant improvement is best accomplished by developing and testing specific changes.* Many improvement efforts become bogged down because the people involved are looking for the "right" solution instead of looking for and testing a number of good ones (specific changes). In this improvement effort, the change to allow students to select their dissertation topic in the first two years was tested and implemented.

2. *The team utilized the change concepts of doing tasks in parallel, synchronization, and standardization (create a formal process).* They asked the question, "Why do we have to treat the completion of course work and the beginning of the dissertation research as two distinct, nonoverlapping activities?" It not only shortens the total time to obtain a Ph.D. to overlap these activities, but it also leads to less attrition and better research. The team tried to determine when the activities should begin to overlap. They learned that sometime in the second year would be the time to choose a dissertation topic. In cycle 2, the team also added more structure to the process.

3. *A wide range of conditions should be included in a test.* The team collected data on a number of measures both before and after the changes to the program. They included in the test eleven students and four professors from different pro-

grams. This increased their degree of belief that the changes would result in improvement once implemented throughout the university.

4. *Cooperation was vital to the success of this improvement effort.* Cooperation between the faculty and students was needed in order for the changes to be successful. Cooperation was built through more frequent interactions.

5. *Intermediate measures can be used to predict the impact of changes on the measures of quality.* An intermediate measure can be defined as a measure that is related to the measure of quality either empirically or theoretically. The intermediate measure is used because it is easier to obtain, because there is a long delay between the change and its effect on the measure of quality, or because the measure of quality is measuring a rare event. In this case study, it could be a long time before an impact of the changes is seen on the measures of quality (quality of research, attrition rates, and time-to-degree). Therefore, some intermediate measures (time to choose a topic, number of changes, delay in starting, early indications of the quality of research, and the likelihood to complete the degree) were used.

Conclusion

Part Two has discussed some methods for improving systems. This chapter presented some case studies using these methods. Part Three describes how an integrated approach to improvement can be developed that will help organizations eliminate quality problems, reduce costs, and even change the expectations of customers. The chapters present a system designed to help leaders integrate improvement into the organization's business plan.

AN INTEGRATED APPROACH TO IMPROVEMENT

The first two parts of this book explored a framework for making effective change. The Model for Improvement, with the three questions and the PDSA Cycle, was explained and applications were described. The applications relied on the skills of developing, testing, and implementing change.

This third part of the book presents approaches to integrating improvement efforts into a system of improvement. Chapter Nine introduces the basis for this integration: the concept of "value" and the three categories of improvement:

Category 1:   Eliminating quality problems
Category 2:   Reducing cost while maintaining or improving quality
Category 3:   Expanding customer expectations

These three categories are explained in detail in Chapters Ten, Eleven, and Twelve, respectively. The approaches to improvement in these chapters are refinements of the methods for developing and testing changes introduced in Part Two. Chapter Thirteen describes activities for integrating the improvement initiatives in an organization.

CHAPTER 9

Integrating Improvement to Increase Value

There are a number of reasons to think about integrating improvement initiatives in an organization:

- Finite resources are available for improvement; these resources should be focused on the initiatives that best help accomplish the aim(s) of the organization.

- The organization must continue to operate as improvements are made; improvement activities must not stop the organization from accomplishing day-to-day business activities.

- The systems that make up organizations are complex; it is important not to suboptimize one part of an organization at the expense of the other parts.

- The different aims of a business can be balanced by selecting improvement initiatives in each of the three categories.

In a business setting, improvements are made to products and services to improve their *value* to customers. This chapter discusses what value is and why organizations should focus on improving it. The chapter also presents approaches to guiding organizations in improving the value of their products and services.

Bob was in charge of organizing business luncheons for his company. One of his most important tasks was to select a restaurant. A new French restaurant near the office had excellent food, but the prices were very high. The prices at Jenny's, conversely, were reasonable, but the food was at best mediocre. After reviewing a number of other alternatives, Bob realized that trying to balance quality with price was not an easy job. A colleague told him about a restaurant about a mile from the office called The Forum. Bob visited there for lunch and found the food very good (almost as good as the French restaurant) and the prices moderate. He knew this could be an appropriate restaurant for the business luncheons.

Whether the provider is a restaurant, a hospital, a manufacturing company, or a bank, customers are constantly judging products and services by their quality and their price. Decisions about quality and price are fundamental to success in business. Customers make purchasing decisions and other judgements by considering both quality and price.

Quality is the measure of how well a product or service matches a need. Quality is defined very broadly throughout this book, to include such dimensions as product features, timeliness, personal interface, consistency, and so on. (Chapter Twelve expands on this definition of quality.)

Price is what the customer has to pay for a product or service (usually in money). This concept of price includes the price tag as well as the "cost to use" the product or service. For example, if a product must be repaired or adjusted in some way before it is used, the price includes the purchase price as well as the cost to repair or adjust. The "cost to purchase" (including time, shipping charges, travel expenses, and so on) might also be considered part of the price component.

Jim, a purchasing agent for his company, has been asked to buy an item at the lowest cost available. The price tag of the item at the store across the street from his company is $100. He can buy the item from a catalogue for $90 plus shipping charges (a minimum of $15 per order). Which opportunity offers Jim the lowest total price? Since the items have identical quality, which is the best value? Jim realizes that he has to consider more than the price tag.

For a business that produces products and services for the marketplace, the establishment of the prices for those products and services is fundamental to the success of the business. The marketplace (customers, competitors, and community) sets a narrow price range for many products and services (such as commodity items). For other products and services, the producer or seller has a lot of flexibility in setting the price. Most organizations have a well-defined pricing process that includes such considerations as the cost to produce and service different customers, customer price sensitivity and perceptions, the pricing structure of the company's other products and services, expected reactions of competitors to price changes, and emotional responses of customers.

Value is the relative worth, utility, or importance of something. The concept of value combines quality and price—in other words: *value = quality/price*. This equation emphasizes the direct influence of quality and the inverse effect of price, but the precise relationship is usually more complex. It is easy to see from this relationship that higher quality does not necessarily mean higher value; the price also has to be considered. The food at the French restaurant may be of higher quality than the food at the Forum, but is it of higher value? To determine this, the prices at each restaurant must be considered. Which restaurant has higher value is a judgement that has to be made by the customer. Bob made such a judgement when he selected The Forum for his company's business luncheons.

Bob met with the owner of The Forum to plan company luncheons for the next year. When Bob complimented the owner on the success of her restaurant, she commented that things had not always been this good. During the previous couple of years she had attempted to advertise more to increase the restaurant's popularity. This did not seem to have much of an impact. So, she decided to focus on making improvements that really affected her customers. If the food and service she provided was of high quality and she could keep her prices reasonable, people would choose her restaurant instead of her competitors'.

So, over the previous year the restaurant had made changes in how the food was prepared, how the waiters and waitresses were trained, and how it dealt with suppliers. People commented about the improvements in the food and service and the reasonable prices. The owner found that this strategy resulted in increased sales and market share.

The owner of the restaurant had learned a valuable lesson: improving value sets off a chain reaction. By improving quality, reducing prices, or both, an organization can achieve other goals such as growth in revenue, greater market share, and more profitability. (This chain reaction is summarized in Figure 9.1.) As a new customer, Bob's company will now also benefit from these improvements.

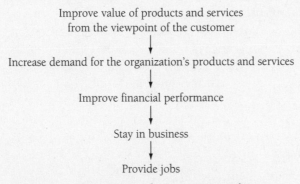

Improve value of products and services
from the viewpoint of the customer

↓

Increase demand for the organization's products and services

↓

Improve financial performance

↓

Stay in business

↓

Provide jobs

Figure 9.1. *Chain Reaction from Improving Value.*

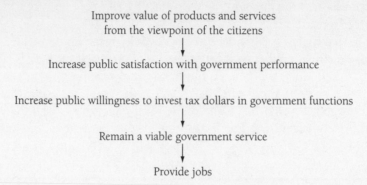

Figure 9.2. *Chain Reaction for Improving Value in a Government Organization.*

As organizations make improvements to reduce their costs, they could decide to take all the financial benefits in increased profits. But improved value is the result only if some of the benefits are passed on to customers. These benefits could be passed on as higher quality (such as additional features) or in the form of reduced prices. Approaches to improving quality or reducing prices that do not involve improvements to processes or products will not set off the chain reaction. For example, increasing inspection to improve outgoing quality may not result in improved financial performance; or a price reduction to increase sales may improve value in the short term, but not improve overall financial performance of the organization. To set off the chain reaction, increased value must persist in the long term. This requires making improvements that reduce costs, increase the capacity of processes within the organization, or improve the quality of products or services.

The specifics of the chain reaction in Figure 9.1 may change for organizations in government, health care, and education, and others. Figure 9.2 is an example of what the reaction may be like for a government organization. A good learning exercise is to write this chain reaction using the situation and language relevant to your organization.

How can value be measured? The concept of value is meaningless unless people are involved. Value is always relative to a particular person, time, location, and other conditions. When does one value having an umbrella in one's briefcase or backpack? Value is best measured and studied by evaluating its two components—quality and price. Chapters Ten, Eleven, and Twelve discuss the types of measurements and data that are useful for value in different situations. In particular, Chapter Twelve discusses the multiple dimensions that are included in the broad concept of quality. Chapter Thirteen discusses the use of a family of measures by an organization to monitor the organization's performance in improving value to customers.

The Aim of Improving Value

If an organization is concerned with improving the value of their products and services, then a broad statement of their aim could be, *Make changes that result in improvement from the viewpoint of the customer.* Although this statement may be simple, achieving it certainly is not. To better understand what is difficult about this aim, let's explore some of the key words in the statement.

Change. Change is never easy. It may be difficult to think of a change that anyone would predict would be an improvement. It is often difficult for people to initially accept change.

Everyone associated with the school was discouraged because standardized scores had not improved over the last few years. The principal understood that the extra training teachers were receiving and the additional practice tests being administered were not helping. She wondered if the faculty was ready for a change that would really have an impact on student achievement. She also wondered what kind of change would be required.

Improvement. All improvement requires change, but all changes do not result in improvement. To be considered an improvement, the change must lead to higher value to someone—better quality, a lower price, or both. Some changes can make matters worse. Many new products and services do not live up to expectations or they have unanticipated side effects. There is always some risk involved when changes are made.

A company with a recognizable brand name decided to change its packaging. They thought that new packaging would revitalize the product. When they introduced the changes, the sales of the product declined. It seems that customers believed it was not the same reliable product they were used to.

Customer. A customer is the person or entity (such as another process) that receives, buys, or uses the outcome of a process. For most organizations, there is a chain of customers (such as the distributor, the wholesaler, the retailer, the purchaser, and the consumer), and there are different types of customers at each level of the chain, and multiple customers for each type. Some customers may be internal to the organization. These different customers will have different views about what determines value, and these views will change over time. Customers judge products and services after they experience them. They can change their mind anytime something of higher value comes along.

A phone company had provided service to Margaret's business for more than ten years. Margaret had very few complaints. One day, another company interested in providing phone service contacted her. They promised more features at less cost. After a two-month trial, Margaret switched her business and her home service over to the new company.

What is expected to happen to an organization that focuses on the aim of making changes that result in improvement from the viewpoint of the customer? Figure 9.1 summarized the chain reaction that should occur. The second part of this book presented methods for overcoming some of the difficulties of achieving the aim of improving value. To achieve the expected benefits in organizations, these methods need to be integrated into a system of improvement. It is helpful, therefore, to look at improving value in more detail.

The Three Categories of Improvement

The broad aim of improving value can be classified into the three major categories introduced earlier:

1. Eliminating quality problems that arise because we fail to meet the expectations of customers
2. Reducing costs significantly while maintaining or improving quality
3. Expanding customer expectations by providing products and services that customers perceive as unusually high in value

An organization that is focused on improving value will often have activities in each of the categories. The specific chain reaction expected from improvements in each of the three categories is different. These chain reactions are discussed in more detail in Chapters Ten, Eleven, and Twelve. It is important to note at this point, however, that improvements in all three categories are required to achieve the chain reaction illustrated in Figure 9.1. For example, doing a good job in Category 1 (eliminating quality problems) does not guarantee a business success if the demand for the organization's products and services disappears.

Category 1: Eliminating Quality Problems

The aim in the first category is to make changes that significantly reduce the occurrence of problems such as errors in shipments, long waiting times, defects in a product, or lost paperwork. Reducing quality problems often has the side effect of reducing the costs associated with resolving the problems. This further improves value.

A center that collects blood was experiencing complaints from new donors. It seemed that some prospective donors had to wait up to an hour before blood was taken. Three people at the center were involved in the preparation process: 1) a nurse's assistant would check the veins of the donor, 2) a physician would do a short health evaluation, and 3) a phlebotomist would then recheck the person's veins and extract the blood. Sometimes the phlebotomist would reject a prospective donor for unsuitable veins. This could happen after the person had waited close to an hour. The people at the center decided to make changes to simplify the process. The result was that a phlebotomist now checked the donor's veins first instead of the nurse's assistant. If the veins were unsuitable, no health evaluation was done. People no longer had to wait only to be rejected. Also, because fewer health evaluations were done, the physician was now better able to keep to his schedule. This resulted in reduced waiting times and an increase in the number of patients that could be seen. (See Chapter Eight for a case study on this process.)

Data for focusing efforts in the first category of improvement are usually readily available. Some examples of sources of data are traditional quality control measures, customer surveys, or as in the case of the blood donation center, complaints. The types of changes to the system that are typically developed include simplification and standardization of processes, training, mistake proofing, and preventive maintenance. Methods for developing changes to solve quality problems are discussed in Chapter Ten.

Category 2: Reducing Costs While Maintaining or Improving Quality

The second category is concerned with making changes that reduce costs. Any organization can reduce costs if it is willing to sacrifice quality by such methods as cutting resources, buying cheaper materials, or postponing maintenance. It takes substantial skill and knowledge to reduce costs while maintaining or improving quality. Cost reductions allow the producer an opportunity to offer products and services to customers at lower prices. If quality is maintained, value is improved.

To boost sales, a manufacturing company ran specials on their products at the end of each quarter. The result was that more than 70 percent of the product shipped during each quarter was shipped during the last month. This greatly increased the labor and inventory expense in the system. The company decided, in agreement with its customers, to offer low prices every day. After this change was made, the level of sales was maintained but the surges in shipments at the end of each quarter were eliminated. With savings in labor and inventory costs, the company was able to maintain their everyday low prices and enhance the return to their investors.

Standard cost figures from an accounting system can be a source of useful data in this category. However, other measures such as the amount of excess capacity due to surges in flow of work and the amount and locations of unfinished work are also useful. In a labor-intensive industry, changes that are important in this category are those that remove work that does not add value or contribute to the desired outcomes. For example, changes could be sought that reduce the nonproductive time looking for tools. Other types of changes include smoothing the work flow; substituting less-expensive materials or supplies that serve the purpose as well as more expensive ones; extending specialists' time on their assigned tasks by shifting some of their support tasks to lower-skilled or lower-paid people; cross training; and reducing inventory. Chapter Eleven discusses methods for developing changes to make significant cost reduction while maintaining or improving quality.

Category 3: Expanding Customer Expectations

The third category is concerned with the development of innovative products and services that attract customers to the business. To improve value, increases in quality due to new products or services have to be balanced with price increases. Customer expectations can also be changed by developing innovative ways of providing existing products and services so that customers perceive them as being of unusually high value.

A travel agency realized that many of its clients were inconvenienced by having to make their travel arrangements during normal business hours. Although nobody complained about this inconvenience, the agency decided to establish an 800 telephone number that would allow anyone to make arrangements any time from wherever they were. The tickets would then be delivered to the person's office on the next business day. Customers were delighted with this new service. The agency was also happy because the increase in productivity during regular business hours more than offset the cost of the 800 number. More importantly, word spread about this new service, and the travel agency's business grew.

In Category 3, the data that are useful are similar to those obtained in the first two categories, with one important difference. While data for Categories 1 and 2 are usually available in the provider's system, useful data for the third category are obtained from the customer's system. Providers must consider changes that reduce not their own but their customer's costs and quality problems. Consideration must be given to problems that customers might not complain about. Customers are often not aware that their needs are not being met by existing products and services. So, asking them or waiting for them to complain will usually not provide the information necessary to develop new products and services.

Data for Category 3 improvements can be obtained by studying the problems, costs, and needs in the customer's system, and by studying quality measures, trend-setting people or magazines, and emerging technologies. Methods for obtaining data from the customer's system and types of changes for this category are discussed in Chapter Twelve.

Summary of the Three Categories

As the leaders of an organization think about how to make changes that result in improvement from the viewpoint of the customer, on which category should they focus the organization's resources? Many times, the focus is obvious. An organization that has been experiencing customer complaints, excessive rework, customer returns, high warranty costs, late deliveries, and lawsuits should usually concentrate their resources on Category 1 improvements. Organizations that cannot compete in the marketplace because of the prices they have to charge to cover their production costs should definitely focus on Category 2. An organization that wants to grow or increase market share should include some Category 3 improvements in their improvement initiatives. Chapter Thirteen discusses a planning process that can be used to direct the organization's resources to the improvement category that will best move the organization toward the broad aim of improving value. Typically, an organization will have some improvement activities in all three categories.

The Effect of Improvement on People

How are people in an organization affected as the organization focuses on making changes that result in improvement from the viewpoint of the customer? The changes in each category produce particular social consequences. An improvement strategy requires a different set of planned actions for each category to address the human dimension of change.

Category 1: Eliminating quality problems. The work in this category is usually focused on an individual unit, process, or product. The need for change is obvious to everyone once the problems are made visible (through measurement or improved communications). It is relatively easy to get people in all parts or the organization involved in developing, testing, and implementing a change since knowledge of the current system is usually an important part of the improvement effort. It is important for managers to keep the focus of the changes on improving the system rather than blaming people for the problem. The types of changes typical in this category (standardization, mistake proofing, training, and so on) often result in a better work environment. It is also relatively easy to prepare the people affected by the change for the implementation because of the small scope and degree of change. However, improvements in this category may result in the need for fewer workers. For example, if currently 10 percent of reports are reworked, an improvement that eliminates rework might result in the need for 10 percent fewer workers (assuming that demand remains constant). Procedures must be put in place for redeploying these resources to productive work, but not everyone will appreciate losing their old job.

Category 2: Making cost reductions. Changes in this category often affect large parts of the organization and can be very devastating to people in the organization. Communicating the need for change and preparing the organization for implementation are major efforts that have to be carefully orchestrated. Everyone affected in the organization should be give an opportunity to understand the external forces that often drive the need for change. When cost reduction is achieved by eliminating waste or cutting noncore resources, managing the displacement of people in the organization is often the most important aspect of the change. Cost reductions can also be achieved by increasing the capacity of the organization without adding resources. By increasing yield and reducing cycle times, unit costs can be reduced without a big effect on resources. This results in a better competitive position and increased job security. Changes of this type offer a positive focus for Category 2 improvements.

Category 3: Expanding customer expectations. Changes in this category are potentially exciting and beneficial to the people in the organization. The objective is to "grow" the business with new products and services. This innovation requires time, risk-taking, new ways of thinking, experimenting, and acceptance of failure. A organization needs an entrepreneurial spirit in order to develop changes in Category 3. There can be friction and resentment between the people involved in the change activities and the people who have to keep the business running. Some organizations have been successful using informal groups (known as "skunk works") outside the organizational structure to focus on Category 3 improvements. The implementation of changes in this category usually offers new opportunities and challenges to people in the organization.

Chapter Thirteen, which discusses the leadership of improvement in an organization, includes guidelines and suggestions for managing the human dimension of change. Chapter Seven also discussed the social aspect of implementing change.

Conclusion

All organizations are continually being judged by their customers on the value of their products and/or services. Focusing on improving value from the viewpoint of the customer allows organizations to achieve their other goals. Considerable progress has been made in developing methodology for making improvements in each of the three categories discussed in this chapter. The balance of this third part of the book shows how these methods can be integrated into a system for improvement.

CHAPTER 10

Eliminating Quality Problems

The light on the passenger-side door of Steve's new car was staying on after the door was closed. It even stayed on after the engine was turned off. Steve was worried that the light would run the battery down overnight. Because he relied on his car to get to work, he made an appointment with the dealer to have the light fixed the next morning. He called Sally who worked with him and lived nearby to ask for a ride to work. She agreed, but said that they must leave by 7:00 because she had an important meeting to attend.

When Steve arrived at the dealership the next morning, he found that six people were ahead of him in line. None of them were happy, but two were particularly upset because they were returning to have a problem fixed that had not been fixed correctly the first time. It seemed that the person who normally checked in the cars was sick and his replacement could not find the necessary forms. At 7:30, a half hour later than he had promised, Steve and Sally left for work.

Everyone has experienced such quality problems in their lives. Some additional examples are:

- Delivery of furniture that is two hours later than promised

- Long lines at the post office, bank, or grocery store

- A missing part for a child's toy (discovered at 5:00 Christmas Eve)

- Incorrect information in the newspaper

- Poor advice from an accountant that results in an IRS audit

- Wrong drug administered in the hospital

- College classes filled at registration
- A VCR that is too complex to program
- Bugs in computer software
- Electrical power outages
- Lost baggage on an airplane flight

These are all quality problems because the product or service did not perform according to the customer's expectations. Such expectations are developed through past experience with the product or service or by promises made by the seller. Steve's experience with the repair departments of car dealerships led him to expect that the time to leave his car and complete the paperwork would be about fifteen minutes.

One of the most basic tasks for any organization seeking to improve the quality of its products and services is to eliminate quality problems that arise because customers' expectations are not met. All too often the approach to accomplishing this aim is to blame the employees involved, institute some form of checking or inspection, react only to resolve immediate problems, or deny that the customer had a right to the expectations in the first place.

This chapter addresses the use of the Model for Improvement and associated methods when the answer to the question, *What are we trying to accomplish?* is, "We are trying to eliminate quality problems." It provides guidance on how to collect data, develop changes, and identify the types of cycles to run when working to eliminate some specific quality problems.

George arrived at work at 7:30 to find a long line of unhappy customers waiting to leave their cars to be repaired. He had been the manager of the department for three years and it seemed that every day there was a problem to solve. Some days he at least had some time to get a cup of coffee before attacking the problem, but not today.

George quickly found the registration forms and helped June serve the waiting customers. After the cars had been checked in, he and June transcribed the notes she had made on paper before the forms were found. Since she had not had the forms when talking to customers, some important information was missing for some of them. After waiting in line, these customers would not be happy to get a call at work. George realized that he could not let this continue any longer. He had to take some action.

The next day he instituted the following three actions:

1. The supervisor must test drive and approve each repair job after the mechanic completes it. For repairs costing more than $700, George must give his approval after the supervisor has given his or her approval.

2. The mechanic to whom the fewest cars were returned for repair of the same problem would receive a cash award.

3. Any mechanic with three or more returns in a month would be put on probation, and he or she would be fired if performance did not improve in the next month.

The assumption underlying George's actions was that most of the problems were caused by the people (poor workmanship). Although attention to the task and putting forth an earnest effort is obviously needed, lack of attention or effort is not usually the major source of quality problems. The causes of these problems are most often found in the processes of work, in the design of the product or service, or in unrealistic promises about the performance of the product or service.

Three months after implementing the actions, the situation was not any better. In fact, George felt that it was actually worse, because returns were about the same and two of his better mechanics were on probation. Also, he had just been reprimanded by his boss because complaints about the service department were up for two months in a row. Fortunately, George had just read an article in a trade journal about a service department that had significantly reduced the number of returns by redesigning some of the processes in the department with the help of the supervisors and mechanics. They had also used something called the Model for Improvement that was based on three simple questions.

Although he did not believe that the obvious deficiencies mentioned in the article would be found in his department, he decided to try the model to eliminate some of the quality problems that were occurring. The aim was to significantly reduce the number of cars that had to be brought back to have the same problem fixed. George decided to run a cycle to analyze the company's records on repairs.

George was amazed at what he found in the records. More than half of the returns were on repairs for leaks in the engine or transmission. There were simple ways to fix leaks. Someone must be goofing off! He went out to the repair area and talked to the mechanics. The first person he encountered had the following observation: "George, repairing the leaks is not the problem; finding them is." This comment was confirmed by the other mechanics. George asked for volunteers to stay for an hour or two after work and discuss ways to improve the process of finding leaks. All but two of the mechanics could make it, and they wrote their ideas down and gave them to George before they left for the day.

George could not believe the number of good ideas that surfaced in less than an hour. The second hour was used to plan a test of the following three changes as part of a PDSA Cycle:

1. Every morning, designate one of the lifts for cars brought in to have a leak fixed. Put the car up on the lift and have the customer explain where he or she thinks the leak is.
2. Rent a piece of equipment that allows a probe to be inserted into the engine to display the inside to identify the source of a leak.
3. For any customer that returns with an unfixed leak, mix a florescent dye into the oil so that if the repair is still unsuccessful, the dye can be used to trace the source of the leak.

After one month the results were studied and the group agreed to the following changes during the Act phase of the cycle:

- Buy the equipment to probe the inside of the engine.
- Extend the policy of using the dye to first-time repair of leaks when the probe did not result in a definitive location of the leak.
- Drop the procedure of putting the car on the lift and asking the customer to point out the location.

Another cycle was planned to implement these changes. After two months, returns were down 20 percent, productivity was up, and George held another meeting after work to talk about the next opportunity to reduce returns. The two mechanics who had been put on probation were taken off. Of course, they had had the most returns, but they were among the best mechanics, so they were assigned the leaks that were most difficult to find.

George had made an important discovery about the relationship between quality and cost. When one eliminates quality problems by blaming people, instituting inspection, or other quick fixes, quality is sometimes improved in the short term, but costs go up. When quality problems are eliminated by redesigning the product or service, quality improves, costs are reduced, and productivity increases. This relationship has been called the *quality-productivity chain reaction* by Deming. Figure 10.1 contains a diagram of this relationship. Deming's theory states that if an organization or group focuses on the improvement of quality, reduced costs and higher productivity will follow.

To redesign a system to get the benefits of the chain reaction, one must develop, test, and implement changes to the system. To accomplish each of these steps successfully, the collection and analysis of data is essential. These data may be collected either as part of a cycle to build knowledge to develop the changes, or as part of a test to determine if the changes are improvements.

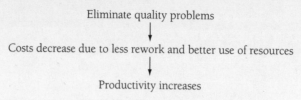

Eliminate quality problems

↓

Costs decrease due to less rework and better use of resources

↓

Productivity increases

Figure 10.1. *The Quality-Productivity Chain Reaction.*

The Use of Data in Eliminating Quality Problems

The primary use of data in eliminating quality problems is to focus the efforts on particular aspects of the system that are most in need of redesign. In the automotive repair shop, George was able to focus the group on developing changes to improve the detection and fixing of leaks by analyzing some data that were already available to him. The first Pareto chart in Figure 10.2 resulted from the first step in George's analysis. He looked at the records for cars that were brought back to the shop because the original problem had not been fixed, and he studied what part of the car was involved in the repair. He found that the motor and transmission repairs had the highest frequency of returns. Although this analysis was a good start, it was not detailed enough to provide sufficient focus for the effort to reduce returns.

The second Pareto chart in Figure 10.2 resulted from a more detailed breakdown of the motor and transmission problems. It was on the basis of this analysis that George was able to raise the question about leaks to the mechanics.

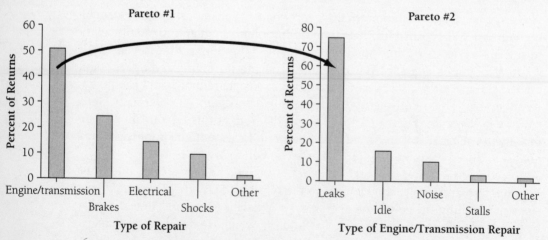

Figure 10.2. *Analysis of Types of Repairs to Automobiles.*

The case of the automobile repair shop is quite typical in that organizations usually already have on hand the data that are needed to establish which aspects of the system require improvement. Some of the sources of data that are useful for focusing efforts on eliminating quality problems are customer complaints; failure modes; responses to customer surveys; questions received on 800 numbers; inspection results; warranty claims; employee observations; records of refunds; rates of back orders, returns, and on-time deliveries; and lawsuits. Although most organizations have these types of data on hand, they are not necessarily readily available. They may be scattered in file cabinets or in various computer files, and they may be available for only a short time.

Don had recently purchased some new software to do word processing. He liked the software but was having trouble using the feature that set up the text in columns like a newspaper article. He had read the manual and made some headway, but he was still having some problems. Although the company had recently started charging for advice on its 800 technical support phone number, Don's frustration level was rising, so he decided to pay the charge and get some help.

Rosa answered Don's call, asked for his identification number, and listened to him describe the problem. (The identification number was used to bill him for the advice.) The problem was one she had dealt with before and she was able to help him quickly. Don was very pleased to be able to finally use the columns feature and he thanked Rosa, but he added that what she had told him should be in the manual. Rosa was happy she had been able to help. That is why she liked this job. She did not have much time to savor the satisfaction. The phone was ringing and she was off to another call.

As far as Don was concerned, the technical support line had served its purpose. He had the answer he needed and had obtained it quickly from a pleasant and courteous person. Unfortunately the valuable data contained in the interaction between Don and Rosa was lost once Don hung up and Rosa answered the next call. No one in the organization would know that Don had had a problem with the columns feature in their software product, even though he called and told them. For the software company, such data would essentially be free if they had a formal system for collecting it. The data from Don's call and the thousands of other calls received on the 800 line could be very valuable in focusing efforts to redesign aspects of the organization's products or services.

In this example, the data that was needed to solve the immediate problem was not used to focus resources to prevent the problem from occurring in the first place. It usually takes a formal process to collect and store this data. Following is the outline of a system for collecting and analyzing data from returns, based on a system used by Supelco Inc. of State College, Pennsylvania. (Supelco manufactures products and sells them through a catalogue.)

Definition of a return:	Customer contacts the company asking that the product be returned or replaced.
Recorders of data:	Any employee, but usually people in technical service and order processing.
Data collected:	Customer information, product type, and lot number. Information on the order, such as date, person who ordered the product, description of complaint, checklist on where the complaint should be routed.
Storage medium:	Computer database.
Analysis methods:	Control charts on the number of returns each month, and Pareto diagrams of the type of complaint. Data can be organized by business unit, type of customer, type of complaint, product, or service.
Action:	1. The information on the individual return is routed to the appropriate group for resolution. After action is taken, the customer is contacted to confirm that their problem has been solved.
	2. The data from all the returns are analyzed and used to set priorities for improvement.

This list includes two of the most important types of data to aid in eliminating quality problems: data on how often the problems occur, plotted over time; and data that describes or characterizes the problems.

Plotting Data Over Time

An essential step in the analysis of data on quality problems is to plot the frequency of occurrence or the severity of the problem over time. The purpose of this analysis is to ascertain whether special causes should be investigated or whether the problems are built into the system in a predictable way. Failure to plot the data over time will significantly reduce the success in eliminating quality problems.

Figure 10.3 contains the run chart that was used by a group in a medical office. The aim of their effort was to reduce the amount of time people waited before seeing a doctor for a scheduled appointment. After considering a variety of indicators of progress, they decided to run a cycle to collect data on the maximum time that any patient had to wait. This measure was chosen on the basis of usefulness and ease in obtaining and recording. One point was plotted for the

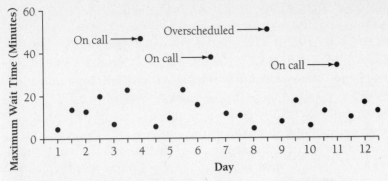

Figure 10.3. *Maximum Waiting Time for Patients in a Medical Office.*

morning appointments and one point for the afternoon appointments. There were three doctors in the office, and the maximum time a patient had to wait was the maximum time for any of the three.

The run chart highlights four data points that are outside the normal pattern of variation (they are much higher than all the rest). The reason these data were so high was found to be related to one of the doctors being on call for the emergency room in the nearby hospital that day. The use of the run chart, combined with the notes about the observations, allowed the group to focus and sharpen the fundamental question concerning changes before attempting to answer it, as shown in the following sequence:

- Before stating the aim of the effort: *What changes can we make that will result in improvement?*

- After stating the aim of the effort: *What changes can we make that will result in shorter waiting times for patients?*

- After analysis of the run chart: *What changes can we make that will result in shorter waiting times for patients on the day one of the doctors is on call?*

The group could now develop cycles by answering a very focused question. They had built up their knowledge of what aspect of the system was in need of change.

Using Data to Characterize the Types of Problems

To focus efforts to eliminate quality problems it is useful to study data on characteristics of the problem—to answer the questions *who, what, where,* and *when.* Does the problem occur only with specific customers or with specific providers of the service or product? What happened that caused the customer to have the problem? Is there a particular location where the problem most frequently occurs? Is there a particular time when the problem most frequently occurs? These data would usually be collected as part of a cycle to build knowledge to develop a change. A run chart was used to provide answers to some of these questions in the example of the doctor's office.

Another useful way to answer the above questions is by recording data about the incident and doing a Pareto analysis. This is what George did in analyzing the data from the returns to the repair shop. He found that a frequency of occurrence was related to a particular part of the car. George was then able to focus and sharpen the fundamental question according to the following sequence:

- Before stating the aim: *What changes can we make that will result in improvement?*

- After stating the aim: *What changes can we make to assure that the repairs are done correctly to eliminate returns?*

- After doing the first Pareto analysis: *What changes can we make that will reduce the returns for repairs to the engine and transmission?*

- After doing the second Pareto analysis: *What changes can we make that will reduce the returns for repairs of leaks in the engine and transmission?*

- After talking to the mechanics: *What changes can we make to better identify the source of the leaks in the engine and transmission?*

After his analysis, George was able to come to the meeting with the mechanics with a very focused question. Because he had such a focused question, they were able in less than two hours to propose changes and plan a cycle to test those changes.

The uses of data described here help to focus the fundamental question about changes that should be made. Sometimes the focusing process alone produces obvious modifications to be made. In any case, developing the changes is usually not a trivial matter. Before discussing some methods for developing changes to eliminate quality problems, let us first deal with an important issue regarding quality problems.

Immediate Reaction to Quality Problems

There are two facets to addressing quality problems:

1. Solve the immediate problem for the customer.
2. Design or redesign the system to prevent the problem from occurring in the future.

   The design of a system to quickly solve a problem for a customer may be a
very substantial improvement for an organization. During the Carter administration, a study was conducted by Technical Assistance Research Programs Institute (TARP) for the U.S. Office of Consumer Affairs. The study highlighted the
benefit that occurs to organizations that react quickly and take care of customer
complaints. Among the findings of the study were the following points:

- Many consumers who experience problems with products or services do
  not complain.

- Customers who complain are more likely than those who do not complain
  to do repeat business with the company that upset them, even if the problem is not solved to their satisfaction. For those customers who formally
  complain, most do business with the organization again, depending on the
  potential financial loss to the customer, if their complaint is addressed and
  solved. Figure 10.4 shows that between 54.3 and 70 percent of customers
  whose complaints are solved repurchase from the same company; the percentage drops to 19 to 46.2 percent for customers who are not satisfied as
  a result of their complaints. Of those who do not complain, between 9.5
  and 36.8 percent repurchase. This percentage increases if the organization
  solves the problem quickly. The data in the figure support a point made by
  the TARP study in 1979: *While many managers view complaints as a drain
  on valuable corporate resources, these survey data suggest that complaints may
  instead be a valuable marketing asset. Among households experiencing consumer problems, those that submitted complaints exhibited the strongest continuing brand loyalty.*

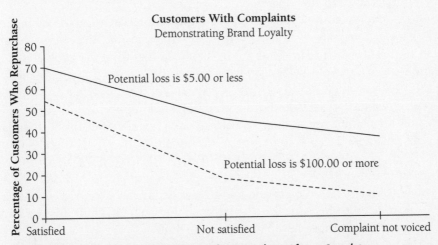

Figure 10.4. *Percentage of Customers Who Repurchase After a Complaint.*

- Customers who are dissatisfied and complain tell twice as many people about their negative experiences as satisfied customers who tell about their positive experiences.

- Most complaints are registered at the place where the product was bought or the service was received.

- 87.3 percent of initial complaints were registered at the point of purchase.

- Fewer than five percent of the complaints about large-ticket durable goods or services ever reach the manufacturer.

- There are three principle reasons why consumers experiencing product or service problems do not complain:

  Complaining was not worth their time or effort.
  They did not know how or where to complain.
  They believed that complaining would not do any good; no one wanted to hear about their problems.

The payoff is large for an organization that has a system in place that resolves customer complaints and provides information to facilitate learning. The Model for Improvement should be used to develop, test, and implement changes as part of the design of such a system.

When a customer experiences a quality problem, the damage has been done. However, an organization can compound the damage or decrease it, depending on how it handles the situation. Solving the immediate problem for the customer should be the first priority. Ironically, resolving the problem quickly and providing extra service to the customer can actually turn the problem into a very positive experience for the customer.

Some examples of immediate reactions to quality problems are shown in Table 10.1. Some actions may seem like overkill, but this is exactly the point. The customer must at least be relieved of the burden resulting from the problem. However, to recover some of the lost goodwill, the customer should receive something extra, something they would not have received had the problem not happened.

A good example of this kind of handling of a quality problem is the reaction of airlines to overbooked flights. Airlines sell more tickets for a flight than there are seats available because some people do not show up for the flight. The airlines do not penalize them. The customer can use the unused ticket on another flight. Without overbooking, the airline would lose significant revenue. Usually, this practice causes no problem and there are seats for everyone. However, sometimes more people show up for the flight than expected. This causes a major quality problem for those not able to take the flight.

In the past, the airline would explain to the people who did not make the

Table 10.1. *Company Reactions to Quality Problems.*

PROBLEM	IMMEDIATE ACTION
Delivery of furniture that is two hours later than promised	Apologize, keep customer informed as to when the furniture will be delivered, or offer to reschedule at another convenient time (even outside of normal delivery hours) and be within ten minutes of the promised time.
Long lines at the post office, bank, or grocery store	Anyone not busy serving a customer drop what they are doing and help those who are serving customers.
Missing part for a child's toy (discovered at 5:00 P.M. Christmas eve)	Drive the part over to the customers house or offer to let them use the floor model until a new part arrives in addition give them a small toy for free
Incorrect information in the newspaper	Print the correction, give some free advertising
Poor advice of an accountant results in an IRS audit	Pay any fines, provide free support during the audit, assume the blame for the mistake
Wrong drug administered in the hospital	Quick reaction to prevent health problems, if not potentially harmful, doctor and nurse provide assurances, send flowers to the room
Classes filled at registration	Provide counseling as to what other schedules would meet graduation or program requirements, entice other students to switch
VCR that is too complex to program for the typical person	Provide telephone support, accept the product back for credit or cash
Bugs in computer software	Free upgrade, help the user to minimize the impact of the problem
Electrical power outages	Develop plan for quick return of service, keep customers informed of the status of the service, pay for damaged electrical devices
Lost baggage on a flight	Keep customer informed of baggage location, deliver the baggage to the residence, provide toiletries if needed

flight why they had to overbook, and the angry customers would be put on the next available flight. Now, the gate attendant asks if there is anybody willing to give up their seat in exchange for a free trip anywhere in the United States. There are usually several people willing to take the offer. They have a good story to tell their friends, and there are no unhappy customers. The investment by the airline in the free ride is a good one.

Following are some guidelines for dealing with customers' who have experienced problems with quality:

Do

- Have a process for dealing with quality problems.

- Listen empathetically while allowing the customer to vent.

- Acknowledge problem, sympathize with customer, and apologize.

- Go overboard to solve the problem.

- Keep the customer informed of the status of the resolution of the problem.

- Give the customer something that they would not have been entitled to if the problem had not occurred (such as refunds, credits, a product).

- Give persons who respond to customer complaints the authority to compensate the customer within certain guidelines without supervisory approval.

- Train persons who interface with customers.

Don't

- Tell the customer they should have read or followed the directions.

- Make the customer feel stupid.

- Make excuses by explaining your system and why the problem happened.

- Create a new problem or the same problem from the quick solution.

- Get angry at the customer.

- Have the customer assume the inconvenience caused by the problem.

- Tell the customer "Its not our policy to. . . ."

- Blame the customer.

None of the actions just listed or those suggested in Table 10.1 prevent the problem from occurring or recurring. They only reduce the amount of dissatisfaction experienced by the customer.

Developing Changes to Eliminate Quality Problems

To prevent quality problems from occurring, products, services, or processes within the system must be redesigned. There are a variety of ways in which this can be accomplished. Many of the change concepts contained in the resource guide at the end of the book apply to the development of changes that eliminate quality problems. The following are a few concepts that have proven to be particularly useful in this effort (the numbers in the third column correspond to the order in which the concepts appear in the resource guide):

General Grouping	Change Concept	Concept Number
Producer/customer interface	Coach customers	39
	Reach agreement on expectations	42
	Optimize level of inspection	44
	Work with suppliers	45
Focus on variation	Standardization	51
	Stop tampering	52
	Improve predictions	54
	Contingency plans	55
Mistake proofing	Reminders	59
	Differentiation	60
	Constraints	61
	Affordances	62
Miscellaneous	Eliminate multiple entry	2
	Change set points or targets	11
	Conduct training	31
	Optimize maintenance	48
	Disguise defects or problems	69

These approaches to eliminating quality problems are discussed in the appendix. This chapter will focus in more depth on the development of changes that address the reduction of unwanted variation and the reduction of mistakes.

Reducing Unwanted Variation

Unwanted variation is a source of many quality problems. For example, a furniture store may promise delivery between 9:00 A.M. and 1:00 P.M. If the store fails to meet that promise, a quality problem occurs. The late arrival of the shipment could be a result of a special cause of variation, such as an accident, or it could be due to a system of delivery that has common causes of variation that predictably produce a certain percentage of late deliveries. Other examples of unwanted variation include differences in the dimensions of an automotive component, in the fat content of butter, in the color of different rolls of the same pattern of wallpaper, and variation in waiting times.

When attempting to develop changes that reduce variation, an assessment of whether the process is stable or unstable is usually helpful. This assessment allows the improvement efforts to focus on the specific circumstances that produce special causes of variation and result in an unstable process. For stable systems that are simply incapable of meeting the expectations, more fundamental changes will be needed. For unavoidable special causes such as traffic accidents or severe weather, contingency plans will need to be developed to prevent quality problems.

The following four change concepts have been found particularly useful in developing changes that reduce unwanted variation: standardization, "stop tampering," "improve predictions," and contingency plans.

Standardization (Develop a Formal Process) Variation may exist in a process because the process is not operated the same each time. Standardization of the process to reduce the variation of operation will usually result in reduction of variation in its output. In some cases, the variation in operation is so severe that it could even be said that no process exists, and a formal process for carrying out the work must be created.

Flowcharts are useful tools for documenting and developing processes. However, documenting every step in a process and asking for adherence to the standardized process is not an efficient way to reduce variation in performance. Some steps in the process are vital to the outcomes and others are not. It is wise to standardize only those steps that are highly related to the outcome. This makes it possible to focus on what really matters and to build in some flexibility to satisfy personal preferences for activities that are less important.

Stop Tampering Efforts to reduce variation can sometimes have the opposite effect: the variation in the system increases. This adverse effect of well-intentioned activities occurs predominantly from reacting to a single measurement or event— for example, a company's sales forecast for one month was 10 percent higher than actual sales, so subsequent forecasts were adjusted down 10 percent.

There will always be fluctuations in the outcomes of a system due to the common causes of variation that are present, and in some systems, there may be additional sources of variation due to special causes. As noted earlier, organizations must be able to recognize whether a system is stable or unstable to effectively choose actions that will reduce variation. If the system is stable, reacting to each measurement or event will increase variation. Deming called this response "tampering," which Webster's dictionary defines as "interfering so as to weaken or change for the worse."

Tampering can be reduced or eliminated by use of a control chart to reliably differentiate between stable and unstable systems. A simple but effective method for preventing tampering and eliminating special causes is *statistical process control,* a control system that uses charts to guide actions aimed at reducing variation.

Improve Predictions A common type of quality problem is waiting for a product or service longer than expected. These delays frequently occur because of poor prediction of demand or poor coordination of parts of the system. For example, if during a visit to a family doctor it is determined that you need to visit a specialist, a call to the specialist for an appointment should produce some options for a visit in the next few days. However, in many health care systems a call typically produces a delay of weeks before seeing the specialist. The delay occurs because the specialist is not integrated with the rest of the system. Appointments are scheduled only when a patient has been identified, rather than holding appointment times open in anticipation of possible patients. The system places predictable demands on the specialist's time—predictable even before the identity of the referred patient is known. For example, an HMO that signs up several families with children will place a predictable demand on the specialists time in the future, for physicals, vaccinations, and so on. The level of the demand can be determined by studying the historical data with the aid of a run chart or a control chart. This information could be used to add to the specialist's schedule a number of open appointments to meet this demand. All that would be missing is the name of the specific patient who will take the slot. Understanding of variation in systems allows one to see that this approach is not a call for more resources but actually a more efficient use of existing resources.

Prediction of demand is most easily done for a stable system. However, some knowledge of the occurrence of special causes such as seasonal fluctuations can also be used to improve the predictions.

Contingency Plans Some events are unavoidable. There may be a traffic accident, or a snowstorm or other natural disaster; someone may have a heart attack on an airplane; a fire seen only once every hundred years may break out; or the electric power may fail. These events are special causes and their times of occurrence are usually unpredictable. Nevertheless, these events should not be thought of as excuses for quality problems. Contingency plans or processes can be developed to mitigate the effect of these occurrences. For example, a delivery driver listens to the traffic reports on his radio. If an accident is reported on his route, he switches to an alternate route that he has mapped out in advance.

Contingency plans are particularly useful for processes that are unstable or that are susceptible to rare but devastating events. For some organizations, such as fire, rescue, and health care operations, providing contingency plans is central to achieving their purposes.

Reducing Mistakes

Another source of quality problems is mistakes. Mistakes occur when actions do not agree with intentions, even though the person is capable of carrying out the task successfully. Mistakes occur subconsciously. A person who has just gotten money from an automatic teller machine (ATM) forgets her bank card at the booth. She is capable of remembering it. She almost always does remember it. But sometimes she slips and makes a mistake. Other examples of mistakes are incorrect bills, wrong merchandise delivered from a mail order business, or wrong medication given to a patient in the hospital. One of the authors recently was having a light lunch at a medium-priced restaurant with a college roommate whom he had not seen in years. He offered to treat for lunch but was surprised to receive a bill of $260. It seems that the two cups of potato soup had been recorded as 222 cups.

Although mistakes are the result of human actions, they occur through the interaction of people with the system. Some systems are more prone to mistakes than others. We can reduce mistakes by redesigning the system to make mistakes less likely. We refer to this type of system design or redesign as *mistake proofing*. This idea is captured in a slightly modified version of an old, familiar saying: "To err is human, to prevent is design." Consider the problem of forgetting one's credit card at the ATM. ATMs work in two different ways. With some machines, you remove your card and then your money comes out. With others, you remove the money and then the card comes out. Which type do you think results in more credit cards being left behind? The design will control the magnitude of the mistakes.

Since mistakes are predominantly subconscious slips, mistake proofing is aimed at reducing the likelihood of these subconscious slips rather than changing conscious behavior. Four important methods for mistake proofing include the use of reminders, differentiation, constraints, and affordances. These methods are briefly discussed here, and examples of applications of each are given in the resource guide.

Reminders Many mistakes are made by forgetting to do something. Reminders are aids for remembering. They can come in many different forms. A reminder can be a written notice or a phone call, a checklist of things to accomplish, an alarm, a standard form, or the documented steps to follow in a process.

Reminders are simple to develop and easy to use, but they do require conscious effort to be effective. Reminders can be overlooked or ignored. For example, a standard process can be defined, but people may have trouble breaking old habits or they might chose not to refer to the flowchart or other documentation.

Differentiation Mistakes can occur when we are dealing with things that look similar. We may copy a number wrongly or grab a wrong part because of their similarity or close proximity to other numbers or parts. Mistakes can also occur when actions are similar. We may end up in the wrong place or use a piece of equipment in the wrong way because the right directions or procedures are similar to others we might have used in a different situation. For example, a person might drive to work on Sunday morning instead of driving to the bakery. These types of mistakes are called *mistakes of association.*

Our minds will at times associate the required things and actions with similar but inappropriate ones. Familiarity that results from experience can actually increase the chance of committing mistakes of association. To reduce mistakes, steps should be taken to break patterns. This can be done by, for example, color coding, sizing, using different symbols, or physically separating similar items.

Constraints A constraint restricts the performance of certain actions that lead to mistakes. For example, public buildings are required to have a gate on the stairs leading to the basement floor from the ground floor. This reduces the mistake of descending past the exit when evacuating the building in case of fire or other emergency. Having to remove the ATM card before the money comes out is another example of a constraint.

Constraints are an important method for mistake proofing because they can limit the subconscious actions that result in mistakes. This includes making sure that the steps performed in a process or in using a product are accomplished in the correct sequence. Constraints usually do not require conscious behavior to be effective in reducing mistakes. An important attribute of an effective constraint is that it restricts the undesirable action while not impeding appropriate action.

Affordances An affordance provides insight, without the need for explanation, into how something should be used. In contrast to a constraint, which limits the actions possible, an affordance provides visual prompting for the actions that should be performed. Once a person sees the fixtures on a door, he or she should be able to determine whether it opens in, opens out, or slides. There should not be a need to refer to labels or to use a trial-and-error approach. If a process or product can be designed to lead the user to perform the correct actions, fewer mistakes will occur.

The following example illustrates the use of mistake proofing to eliminate a quality problem.

Example: Eliminating Blood Transfusion Mistakes

A hospital gave blood transfusions to some patients as part of their treatment. Giving a patient blood that was meant for another patient is one type of mistake that can occur. In six years there had been three instances in which a nurse at this hospital had mistakenly given the wrong blood to a patient, even though it was correctly labeled by the lab. This was a mistake rate of 1 in 52,000. Although the mistakes were relatively rare, they needed to be totally eliminated because receiving the wrong blood type can be fatal.

The hospital had provided extensive training that included the proper approach to verifying that the correct blood was being given to the patient. However, this approach had not been sufficient to prevent the mistakes. It relied on changing conscious behavior. It is easy to become complacent about a mistake that is so rare.

To address this problem, the hospital built some inspection into the system. Any time a nurse was to start a transfusion, she was required to have another nurse verify that the identification on the blood matched the identification on the patient. This also proved to be not sufficient to stop the mistakes; one occurred after the policy was in effect. For rarely occurring catastrophic mistakes, a constraint is needed that does not rely on conscious behavior.

The hospital decided to take a look at the system and used the Model for Improvement as a guide.

What are we trying to accomplish? We are trying to eliminate the giving of incorrect blood to patients undergoing transfusions in the hospital.

Guidance: Focus on mistakes that occur after the blood leaves the Blood Bank. This does not, however, preclude changes in the processes in the Blood Bank. Also, since the mistake rate is very low, develop a change that builds a constraint into the system that does not rely for success on the conscious behavior of the nurses.

How will we know that a change is an improvement? As part of normal safety procedures in the hospital we will record mistakes and plot the time between mistakes on a control chart. Because the mistakes are so infrequent, this measure will take a long time to show that the change has had a beneficial effect. The control chart will be useful for detecting a special cause increase in the mistakes. We may be able to increase the sensitivity of the measure by combining data with other hospitals that are already using or will use whatever change we develop.

We will determine that the change will not significantly increase the time to start a transfusion.

What changes can we make that will result in improvement? One of the pharmacists who was working on the project had read of a locking device for the bag that contained the blood to be transfused. The lock is attached in the Blood Bank to the top of the bag containing the blood. A three-letter code is then programmed into the lock that matches the code on the patient's identification bracelet. Once the blood reaches the bedside, a nurse must remove the lock before the blood is ready for use. To remove the lock, the nurse must dial in the three-letter code found on the patient's bracelet. If the patient's code matches the code programmed in the pharmacy, the lock can be removed. Using this technology would create a constraint in the system that seemed to fit well with the expected outcomes of the effort. The group decided to gather some information on the device.

Cycle 1

Plan: To gain some information, the group decided to schedule a meeting with the manufacturer of the device and to visit three hospitals that were already using the device. They would focus on how well the device prevented mistakes, the ease of using the device for the nurse, and the cost.

Do: The meeting with the manufacturer was delayed once, but only for a few days. They were only able to visit two of the three hospitals.

Study: The results of the visits were encouraging. None of the hospitals had made a mistake in the year since the devices were installed. However, because of the low frequency of mistakes in the past, this could have been the result of good fortune rather than the device.

The device added only a small amount of time to starting a transfusion. If the check by the second nurse could be eliminated, then the device would actually save time. Some nurses at the hospitals using the device reported having to send the blood back to the Blood Bank because they could not remove the lock even though the code was correct. However, they said that the manufacturer had made some improvements and that no problems had occurred in the last four months.

The cost of the device was within the bounds of what the hospital could afford to invest in the problem.

Act: The group decided to move forward with testing the device at their hospital.

Cycle 2

Plan: The technology was purchased from the vendor. The vendor agreed to take back the main part of the technology (except the locks) within six months if it did not meet the aim. Enough locks were purchased to test the system on one nursing unit. The test would run for four months.

A procedure was established for using the technology based on suggestions from the manufacturer and the observations made at various hospitals. The existing verification procedure was continued throughout the test.

The following data was to be collected during the test:

- Number of incidents of incorrect blood given to patients (expected to be zero)
- Number of times either the check by the nurse or the code prevented a mistake
- Observations by nurses concerning how the system could fail to prevent a mistake
- Observations by nurses and pharmacists on ease of use

Do: The plan was carried out with no major problems.

Study: No incidents of wrong blood administered were reported. There was one incident of a nurse identifying the wrong patient to receive the blood. The mistake was caught by the verification of the second nurse and the lock would not open. The technology was easy for both the nurses and the pharmacist to use. The small amount of extra time was accepted as a small price to pay for eliminating the problem.

One possibility for a mistake to occur was identified. If the pharmacist programmed an incorrect code into the lock and the nurse misidentified the patient with that code, the lock would come off. The chance of both these mistakes occurring at the same time was very unlikely. The three-letter code was not used by the nurse to identify the patient, only to remove the lock. The two mistakes were therefore thought to be independent. That is, if one mistake was made, it was no more likely that the other mistake would occur.

Act: The equipment was retained and additional locks were purchased. The procedure became the standard process on the nursing unit on which it was tested. The verification by a second nurse was dropped on this unit.

Cycle 3

A third cycle was used to implement the change throughout the hospital. The procedure described in cycle 2 was used for each nursing unit. The only modification was that the introduction to these units was ten weeks rather than four months.

Conclusion

Any organization that wants to improve must have at least a minimum level of competency in the ability to prevent quality problems from occurring. The collection and utilization of data are central to any system designed to continually reduce quality problems, as are processes for taking action in both the short and long term. The Model for Improvement and change concepts are effective tools for developing changes that address quality problems.

This chapter has focused on eliminating quality problems to ensure customer satisfaction. The next chapter discusses a challenge faced by many people in business: How do we reduce costs while maintaining or improving quality?

CHAPTER 11

Reducing Costs While Maintaining or Improving Quality

George was pleased that the number of cars returned for repair because the problem was not fixed initially had decreased substantially (see the beginning of George's story in Chapter Ten). He had other quality problems to address, but most of his customers seemed to be reasonably satisfied for the time being. His major worry was that his costs were too high and that he was making only a meager profit.

Income from his automobile service business was extremely important to George if he was going to continue to provide high-quality service. Automobiles were getting more complicated all the time. They now even contained computers, so his business needed sophisticated (and expensive) electronic diagnostic equipment. The equipment for solving the problem of identifying leaks had not been cheap. To do a good job, a mechanic required training in electronics. All of this required investment, and there was not enough income to keep up to even minimum standards, much less to invest in providing extremely high-quality service.

George was experiencing a problem that is faced by most people who run businesses: keeping costs under control while providing quality products and services to customers. Without cost reduction and control, a business does not generate sufficient profits to invest in new technology or improvements. As pointed out in Chapter Ten, good quality does not necessarily mean high cost. When George and his mechanics solved the problem of returns for leaks, quality went up and cost went down. Almost anytime a quality problem is solved by changing the system to prevent the problem from occurring in the first place, cost will go down as a result of the chain reaction that is set off. (This chain reaction was illustrated in Figure 10.1.)

The cost reduction that occurs as a result of the chain reaction from reduction of quality problems may not be enough, however, to improve a company's financial situation. This is particularly true for organizations that have eliminated

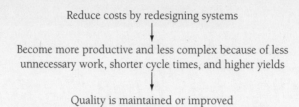

Reduce costs by redesigning systems

↓

Become more productive and less complex because of less
unnecessary work, shorter cycle times, and higher yields

↓

Quality is maintained or improved

Figure 11.1 *Chain Reaction for Improvements Focused on Cost Reduction.*

most of their major quality problems. Some resources usually need to be focused
on changing the system with the primary aim of cost reduction while maintaining or improving quality. Figure 11.1 shows the chain reaction expected for these
type of improvements.

In addition to financial costs, many organizations are concerned with reducing the social costs related to their business. The areas of concern include occupational health and safety, and environmental pollution. When addressing these
concerns, the organization faces the dual task of reducing the social cost while
maintaining or improving quality.

This chapter addresses the use of the Model for Improvement and associated
methods when the answer to the question, *What are we trying to accomplish?* is
"We are trying to reduce financial or social costs while maintaining or improving quality." Specifically, it explores what data is useful to collect and analyze in
cycles, and what changes might be considered for testing and implementation
as part of any effort to reduce costs and maintain quality.

A Systems Approach to Cost Reduction

George was almost totally absorbed by the need to reduce costs. He could not seem to
come up with any ideas for making a major impact on his operating costs. He thought
about laying off some mechanics, but he already could not keep up with the workload
with the mechanics he had. He also heard of some other repair shops in town that were
purchasing rebuilt parts, using them in the repairs, and charging the customers for new
parts. He would rather go out of business than run his company that way. The only
approach he could think of was to increase the productivity of his mechanics. He talked
to them about ideas they had for increasing their productivity. Some of the ideas were
helpful, but they produced only small increases in productivity.

George felt that the only alternative left to him was to put in a productivity incentive
system. Based on his experiences with eliminating the returns for leaks, he was concerned
about this approach. But he did not have any realistic alternatives. Shop standards existed
for each of the jobs that the mechanics performed. The standards specified the time it

should take to perform the job (for example, an engine tuneup). The incentive system was based on performance to standard. Each mechanic would sign in with the supervisor when the job was started and sign out when it was completed. At the end of the month, the mechanics were paid a bonus based on the extent to which they beat the standard times for the jobs they had performed.

After two months, George reviewed the data on costs and was astounded. On average the mechanics were performing 10 percent better than the standards the first month and 15 percent better the second month. It appeared that the incentive plan had worked! There was a problem, however: his overall costs were up. How could this be? When George looked at the financial report in more detail, he saw that his labor costs had increased. His expenses for parking cars had increased. (George's shop was in an urban area and parking was scarce. He contracted with the local parking garage to park the cars that could not fit on his lot.) He was also baffled by complaints from customers that their cars were not ready when promised—all this, even though the mechanics were more "productive." He decided that it was time to get the mechanics together for a discussion about what was happening.

George needed to make significant cost reductions, and he was not finding it easy. His first cycle to test the incentive system was not encouraging. Anyone can reduce costs if they are willing to sacrifice quality, but it takes substantial skill and knowledge to reduce costs while maintaining or improving quality. Often, cost reductions in one area of the organization just transfer costs to another area.

George considered or used some of the typical means that organizations use to reduce costs:

- Instituting layoffs, leaving the remaining people to work harder or cut corners

- Using productivity incentives

- Cutting back on service—for example, having customers pump their own gas

- Giving people less product for the same price—for example, smaller candy bars

This is not to say that these approaches are always wrong. In an organization that is grossly overstaffed, across the board layoffs may be the only alternative. Sometimes this occurs because of major swings in the marketplace, but more often it seems that the organization was not planning for the future.

Productivity can be increased by people increasing their focus on the work. In the short run, incentives can often accomplish this, but they almost always have unwanted side effects. Cutting back on service may cut costs but will antagonize customers. Gas stations have had to charge less for self-service, thus losing some of the benefits of the cost reduction. The poor reputation of cost-reduction efforts are mostly due to the methods used and the results obtained, not to the aim itself.

George invited the mechanics and the supervisors to work together after closing one evening and discuss the cost figures. He presented the data and asked them how productivity could be up while at the same time costs were up, including labor costs? At first, they were not quite sure. After a few questions on how the numbers were obtained, the mechanics had some answers. One of the major problems they mentioned was that they often had to wait to get a car on the lift in order to begin their work. Many of the mechanics had specific specialties that they performed. Some could do the oil changes and engine tune-ups but could not do major repairs. Others who were specialists—for example, in electronics—thought that routine repairs were beneath them.

Because of this specialization, a car often had to be put on and taken off the rack several times to complete the work requested by the customer. The mechanics tried to coordinate their work even though no satisfactory scheduling process was available to help them do that. Since the new incentive system was put in place, people paid less attention to coordinating their work and focused primarily on getting their part of the service job done quickly.

George asked them about the increase in parking fees. Since there was less coordination among the specialties, the cars were being put on and taken off the lift more often. This slowed down the repair time for the car, which resulted in more cars waiting for repair. They had run out of space in their normal parking lot and were using the one down the street for the overflow. They paid for the additional spaces at market rates for parking. After hearing the explanations, George realized how they could achieve significant cost reduction without sacrificing quality or using shady business practices.

George had learned some significant lessons about reducing costs. These lessons were similar to the ones he had learned about solving quality problems:

- Reducing costs while maintaining or improving quality takes making changes to the system, not exhorting people in the system to produce more.

- Increases in productivity of individual components do not necessarily mean increase in productivity for the system.

- Using incentive systems to increase productivity almost always results in unwanted side effects.

- Having excess work in progress (parked cars in this case) increases costs.

George had learned what not to do, but what are some useful ways of designing or redesigning a system to make it more cost-effective? When people think about cost reduction, they often think about decreasing something: people, materials, service. These methods can be effective, particularly for parts of the system not directly related to producing or delivering the product or service. However, there is no rationale for concluding that cost reduction done in this way assures that quality is maintained or improved when these methods are applied to the core process of producing and delivering the product or service. When focusing on reducing costs associated with producing the product or service, it is useful to have as a common theme *increasing the capacity of the system*. This approach will increase the possibility that quality can be increased while costs are reduced.

In a bank, increasing capacity would mean increasing the number of customers that could be served by the same number or a smaller number of tellers. In a hospital it would mean increasing the number of people that could be cared for with the same number or a smaller number of beds and people. In a school it would mean increasing the number of students educated with the same number or a smaller number of teachers. In a manufacturing plant it would mean an increase in the amount of production for a fixed or smaller amount of equipment and labor. In an electrical utility it would mean increasing the number of customers served by the same number or a smaller number of generating plants and staff.

Although the above examples are similar to typical productivity increases, the use of the word "capacity" allows for reflection not only on the current performance of the system but also on its potential—what it could be. This approach helps organizations to identify hidden resources and opportunities for reducing costs. Increasing capacity is only indirectly related to cost reduction. The means of taking advantage of the increased capacity to reduce costs depends on whether the demand for the organization's products and services is increasing or not:

- If demand is increasing, use the excess capacity to produce more service or product with the same resources, thus lowering the unit cost.

- If demand is level or decreasing, remove the resources associated with the new excess capacity, lowering total costs and unit costs.

- Regardless of demand, work to minimize the resources that do not add value to the customer or contribute to capacity.

The best situation is when the business is growing because its customers perceive that its products are of high value. In this environment, people whose work is eliminated as a result of the increased capacity can be retrained to perform new jobs. This requires investment on the part of management and flexibility on the part of workers.

If an organization is not growing and does not expect to grow in the near future, some of the following means can be considered to soften the trauma experienced in the organization as improvements in capacity are made:

- Reduce overtime.
- Allow people to take leave without pay.
- Reduce the use of contract labor.
- Use attrition to reduce staff.
- Find people jobs with suppliers
- Give an early retirement incentive.
- Give incentives for people to voluntarily leave the organization.

These approaches are used more effectively when the organization can anticipate the need to reduce staff. Too frequently, organizations hire new people right up to the time they have a large layoff.

The concept of increasing capacity can be used to help provoke ideas on how to redesign the system. Capacity can be thought of as a function of resources, first-pass yield, and cycle time:

$$\text{Capacity} = \frac{\text{Core resources x yield}}{\text{Cycle time}}$$

This formula for capacity should not be viewed in a strict mathematical sense but as a concept that is useful in planning. For example, a truck fleet wanted to evaluate different strategies for improving its capacity to make deliveries.

Key decision: How many trucks should we have in the fleet (each truck costs about $60,000 per year) to service our customers and optimize our costs?

Current situation: Too many trucks increases costs, too few trucks results in late deliveries, unhappy customers, and a potential loss of future business.

Core resources: 100 trucks

Yield: 90 percent of the trucks complete the delivery with correct materials and with no delays or accidents.

Cycle time: The average time to complete a delivery is ten days.

In other words:

$$\text{Capacity} = \frac{\text{Core resources (100 trucks) x yield (0.90)}}{\text{Cycle time (10 days)}}$$

= 9.0 Trucks/day

Table 11.1 summarizes the information used during this evaluation. Notice the leverage from reducing cycle time as it relates to capacity. A reduction of one day in the average cycle time allows for an increase from nine to ten deliveries a day. Without such an evaluation, the typical response is just to add more resources, which would of course add costs. Generally, ideas for improving cycle time and yield should be developed, tested, and implemented before additional core resources are purchased.

The resources (in this case, the trucks) that determine capacity are noted as "core resources." Not all resources are used to deliver value to customers, nor do all resources contribute to the capacity of the system. Some significant cost reduction can be achieved by reducing resources that do not contribute directly or indirectly to the purpose of the system, either because they are related to work that is not necessary or because they are wasted in other ways.

Another example in which the capacity formula could be used is to evaluate a bank's ATM service. The number of transactions that a bank can process in an hour depends on the number of tellers and ATM machines (core resources), the time it takes to process the transactions (cycle time), and the percentage of transactions that are initially done correctly (yield). Capacity can be increased by increasing the number of tellers or ATM machines, decreasing the time it takes to perform the transaction, or reducing the errors (higher yield). Increasing the tellers would increase capacity, but it would also raise costs. Since the aim is to

Table 11.1. *Using the Capacity Formula to Evaluate System Redesign Alternatives for a Trucking Company.*

STRATEGY	RESOURCES (# OF TRUCKS)	YIELD (PROPORTION)	CYCLE TIME (DAYS)	CAPACITY (TRUCKS/DAY)
Current Baseline	100	0.9	10	9.0
Add Core Resources	110	0.9	10	9.9
Improve Yield	100	0.97	10	9.7
Reduce Cycle Time	100	0.9	9	10.0

reduce costs, the focus would be on increasing the time the existing tellers could dedicate to the core process, shortening the time of the transactions, or reducing errors.

The ATM example describes a fairly simple process. Large cost-reduction efforts are often concerned with redesign of much more complicated systems. Suppose, for example, that the system whose capacity is being improved is the system of providing loans to finance a construction project. The system involves several processes, including the initial application, the feasibility assessment by the bank, the approval (or disapproval) of some amount of money, the obtaining of insurance, and the conferring of the loan.

The formula for calculating capacity applies to this more-complicated system. It is highly likely that many of the resources in this system do not contribute to making an appropriate loan in a timely manner. A first step is to remove these nonessential resources. Next, run a cycle to determine the *bottleneck* or *constraint* in the system by observing where the work is backing up. Then, focus the efforts at the bottleneck to increase the capacity of the system. Using the concept of bottleneck allows large systems to be redesigned with almost the same ease as smaller processes. (Bottlenecks will be discussed further later in this chapter.)

With the systems approach to cost reduction as the framework, the next two sections discuss applications of the Model for Improvement to reducing costs while maintaining or improving quality.

Sources of Data in Cost-Reduction Efforts

When approaching the task of reducing costs in such a way that quality is maintained or improved, the logical first step is to understand what the sources of costs are. Data from the usual financial reports analyzed in a traditional manner are helpful in pinpointing areas for the most emphasis. In a labor-intensive industry, one would pay close attention to the costs associated with wasted or unnecessary labor and cycle times. In a capital-intensive industry, one of the primary sources of cost reduction is making better use of equipment and facilities. In an industry in which the cost of raw materials is a major component of costs, the costs associated with low yield and the waste of materials should come under scrutiny. In any serious cost reduction effort, attention will be paid to all of these areas, but the emphasis would be dictated by whether an organizations largest costs are in processing (labor/equipment) or in materials. This useful, well-known method of analysis will not be discussed any further here. Instead, the focus will be on obtaining data for analyzing how to increase the capacity of the system.

If a systems approach to cost reduction is taken, specific data relating to capacity of the system are needed. These data will not have dollars associated with them. They will be in units such as time, percentage, or units per hour. These data are useful to collect and study in a cycle, to test a change or to build knowledge to help develop a change that is aimed at increasing the potential capacity of the system. Efforts focused on increasing capacity will not only result in cost reduction but could also result in improved quality by reducing cycle times and raising yields.

Table 11.2 outlines some sources of data that can be used to assist in increasing capacity depending on where an organization's costs are concentrated. (Remember, capacity is a function of resources, yield, and cycle time. The technical section at the end of this chapter contains some additional information for collecting data to decrease cycle time.)

The data discussed in this section relate primarily to costs or capacity of the system. It is important to remember, however, that the aim is to reduce costs while maintaining or improving quality. It is therefore necessary to include measures of quality of the product or service as part of any cycle to test a change aimed at reducing costs. This will ensure that quality has not been compromised.

The next section discusses the development of changes that reduce costs while maintaining or improving quality.

Table 11.2. *Sources of Data for Focusing on Increasing Capacity.*

PROCESSING (LABOR/EQUIPMENT)		
RESOURCES	**YIELD**	**CYCLE TIME**
1. Unavailability of equipment (equipment down time)	% returns (percentage of cars returned after repair)	Total cycle time (length of stay in hospital)
2. Utilization rates (% of time bank tellers actually serve customers)	Repeats (calls placed correctly on the first try)	Set-up time (time to prepare a hotel room for the next guest)
3. Unavailability of people to complete core tasks (people required to do non-value work)	Rework (percentage of engineering drawings that have to be redrawn)	Processing time (time spent with a physician)
MATERIALS		
1. Material cost per unit (cost of plastic for each toy made)	% rejects (percentage of parts made that have to be reworked or destroyed)	Shelf-life (amount of material detroyed due to expiration dates)
2. Machine time required per unit (reactor time required for each chemical batch)	Conversion rates (lbs of product produced per raw materials used)	Set-up time (lead time to order materials for a job)
3. Maintenance costs associated with each area of the process	Waste (product damaged in handling)	Inventory age (average age of inventory in storage)

Developing Changes

After reviewing the data on costs after two months of his productivity incentive system, George realized that this change would not result in the reduction of costs for which he had hoped. He asked the mechanics to help him develop some changes to the system that would increase the efficiency of the entire system and increase its capacity. They came up with the following changes:

- Divide the mechanics into teams and assign each team one or more lifts with the aim being to put the car on the lift only once.
- Cross-train the mechanics so they can each do more jobs.
- Develop a scheduling system to support the coordination of work.

These changes were developed and tested as part of two Cycles. The first cycle related to working in teams and cross-training. The second cycle tested the scheduling system. George, the supervisors, and the mechanics each had a role to play. The entire group would meet once every two weeks to discuss progress and make further changes as necessary.

After six months, George was pleased with the progress. They had run several cycles that resulted in accomplishing a significant amount of cross-training and in removing most of the bugs from the team concept for repair of cars. The average cycle time (time from when the customer drops off the car until it is ready for pickup) was down from twenty-four hours to fifteen. Expenses for parking were lower than they had ever been. George predicted that when the scheduling system was put into place, the cycle time would be reduced to ten hours.

Due to the reduction in cycle time, the capacity of the system had been increased. Customers were pleased with the quicker turnaround on repairs. George canceled the ad he was going to put in the paper to hire two additional mechanics to replace two who had left. Through these changes, he had significantly reduced both his labor and parking costs.

George and the others at the repair shop were able to reduce costs and improve quality (service time) by making changes to the system. The changes resulted in better use of labor and reduced cycle time. The reduced cycle time translated into increased capacity for the system and better service for customers.

The next section will provide some ways of answering the question, *What changes can we make that will result in improvement?*—or more specifically, *What changes can we make that will result in increased capacity?* (Changes that are directly related to reducing rejects, or low first-pass yield, are not discussed because they were covered in Chapter Ten.)

Reducing the Waste of Resources

One of the changes that George and his mechanics developed involved teams and a scheduling system that would prevent the car from being put on and taken off the lift several times during a repair. This extra work did not add value to the customer; it only added inefficiency to the system.

Most systems include a lot of work that does not add value to the customer and is essentially wasted labor. Examples are duplication of effort, reports that no one reads, people waiting, and fixing errors. In a labor-intensive industry, taking work out of the system is a primary strategy for cost reduction. By taking out the unnecessary work, quality can be maintained or improved and costs reduced.

In many cost-reduction efforts, people are taken out of the system before the work is. This often results in the following side effects:

- Work is rearranged rather than reduced.

- Since fewer people do the same amount of work, people cut corners and sacrifice quality.

- Some areas are understaffed and some are overstaffed.

In some cases, a search for work that does not add value makes it obvious that resources are being expended unnecessarily. For example, producing reports that nobody uses can be identified and eliminated. It is more common, however, that the unnecessary work is "necessary" because of a poorly designed system. Consider the example of a group of people responsible for answering the variety of calls that come into a hospital's main telephone number.

The hospital had worked at streamlining how the operators answered the calls by providing a new information system and addressing the major issues that prevented the operators from answering the calls effectively. One might suppose that the remaining work associated with answering the calls is "necessary" work. This is true only if the number of calls coming into the switchboard is taken for granted. But are they all necessary?

After running a cycle to determine the reasons for the calls, it was discovered that more than 10 percent of the calls were from people asking for directions who had been scheduled by their doctor to be admitted to the hospital. A significant number of these calls were eliminated by providing printed directions to the doctors who had admitting privileges to the hospital.

As this example illustrates, any specific work is necessary only because the current system is designed to need it.

Just as with people, if equipment is not available when it is needed, the capacity of the system is affected. Therefore, focusing on reducing downtime of the equipment used to produce the product or service will result in the opportunity to reduce costs in the system. To increase capacity, it is important that the efforts are directed at the resources that are the bottlenecks. The following change concepts have been found to be particularly useful for redesigning a system to reduce the waste of resources; details on each of the concepts can be found in the appendix (the number of each concept is provided in the list):

Removing Unnecessary Work
- Minimize handoffs (14)
- Smooth the work flow (18)
- Eliminate overkill (3)
- Focus on the core process (34)

Reducing Equipment Downtime
- Optimize maintenance (48)
- Develop contingency plans (55)
- Use a coordinator (41)
- Reduce setup or startup time (46)

Reducing Costs Associated with Materials

In manufacturing industries, the cost of raw materials is often an appreciable proportion of the operating expense of the organization. Small reductions in the percentage of this material that is wasted can often mean significant cost savings. Raw material is wasted in a variety of ways. It can be wasted when product is scrapped because of defects. It can also be wasted when part of the raw material is not used during processing—for example, the fabric that is trimmed or cut off of borders and edges. Another source of waste that has a large environmental impact is partially processed material. In a chemical plant, there may be some material that has not reacted and must be disposed of. In a furniture manufacturing plant, some of the wood is sanded and turns to dust that must be captured and disposed of.

Service organizations expend a significant amount of money on supplies, including equipment. They also budget for energy for heating and lighting. Most of the people who work for these organizations do not even know the cost of routine supplies such as paper for the copy machine. Since people do not pay for these supplies themselves, it is easy to establish a pattern of waste. Eliminating this waste can often be an easy source of cost reduction.

Another substantial cost associated with materials is the cost of inventory of finished goods that will be sold to customers, inventory of supplies, and inventory of unfinished product or work. Inventory of finished goods is usually associated with manufacturers. However, home builders, grocery stores, restaurants, publishers, newspapers, and repair shops also have finished goods inventory. Examples of inventory of unfinished product or work include products at an intermediate stage in a manufacturing process, partially finished books or papers, partially completed additions to houses, partially completed reports, partially completed repairs, bank loans being processed, criminal cases being tried, partially completed information systems, and bills in the legislature.

Inventory adds to the costs of an organization in several ways. The capital associated with the inventory could be in the bank earning interest. The space to store the inventory incurs a cost. Some inventory is damaged in storage or becomes obsolete. Most important, labor is needed to keep track of the inventory, manage unfinished projects, or move inventory from place to place. Excess inventory results from several causes, including

1. Intentionally or unintentionally ordering or producing more than is needed
2. Inefficient or undependable arrangements with suppliers
3. Stocking of a variety of brands of the same item for reasons unrelated to customer satisfaction
4. Poor scheduling processes

The following change concepts have been found to be particularly useful for redesigning a system to reduce costs associated with materials. Details on each of the concepts can be found in the appendix.

Reducing Waste
- Match the amount to the need (9)

- Set up timing to use discounts(47)

- Eliminate overkill (3)

- Recycle or reuse (5)

- Substitute different materials (6)

Optimizing Inventory
- Match inventory to predicted demand (23)

- Use a pull system (24)

- Reduce unwanted features (25)

- Reduce multiple brands (26)

Reducing Cycle Time

The cycle time of a process is the elapsed time from when the inputs are ready for processing until an outcome is produced from those inputs. Cycle time is composed of both production time and wait time. In a bank, the cycle time to process a transaction at the teller's window is the sum of the time the customer waits in line and the time at the window. In George's repair shop, it is the time between when the car is dropped off and when it is ready to be picked up. In a hospital, the cycle time would be the time between admission and discharge of the patient.

The cycle time for an order of shirts from a catalogue is the elapsed time from when the order is placed until it is received. From the viewpoint of the customer, all of the cycle time is wait time. From the point of view of the catalogue house, the same cycle time might be divided into wait time before someone begins work on the order and the processing time of retrieving, packaging, and sending the merchandise.

The capacity of a system increases as its cycle time decreases. Quality and customer satisfaction usually increase as cycle time decreases. (Note: in service industries, quality levels can decrease if cycle time is reduced by rushing the customer.) Thus, cycle time is an important method for reducing costs while maintaining or improving quality.

The following change concepts have been found to be particularly useful for redesigning a system to reduce cycle time. Details on each of these concepts can be found in the appendix.

Reducing Cycle Time
- Find and remove bottlenecks (16)

- Do tasks in parallel (19)

- Reduce setup time (47)

- Move steps in the process closer together (15)

- Implement cross-training (31)

- Minimize handoffs (14)

- Synchronize (12)

The Role of Technology in Cost Reduction

The use of new or existing technology is a significant means of developing changes that reduce cost. Examples include equipment that saves labor, new materials that are less costly or less toxic than those that they replace, and information technology that reduces waiting time. Appropriate use of technology is an integral part of the systems approach to cost reduction. It has a role to play in improving each of the three components of capacity: core resources, cycle time, and yields.

A hospital removed some of the work involved in the delivery of medications to patients by testing and then implementing an automatic dispensing system. The equipment (a sophisticated vending machine) was stocked with the most common medications needed on each unit. This eliminated the need for calling the hospital pharmacy and having someone deliver the medication to the unit.

Using technology to replace labor is no substitute for changes that eliminate unnecessary work. It is not very beneficial to automate work that does not need to be done in the first place. Before the vending machine was installed, the doctors and pharmacists had reduced the amount of medications used by eliminating what was unnecessary or wasted. After this 15 percent reduction in medication use, the removal of the remaining unnecessary work was fruitful.

The social or financial costs associated with materials used in a product can be reduced by taking advantage of technological breakthroughs that result in new materials that are less costly or less toxic.

Equipment that can perform tasks much more quickly than humans is a vital source of system redesign to reduce cycle times, if the process time is the primary component of the cycle time. The familiar use of bar codes speeds up the checkout at the local supermarket. Technology changes must be integrated with other aspects of system redesign. Technology that contributes to reducing cycle time at the bottleneck of the system increases the overall capacity of the system. Speeding up one nonbottleneck step in the process only causes wait time in the system and may even increase cycle time. (George saw this happen in his repair shop.)

Technological innovations that enable fewer errors, better mixing, more uniform heating, higher pressures, or more precise machining increase yield if properly integrated into the system. Technology that substitutes for or supplements human labor in nonmanufacturing industries also has potential for increasing yields. Information technology is particularly useful for this purpose. Forms of information technology allow the travel agent to find the best itinerary, the person picking stock in the warehouse to locate the proper merchandise, the checkout clerk to record the proper price, and the customer service representative to give the proper answer to a customer inquiry.

Information technology (IT) is now providing ways to reduce *coordination costs* for entire systems of organizations. The need to coordinate information, decisions, and resources from the time an order is taken to deliveries to customers is being aided in many systems. In the recent past, organizational hierarchies of management (sometimes six or more levels) would coordinate information and decision making. E-mail, computer networks, and other IT advances are providing access to information for everyone in the system. This speeds up decision making and reduces the need for levels of managers who used to be middle men for handling information. Many reengineering efforts are providing good examples of using information technology to reduce coordination costs.

Example: Cost Reduction at an Airline

Significant cost reduction was a key initiative for an airline that wanted to offer low fares while still making a profit. The airline concentrated its efforts on increasing capacity, following a systems approach to cost reduction. Capacity of an airline can be measured in the number of passenger miles per day that the airline is capable of flying. The utilized capacity is the sum of all the miles actually flown by each of the airline passengers. Therefore, capacity of the system is a function of how many flights the system was capable of flying and how many people could be carried on each flight. Cycle time was divided into wait time (time at the gate unloading, preparing the plane for the next flight, and boarding) and flight time.

Before establishing some teams to focus on the cost reduction, the managers of the airline reviewed available data on resources, cycle time, and yields. Some of the key resources were people (flight crews and ground crews), planes, gate slots at airports, and takeoff and landing privileges at airports. The managers collected data on the cost of these resources for each airport. Then they collected data on cycle time along a key route. They found that the average cycle time between the two cities was 135 minutes, 33 percent of which was wait time at the gate. Only about two thirds of a very expensive asset, the plane, was being used to earn money.

They also studied problems related to cancelled flights. Cancelled flights relate to yield for an airline. For this study, a version of yield was defined as the number of scheduled flights that were actually completed. (They counted the flight even if it was late. Late flights were being addressed under an initiative relating to eliminating quality problems.) They found that about 1 in 150 flights were cancelled. A Pareto analysis showed that the three major causes were mechanical problems, unavailable crews, and weather.

Because wait time was such a large component of cycle time, the top managers of the airline decided to form a multifunctional team to reduce the wait time. They believed that focusing on wait time would also identify some unnecessary work that could be removed. The maintenance organization was asked to focus on reducing the number of flights cancelled due to mechanical problems.

What are we trying to accomplish? The airline wanted to reduce the cycle time between landing in one city to landing at the next destination by focusing on the reduction of turnaround time of an airplane at the gate. Shortening the wait time from 45 minutes to less than 25 minutes would mean that many planes could fly an additional flight per day.

Guidance
- Use flight crew to communicate the needs to the ground crew—for example, how many new meals are needed?
- Perform only work that is needed for safety and passenger service—eliminate overkill on the ground.

How will we know that a change is an improvement?

- The primary measure of success for the team is cycle time.
- A measure that relates to cycle time and to the aim is the wait time at the gate.
- Various components of the wait time will also be measured.
- Customer complaints will be monitored to ensure that service does not deteriorate.

What changes can we make that will result in improvement?

Airline personnel performed many tasks while the plane was at the gate, including getting passengers on and off the plane, finalizing the flight plan, cleaning the interior of the plane, catering, fueling, maintenance, and loading and unloading baggage. The team developed a flow diagram of these various tasks and who performed them.

Cycle 1: Increasing Knowledge

As a result of the meeting, the team decided to run a cycle to determine the components of the wait time. Two of the flight attendants on the team volunteered to collect the following data:

1. Time that a plane entered the gate and the pilot gave the signal for passengers to stand.
2. Time that the last passenger left the plane.
3. Time that the first passenger entered the plane for the next flight.
4. Time that the plane pushed back from the gate.

For any flight, the difference between items 1 and 2 would be the time to *disembark*; the difference between items 2 and 3 would be the time to *prepare* the plane; and the difference between items 3 and 4 would be the time to *board*. These data were to be collected for two weeks on any flight on which they were working. One of the flight attendants also recorded two important observations during the cycle: the boarding process was hampered by people seated in the front of the plane boarding before people seated in the back, even though people were supposed to board by row numbers. Also, delay was caused by people with luggage that did not fit under the seat or in the overhead compartment.

Figure 11.2 shows the key measurements on run charts for disembark time, preparation time, and boarding time that were started in this cycle.

Cycle 2: Developing Changes

The second meeting of the team was devoted to developing changes. Based on the results of the first cycle, they decided to focus their changes on preparing and boarding the plane. They had been given some ideas to consider in the charter and several of the team members had additional ideas. They also used change concepts related to reducing time and removing work to provoke some new ideas. The following change concepts were posted in the meeting room:

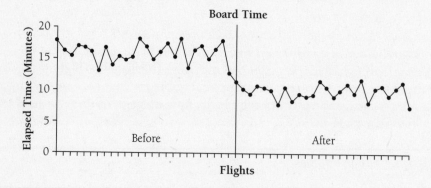

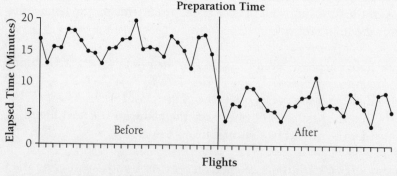

Figure 11.2. *Before and After Charts for Disembark Time, Preparation, and Boarding.*

Reduce Cycle Time
- Find and remove bottlenecks (16)

- Do tasks in parallel (19)

- Reduce setup time (46)

- Move process steps closer together (15)

- Cross-train (32)

- Minimize handoffs (14)

Remove Work That Does Not Add Value
- Consider people as in the same system (20)

- Smooth the work flow (18)

- Eliminate overkill (3)

- Focus on the core process (34)

The meeting resulted in the following changes (listed in order of predicted impact) to be tested in future cycles:

1. *Begin cleaning the plane while the passengers are disembarking* (do tasks in parallel). Previously, the cleaning crew waited until all passengers were off the plane and then entered the plane and began cleaning. Thus, cleaning began ten minutes after the plane landed. The cleaning crew would now enter the rear of the aircraft through the emergency exit. They would follow the departing passengers down the aisle, so cleaning would be nearly complete when the disembarking was complete.
2. *Place a luggage sizer at the gate to screen out oversize luggage* (remove a bottleneck). Passengers with large bags would be asked to see if they fit in the sizer. If they did not, they would not fit in the overhead bins. The bag would then be put in the luggage compartment of the plane.
3. *Assess catering needs in flight and call to caterers during flight* (do tasks in parallel). The traditional approach was to let the caterers enter the plane after it had landed and assess the catering needs. As part of the change, the flight attendants would assess the needs and the co-pilot would call in the results to the catering crew at the airport. This reallocation of work was expected to save five minutes of catering time on the ground.
4. *Enforce the boarding-by-seat assignment—back rows first* (focus on the core process). For full flights, the gate attendants were to enforce politely the existing procedure on boarding by rows.

Cycle 3: Testing the Changes

To keep the test to a small scale, the changes were tested on planes shuttling between two selected cities. Data were collected on the time to disembark, the time to board, and the elapsed time between the last passenger disembarking and when the plane was ready for new passengers. During the test, passengers did not board immediately; only the potential to board them was assessed.

The run charts in Figure 11.3 contain the data from before and after the test. The average time for disembarking was still approximately six minutes; the average time to prepare the plane was reduced to approximately seven minutes; and the average time to board the plane was reduced to approximately ten minutes. The charts indicated to the team that the twenty-five-minute wait time goal could be met, possibly with a few minutes to spare.

Cycles 4 to 6: Further Testing of the Changes

Three other cycles were run to test the changes between different cities and with some connecting flights. The results of cycle 3 were duplicated in these cycles. However, to account for some variation in arrival times of connecting flights, not all of the wait-time savings could be exploited.

Cycles 7 to 9: Implementing the Changes

Three cycles were used to implement the changes. Implementation included changing schedules to take advantage of the decreased total wait time summarized in Figure 11.3. Cycle 7 was successful in allowing the planes on the route to fly seven flights a day rather than six. The additional two cycles were used to spread the changes throughout the airline's network. Customer complaints were

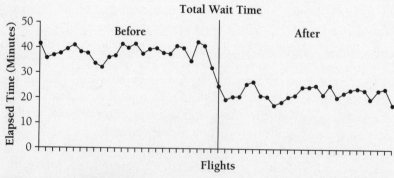

Figure 11.3. *Total Wait Time.*

monitored carefully during these cycles to assure that the quality of the service did not deteriorate in any way.

The following are some of the lessons learned from the implementation cycles:

- About 50 percent of the routes could take full advantage of the time savings and gain an extra flight per day for each plane.

- Routes that did not add extra flights were able to use the time savings to increase on-time arrivals.

- Routes that added an extra flight needed a longer wait time during the middle of the day to give the plane a more thorough cleaning and to provide some catch-up time if schedules slipped.

The extra flights and other benefits from the work resulted in almost a 10 percent capacity increase in eighteen months. By better utilizing the planes, pilots, flight attendants, and ground crews, the airline was able to decrease its average costs per passenger mile. It was able to utilize in a cost-effective way the increased capacity gained from improving the turnaround times. These cost reductions were obtained without any deterioration in the quality of service.

Technical Aspects of Cost Reduction

This section contains some additional material on reducing costs that is of a more technical nature than the material that has been presented so far. Three subjects will be covered: bottlenecks, data for the reduction of cycle time, and some commonly used definitions.

Bottlenecks

A bottleneck (also called a constraint or rate-limiting step) is that part of the system that has the smallest capacity relative to the demand for its resources. The capacity of any system is determined by the bottleneck in the system, the part of the system that provides the constraint to increased capacity for the entire system. The hourglass in Figure 11.4 provides a simple way to visualize a bottleneck. An hourglass is an instrument for measuring time. It is a glass vessel having two compartments that are connected by a small opening that allows sand to flow from one vessel to the other. The volume of sand through the hour glass is determined by the diameter of the small opening that connects the vessels.

To increase volume (or reducing time) requires focusing on the bottleneck, the opening between the two vessels. Everyone encounters bottlenecks in every day life. Some examples are given in Table 11.3.

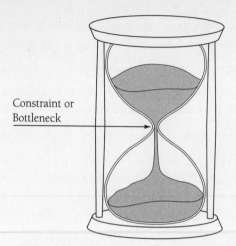

Constraint or
Bottleneck

Figure 11.4. *Hourglass as a Constraint Example.*

In a systems approach to cost reduction, it is fundamental that the bottleneck in the system be identified and become the focus of the activity. This is especially true for redesigning large systems. Data on bottlenecks is best collected and analyzed as part of a cycle to build knowledge for developing a change. A simple way to collect data in a cycle to identify a bottleneck is to observe where people are waiting or where material or work is piling up. Once the bottleneck is

Table 11.3. *Some Examples of Bottlenecks.*

A highway changing from three lanes to two

A supermarket checkout

A bank teller's window

The bathroom at 7:00 A.M.

One car for a family with three drivers

The school hallway between classes

The drain of a sink

The entrance to a football stadium

A hotel lobby at checkout time

Telephone information hot lines

Parents' time available to spend with children

A reactor's capacity

known, the capacity of the system can be increased by developing changes that remove the bottleneck or increase its capacity.

In the story presented at the beginning of the chapter, George could determine the bottleneck in his repair shop by checking the cars that were in the parking lot or the shop and determining who or what they were waiting for. It could be availability of a lift, a part, or a mechanic with a particular skill.

In a manufacturing plant the bottleneck can be determined by observing where the unfinished product is piling up, waiting to be further processed. In an administrative process the same approach can be used by searching people's inboxes to see at which stage in the process the work is piling up.

In the Department of Motor Vehicles in most states, a driver goes through several steps to renew a driver's license, including filling out some paperwork, taking an eye test, and having a picture taken. The bottleneck in any such office could be determined by observing at which step the lines are the longest. If the eye test was the bottleneck, resources from other nonbottleneck steps could be used to help with eye tests. Improvements in cycle time and yields of the eye tests would also result in increased capacity of the system. The capacity of the system could be increased by using resources from nonbottleneck steps to help administer eye tests. Reductions in the time to give an eye test and in those tests that have to be repeated would also result in increased capacity of the system. In this situation, consideration could also be given to reducing demand for the eye test, perhaps by allowing people to bring proof of vision from their doctor if they have seen him in the last six months.

Figure 11.5 contains the data that was collected by an organization that gave advice to clients to help them comply with government regulations. Consultants from the firm would visit a client's site and assess the situation. The organization would then put together a report of their findings and their recommendations. The aim was to reduce the time it took to get the reports to clients after the site visit. There were many reports in the system at any one time. The effort began with a cycle to determine where the bottleneck was. The plan included finding out where all the reports were in the system. During the study step of

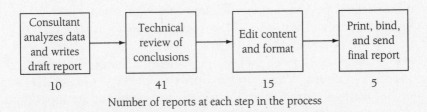

Number of reports at each step in the process

Figure 11.5. *Finding the Bottleneck in the Report Production System.*

the cycle the team analyzed the data by writing down the number of reports at each stage in the process. The data made it clear that the technical review process was the bottleneck.

Using Data to Reduce Cycle Times

Several different but rational definitions of when to start and stop measuring cycle time can usually be suggested for any particular application. Sometimes it can be a little tricky to define cycle time. It is usually best not to agonize over the definition; rather, choose a definition that makes sense and refine it as more is learned about the system.

Before developing changes that reduce cycle time, analyze the cycle time for the relative contributions of wait time and production time. This helps to establish the proper focus. This analysis is sometimes very straightforward. Often there is wait time, and then processing time, as in a transaction at the teller's window in a bank or an office visit to a physician. In other cases the analysis is not so simple, because there are multiple steps in the process and the wait times can occur between the steps. In these more difficult cases, wait time can be indirectly assessed by the following process:

1. Measure the total cycle time.
2. For each step in the process, measure the production time.
3. Add them together to get the total processing time.
4. Compute the wait time by subtracting the production time from the cycle time.

A producer of custom products that customers ordered in small quantities performed this analysis and found a cycle time of between ten and fifteen days and a production time of four hours. This is an extreme case, but it is not unusual for most of the cycle time to be composed of waiting time. This excess waiting time adds complexity and cost to the system.

Commonly Used Definitions for System Performance

A number of terms have been used to describe the performance of a system. They are defined a variety of ways in different applications. For clarification in this chapter, the following definitions are given:

Capacity can be an illusive concept. Traditionally, it has been a theoretical concept used for planning. The term can apply to any type of resource—space, equipment, materials, or people. It is usually thought of as an upper limit, but it is a limit usually defined by management for planning purposes. In describing operations for a specific period of time, the term *practical capacity* is used. Practical capacity is the maximum level of efficient operations. The approach to cost reduction presented in this book uses capacity of the system to mean the potential of the system to produce, given certain resources, yields, and cycle times. Other terms that relate directly to capacity are:

Utilization refers to how much of the theoretical capacity (or sometimes practical capacity) was actually used during a given period.

Productivity is the ratio of output to input for a given period, where input can consist of labor, material, capital, and/or support services.

Efficiency also describes the relationship between inputs and outputs. The fewer inputs (resources) used to obtain a given output, the greater the efficiency.

When these terms are used to describe the performance of a process, output is usually measured in *standard units produced* (note: when labor is the most important resource, standard hours are used). That is, standards are established for the various types of outputs. With these definitions in mind:

$$\text{Efficiency} = \frac{\text{Standard units of output produced}}{\text{Resources used}}$$

$$\text{Utilization} = \frac{\text{Resources used}}{\text{Resources available}}$$

$$\text{Productivity} = \text{Efficiency} \times \text{Utilization}$$

$$= \frac{\text{Standard of output produced}}{\text{Resources available}}$$

Conclusion

The methods presented in this chapter can be combined with those in Chapter Ten to offer an organization a strategy that will reduce quality problems and decrease costs. This may not be enough, however, to keep an organization competitive. The next chapter fills in the missing pieces.

CHAPTER 12

Expanding Customer Expectations to Increase Demand

The elimination of quality problems and reduction of costs had brought success to George's repair shop (see Chapters Ten and Eleven). Returns for repairs not done correctly were rare. The average time a car was in the shop for a specific job was down from sixteen hours to eight hours. This translated into a 30 percent increase in capacity for the shop. The result was a healthy profit margin. Part of this profit went to the employees as part of a gain-sharing plan, but the bulk of it was reinvested in the shop, mostly in new equipment. George knew that in business, things never went this smoothly for long.

In a brief moment of tranquility at the end of the day, George was in his office thinking about his latest problem. The increased capacity and reduction in rework meant that the mechanics were not keeping busy full-time. This situation would be exacerbated when Frank, one of his best mechanics, came back from medical leave. A layoff as the consequence of everyone's efforts appalled George. The ring of the phone pulled him out of these depressing thoughts.

It was Sid, one of George's most loyal customers and a good friend. Sid's vision of a relaxing barbecue had been shattered by the stream of oil running from under his car, which was parked outside the office building where he worked. He had returned to the building to call a cab, but had decided to call George first. George told Sid to wait, and then hopped into the tow truck and headed to the office complex. He took some oil and some parts with him, in case it was just a simple problem. When George arrived, he found that the problem was just a worn seal that needed to be replaced. He was able to fix it on the spot. Sid enjoyed his barbecue that night after all.

The next morning, George burst into the office and called a quick meeting. He had an idea for a new service that could increase business and help preserve the jobs at the shop. He explained his rescue of Sid the previous night and the idea that had come to him on the way home. The parking lot was full of cars whose owners deferred routine maintenance because of the inconvenience of getting to work without their cars. Why not do the oil changes or other routine jobs right in the parking lot during working hours?

Initially, the idea was received with skepticism, but gradually the mood progressed to acceptance and even excitement. George put together a team to develop and test the new service. They would use the Model for Improvement just as they had done for the cost-reduction efforts. Once the team had agreed on its aim, defined some measures, and developed a prototype of the new service, they planned the first cycle.

George called the property manager at the office complex and ask her for permission to run a test. She was very hesitant at first. All she could think of was the potential problems, but George prevailed. She agreed to a test for one week, as long as George would include her car in the test; it was badly in need of an oil change and some new wiper blades.

The third category of improvement—expanding the expectations of customers by providing products and services that customers perceive as unusually high-value—is the most difficult category. It requires study of the customer beyond what is necessary for eliminating quality problems or for reducing costs. New, creative ideas are needed. Success in solving quality problems and reducing costs without developing new products to create more consumer demand too often results in organizational gain but personal loss for the workers. People lose their jobs when organizations get more efficient without creating new opportunities.

The addition of this third category of improvement to eliminating quality problems and cost reduction creates a unified system of improving value. This system includes incremental improvement of the quality of existing products, substantial improvements in quality through innovative new products and services, and the ability to offer low prices because of substantial cost reductions from reengineered systems. High value is obtained through the combination of high quality and relatively low price. High-value products and services create demand and thus allow an organization to stay in business and create jobs. To accommodate this comprehensive view of quality and price, the chain reaction must include the concept of value. This chain reaction is illustrated in Figure 12.1.

This chapter discusses some methods for expanding the expectations of customers. The methods presented can be applied continually and routinely by a variety of people. The output of this category of improvement is a predictable stream of new products and services that raise the expectations of customers because of their very high value. Other writers have called this approach to improvement "attractive quality creation."

A strong customer orientation is vital to success in this category. One manifestation of this orientation is the method of collecting data to determine the opportunities. Much of the data used in eliminating quality problems or reducing costs are available in the producer's system. The data used for Category 3 improvements must be collected in the customer's system, often by observation

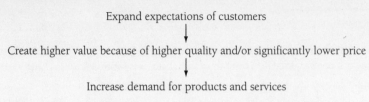

Expand expectations of customers

↓

Create higher value because of higher quality and/or significantly lower price

↓

Increase demand for products and services

Figure 12.1. Chain Reaction for Third Category of Improvement.

or by putting oneself in the customer's place. Customers are not a reliable source of ideas for how to expand their expectations. Experiences with present and past products and services have set their expectations. The providers of products and services will of course be delighted with any ideas that come from customers. However, in this category the input of customers is most useful once a prototype of a new product or service has been developed and the customer can react to a tangible item. The collection of such data will be discussed later in the chapter.

George planned two pizza nights for the next month, one to plan the test and one to study the results. Excitement pervaded the discussion and pizza sustained the energy. The group planned the test and scheduled it to begin in a week and a half, on a Monday. They would rent a van to carry tools and supplies. Only oil changes, checking of fluid levels, and some minor exterior repairs such as replacement of windshield wiper blades were included in the test. The property manager of the office complex publicized the pilot study in the complex's newsletter and asked for volunteers. There were still some details to be worked out. A group of three mechanics volunteered to describe in some detail, and using a flowchart, the process for servicing cars at the office complex, and to make some suggestions for efficiently changing oil without a lift. Everyone involved expected a few difficulties to arise during the test, but they were anxious to anticipate and prevent as many as possible.

The data collected as part of the test included the results of a short phone survey of the customers, the types of repair requested, the time needed to make the repairs, and the observations of the mechanics about how well the process had worked.

Informal reports of the test were mostly positive, but some problems surfaced. The results of the phone survey showed that customers were for the most part very enthusiastic about the service and would use it again. The mechanics realized that they could expand the type of repairs they offered, and they could have more parts available in the van. The major problems, however, were collecting the keys from the customers and finding the cars in the parking lot. During the test, the receptionist at each building had agreed to hold the keys for the crew and note the location of the car. This turned out to be too burdensome for the receptionists. The idea of using a lockbox developed, and one was installed in the lobby during the last few days of the test. Customers made their appointment the day before and dropped their keys in the box as they came to work. Also, a separate area of the parking lot was designated for the cars that were to be serviced that day.

George and the mechanics decided to run another four-week cycle to incorporate and test the additional changes made based on what they had learned during the first test. George called some other office complexes and some large employers in town to see if they too would be interested in the service. Everyone was to think about opportunities for expanding the idea of taking the service to the customer into other settings. Luckily, Frank would be returning from medical leave and could pick up some of the work in the shop for the mechanics who were now on the road.

George's story contains several elements that relate to expanding the expectations of customers:

- The idea for the change was stimulated by observations of the customer's system, not the provider's system.

- The idea for the new service was novel, but not extraordinary.

- It is unlikely that a customer would have suggested the new service in response to a customer survey.

- The design of the new service occurred in two parts: the idea or concept for the new service was developed first, and then the detailed processes for delivering the new service were designed.

- The concept was tested on a small scale using rough prototypes.

Before discussing further each of these aspects of expanding customer expectations, and the applicable data-collection methods and concepts for developing change, this chapter probes more deeply into what quality and value mean in various settings, and how an organization can match products and services to needs in the marketplace or society. This deeper understanding of quality is not as important in eliminating quality problems and reducing costs, but for those who wish to excel at the more difficult work of Category 3, it will provide a useful foundation.

Quality and Value

When an organization is trying to expand customers' expectations, it may need to design a new product or service. But what is it about a product or service that causes it to expand customers' expectations? What is it about a product or service that makes it high quality? These questions are relatively easy to answer after a product or service is in the hands of the customer. The important task, however, for the marketer and designer of a product or service is to find answers to the following questions: What is it about a product or service that *would* make it high quality? What is it about the product or service that *would* cause it to expand customers' expectations? How can quality be defined for a product or service that does not yet exist? The process of answering these questions begins with the development of a definition of quality.

It is easy to slip into a very philosophical and abstract discussion of the meaning of quality; but while this discussion might be of interest to some, it does not serve the purpose of providing practical methods for expanding the expectations of customers. The following discussion of how to define quality when the product or service does not yet exist begins with an examination of how to define quality for an existing product or service.

Defining Quality

The development of an operational definition of quality that is practical begins with a set of measurable characteristics, sometimes called *measures of quality* or *quality-characteristics*. For example, measures of quality for a calculator might be speed, accuracy, complexity of the computations it can perform, clarity of display of the results, and ease of use. These characteristics would form the basis of judging the quality of the calculator.

They would also provide a way of judging what customers desire but do not expect. Perhaps customers expect that a calculator that can perform complex computations—for example trigonometric functions—will be more difficult to use than one that only performs simple arithmetic computations. A calculator that performs complex computations but is also easy to use for simple arithmetic computations could expand the expectations of customers.

Measures of quality can also be used to determine what is important about a product or service to different types of customers (segments of the market), and to design products and services for the different types of customers. Following are some examples of measures of quality for a variety of products and services:

Vinyl flooring	Appearance, stain resistance, ease of cleaning, resistance to scratches, durability, ease of installation
Health Maintenance Organization	Extent of prevention of health problems, ability to diagnose health problems, ability to solve health problems, personal interface, access to care, choice of doctors

| Checking account | Diversity of uses, ease of access to funds, security of funds, ease of record keeping, availability of credit, time to make purchase |
| Newspaper | Factual, fair, interesting to read, breadth of coverage, depth of coverage, thought-provoking editorials |

The following list identifies and defines a number of generic "dimensions of quality" that may assist in defining quality for a particular product or service:

Dimension	*Meaning*
1. Performance	Primary operating characteristics
2. Features	Secondary operating characteristics, added touches
3. Time	Time spent waiting, cycle time, time to complete a service
4. Reliability	Extent of failure-free operation over time
5. Durability	Amount of use before replacement is preferable to repair
6. Uniformity	Low variation among repeated outcomes of a process
7. Consistency	Match with documentation, forecasts, or standards
8. Serviceability	Resolution of problems and complaints
9. Aesthetics	Relating to the senses, such as color, fragrance, fit, or finish
10. Personal interface	Punctuality, courtesy, and professionalism
11. Flexibility	Willingness to adapt, customize, or accommodate change
12. Harmlessness	Relating to safety, health, or the environment
13. Perceived quality	Inferences about other dimensions; reputation
14. Usability	Relating to logical and natural use; ergonomics

These dimensions support a broad definition of the concept of quality that can include all aspects of the performance, appearance, and variation associated with products and services. The dimension of "features" can be further divided to include such aspects as the size and location of a product or service.

One way to use these dimensions is to develop measures of quality for a particular product or service based on input from customers and then to check these measures against the list just provided. Another approach is to define what each of the dimensions means relative to a particular product or service and then to organize information obtained from customers using the fourteen dimensions as categories.

When developing a list of measures of quality, do not make it too long. The measures will be used to identify potential improvements to the product or service. While all or many of the dimensions may apply, the designer must focus on a small number of them. Excelling in one or two dimensions is usually enough to differentiate a product or service. A set of four to seven specific measures is usually sufficient for a particular application.

The discussion up to this point has been about using measures of quality for an existing product or service. To significantly expand the expectations of customers, however, new products and services are often required. How can the quality of a product or a service be discussed before it even exists? To do so requires an understanding of the *need* that the product or service will fulfill. The discussion of need is at a higher level of abstraction than the discussion of measures of quality. However, the concept of need has important practical applications, as will be shown later in this chapter.

Identifying the Need

Many people have checking accounts; many people have credit cards. What do they do with them? Why do they need them? Usually people use checking accounts and credit cards to make purchases and pay bills. The need is not for the checking account; the need is to pay bills. Since credit cards were developed, many people have used them rather than checks to make purchases. The development of credit cards changed the expectations of many people about services to pay bills.

Every successful product or service is based on satisfying a need of a customer or of society. Customers choose an organization's products and services to satisfy that need. A service may be quickly supplanted by a new service aimed at the same need, however. It is easy for an organization to fall into the trap of assuming that the customer's need is for the organization's present product or service. Although new products come and go, the need remains.

The need may be for personal transportation, for the disposal of garbage, for a pleasant work environment, for the transfer of knowledge, or for the separation of chemical mixtures. Usually several products or services in the marketplace are aimed at the same need. The following list identifies some needs and a few of the products and services that are intended to meet those needs:

Need	Product or Service
• Perform handheld computation	• Abacus, slide rule, calculator, microcomputer
• Transfer of knowledge and promotion of lifelong learning	• Public education, library, television, Internet
• Health care	• Hospital, clinic, home care, health club

- Information about the affairs of the world
- Personal transportation

- Floor coverings
- Paying bills and making purchases

- Newspaper, television, magazines, Internet
- Walking, city bus system, automobile, bicycle
- Vinyl tile, ceramic tile, carpet, wood
- Cash, checking account, credit cards, cash, interactive television

The following questions are helpful in defining the need underlying a particular product or service:

- How do customers use the product or service?

- Why is this product or service important to customers?

- What other product or service could be used instead?

The answer to the last question should go beyond the same product or service offered by competitors. In defining a need, there must be a balance between a definition that is so abstract that it is not useful and a definition so specific that it assumes that the existing product or service is a fundamental need.

How can the concept of need and the dimensions of quality be tied together? Consider the following example. People need floor coverings in their homes. This need can be satisfied by a variety of products: rugs, vinyl tiles or sheets, wood, ceramic tile, or paint. Some possible measures of quality include appearance, resistance to stain, ease of cleaning, resistance to scratches, durability, and ease of installation. Note that these measures of quality refer to the *need* for floor coverings. They can be applied to any product addressing this need, but they are not dependent upon a particular product. They are thus measures of quality that can be used for products that do not yet exist. Such measures are important when an organization is trying to expand customers' expectations by designing new products. Figure 12.2 provides an example of how these measures of quality can be used to determine opportunities for expanding expectations. The figure portrays five existing products designed to satisfy the need for floor coverings relative to two measures of quality: appearance and ease of cleaning. There seems to be a tradeoff between these two measures of quality for these products—that is, either the floor covering has good appearance or it is easy to clean. A product that is both easy to clean and attractive could change the expectations of customers. The change could come from the redesign of an existing product or the design of a new product.

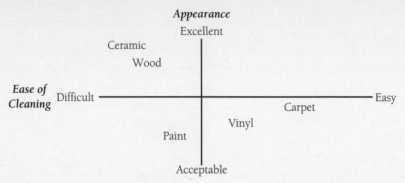

Figure 12.2. *Determining the Need for a Floor Covering Relative to Measures of Quality.*

A chain of bookstores was looking for ways to grow their business. They studied their customers and determined that the need the stores were fulfilling was for entertainment, not books. The measures of quality that were important to customers included people with similar interests with whom to mingle, a relaxing atmosphere, availability of new offerings, and the opportunity to treat themselves to something interesting or unexpected. The company began to change its stores to enhance the shopping experience. The redesigned bookstores included open spaces, cafes, and plenty of places to sit and relax. Focusing on the need and then matching the design of their stores to the important measures of quality relative to this need allowed them to become one of the world's largest booksellers.

This discussion of need and measures of quality is based on the principle that quality is improved by *ongoing matching of products and services to a need in the marketplace or in society.* When the consideration of price is added to the matching process, the focus becomes the enhancement of value. The better the match of the product to the need with respect to either quality or price, the higher the value and the more the customer will want the product or service. How well the product or service matches the need is determined by the important measures of quality and the price. Matching the need becomes the target for improvement.

The next section builds on this foundation by discussing a general approach to Category 3 improvements.

A Roadmap to Expanding Customer Expectations

The approach in the first two categories of improvement was to use data to determine the quality problem or opportunity for cost reduction, and then to use the change concepts to determine how to make changes that would lead to improvement. The *how* was usually the biggest challenge. In Category 3, deciding *what* is also an issue. Determining what results, outcomes, features, or entirely new products and services would expand the expectations of customers and determining how these results might be obtained (by what methods) may be quite challenging and require a significant amount of creativity. In the earlier story, George first had to come up with the idea of a mobile service (the *what*), and then he had to figure out a process to make it feasible (the *how*).

Figure 12.3 summarizes a general approach to improvements aimed at expanding customers' expectations. The Cycle for Learning and Improvement supports this approach through specific cycles in each phase to gain knowledge, conduct tests, and implement changes. The approach consists of four stages. The first two stages discover and clarify what changes need to be made. The last two stages focus on how to make the changes.

Developing What Will Expand Customer Expectations

Where do ideas that allow organizations to expand the expectations of their customers come from? Think of the famous inventors that gave us the telephone, airplane, and computer. Certainly an organization should take full advantage of one of these geniuses when they are available. Technology also offers opportunities for developing ideas; research and development groups study ways to incorporate new technologies or to extend existing technologies in their organization's products and services. Both of these sources provide opportunities for developing ideas for *whats* that might expand customers' expectations. There are, however, some things that the rest of us can do while we wait for ideas from our organizations' geniuses and from new technologies.

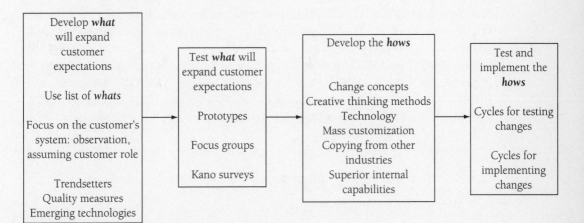

Figure 12.3. Roadmap to Category 3 Improvements.

To expand the expectations of customers in any particular setting, what should be accomplished is determined by the interaction of data with knowledge of both the customer and the marketplace. The following list contains some *whats* for expanding the expectations of customers. It is meant only to stimulate creative thinking about what will be necessary. It could also serve as a checklist to use when collecting data.

- Solution to a problem or reduction of cost in the customer's system

- Customization of the product or service to the individual customer's measure of quality

- Dramatic reduction in waiting time (anytime)

- New features

- Elimination of undesirable side effects

- Dramatic reduction of variation in performance

- Unusually good outcomes, for example, in health, education, and crime reduction

- Unusually good matches to selected measures of quality, for example, performance, reliability, or aesthetics

- Unusual convenience (anyplace)

- Particularly high value (any of the above combined with a relatively low price)

Making a list of *whats* that fit the appropriate market or industry is a useful exercise for organizations to use to uncover some opportunities to expand the expectations of their present or future customers.

The *whats* just listed, such as solving a problem in the customer's system or dramatic reduction in waiting time, are for the most part results. Following is a list of sources of data that are useful for gaining knowledge in order to understand the potential opportunities to expand customers' expectations:

- Study of the customer's system: problems, costs, and needs

- Trendsetting people or magazines (lead users)

- Science fiction books and films

- Quality measures related to the need

- Emerging technologies

- Reports and books by "futurists"

Study of the Customer's System In Categories 1 and 2, the focus is usually on the provider's system. What aspect of the system is causing the problem? Where are the costs and what waste can be taken out of the system? In Category 3, the focus is on the customer's system: the needs that are present, the problems in the system, and how those in the system define quality. Many of the approaches to collecting data that were used in the first two categories will also be used in Category 3. The difference is the location of the data collection.

A simple survey of customers and some recording of problems by the agents taking calls might be sufficient to uncover some problems experienced by the customers of a travel agency. Perhaps they often get put on hold when they call the agency, or maybe some of the flight reservations are in error or do not take advantage of available discounts. The travel agency might also collect data to reduce cost. They could collect data on when calls arrive and then develop a way to smooth the flow of calls, or they could develop a contingency plan for dealing with the peaks in calls without adding staff. Perhaps they could use part-time workers operating from their homes during this time. They could collect data on the length of calls. What problems do the travel agents experience getting the correct information for customers? What slows them down or forces them to call a customer back at a later time?

These data on problems and opportunities for cost reduction may lead to some changes that help a travel agency meet the expectations of its customers while also making a profit. However, the changes spawned from these data will probably not expand customers' expectations of the services provided by a travel agency. To do so, the agency must collect data found in the customer's system.

Two of the most powerful ways to better understand the customer's system are to observe the customer or to take the place of the customer. Observation means obtaining information from customers by watching them use the organization's product or service. This can be done both with and without the customers' knowledge. Taking the place of the customer, or trading places, is another useful means of obtaining information about the customer's system, this time through direct experience.

For example, members of the travel agency could go to the travelers' homes or places of business. They could focus on how travelers are using the agency's services overall (understanding the need), not just on how customers are responding to the agency's current offerings of services. They could observe the planning for the trip, the securing of the reservation and the tickets. They could accompany a customer on a trip. The data would consist of recorded observations of the customer relative to the trip.

A better understanding of the needs and problems the agents observed, especially those normally considered outside the responsibility of the travel agency, is a source of ideas for new or redesigned services. Perhaps the agent observed the traveler's difficulties in securing a taxicab at a train station after arriving late at night. The travel agency might use the change concept "develop alliance/cooperative relationships" and arrange with a local taxicab company to provide rides for their clients. The traveler could receive their taxi reservation along with their train ticket.

This data collection is not very sophisticated, but it is unusual. How many travel agencies have made the investment to understand the customer's system at this level of detail? The following list contains some examples of these two approaches to obtaining data from the customer's system:

Observing the Customer
- Travel agent taking a trip with a customer

- Engineer watching the customer install the garage door opener

- Designer watching the customer program the VCR

- Administrator spending a day with a patient who has just been discharged from the hospital

- Members of the IRS watching people fill out the new tax form

- Teachers observing the family lives of students

- Programmers observing people using a newly acquired software program

Assuming the Role of the Customer
- A new designer assembling the gas grill his company manufacturers

- Automobile company executives driving cars with fifty thousand or more miles on them

- Mayor of San Diego posing as a homeless person using available government services

- The president calling the company's main telephone number

- Manager returning a damaged product to one of his stores

- Physician spending time as a patient in the hospital

- Congress abiding by the laws they pass

Both of these methods of obtaining data in the customer's system are useful for obtaining information of which the customer may not even be aware. Observation offers a number of advantages as a means of obtaining information:

- Information can be obtained under realistic conditions.

- The observer needs less skill than an interviewer to obtain the information.

- It is useful for generating ideas for innovation if the observer possesses technical knowledge.

- It is simple to carry out.

- Videotape may be used to document observations and for later analysis.

Possible disadvantages of this method are that the presence of an observer may create artificial conditions, that the conditions under which the observations are made are time limited, and that the observer will likely miss important but infrequently occurring events.

A manufacturer of medical supplies encourages its salespeople on sales calls to hospitals to observe how the medical personnel treat the patients. When the salespeople observe a need for which there is no product, they contact the company's research and development office to begin the design process. The salesperson who knows both his own business and his customer's business does not need much statistical data to reach an informed conclusion about what he sees and hears in the hospital.

A designer and manufacturer of consumer durable products pays hundreds of consumers to fiddle with computer-simulated products at the company's "Usability Lab" while engineers record the users' reactions on videotape. The company has used its consumer expertise to differentiate its products from the products of its competitors.

Taking the place of the customer to obtain information can provide rewarding experiences as well as new knowledge. It allows a very personal view of the customer's system. When taking the role of the customer, providers can experience the full range of human responses, from frustration and anger to satisfaction and delight. Some advantages of this approach to obtaining data include:

- It allows the provider to experience feelings that could not be expressed in an interview.

- It is useful for building or enhancing relationships with customers.

- An important but minute level of detail can be experienced.

- A single experience can potentially provide more information than hundreds of surveys.

Some concerns when using this approach are that the presence of the person assuming the role may create artificial conditions, that certain skills may be required to become a customer, and that the experience may be too short to form a useful perception. Sometimes, familiarity with the product or service may make it impossible to assume the position of a first-time or infrequent user of the product.

The mayor of San Diego spent forty-eight hours disguised as a homeless person, living on the street and in public shelters. Much of what she previously had learned about the homeless had come from staff reports. She decided to get out there herself so she would not get a filtered version.

A distribution manager of a chemical company assumed the role of a truck driver to better understand the problems that a driver experienced when he picked up product at one of his terminals.

Trendsetters Once a year, attention is focused on Paris as fashion designers unveil their latest collections of clothing. Most of the clothes that are shown are not purchased by the general public. Some of the clothes are so extreme that it is hard to imagine anyone wearing them. However, these new collections provide important data for clothing designers and manufacturers everywhere. They indicate trends in fashion. They define new expectations for customers.

In other industries as well—such as cars and household furnishings—new fashion trends result in new customer expectations. Data to spot these trends can come from the people who influence trends, such as fashions designers, magazine editors, or public figures (John Kennedy's failure to wear a top hat during his inauguration changed people's expectations of what constituted formal wear). Data can also be obtained by observation.

An executive of one of the American automotive companies was attending the Super Bowl football game at the Silverdome in Pontiac, Michigan. He noticed three people looking at the crowd and taking notes. They were paying little if any attention to the game. Curiosity finally got the best of him and he asked them what they were doing. They were in the clothing business and they were in the process of designing a new line of sportswear. They thought that people at the Super Bowl might be trendsetters, so they were recording details about what people were wearing.

"Trendsetting" is a word normally used in the fashion industry to refer to the types of people that other industries call "lead users." Lead users might develop an application that is presently not available by adapting an existing product to meet their needs. An example is the customization of computer software. People who are skilled in programming and intent upon customizing commercially available software to their specific needs could provide information about how to improve the software to expand the expectations of other customers. Another example is the information that automobile manufacturers get from auto racing. Many of the features found in the family car were first developed and tested for use in race cars.

Quality Measures Related to the Need Traditional surveys of customers about what they like or dislike about existing products or services are not very helpful in determining how to expand expectations. However, using the customer's input to define quality using specific measures can be very helpful. This definition of quality can be used to obtain a deeper understanding of what new products and services customers might value. Market segments can be defined based on the variation of customers' definitions of what would match the need, and the need plus the specific quality measures can then serve as a target for those who are designing the products and services. For example, the assessment of different floor coverings relative to two measures of quality illustrated in Figure 12.2 revealed where the potential is to use new products to expand the expectations of customers. This analysis could of course be carried out with more than two measures of quality.

Emerging Technologies A new technology or an innovative adaptation of an existing technology can be the foundation of an improvement that expands the expectations of customers. Technologies developed over the past twenty years such as information storage and transfer, wireless telecommunications, artificial knowledge, solar energy, and electronic miniaturization offer unlimited opportunities for applications to new products and services. Sometimes, new technologies are made known and available to the passive observer by the developer of the technology. Trade shows are an obvious place to gather data on new technologies. However, for organizations that wish to take more initiative in adapting technology to better match the needs of customers, a more determined approach to gathering data is needed.

One approach is to identify a specific technology that is still under development and make a special effort to follow the progress or perhaps volunteer to be a test site. For example, organizations that rely on frequent communication with customers as a key part of their service—such as law firms, groups of consultants, and other professional services—might make a special effort to keep abreast of developments in video conferencing. Establishing close ties with research universities or government research organizations such as the National Institute of Standards and Technology is another way to gain data on potentially useful technologies. These institutions could also be approached with a problem and asked what technological solutions are available. Another source of data is organizations that specialize in technology transfer. These organizations often broker the results of pure research at universities into commercial applications.

Testing What Will Expand Customer Expectations

Once an idea (the *what*) about how to expand customer expectations has been generated, how can the degree of belief that the product or service will be accepted in the marketplace be increased? And when many different ideas have been generated, how can their relative merits be established? How can organizations determine which ideas to develop further? The next stage in the general approach to Category 3 improvements is to run cycles to test the *whats*.

There are a number of approaches to testing ideas for new products or services with customers. The most common way is to create rough prototypes of the product or service and run tests on a small scale. Focus groups or observation of potential customers reacting to and using these prototypes can provide useful feedback on the ideas. This can be a difficult task if the *hows* for producing or delivering the product or service have not yet been developed. It can be very difficult for the customer, when first exposed to an idea, to appreciate how it will be useful. In the example of George's mobile repair service, a friend's emergency resulted in a chance to both discover and test the *what*. Additional cycles tested both the *what* and the *how* of his creative idea.

An approach called *conjoint analysis* has been used by marketing research groups since the 1970s. This technique allows potential customers to examine a set of alternative product configurations and rank them by their preference. By including a price with each configuration (that is, with each level of selected quality-characteristics), the value a customer places on each alternative can be studied. A customer preference model can be developed and used to predict satisfaction with alternative configurations. (Sources of further information on conjoint analysis are included in the notes at the end of the book.)

Special survey methods can also be used to test the *whats*. Noriaki Kano of the Science University of Tokyo developed a survey method that defines three classifications of quality-characteristics of a product or service:

1. One-dimensional quality-characteristic. Results in customer satisfaction when fulfilled and dissatisfaction when not fulfilled.
2. Attractive quality-characteristic. Results in customer satisfaction when fulfilled but is acceptable as is when not fulfilled.
3. Must-be quality-characteristic. Taken for granted when fulfilled but results in customer dissatisfaction when not fulfilled.

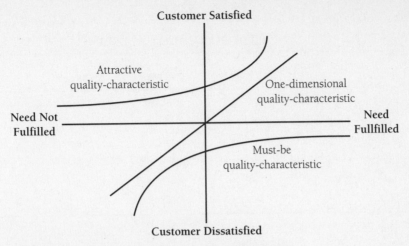

Figure 12.4. *Kano's Two-Dimensional Recognition Model.*

Figure 12.4 shows how these quality-characteristics are defined on a two-dimensional scale.

A survey using this model requires a pair of questions—one negative, one positive—for studying each quality element, such as the following from a typical Kano questionnaire. Customers are asked to circle the phrase that best describes their feelings:

1a. How would you feel if you had a VCR in your room?
    Delighted   I expect it and like it   No feeling
    Live with it   Do not like it   Other

1b. How do you feel when you do not have a VCR in your room?
    Delighted   I expect it and like it   No feeling
    Live with it   Do not like it   Other

The results of the questionnaire are classified into one of seven possible outcomes—skeptical, reverse, attractive, indifferent, one-dimensional, must-be, and other—using a two-way table for each pair of questions (see Table 12.1). If the data produce either the attractive, one-dimensional, or must-be outcome, the quality characteristic has been successfully classified into one of the three categories shown in Figure 12.4. If one of the other four results occurs, the quality characteristic was not successfully classified.

The following example shows the use of this survey methodology to study potential attractive quality elements at a hotel. The potential attractive elements were developed at a brainstorming session of the hotel managers. The survey forms (see Exhibit 12.1) were placed in the room information packet given to

RESPONSE TO POSITIVE QUESTION	RESPONSE TO NEGATIVE WORDING OF QUESTIONS					
	DELIGHTED	EXPECT IT AND LIKE IT	NO FEELING	LIVE WITH IT	DO NOT LIKE	OTHER
Delighted	Skeptical	Attractive	Attractive	Attractive	One-dimensional	Other
I expect and like it	Reverse	Indifferent	Indifferent	Indifferent	Must-be	Other
No feeling	Reverse	Indifferent	Indifferent	Indifferent	Must-be	Other
Live with it	Reverse	Indifferent	Indifferent	Indifferent	Must-be	Other
Do not like	Reverse	Reverse	Reverse	Reverse	Skeptical	Other
Other	Other	Other	Other	Other	Other	Other

Table 12.2. *Summary of Hotel Survey Results.*

QUALITY ELEMENT	ATTRACTIVE	ONE DIMENSION	MUST-BE	INDIFFERENT	REVERSE	SKEPTICAL	OTHER	TOTAL	TREND
1. VCR	88	11	4	123	5	2	1	234	Indifferent
2. Work desk	33	17	128	48	7	1	1	230	Must-be
3. Coffee in-room	47	82	15	67	8	1	5	225	One-dimensional
4. Speaker phone	86	11	4	113	12	2	1	227	Indifferent
5. Shampoo/ Conditioner	17	27	137	17		8		210	Must-be
6. Van check-in	129	13	5	74	12	2	6	231	Attractive
7. Fax in room	130	3	2	70	38	17		220	Attractive

each guest during check-in. The response rate was about 10 percent, which was higher than previous in-room surveys. Over a two-month period, 235 completed survey forms were received. Table 12.2 shows the analysis of these data. The answers to the open-ended questions were analyzed first by grouping them according to common themes and then prioritizing the data based on the number of entries for each theme to indicate the primary areas for focus.

The results of the survey indicated that elements 6 and 7 (check-in in hotel van and fax in room) are attractive to guests and can be considered as means to expand customer expectations. The work desk and the shampoo/conditioner are elements that guests already assume will be available in their room. Most guests

Survey Form for Kano Questionnaire Used at a Hotel.
Please let us know what you think. Circle the phrase that best describes your feelings.

1a. How would you feel if you had a VCR in your room?
Delighted___ I expect it and like it___ No feeling___ Live with it___ Do not like___ Other___

1b. How do you feel when you do not have a VCR in your room?
Delighted___ I expect it and like it___ No feeling___ Live with it___ Do not like___ Other___

2a. How would you feel if you had a work desk in your room?
Delighted___ I expect it and like it___ No feeling___ Live with it___ Do not like___ Other___

2b. How do you feel when you do not have a work desk in your room?
Delighted___ I expect it and like it___ No feeling___ Live with it___ Do not like___ Other___

3a. How would you feel if a coffee maker was in your room?
Delighted___ I expect it and like it___ No feeling___ Live with it___ Do not like___ Other___

3b. How do you feel when there is no coffee maker in your room?
Delighted___ I expect it and like it___ No feeling___ Live with it___ Do not like___ Other___

4a. How would you feel if you had a speaker phone in your room?
Delighted___ I expect it and like it___ No feeling___ Live with it___ Do not like___ Other___

4b. How do you feel when a speaker phone is not available in your room?
Delighted___ I expect it and like it___ No feeling___ Live with it___ Do not like___ Other___

5a. How would you feel if shampoo and conditioner were available in your room?
Delighted___ I expect it and like it___ No feeling___ Live with it___ Do not like___ Other___

5b. How do you feel when shampoo and conditioner are not available in your room?
Delighted___ I expect it and like it___ No feeling___ Live with it___ Do not like___ Other___

6a. How would you feel if you could check-in while riding in the airport van?
Delighted___ I expect it and like it___ No feeling___ Live with it___ Do not like___ Other___

6b. How do you feel when you have to check in at the front desk?
Delighted___ I expect it and like it___ No feeling___ Live with it___ Do not like___ Other___

7a. How would you feel if you had a FAX in your room?
Delighted___ I expect it and like it___ No feeling___ Live with it___ Do not like___ Other___

7b. How do you feel when you have a FAX service available at the front desk?
Delighted___ I expect it and like it___ No feeling___ Live with it___ Do not like___ Other___

What delightful surprises did you have during your stay with us?

What disappointing surprises did you have during your stay with us?

Thank you for your help in making our hotel a great place to stay!

Exhibit 12.1. Survey Form for Kano Questionnaire Used at a Hotel.

are indifferent about having a VCR (element 1) and a speaker phone (element 4) in the room, but since a large number of the survey responders found the VCR and speaker phone attractive, customizing rooms to offer these features to interested guests might be considered. Element 3, having a coffee maker in the room, was one-dimensional; guests were disappointed when it was not there and happy when it was.

The Kano survey technique provides a valid method of testing new ideas and quality concepts with customers to determine if the ideas might provide the potential to expand their expectations. In addition, the open-ended questions on the questionnaire can provide useful information about quality elements that have not yet been considered.

A note of caution: Customers do not always know what types of products and services they will want to purchase in the future. It is difficult for many customers to be imaginative. Results of focus groups and tests of prototypes can be misleading. When Coca-Cola tested "New Coke" in the 1980s, the results were very favorable, but consumers did not buy the product when it was released. Experience has shown that observation of customers is often more reliable than customer responses to surveys.

A deep understanding of the need that the product or service is intended to fulfill can provide better insight into ideas for *whats* than feedback from potential customers. This is especially true for innovative products. Frozen food, microwave ovens, the VCR, and fax machines all received negative responses when initially presented to potential customers. Sometimes the best strategy is to develop a strong belief in the idea and move ahead with developing the *hows*. Then, potential customers can experience the new product or service during pilot tests.

Developing the Hows

Depending on the specific *what*, change concepts can be used to develop the *hows*, just as they are used to eliminate quality problems and reduce costs. Following is a list of some of the change concepts that would be useful in this category of improvements (the numbers in parentheses refer to the change concepts discussed in the resource guide at the end of the book):

- Alliances and other cooperative relationships (37)
- Mass customize (63)
- Outsource for "free" (43)
- Influence or take advantage of fashion trends (67)

- Offer the product/service anytime (64)

- Offer the product/service anyplace (65)

- Other change concepts needed for solving problems or reducing costs

Although these and other change concepts are discussed in the resource guide, the first two concepts in the list deserve more in-depth coverage for Category 3 improvements.

Alliances and Other Cooperative Relationships Opening up an organization to interaction with and influence from outside groups can produce many ideas for developing changes. The people in organizations build certain capabilities and develop common thought patterns. These capabilities and thought patterns, while useful for running the day-to-day business, may inhibit innovative changes. Forming alliances with other organizations with different capabilities or thought patterns is an effective way to find the *hows* of expanding the expectations of customers.

The most common form of this method is cooperation with suppliers, especially during the design of a new product or service. However, alliances between organizations that have different capabilities and that traditionally have not worked together can be particularly fruitful in changing the expectations of customers. Examples of such alliances include government services sharing a common building and offering "one-stop shopping" to citizens; a supermarket chain and a Health Maintenance Organization (HMO) cooperating to allow nurses from the HMO to give childhood immunization and flu shots in the supermarket; and a cable television company and an information systems company forming an alliance to provide information services to cable TV subscribers.

Cooperation with competitors is another fruitful source for expanding the expectations of customers. For example, customers would like access to a certain service twenty-four hours a day, but it is not economical for an individual business to stay open all the time. Businesses offering this service could cooperate to ensure that the service is available to customers at all times.

Mass Customize Most consumers of products and services would agree that quality increases as a product or service is customized to the customer's unique circumstances. Most consumers would also expect to pay more or wait longer for these customized offerings than for a mass-produced version. Mass customization means combining the uniqueness of customized products with the efficiency of mass production. New technology may contribute to the ability to mass customize—an example is genetically engineered drugs. Following are some other methods of mass customization.

1. *Differentiating the product or service at the last moment.* One reason that a customized product or service can be costly to produce is that many combinations and a great deal of complexity are generated. By customizing at the last possible moment, standard semifinished products can be produced at relatively low price and then customized relatively cheaply.

A company that produced paint worked with their retailers to customize colors of paint to closely match the colors desired by customers. Customers brought samples of the desired colors, for example, fabric or a picture in a magazine. The retailer used a color-matching instrument consisting of an optical device and color-matching computer software to analyze the sample and suggest the appropriate mix of standard paint and pigments. This service not only increased customer satisfaction but also cut costs by significantly reducing the number of different colors that were needed in inventory.

---

2. *Using modules.* This method is related to differentiating at the last moment. The modules are mass produced and the customization is done by using different combinations of the modules.

A publishing company serving the college market found a way to customize textbooks to the course being taught. Rather than have authors write a complete textbook, they commissioned specific modules. The professors were then given the opportunity to choose from a number of different modules to assemble the text for the course. Besides the increase in quality from customization, this approach reduced the cost and time of publishing subsequent editions.

---

3. *Building knowledge of the most-likely choice.* Theoretically, there may be a limitless number of choices that people can make for a customized product. In reality, there will be a distribution of choices. Many people will choose the same "custom product." Some of the cost of customization comes from not being able to predict the distribution of choices. Costs can be significantly reduced if an accurate prediction of the distribution can be made.

A manufacturer of sportswear emphasized color rather than form in the aesthetics of its product. Many different colors and combinations of colors were made available. The steps in the manufacturing of the clothing were reordered to make dyeing the last step.

Large amounts of undyed clothes were made and some were dyed and sent to the stores. Based on the distribution of choices by customers, the remaining clothes were dyed.

---

4. *Exploiting knowledge of the cause and effect system.* Some products and services are designed to have an effect—for example, an antibiotic is designed to cure an infection, and a French class is designed to teach people to communicate in a second language. Better understanding of the cause and effect mechanisms and how they differ for different circumstances allows customized applications of the product or service.

A successful tennis camp was looking for ways to improve the teaching of tennis to adults. They recognized that individuals have different learning styles. Some learn best by hearing, others by seeing, and others by doing. The predominant learning style of each student attending the camp was ascertained at the same time their level of skill was determined. Students were grouped not only by skill level but also by learning style, and instruction was tailored to the predominant learning style of the group.

When attempting to obtain dramatic results, the usual approach to developing changes using change concepts and subject matter knowledge may need to be augmented by some other methods, such as the following:

- Creative thinking

- Technology

- Learning from other industries

- Taking advantage of superior internal capabilities (such as manufacturing or information systems)

Creative Thinking Methods for drawing out people's creativity were discussed in Chapter Five. These methods are particularly important for developing changes that result in products or services that expand the expectations of customers. They are grounded in provoking new thought patterns. The *whats* listed earlier are meant to provoke people into thinking differently about the products and services they offer.

Provocations can be developed by thinking more deeply about what quality means in a certain circumstance or for a certain group of customers. Discussing the underlying need that a product or service fulfills can free people from focusing on only existing products or services, and provoke ideas for new ways of satisfying the need. As discussed earlier, this can be done by defining quality with measurable characteristics and assessing where gaps exist with existing products (such as in the example of assessing floor coverings). By identifying these gaps, people can focus their creative energies on areas in which customers' current expectations are low. (An example of a method that can be used for creative thinking will be provided later in the chapter.)

Technology Exploiting new technologies or transferring technologies from other industries is a significant source of *hows* for expanding the expectations of customers. Usually, the technology has been developed somewhere else and is simply adapted to the new setting. For example, materials that were developed for sending people into space are now used in clothing, emergency supplies (such as the "space blanket") and even recreational equipment such as tents.

Sometimes it is the creative transfer of existing technology that provides the means for a new or enhanced product or service. Automatic Teller Machines (ATMs) are used in banks to dispense money to customers "anytime." The technology underlying the ATM could be adapted and transferred to other industries in which dispensing a product or service anytime would be a source of expanding customer expectations. Why not dispense gasoline, library books, rental cars, or common grocery items that way?

Learning from Other Industries The study of other organizations for the purpose of identifying practices or generating ideas that could be adapted and result in improvement to the organization doing the study is sometimes called *benchmarking*. Within an industry, changes spread relatively quickly. When one automotive company supplies antilock brakes, other companies will follow so as not to lose customers. Once a particular type of clothing is made popular by a retailer, other retailers must follow. Because of this rapid spread of new ideas, learning within an industry is almost a necessity in continuing to meet customer expectations and therefore avoid quality problems.

The rapid spread of ideas within industries, however, negates the wisdom of relying only on industry-specific learning to expand customer expectations. It is much more fruitful to study practices in other industries and adapt them. An organization seeking to find ways to make better decisions in a short time under pressure might study the processes used by basketball coaches and military field officers. Rental car companies seeking to find ways to dispense the keys to cars automatically so that customers can rent a car anytime with no waiting might study the ATM technology used by banks. A hospital seeking to find ways to quickly prepare a room for a new patient after the previous occupant has been discharged might study the processes used by a manufacturing organization known for its short setup times.

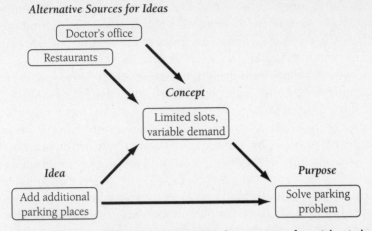

Alternative Sources for Ideas

Doctor's office

Restaurants

Concept

Limited slots, variable demand

Idea

Add additional parking places

Purpose

Solve parking problem

Figure 12.5. *Application of Concept Triangle to Learning from Other Industries.*

The *concept triangle* is a creative-thinking method that helps to generate new ideas that relate back to a particular purpose. The power of the method is that it helps to separate current ideas from the concepts to which they are attached. Once a specific idea is produced, the overall concept that inspired it is identified. This illumination of the concept is then used to produce more specific ideas.

An especially useful application of the concept triangle is when it is used to relate particular ideas from one industry (the *whats*) to solutions (the *hows*) from another industry. Figure 12.5 illustrates the use of the concept triangle in solving a parking problem at a university. The idea of making more parking spaces available was proposed as a solution to the problem. The team working on this problem then extracted the concept of "limited slots with variable demand" from this idea. Next, the team thought about how other industries have solved problems related to this concept. Two situations were identified: scheduling patients in a doctors office and managing customers in a restaurant. The team selected a leading HMO and a restaurant in town noted for its service and studied their approaches to dealing with "limited slots with variable demand."

Taking Advantage of Superior Internal Capabilities Improving internal capabilities is usually associated with solving problems or reducing costs. However, if superior capabilities exist for functions such as manufacturing, distribution, or information systems, they can often be exploited to provide products and services that would not be feasible without such superior levels of performance. For example, Federal Express created a new service built on a superior delivery system and Walmart gained its share in the retail goods market with a superior inventory and distribution system driven by information technology.

Customized products produced at low cost place a heavy burden on manufacturing. Production must be switched quickly from one product to another. There is no time to cover up problems in short production runs. Manufacturing organizations that can perform with a high level of flexibility can take advantage of this capacity to offer a wide selection of products at a reasonable cost.

Organizations that have excellent capability using information systems or other methods of information development and transfer can exploit that capability to change the expectations of customers about the information that is provided with the product or service. For example, washing instructions on garments and nutritional labeling of food products are common now and much appreciated by customers. People can consistently wash garments in an appropriate fashion, and their clothes last longer and look better. Using the information obtained from food labels, people can have more control over what they eat. (Note: these changes came about because of government mandate not because producers realized a chance to enhance their products with better information.)

Testing and Implementing the Hows

The last stage in the process of making improvements that change the expectations of customers is to test and implement the new or redesigned products and services. The focus in this stage is on integrating the *hows* into the organization's current system of production and delivery of products and services. Further development of the *whats* to match the need for particular customers or market segments can also be done at this stage.

The cycles for testing discussed in Chapter Six and the cycles for implementation discussed in Chapter Seven provide the methods used at this stage. The marketing functions in an organization usually play a leadership role in introducing these new products and services to customers. Appropriate advertising and promotion are important if innovative new ideas are to be accepted by customers who have not recognized the unfulfilled need.

Case Study: Improving Service at a Hotel

A small hotel, one of three in a town whose major employer was the large state university, had been focusing on improvement for the past three years. The hotel managers had eliminated many of the quality problems that had nagged them in the past. As a result, complaints from guests (that is, customers) were down by more than 50 percent. The management team had also redesigned many of the hotel systems to reduce costs in their operations. For example, one of the cost-reduction measures included locating the laundry room in a storage area near the front desk. This enabled employees (who at this hotel wore many hats) to do the laundry while working the registration desk at night, a slow period that offered ample free time for this task. The reduction in costs from this improvement effort allowed the hotel to maintain competitive rates.

Even with these efforts, the hotel was still only booking 70 percent of its capacity, and that percentage was highly variable. On football weekends and at other times when there were major university functions, the hotel was booked solid. At other times, it was booked well below the average 70 percent. There was some tourism in the area, but most of the steady business was from business travelers, about 65 percent of the hotel's total business. The managers decided to focus on the business travelers and go beyond simply meeting their expectations. They predicted that this approach would increase the hotel bookings. They considered making the hotel more suitable for large conferences, but for a variety of reasons they discarded that approach. The managers created a team that used the Model for Improvement to organize their improvement effort.

What are we trying to accomplish? The goal was to expand the expectations of the hotel's business guests by offering new services or features that make their business travel easier and more productive.

Guidance: Improvement would be focused on the individual traveler. Some improvements were expected to also benefit small groups that stayed for business meetings. A booking rate of more than 80 percent was perceived as desirable to remain profitable in the future.

How will we know that a change is an improvement? The primary measure of success for the improvement team assigned to this initiative was the percentage of capacity utilized. Historically, it had been about 70 percent. The team started a run chart using capacity data for the previous four weeks. A booking rate of more than 80 percent would provide a good operating profit and allow the hotel to consider investing in some of the conference services they had deferred.

Developing What Will Expand Customer Expectations

What changes can we make that will result in improvement? Some of the members of the team had traveled on business in previous jobs and two had traveled as part of their jobs with the hotel. Based on these experiences, they felt they had some data that was acquired by putting themselves in the role of the guest. They used this knowledge to discuss some features that might be of interest to business travelers. One member suggested putting a fax machine in each room. He noted that the number of faxes that were being sent and received at the front desk was increasing. The team decided that a creative thinking session to expand on this idea would be a good way to develop some more ideas for changes.

The team held a meeting to develop some ideas for changes. One of the members skilled in creative thinking offered the provocation of making the hotel "the office away from the office." This provocation brought out some ideas about features that could be offered in the hotel room, but also led to an interesting conversation about getting in and out of the hotel, which was very different from getting in and out of an office. The discussions that took place during two team meetings resulted in the following ideas for changes:

1. Provide a fax machine in each room.
2. Provide a speaker phone in each room.
3. Allow people to rent rooms in twenty-four-hour blocks.
4. Allow guests to go directly to the room at check-in without stopping at the front desk.

These four changes were the *whats* that the team felt could potentially change the expectations of guests. They knew of no hotel that had all four features as part of their service. There was some discussion of the *hows* of accomplishing the changes that they felt would be very attractive to their business guests. Some on the team reacted critically to the changes, particularly concerning the check-in and check-out procedures. However, they skillfully managed the three modes of thinking (creative, logical positive, and logical negative) that were present and agreed on the next cycle.

Testing What Will Expand Customer Expectations

Cycle 1 The team decided that before they worked on the *hows* for accomplishing the four changes, they would run a cycle to test whether business travelers would feel that the four changes were actually attractive. The survey they used is shown in Exhibit 12.2.

Over the course of the next month, the survey was administered to thirty business travelers. Fifteen of the travelers were steady guests who were deliberately selected and the other fifteen were chosen at random.

After studying the results, the team concluded that the new check-in and check-out procedures and the fax machine in the room would be very attractive to business guests. The speaker phone got mixed results in the survey and was abandoned for the first round of testing. In response to the open-ended question, several people said they had fax capability in their laptop computer and needed only the ability to plug the computer into a phone jack.

Developing the Hows

Cycle 2 The team needed to develop the *hows* for the three changes that the business travelers had found attractive. The team had three meetings and also worked between meetings to plan the cycle. They found out that they could rent fax

---

Survey to Test the Attractiveness of Hotel Changes to Business Travelers.
Answer each of the following questions using the following scale:

1. I dislike it that way

2. I can live with it that way

3. I am neutral

4. I would be delighted if it were that way

5. I expect it that way and it must be that way

6. Other

1. Check-out time:
   When your check-out time is twenty-four hours after check-in, how do you feel?
   When you have a fixed check-out time regardless of when you check-in, how do you feel?
2. Speaker phone:
   When you have a speaker phone in your room, how do you feel?
   When you do not have a speaker phone in your room, how do you feel?
3. Fax machine:
   When you have a fax machine in your room, how do you feel?
   When you do not have a fax machine in your room but can send faxes at the front desk, how do you feel?
4. Check-in:
   When you can go directly to your room and then call the front desk to check in, how do you feel?
   When you must check in at the front desk, how do you feel?
Do you have any other suggestions for improvement?

Exhibit 12.2. *Survey to Test the Attractiveness of Hotel Changes to Business Travelers.*

machines for one month to test in a few rooms. A lot of creative thinking was needed, particularly to develop the means to enable travelers to go directly to their rooms. The three modes of thinking—creative, logical positive, and logical negative—were managed during the meetings by all members of the team (one of the members with more experience paid special attention to it).

One of the provocations used in the first meeting to promote creative thinking was "let the room come to the guest." This did not produce any ideas for the check-in or check-out procedures, but it did generate a new idea: putting a small number of rooms at the airport and forming an alliance to clean them with the company that maintained the airport. Implementing the new check-in and check-out ideas would make this new idea even more feasible. The idea was presented to the hotel manager and formed the basis of a new improvement project.

The team met with the head of housekeeping to discuss the impact of changes in check-in and check-out procedures. The operational changes to accomplish the new check-out procedure were relatively simple. The major processes that were affected were cleaning and room scheduling. Some relatively minor changes were developed that might actually smooth the work load of the cleaners, possibly making them more efficient.

The operational changes to accomplish the check-in process were more drastic. The team almost abandoned the change but was spurred on by the strong support for the change in the survey. To provoke some new thought patterns, the team thought about how other industries approached similar problems. One member had recently rented a car and was able to use her credit card in an ATM-like machine to choose a car and get the key without stopping at the rental desk. This discussion resulted in some movement in the team's thinking and some ideas for practical changes to their system to accommodate the new check-in procedure. Most of the solutions addressed how to get the room key to the guest if they did not stop at the desk.

One of the members, in an attempt to get some more creative ideas, used the "attack the solution" provocation by saying "one does not need a key to get into the room." The team then developed an idea of using an approved credit card to get into the room. Available rooms and their features could be posted on an electronic board in the lobby, and the guest could simply choose one that best matched his or her needs. This approach also had some promise for letting guests choose the features they wanted (such as the few who really wanted a speaker phone). In a sense, guests could customize their rooms. This change would take some adaptation of technology that was currently being used in other industries. The team planned some background work but did not test the change in cycle 2.

Testing and Implementing the Hows

The plan for cycle 2 was completed. During the next month, ten fax machines would be rented and installed in some rooms. These rooms would be offered to the steady business guests who had responded to the survey, as well as two additional guests each day (selected at check-in). The first ten guests each day would be given the new twenty-four-hour check-out option on a trial basis. The data would be reviewed daily at first, and then less frequently as problems with the new procedures were eliminated. Guests would be asked if they had used the fax and how they felt about having it in the room. Guests would also be asked about the check-out procedures, and data on their check-out times would be recorded.

After two weeks it became apparent that both of the changes were being well received by guests. Forty percent of the guests used the FAX in their room when it was available. Some who did not use it said they would have had they known it was going to be in the room. Almost all were delighted that it was available. People who checked in late at night but did not have a meeting until the next afternoon were particularly delighted by being able to check out late the next day at no extra charge (as were business travelers who had brought members of their family with them). Only 15 percent of guests checked out later than they would have under the old procedure, but many mentioned that they were pleased to have that flexibility available. The team members decided to let the test run to completion, but they recommended that fax machines be purchased and began developing plans to make the check-out procedures permanent.

Cycles 3 and 4 The team used these two cycles to implement the two changes tested in cycle 2. Cycle 3 included making decisions about how many fax machines to install, and equipping rooms so that laptop computers with fax capabilities could be used. Also during these cycles, the team developed marketing materials to advertise the new, attractive features to potential guests.

Cycles 5, 6, and 7 Cycles 5 and 6 focused on the new check-in procedure. During cycle 5, selected guests used their credit cards to get into a room after choosing the room from a display near the elevator in the lobby. This test was successful, and cycles 6 and 7 were used to implement these changes.

Figure 12.6 contains a run chart of weekly occupancy rates for the two months before the changes began, the two months while the changes were being tested and implemented, and the two months after the three changes were implemented.

The team felt that they had been successful in making changes that their guests found attractive. Plans for new improvement initiatives to expand the expectations of guests included the following:

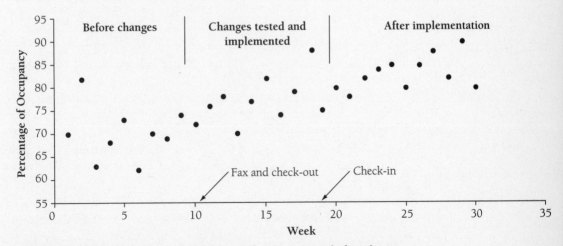

Figure 12.6. *Run Chart for Hotel Occupancy Before, During, and After Changes.*

- Rooms at the airport

- Changes focused on small conferences in the hotel

- Changes affecting family members traveling with someone on business

Conclusion

This chapter has explored use of the Model for Improvement for Category 3 improvements, in which the aim is to expand the expectations of customers either by developing innovative products and services or by developing innovative ways of providing existing products and services, so that customers will perceive the products and services as having unusually high value. The methods for changing the expectations of customers introduced in this chapter can be applied continually and routinely by a variety of people.

Improvement in Category 3 facilitates the fulfillment of the chain reaction introduced in Figure 9.1—that is, it results in increases in revenue and market share, and growth in job opportunities. A predictable stream of new products and services that raise the expectations of customers because of their very high value is the output of this category. By making such changes, an organization can expect to grow and develop, not just become more effective and efficient.

Coordinating the three categories of change introduced in Chapters Ten, Eleven, and Twelve requires leadership, the final ingredient for integrating improvement into an organization. The next chapter defines leadership and presents methods for creating it.

CHAPTER 13

Guidance for Leaders

The science of improvement is the basis of an important and emerging technology that affords organizations the means of rapidly making improvements. This technology is based, however, on knowledge and know-how, not hardware. It cannot simply be installed in an organization like a new piece of equipment, or built like a new wing on a building. This reality creates some challenges for leaders. This chapter discusses how to establish an organizational environment that is conducive to improvement, and how to build a system to support improvement.

Establishing an environment that is conducive to improvement is dependent upon a number of factors. For that reason, this chapter does not offer prescriptions for leaders, only advice. This advice is based on observations of skilled and unskilled leaders, and on experience in helping organizations excel at improvement. Leading improvement skillfully is more art than science. The leader must strike some difficult balances (such as between short-term demands on time and the need to make improvements in the long term).

Establishing a system of improvement that provides a framework for leading change is a high priority. Five key activities provide the structure for leaders to drive, manage, and support the organization in its improvement efforts:

1. Establishing and communicating the purpose of the organization
2. Viewing the organization as a system
3. Designing and managing a system for gathering information for improvement
4. Conducting planning for improvement and integrating it with business planning
5. Managing individual and team improvement activities

Each of these activities is discussed in detail later in the chapter.

The term "leader" is used in this chapter in the broadest sense: anyone can assume a leadership role. Leaders obtain their power from three sources: (1) authority of position, (2) knowledge, and (3) personality and persuasive power. A successful leader knows to use all three of these sources of power appropriately to make things happen. People in management positions have an obligation to provide leadership, but managers have the opportunity to build on this given base and to become more effective as leaders when they choose to develop and use their knowledge and persuasive power. In many organizations, nonmanagement people have developed their expert knowledge and persuasive power in order to assume a leadership role. History and business literature are replete with stories of these *informal* leaders.

Establishing an Environment Conducive to Improvement

Organizations differ dramatically in their cultures. Differences can even occur between divisions of the same organization. Some hint of an organization's culture may be formally written in the organization's purpose statements or in statements of belief established by the founders. More often than not, however, those in the organization are left to make inferences about the culture from observed behaviors. For an organization's stakeholders, the ability to read the culture and to play one's role can be very difficult depending on how new members are introduced to the organization's "microsociety." The culture may be one in which most decisions are made at the top, or conversely, one in which decisions are primarily made by consensus; it may be a culture in which people are given freedom to try different approaches, or one in which people are expected to follow protocols before making changes; it may support standardization of processes, or it may view standardization as an infringement upon professional judgement.

The leaders of an organization may choose to undertake a major change in the culture of the organization. A system for focusing and managing improvement and the Model for Improvement can be used to guide this cultural change. The application of the science and art of improvement is not limited to any particular culture, however. Part of the art of improvement is to adapt the methods to the strengths and weaknesses of different cultures.

Regardless of the culture, there are some basics that must be in place if an organization is to be successful at the broad objective of *making changes that lead to improvement from the viewpoint of the customer.* This chapter discusses the following attributes of leadership, which contribute to an organizational environment that is conducive to improvement:

- Creating the desire for continuous improvement
- Creating an environment that nurtures mutual respect among people
- Providing encouragement
- Promoting cooperation

The chapter also addresses particular weaknesses that are difficult to overcome.

Creating the Desire for Continuous Improvement

The broad objective to make changes that lead to improvement from the viewpoint of the customer requires an environment in which people are motivated to improve the system and its products. This motivation comes from

- A belief that the purpose of the organization is worthwhile
- An intrinsic desire on the part of people to improve
- A system that allows people to enjoy their work and to take pride in its outcomes
- An environment that provides the time for people to participate in improvement
- Recognition and appreciation of efforts to improve

People naturally enjoy and are motivated by improving what they do. As leaders learn to rely on these intrinsic motivators, they need to rely less on outside, or extrinsic, motivators such as bonuses, awards, competition, and the trappings of success. Reliance on an extrinsic motivator often promotes short-term thinking and competition. An extrinsic motivator can divert attention and energy from the purpose of the organization; attaining the extrinsic motivator frequently becomes the aim.

Creating an Environment That Nurtures Mutual Respect Among People

The leader often is responsible for the success of the entire organization, and at times must be firm in the face of significant opposition to change. This firmness must be balanced by an environment of mutual respect among all members of the organization. Not everyone is equal in experience or competence, but everyone has equal worth as human beings. Given a genuine desire to increase the level of respect in an organization, the following tips can help leaders to attain this goal:

- Let people know that you do not have all the answers. Most organizations are complex and face an ever-increasing rate of change. Everyone must help one another to be successful. This behavior should begin at the top to help create an environment that fosters learning.

- Listen and respond with empathy.

- Minimize negative talk, including put-downs relative to a person's position in the organization, threats, harangues, name-calling, imitating, and comparisons for the purpose of embarrassing.

- Watch your tone of voice when communicating; when trying to persuade, talk in a firm but friendly way.

- Watch nonverbal behaviors such as facial expressions, posture, and gestures.

- Drive out excessive fear and/or complacency in the organization.

- Show sincere interest in the opinions of others and the reasons behind them.

To assess the level of mutual respect in your interactions, envision your communication with someone with whom you have a mutually respectful relationship. Use this way of relating as the standard by which to judge your communication with others.

Providing Encouragement

To encourage is to inspire with courage, spirit, or hope. When changes are being developed, tested, and implemented, people need all the courage, spirit, and hope they can get. Someone who is encouraged feels that they are responsible for something, have a say in how things are done, and have some control over the changes to be made. Conversely, someone who is discouraged feels compelled to keep quiet and do exactly as they are told.

Encouragement and discouragement come from the systems in which people work and from the interactions they have with others. People can be very discouraged when beset with problems occurring from bad systems, especially if there is no time or resources to solve problems or address the overall system issues. A leader can provide significant encouragement simply by improving the systems in which people work and by giving them opportunities to make improvements in their daily work. Ideally, everyone in the organization should be able to point to some change they are testing this week and what they are learning.

Providing good systems and the chance for people to improve is not all that is needed to encourage people in an organization. Encouraging purposeful interaction among people is required for most organizations to make improvements. Leaders may need to change their own patterns of communication and behavior. Some means of obtaining encouraging interactions include

- Asking for help in solving problems and making improvements

- Offering help without taking responsibility

- Showing confidence in people by communicating positive expectations

- Expressing appreciation for efforts and contributions

A bottom-line question that is useful to ask yourself before communicating with someone is, *What can I communicate that will make this person more willing to make improvements?*

Promoting Cooperation

Thinking of the organization as a system or as an *interdependent group of items, people, or processes working together toward a common purpose* makes it easy to see that there are substantial dependencies among people and departments within an organization. It becomes apparent that there are important customer and supplier relationships within an organization. The work of an individual or a group (supplier) is used by another individual or group (customer) in the organization. The two groups are thus linked in a supplier-customer relationship. Understanding these ideas keeps the focus of the system on the customer and helps people avoid suboptimization.

Systems are interrelated people and processes. Changes to one part of a system will reverberate in another part. For example, a loss taken on one part of a system can have a net effect of a gain for the entire system. Many high-impact changes cut across internal organizational boundaries. If a step in a process is a bottleneck, some of the work of that step can be moved to another process. Even if the new process is less efficient, it should reduce the impact of the bottleneck and increase the productivity of the system.

These and other attributes of systems make it obvious that without cooperation among members, an organization will be severely limited in the number of improvements that can be accomplished. Achieving cooperation among people and organizational entities is one of the biggest contributions a leader can make to an organization's ability to improve.

An environment of mutual respect and encouragement is a good start towards fostering cooperation. However, before people can cooperate they must know the common purpose of the system in which they reside. Without knowledge of this common purpose, people will avoid or fail to consider decisions that lead to cooperative improvement of the system.

The Leader's Role

The art of leading improvement requires a leader to have the ability to think about the many combinations of people, processes, customers, suppliers, and other factors in a system and how those ingredients can be integrated to help an organization achieve its purpose, strategic goals, or vision. Leaders who can think holistically in this fashion, who can communicate and persuade others, can accelerate improvement in their organization. Each leader will need to adapt this role to his or her own style, situation, and inclinations. Playing the role will require theory, vision, personal drive, and a practical plan.

In addition to the role of setting an appropriate environment, leaders also have a more *structured* task to accomplish: building the infrastructure to drive and support improvement in the organization.

Building the System of Improvement

There are many things that must happen if an organization is to continually make changes that lead to improvement from the viewpoint of the customer. Establishment of a system of improvement to provide a framework for leading change is a high priority. As mentioned earlier, five key activities can be used by leaders to drive, manage, and support the organization toward this aim. Again, these are:

1. Establishing and communicating the purpose of the organization
2. Viewing the organization as a system
3. Designing and managing a system for gathering information for improvement
4. Conducting planning for improvement and integrating it with business planning
5. Managing individual and team improvement activities

These activities are focused on aligning all of the improvement efforts in an organization so that the changes developed and implemented move the organization in a desired direction. The activities are very interdependent and have to be considered as a system. This approach protects against suboptimization from independently managed individual improvement efforts.

Establishing and Communicating the Purpose of the Organization

Change requires direction. It is the job of the leader to provide direction by recognizing and communicating the purpose of the organization. *The purpose of the organization is the reason the organization exists, the need in society that it fulfills.* Unless the organization fulfills a worthwhile and long-term need, it may not have a market in the future.

Constancy of purpose is the first of Deming's fourteen points for management and the one he emphasized as the most important. If an organization is to function as a system, then everyone in the organization must know what the common purpose of the organization is and how their work helps to achieve that purpose. Developing and communicating a formal statement of purpose provides a common understanding of the business to stakeholders. Developing such a statement is a role for the leaders of the organization, and an obligation of the top managers.

Simply stating the purpose of the organization is not enough, however, to obtain constancy of purpose. It is also necessary to provide an environment in which everyone in the organization can work towards the purpose. It is easy to get focused on daily problems and forget that the long-term existence of the company depends on allocating resources to the future. Constancy of purpose in an organization is aided by leaders doing the following:

- Communicating the purpose throughout the organization

- Using the purpose statement to provide the broad aim for all improvement efforts

- Allocating resources for research

- Allocating resources for education and training

- Balancing short-term needs with long-term improvements in products and services

- Providing opportunities for everyone in the organization to participate in improvement

It is difficult for an organization to have constancy of purpose unless everyone in the organization knows *why* the organization exists. Even in small organizations, people often have different ideas about the purpose of the organization. One way for leaders to communicate the purpose is to develop a statement that would explain the mission; the values, beliefs, or tenets; and the vision of the organization. The *mission* should include the need in society or in the marketplace that the organization is attempting to fulfill, and the core business of the organization. The values, beliefs, or tenets define how members of the organization can be expected to conduct themselves in carrying out the mission. The *vision* provides insight on where the organization is going in the future. Some other possible components of the purpose statement are roles, themes, and slogans.

Following is the purpose statement for Bulk Transport, a fictional trucking company based on two actual companies that transport chemicals and other bulk materials for the process industries:

Mission

Modern society and the process industries require the safe transportation and distribution of intermediate and finished products. Bulk Transport provides the necessary logistical and delivery systems to ensure that we deliver the right products to the right place and on time.

Tenets

Customers and their satisfaction are critical to the long-term prosperity of our company. Satisfaction is achieved not only by meeting the wants and desires of our customers but also through understanding and matching their need for our service.

Associates at Bulk Transport ensure professional service through their knowledge. Knowledge is fostered by a program of ongoing development, education, and training for all Bulk Transport associates.

Safety and the environment are not to be sacrificed as we carry out our mission. Bulk transport provides a system that is aimed at providing safe working conditions for our associates, suppliers, customers, and the communities in which we operate. The environment in which we operate demands that we properly dispose of and recycle materials to ensure that the health of our associates, the public, and the environment is protected.

Profit is the cost of staying in business in the future. All stakeholders of Bulk Transport should profit from their relationship with our company.

Vision

To be known as the carrier of choice for safe, on-time delivery.

Exhibit 13.1. *Purpose Statement for Bulk Transport.*

It sometimes appears unnecessary to spend time communicating the purpose of an organization. Writing down a statement of purpose can appear to be redundant to what is supposedly already known by everyone in the organization. But does everyone really understand the purpose of the organization and their role in achieving that purpose? The purpose should be communicated by educating people in the system about the meaning of the statement of purpose, relating the statement to their work, and sharing the definitions of key words and concepts.

Sometimes, in their desire to be as complete and comprehensive as possible, leaders create purpose statements that are too detailed and not very useful for guiding the organization on an everyday basis. It is sometimes helpful for the leaders to develop a *theme* that simplifies the purpose and makes the focus of the organization more concrete. This allows the everyday actions of people and the improvement efforts to be more easily directed toward a common goal. The following are some examples of themes for different organizations:

Organization	*Theme*
Trucking of chemicals	On-time, clean, dry, and odor free
Police department	To serve and protect
Hospital	Better care at lower cost
Food company	Feeding people better
Automobile company	Quality is job one!
Car rental service	We're number two, we try harder!
School district	Preparing all children to be citizens

If not used continually, the statement of purpose has minimal impact on the organization. The following is a partial list of uses for a statement of purpose:

- To introduce and manage change in the organization (see Chapter Seven for more on this issue)

- To provide input to decisions at all levels of the organization

- To serve as a basis for feedback to those in the organization who conflict with the purpose

- To provide input to strategic and business planning

- As a tool to communicate with customers, suppliers, potential employees, and the community

- As an aid to innovation, by reminding people of the need that the organization's products and services fulfill

- As input to developing a view of the organization as a system

The purpose statement is a useful tool for the leadership to use to communicate and encourage cooperation, mutual respect, and other necessary behaviors to help people in a system to change and to align their energies.

Viewing the Organization as a System

Efforts to raise the important issues within an organization and to develop and implement changes related to these issues must be continuous, coordinated, and focused on the organization's common purpose. To accomplish this, an organization must recognize itself as a system and operate as a system. A system is an interdependent group of items, people, or processes with a common purpose.

The "systems view" is an important way for leaders to think about their organizations. Different departments, people, equipment, facilities, and functions make up an organization. A leader's job is to *integrate* these diverse components so that they accomplish the common purpose of the system. Ultimately, the success of an organization will depend on this integration.

The typical organization chart is hierarchical in nature, depicts the organization as a group of independent departments, and describes the reporting relationship for people in the organization. This view does not support the interdependence of the various parts of the organization or show how work is accomplished. The organization chart can thus be compared to a sports team's player roster. In contrast, a systems view defines the interdependent processes by which work is accomplished. It can be compared to the sports team's play book. Both the roster and the play book are important, but neither is sufficient. Figures 13.1 and 13.2 compare the two views of an organization. Figure 13.1

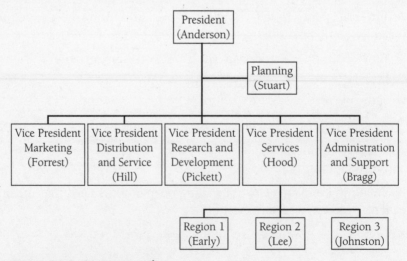

***Figure 13.1.** Organization Chart.*

depicts the organization as an organization chart; Figure 13.2 provides a systems view of the same organization. The second figure is a modification of Deming's figure "Production Viewed as a System." The systems view provides the general framework for describing how an organization works to accomplish its purpose.

Figure 13.2 depicts a general view of any organization as a system. Some important aspects of this view include:

- The need in society is the primary focus and provides the aim for efforts to improve.

- Suppliers and customers are closely connected to the system.

- The feedback loop shows the system for improvement.

- Customer research and planning are prerequisites for improvement.

- Improvement results from design or redesign of some aspect of the system.

- Everyone in the organization should participate in improvement.

When describing how work gets accomplished in a specific organization, it is useful to show the key processes that constitute the system. Leaders should understand how improvement of each process is measured and how it relates to improvement of the system as a whole. A leader's responsibility then is to help develop conceptual designs for changes at the process level.

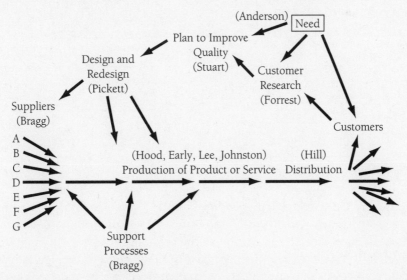

Figure 13.2. The Organization Viewed as a System.

SOURCE: Adapted with permission from Deming, W. Out of the Crisis. Cambridge: Massachusetts Institute of Technology, 1986, p. 4.

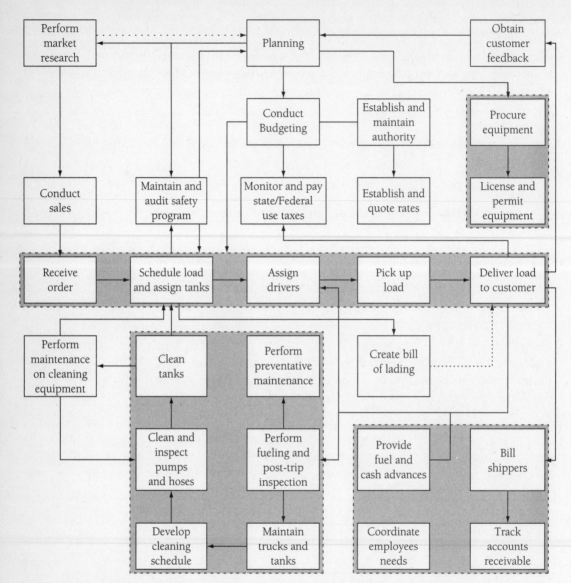

Figure 13.3. *Bulk Transport as a System.*

Figure 13.3 illustrates the system of Bulk Transport by linking the key processes in the organization. The center of the diagram describes those processes that are utilized to accomplish the company's mission, to provide logistical and delivery capability. The processes at the bottom of the diagram are the secondary processes that support the primary processes. The processes at the top of the diagram are the secondary processes that are used to gather customer intelligence, plan the business, and so on.

Bulk Transport may use its system diagram as follows:

1. To apply systems-thinking concepts
2. To encourage recognition of internal customer/supplier relationships and interdependence within the organization
3. To focus problem-solving and improvement efforts on the processes in the organization, not just on individual departments or people
4. To provide a structure of the organization that can be used to implement various programs and for measurement (such as activity-based accounting)
5. To train new employees
6. To standardize systems (on projects, in terminals, and so on)
7. As a data collection form when studying the Bulk Transport system
8. To communicate with customers, suppliers, and other stakeholders about their roles in the system
9. To organizing research information, suggestions, and ideas that are generated in the organization so that they can be incorporated into the planning process

To decide whether a system is moving closer to accomplishing its purpose, some measurement of the system should be done. A common force for suboptimizing a system is the attempt to define its performance by a single measure (or a few measures concentrated in one area). Examples of such measures are return on investment, throughput, percentage of legal cases won, scores on standardized tests, and volume of sales. Given one measure of success, almost any group can be successful in the short-term by improving that measure at the expense of other important measures—for example, profits can be increased in the short-term by decreasing investment in research and development.

Improvement of a system results in the improvement of a family of measures. The family of measures should serve as both indicators of present performance and predictors of how the system will perform in the future. These measures should relate to a variety of dimensions of the system, such as customers, employees, business and financial dimensions, operations, and outside environment. One way to develop a family of measures is to use the purpose statement as a guide. Leaders should review each part of the purpose statement and decide how it could be measured. In the beginning, it is best to identify a set of ten or fewer and establish a system for collecting the appropriate data for regular review. This set of measures can then be added to over time.

It is the responsibility of leaders to ensure that everyone in an organization understands the measures, the important relationships among the measures, and which measures will act as predictors of future performance. Bulk Transport uses the following family of ten measures to understand their organization:

1. Difference between scheduled and actual time of delivery
2. Accounts receivable over sixty days
3. Accidents
4. Breakdowns
5. Number of improvements per associate made to the Bulk Transport system
6. Profits per associate
7. Revenue per associate
8. Turnover rate of drivers
9. Absenteeism
10. Maintenance costs per mile driven

Figure 13.4 displays the first five of these measures using control charts. Each of the measures depends on many processes within Bulk Transport. When considering the health of the company, the measures are viewed as a family. To implement change, during a given period the organization may have to lose ground in one measure in order to improve other measures and the system as a whole. Obviously, everyone would like to have their cake and eat it too, and foster change that avoids tradeoffs—for example, to develop a strategy in which revenue per associate will improve as breakdowns are improved. This would occur as a process for maintaining tractors and tank trailers is developed, tested, and implemented. After the change is implemented and the predicted results are captured, then revenue would change to a new level, preferably as predicted.

Having a common purpose and viewing the organization as a system helps everyone in making decisions and taking actions. Leaders must daily reinforce the view of the organization as a system, at both formal and informal meetings and by example. Monitoring a set of systemwide measures allows leaders to learn whether the changes made to products, services, processes, and subsystems are improving the organization as a whole.

Designing a System to Gather Information for Improvement

An important aspect of focusing on improvement is to find ways to better meet the present and future needs of customers. This requires gathering information from both present and potential customers. Chapters Ten, Eleven, and Twelve discussed sources of data that are useful for focusing improvement efforts in the three categories of improvement. This activity of gathering information focuses on the system to regularly obtain, analyze, and distribute these data.

There are usually two purposes for gathering information for improvement of a system. The first purpose is obvious: to build the knowledge of those who are obtaining the information. The second purpose is to obtain a desired effect on the relationship between those obtaining the information and those providing

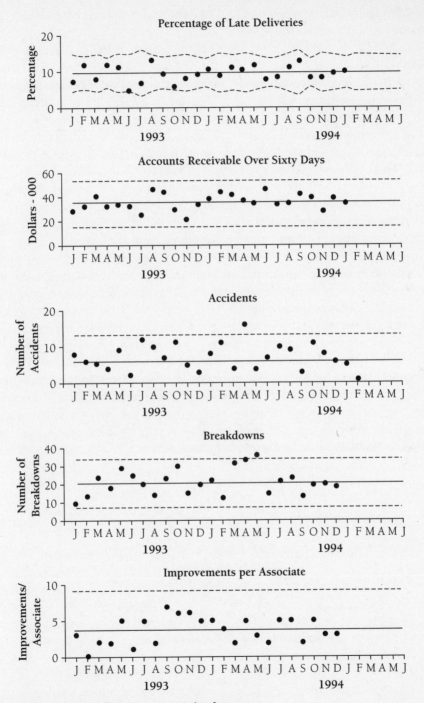

Figure 13.4. *Bulk Transport's Family of Measures.*

the information. Both purposes should be kept in mind when planning to gather information.

Obtaining useful information from people can be difficult. Customers often are not able to articulate what types of products or services could better match their needs. This often results in the primary source of information being negative. Examples of negative sources of information include complaints, warranty claims, and returns. Leaders must react to this information and consider it important in helping to eliminate quality problems. Relying on it totally, however, is not sufficient to provide the basis for a system of continuous improvement that will set off the chain reaction introduced in Chapter Nine.

Methods that are proactive in gathering information are needed. Information should be gathered to monitor the quality of current products and services and to help in the development of new products and services. Figure 13.5 shows the three levels of information that can be obtained from customers.

Generally, these three levels can be related to the three categories of improvement. Problem solving will obviously relate to Category 1, solving quality problems. Urgency oftentimes rules the day and organizations must solve not only problems, but *immediate problems.* If not resolved, problems could result in immediate, undesirable consequences. Category 2, reducing costs, would typically be addressed with current matching issues; that is, issues related to the extent of the match of current products and services to the needs of customers—for example, how can an organization reduce costs related to the products and services it is currently offering? However, information gathered in this area could be used to address Category 1 issues. Future matching would involve products and services of which the customer is usually unaware, and would relate to Category 3, expanding the expectations of customers.

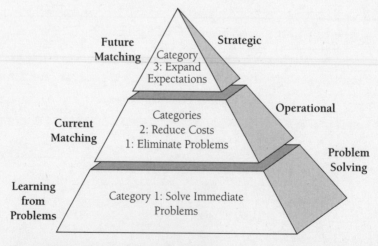

Figure 13.5. *Three Levels of Information.*

A variety of methods may be used to obtain information from people in a proactive way. Informal conversation with people concerning their needs is one method. More formal methods include written surveys, personal interviews, group interviews, observation, and trading places. In order for the information to be useful for improvement, a system must exist for gathering, summarizing, analyzing, and communicating. Such a system should

- Assist in the identification of ideas in the three categories of improvement.

- Gather information from present and potential customers.

- Gather information to support the design of new products and services.

- Gather information from groups such as employees, suppliers, investors, the community, and so on.

- Use information already available in the organization such as existing customer contacts.

- Operate continuously and be coordinated with the organization's everyday activities.

Figure 13.6 illustrates the key parts of the information system used by Bulk Transport. The system supports the efforts of the company in the following ways

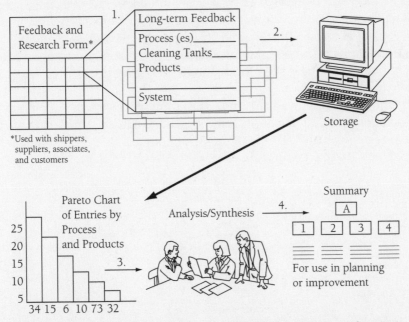

Figure 13.6. *Bulk Transport's System for Gathering and Organizing Information.*

(the list corresponds to the numbers on the figure):

1. It provides a structure for recording feedback from customers as well as observations by drivers, management personnel, salespeople, or anyone at Bulk Transport who interfaces with customers or potential customers.
2. It supports the ability to document both immediate reaction to problems and possible market opportunities for business or improvement in the future. It also enhances the ability of Bulk Transport to store information and retrieve it for later planning and improvement efforts.
3. One output of the system is designed to summarize information for use in the strategic or business planning process.
4. When individuals or teams are chartered to make specific improvements, information is retrieved on products and/or processes so that the voice of the customer is used in developing, testing, and implementing changes.

Planning

Once a system to gather information is in place, the information obtained can then become a useful input to planning for improvement. Planning provides leaders of an organization with a significant opportunity to establish direction, policies, and focus, and to allocate the organization's resources.

Leaders can undertake different types of planning. The purposes of planning can be divided into two categories: planning to operate the present system and planning to improve the system (see Figure 13.7). For example, developing a plan to carry out an advertising campaign supports operation within the present system, while evaluation and improvement of advertising alternatives (policies) is a plan to improve the system for the future. Planning in either category could be short-term or long-term.

By planning for improvement, an organization will stay focused on satisfying its customers. Planning for improvement is not intended to be a substitute for business planning or market planning. It is important that these different types

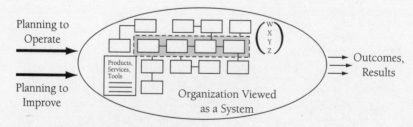

Figure 13.7. *Two Purposes of Planning.*

of planning be integrated into a general system. How can a leader decide if an organization's current planning system has incorporated planning for improvement? The following five criteria can be used to make such an assessment:

1. The system includes objectives to improve the organization from the viewpoint of customers.
2. The system balances short-term and long-term needs.
3. The system identifies what part of the organization will be designed or redesigned.
4. The system provides information to set priorities for the design of new products and services.
5. The system includes the allocation of resources for improvement.

To develop a system of planning that achieves these criteria, leaders must have available to them information from customers, employees, suppliers, and other stakeholders of the organization, and from the environment in which the organization operates. Planning for improvement should accomplish the following:

1. It should provide strategic objectives. What are the *ends* that need to be achieved? What are the focus areas for the organization for the next two to five years?
2. It should identify improvement efforts. What *ways* will be developed to design or redesign the system to accomplish the organization's purpose? Which products or processes must be designed or redesigned?
3. It should identify and assign resources. What *means* will be used to help implement the identified efforts for operating and improving the system? Will more time, equipment, or people be needed?

The three categories of improvement play a key role in providing structure to the planning efforts. Leaders should learn during the planning process in which category to focus their activities. Although the plan will usually focus on one particular category, it will often include activities in the other two categories as well. The change concepts identified in Chapters Ten, Eleven, and Twelve play a key role in finding methods to focus improvement initiatives.

Bulk Transport uses a process of planning for improvement that produces strategic objectives, defines improvement efforts, and assigns resources, summarized in Figure 13.8. The first step in the process is to develop strategic objectives to improve the organization. Figure 13.9 shows how such objectives are based on the synthesis of several strands of information. Some of these pieces of information might be contradictory or even confusing. It is the job of leadership to study the information from the system and then determine a course of action.

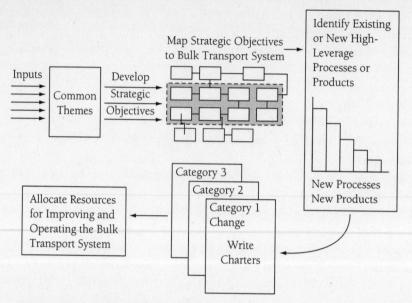

Figure 13.8. *Bulk Transport's Planning System.*

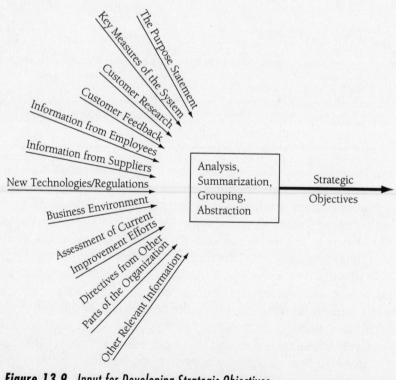

Figure 13.9. *Input for Developing Strategic Objectives.*

Developing strategic objectives for improvement should be viewed as a learning process. This process should include gathering needed information, sharing it with other leaders in the system, and then analyzing, summarizing, and grouping the information so that an appropriate course of action can be developed.

Using this approach, Bulk Transport reviewed all the relevant inputs to their system and developed the following strategic objective, and then related them to the categories of improvement (1 = eliminate problems; 2 = reduce costs; 3 = expand customer expectations):

Strategic Objective	*Category of Improvement*
Improve on-time delivery performance	1, 3
Develop a company-wide system for hiring and developing skilled people	3
Improve ability to develop business in new markets	3
Identify and develop more customer alliances	2, 3
Improve the system for maintaining trucks and tanks at all terminal locations	1, 2

The next step in the Bulk Transport planning process is to answer the question, *What processes, products, and services must be improved to accomplish the strategic objectives?* This step involves mapping the strategic objectives onto existing products and processes as well as potential ones. The purpose is to identify a few products or processes that could be improved in order to meet the strategic objective. Once these high priority processes and products are identified, then the next steps in the planning process are taken: charters are written and resources are assigned.

Writing charters is one of the greatest leverage points for leaders in this system of improvement. A charter (see Chapter Four for more information) usually contains a general description of what is to be achieved and some guidance on what is expected in terms of results and/or boundaries for the individual or team that is going to use the charter. Table 13.1 lists the charters developed by the Bulk Transport system (each charter is usually related to one or more processes or products) and the strategic objectives that are supported by the charters.

The following guidelines have proved to be useful in writing the charter.

1. *Make sure that the current way of doing things is not an alternative.* No matter how poorly it performs, the current system will be the most attractive option to many people. It is familiar, and people have established a routine and "optimized" their work from their individual point of view. Some of this optimization

Table 13.1. *Bulk Transport's Charters and Associated Strategic Objectives.*

CHARTER	STRATEGIC OBJECTIVES SUPPORTED
Improve the process of developing alliances	#4 Identify and develop more customer alliances
Improve the process by which we develop people	#2 Develop a company-wide system for the hiring and development of skilled people #3 Improve our ability to develop business in new markets #4 Identify and develop more customer alliances
Develop a standard method of cleaning tanks for use in all terminals	#1 Improve on time delivery performance #5 Improve the Bulk Transport system for maintaining trucks and tanks at all terminal locations
Use the upgraded information technology system to improve the process by which we quote prices for the pick-up and delivery of hazardous products.	#3 Improve our ability to develop business in new markets #4 Identify and develop more customer alliances
Improve the process by which we schedule and perform preventative maintenance of tanks	#1 Improve on time delivery performance #4 Identify and develop more customer alliances #5 Improve the Bulk Transport system for maintaining trucks and tanks at all terminal locations

may be to work around a bad system. Many individuals or teams approach improvement efforts with the assumption that if they cannot find a better alternative, the current system is the default. With the strong pull of the current system as an alternative, little or no real change results.

If a major improvement is expected, it is the leader's responsibility to ensure that the current system is not one of the alternatives considered by the team. This is best accomplished by saying so explicitly in the charter.

Most of Bulk Transport's deliveries are products that do not require special handling, but 15 percent of the company's business is hauling hazardous products. The planning team was concerned because the company was taking one to two days to get back to customers with a price quote for hauling a hazardous product. Many of the orders were lost because customers found the service elsewhere. A previous team had worked for two months and produced only a letter outlining why quoting prices for hazardous products was so difficult and why the process could not be speeded up. This solution was unacceptable to the planning team. The company might as well get out of the hazardous delivery business if they could not quote the price within a couple of hours. The team wrote the following charter:

General Description

Use the upgraded information technology system to improve the process by which we quote prices for the pick-up and delivery of hazardous products.

Guidance

1. Test and implement a new process to reduce the time to quote from the current one to two days to one to two hours.

2. The team that is assigned to work on this charter will have until March 1 to propose and test a new method. Starting in March, if a better system is not available, the average rate for the last twenty loads will be quoted automatically.

3. Ensure that the new process complies with all federal, state, and local laws.

4. Improvement will not increase resources.

In developing this charter, the planning team had provided leadership. The charter freed the team from the bounds of the current system and encouraged them to use their creativity. One caution: methods such as the one described here must be applied in an atmosphere of mutual respect, as discussed earlier in the section on creating an environment for improvement.

2. *Use ambitious goals in charters to communicate the need for dramatic change.* Improvement is about change. The larger and more innovative the change, the greater the potential for improvement. How big a change is desired? This information should be included in a charter as an expected result or guidance. Often, a numerical goal is an effective way for a leader to communicate the size of the change that is expected. Examples of numerical goals are cutting waiting times by 70 percent and delivering the same quality at 10 percent less cost. A 70 percent reduction in waiting time usually will not come from small adjustments to the system but will instead require significant change. Creative thinking and skillful use of change concepts will be necessary.

Some goals are statements of fact derived from the study of the market environment or from other inputs to the planning activity. These statements of fact are not, however, the only or even the primary way that numerical goals can be established. A leader experienced and skilled in improvement will have a sense of what is possible and how much can be prudently invested in the improvement. The precision of such a goal is not important. A goal to cut waiting time by 60 percent serves the same purpose as a goal to cut waiting time by 80 percent: to communicate the magnitude of the desired change.

Communicating methods to accomplish the goals can take the form of establishing changes that might be tested. If the goal is reduction of waiting time, suggestions of what work could be eliminated, what work could be done simultaneously, or what new technology is available would constitute proposed methods that could be included in the charter with the goal. By establishing that there are feasible ways to attain the goal, the leader encourages others to suggest changes equally as radical. It is important for the leader to realize that at this point it is only necessary to establish the feasibility of the goal, not all the specifics of how to achieve it.

Bulk Transport has incorporated ambitious goals into a few of its charters where dramatic changes are expected. The following charter illustrates the use of numerical goals for improvement in tank cleaning:

General Description

Develop and implement new cleaning equipment and a standard method of cleaning tanks for use in all terminals.

Guidance

1. There are currently thirteen different methods for cleaning our tanks. The team is formed to create one standard method for Bulk Transport.
2. Increase the number of tanks cleaned daily by 20 percent to support planned growth.
3. Incorporate our recent advances in cleaning equipment technology with our supplier. Use information from the newly created Transportation Carriers Network to learn about recent advances in cleaning.
4. The team will keep the leadership group informed by sharing results of development, testing, and implementation cycles.
5. Reduce variation in clean, dry, odor-free tanks to our customers.
6. The team must coordinate its efforts with the preventative and routine maintenance teams.

The planning process that Bulk Transport has carried out has provided three outputs that are necessary for making improvements: strategic objectives, selected improvement efforts (charters), and the resources to accomplish the charters. The selected charters of Bulk Transport amounted to 8 percent of the resources budgeted for the year. Once charters are written and resources are allocated, then the real work of change can begin.

Managing Improvement Efforts

This is where it all comes together, in leadership's ability to deploy and manage the necessary resources to accomplish the stated plan and the selected improvement efforts. It is important for the leaders of an organization to clearly understand that improvements do not occur until individuals and teams start working with the charters created during the planning process. The first four activities needed to build the system for improvement (establishing and communicating the purpose of the organization, viewing the organization as a system, designing and managing a system for gathering information, and planning for improvement and integrating that planning with business planning) focus on aligning the organization to ensure that people are working on the right issues. This alignment is accomplished by emphasizing the organization's purpose, understanding the system, gathering information to create strategic direction, identifying changes, and allocating resources.

Aligning the organization behind the changes called for in the charters begins with providing some background on how and why the changes were selected. Each change effort should be tied to the overall purpose of the organization, and everyone in the organization should be made aware of how the efforts originated from the planning process. People who are selected to carry out the change should be educated on the importance of the effort to the organization, why they were selected, and the importance of their role in achieving the aim of the change effort.

Too much emphasis on alignment can lead to the "getting-ready-to-get-ready disease." Nothing happens except continuous planning, measuring, and so on. Leaders must ensure that alignment is attained, but they must then set the plan in motion. The fifth activity (managing individual and team improvement activities) focuses on managing and coordinating the efforts to develop, test, and implement changes. The leader must stay close enough to the effort to make sure that the Model for Improvement is providing the appropriate feedback structure to keep individuals or teams progressing toward their aim. For specific high-priority projects that have large implications for the organization, the leader must also provide some guidance and detailed help to those working on the project.

The following six methods will help leaders to effectively manage change:

1. *Stay with the project until the concept for change is established.* This advice is particularly important for large design or redesign efforts (sometimes called reengineering). Obviously, the leaders in the organization must play a strong role in answering the question, *What are we trying to accomplish?* However, for these larger efforts the leader must also be sure that the answer to the question, *What changes can we make that will result in improvement?* is sufficiently different from the existing system to warrant the resources expended on the effort.

These reengineering efforts should proceed in two phases: concept design and detail system design. One or more organizational leaders must stay involved in the project at least until the concept design begins to take shape. Even though the team may have been told that they could start with a "clean sheet of paper" and that they should not be constrained by the existing system, they will still be skeptical or apprehensive. They will most often start with relatively conservative changes (even if they have more innovative ones in mind), and then observe the reactions of their peers or top management to their suggestions. They will also take their cues from the type of changes that are suggested by organizational leaders.

Once the requisite courage has been instilled in the team and is reflected in the concept design, the organizational leader can then play a less-active role during the completion of the concept design and during the detail system design.

2. *Encourage tests on a small scale.* It is desirable to test innovative changes on a small scale. "Small scale" refers to the risks associated with the test, not to the size of the change or its level of innovation. One of the inhibitors to innovative change is the fear that the change is so different from what is currently done that a disaster could result. People will be more courageous in suggesting innovative changes if they know that the changes will be tested in a way in which the risks will be low even if the change does not prove to be an improvement.

It is often said that an environment that promotes the taking of risks will foster innovation. It is also true that methods that *minimize* the risks associated with developing and testing changes will foster innovation. Finding ways to test changes on a small scale is not always straightforward, however. See Chapter Six for description of some different ways to conduct small-scale tests.

3. *After a second-order change, make sure that the necessary first-order changes also get made.* It is exciting for everyone involved in developing, testing, and implementing a change that produces significant improvement. This is particularly true if a fundamental change has been made to a large subsystem.

The *study* of the change effort is an important step to ensuring that the change has become embedded in the system. The leader must ensure that this study includes the identification of barriers and other problems that sometimes occur from the implementation of a change—the *ripple effect* of the change on the system. Far less exciting, but just as important, is doing all the detail work that is necessary to make sure that the gains are held. Unanticipated problems will occur because it is impossible to recognize all the processes that will be affected by such a large change. The appropriate leader must help people put in place a system to address these problems as they arise. Most often, the best people to do this are not the people on the team but the people working in the new system. Small, nagging problems—the type that may not usually come to the attention of other leaders in the organization—are likely. Also, while a system is still new, the people working in it will not be familiar with it and will not have developed the same level of problem-solving skill that they had in the old system. When a problem occurred in the old system, someone had usually seen a similar problem and had some ideas about how to fix it. The leader should stay involved until he or she is convinced that people in the new system have the skills and resources to address the routine problems that occur.

4. *Ensure that resources are redirected and redeployed.* When a change is implemented, there is usually an impact on the current configuration of resources allocated for the system being addressed by the change. This impact may include displacement of people, redesign of administrative procedures, or the need to train people for new or redesigned jobs.

As improvement efforts are completed, the leader should determine how the results of the effort will affect the organization. Some issues to consider include:

- What actions by leaders are needed to reap the benefits of the improvement effort?

- What resources (budgets, positions, equipment and supplies, organization structures, and so on) need to be modified due to the improvement effort?

- What permanent changes in the system need to be made to maintain the improvement? Examples include rewriting job descriptions, changing policies, updating procedure manuals, and reorganizing departments and staff.

If the leader does not effectively deal with these issues, the gains from the improvement efforts may not be realized. Resources made expendable from the improvement efforts should usually be invested in further improvements. For an organization that is increasing its market, these resources are often needed for running the business.

5. *Study changes to learn about fundamental causes of problems in the system.* The work of improvement teams and other change efforts provide leaders with an opportunity to learn about the system they are leading and managing. The leadership team should study the work and progress of these improvement teams to learn how the organization works as a system. The elements studied should include:

- *Key processes in the organization and key linkages between processes.* Sometimes when a change is made to a process, an unexpected impact occurs in other processes in the organization. This learning can be used to update the linkage of processes.

- *Underlying forces in the organization that cause problems and create barriers.* What are the management systems (such as accounting, budgeting, appraisal, and so on) that drive the organization? Study of the change can uncover these forces. Leadership should learn how these forces interact and impact the employees of the organization.

- *The impact of the change on the system.* Improvement efforts often result in cost savings, productivity improvements, and other efficiencies for particular products and in particular processes in the organization. How do these changes impact the key measures of the system (the total organization)? Because of the interdependence of the processes and products, the combined improvements will not "add up" at the system level.

- *The economic impact of improvements in quality.* How do the various types of improvements result in changes to business measures such as productivity, fixed and variable costs, and market share?

- *The long-term social consequences of the tangible changes.* What impact do changes made by individuals and teams have on the social aspects of the system?

- *Understanding of the external customer's definition of quality.* What types of changes are recognized by the organization's external customers? What are the important dimensions of quality for the products and services of the organization?

The leadership team at Bulk Transport had an opportunity to learn from the team assigned to work on the problem of quoting rates on hazardous loads. After the customer service manager discussed the charter with the team and communicated the sense of urgency that she and the planning team had about improvement of the quoting process, the team went to work with a renewed sense of purpose. In ten days they returned with a plan for a test of an innovative way to quote prices in which 75 percent would be quoted on the phone and the remaining 25 percent could be quoted within three days.

When the leaders of the organization studied the proposed plan of the hazardous quote team, they discovered that some changes would be required in other key processes within the Bulk Transport system. In addition, they noted some potential barriers for implementation, made some plans to overcome these barriers and discussed these ideas with the team. Study on the part of the planning team paved the way for a smoother implementation. Leaders who take the time to study changes both before and after implementation will usually benefit by learning more about the change and its potential impact on the system.

6. *Evaluate and publicize the status of the improvement efforts in the organization.* Most people appreciate, and need, recognition, but it is often hard to provide. There are two basic reasons for providing recognition to those contributing to improvement:

- *Making improvement and enduring change is hard work* and comes with side effects for both those carrying out the change and those undergoing the change. Those who are carrying out the change usually have to spend time away from their regular duties, which sometimes creates stress. This extra effort should be recognized.

- Examples of successful improvement efforts that others can study and from which they can learn should be created and documented inside the organization. These examples must be communicated to the rest of the organization. Recognition of those involved is a good vehicle for providing this education.

The basic principle to follow when considering recognition for improvement efforts is to use the recognition systems already in place in the organization. There is no need to treat recognition for improvement differently than recognition for other initiatives in the organization. If, however, the current recognition system is inadequate (for instance, if it is extrinsic, with people working for a baseball cap or thermos rather than being recognized for the work they have done), effort should be undertaken to improve the system used for recognition in the organization. One improvement is to learn how to better recognize the job or task accomplished.

Developing, testing, and implementing change is often challenging. The story of Bulk Transport and the work accomplished by its teams that is woven throughout this chapter is typical of changes made in many organizations. The company allocated time and people to their charters and began work. One of the most challenging tasks was in the hands of the team chartered to implement new equipment and standardize the cleaning method. Their task was to achieve the ambitious goals of the charter that entailed getting agreement on the use of one standard method for the terminals to replace the thirteen different methods that were being used. The tank-cleaning process has a big impact on the ability of Bulk Transport to make deliveries and pick-ups on time. The success of this team had a major impact on the achievement of the strategic objective for on-time delivery.

The team's task was to learn how the new equipment would be different from the old and then to develop a standard method for using the new equipment throughout the Bulk Transport system. The changes necessary to implement the new equipment and standard method were developed and then tested. Testing proved useful, but training was deficient in the testing cycles and would need to be enhanced as the new equipment was introduced to the other terminals. After developing a plan to implement the equipment and the standard method the team was well on its way to fulfilling its charter.

The efficiency of the new equipment and the new standard method reduced breakdowns of equipment dramatically. Many areas within Bulk Transport that had previously run two shifts of tank cleaning were down to ten- to twelve-hour days. The number of rejected loads for tanks that were not cleaned was cut in half. The downside of this effort was the need to reduce the number of personnel assigned to tank cleaning. This was accomplished through a policy of attrition. Also, some managers were reluctant to use the prescribed cleaner. It was discovered that some managers had established special relationships with their local cleaner salespeople for the old cleaner and were being slow in moving to end these relationships. One manager refused to use the new cleaner; this required some follow-up action by the president of the company.

The leaders at Bulk Transport highlighted the following key learning points from the work of this one team:

1. *Make sure that the current way of doing things is not an alternative.* The use of the new cleaning equipment took the old system out of the running as an alternative. However, the use of various kinds of cleaning liquids by several groups caused unwanted variation from the company standard of clean, dry, and odor free. When one manager refused to use the prescribed cleaner, a brief visit from the company's president at the manager's Galveston, Texas, terminal revealed that the manager "just didn't understand the benefits of the new system" and would now be happy to comply.

2. *Stay with the project until the concept for change is established.* The leadership team developed the concept for change in the charter.

3. *Encourage tests on a small scale.* The initial testing and implementation was accomplished at three key terminals. After this initial development, implementation at each additional terminal was treated as a learning cycle, and implementation was improved during each successive cycle.

4. *After a second-order change, make sure that the necessary first-order changes also get made.* The team had to work with purchasing to remove the old supplier from and add the new supplier to the approved list.

5. *Ensure that resources are redirected and redeployed.* The new cleaning equipment and associated methods called for a reduction in the head count assigned to the cleaning wash bays. This was due to the reduction in the number of shifts required to clean tanks. The problem of extra associates was addressed through a system of attrition. People without jobs in the short term were utilized to make improvements that had been backlogged and to substitute for absentee associates, and some were transferred to other terminals.

6. *Study changes to learn about fundamental causes of problems in the system.* People directly involved with the change were continually surprised by the impact they had on Bulk Transport associates. This included everything from fear of not being able to use the new system or equipment to outright resistance to using the prescribed cleaner. Preparing people for change needed to be incorporated into developing the system.

Building a system of improvement not only guided Bulk Transport in solving immediate problems; it also allowed the company to align the organization to make improvements intentionally: to set direction through the planning process, to identify the processes and products within the system that needed to be changed, and finally, to allocate resources and write charters. This system for building improvements helps an organization to make improvements that customers care about, and to ensure that people in the organization are working on changes that contribute to customer satisfaction.

Case Study: Building a System of Improvement in a School District

The Leander Independent School District (LISD), located in Leander, Texas, has used the five activities to build a system of improvement for the school district. The primary leaders involved in this effort included the school superintendent, several support managers, principals, and several members of the school board.

Following is the LISD purpose statement:

Purpose

The purpose of LISD is to educate each student to be successful in an ever-changing world.

Vision

Each LISD graduate is prepared to have the academic background and life skills to be a productive learner, an effective communicator, and a responsible citizen.

Graduate Profile

To be an effective communicator, the LISD graduate must

- Read for a variety of purposes and apply reading skills to real-life situations.
- Use a range of writing styles effectively and in a manner appropriate to purpose, situation, and audience.
- Listen attentively and critically for a variety of purposes and respond to speakers appropriately.
- Use effective speaking strategies for a variety of purposes and in a variety of settings.

The LISD graduate is academically prepared to

- Use mathematics, science, and social studies as tools for problem solving, communicating, and reasoning.
- Use the literary, visual, and performing arts to enrich his or her daily life.

As a responsible citizen, the LISD graduate

- Understands the nature of economics as it applies to everyday living.
- Actively contributes to community or school service organizations.

- Makes and evaluates decisions based on ethical principles.
- Understands world issues, identifies the rights and obligations of citizens, and participates in the democratic process.

To be a productive learner, the LISD graduate

- Applies the self-management skills of goal-setting, time management, study skills, and continuous improvement.
- Demonstrates skill in resource management to allocate money, materials, space, and people.
- Manages information by acquiring and evaluating data, organizing and maintaining records, using technology to process information, selecting equipment and tools, and using research skills.
- Designs and improves systems to accomplish goals.
- Uses critical and creative thinking to solve problems.

The LISD graduate

- Makes wise career decisions based on self-knowledge, educational and occupational exploration, and career planning.
- Fosters personal health and self-esteem.
- Demonstrates interpersonal skills needed to work effectively in teams, manage conflict, lead in community and business, and be effective parents.

The need that LISD meets is *preparing the LISD graduate with the academic background and life skills to be a productive learner, an effective communicator, and a responsible citizen.* The graduate profile defines each of these key terms, provides guidance for the development of programs within the district and provides job descriptions for all LISD employees so that they will know what they need to help students accomplish. More importantly, it is used to communicate expectations to the students and their parents.

Viewing the Organization as a System

To help improve the school district, the leaders developed a view of the key processes that were required to accomplish the purpose of the system. This view is presented in Figure 13.10.

Measures of the System

The following list presents the family of measures that LISD uses to understand the performance of its system. This list is a subset of many other measures used to run the school system.

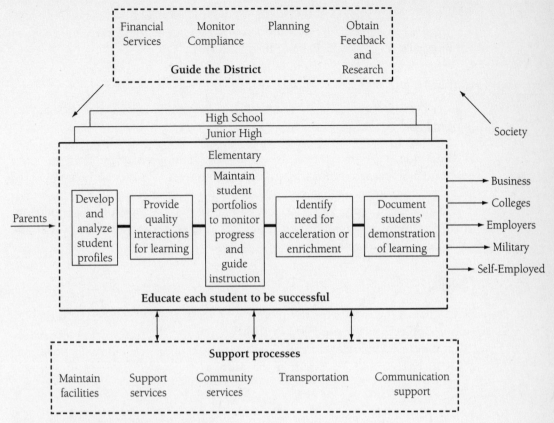

Figure 13.10. *School District as a System.*

Perspective	Measure
1. Student	Attendance percentage
2. Student	Dropout rate
3. Student	Percentage of students involved in extracurricular activities
4. Student	Discipline incidents
5. Operations	Pupil/teacher ratio
6. Operations	Graduation rate
7. Supplier	Kindergarten profile (ready to learn)
8. Employee	Percentage of employee turnover
9. Employee	Percentage of teacher turnover
10. Community	Number of volunteer hours
11. Community	Number of volunteers

12. Community	Percentage of students who go into business, college, trade school, the military
13. Financial	Per-pupil expenditure
14. Financial	Fund balance
15. Financial	Student enrollment

Information

LISD developed a system that collected data from employees, suppliers, students, board members, the community, and local employers. These methods included focus groups, written surveys, industry surveys, and employee forums. The Pareto charts in Figure 13.11 illustrate the responses received to two questions asked of parents in a telephone survey: (1) What do we need to improve? and (2) What do we do well?

Planning

LISD studied the inputs for the planning process and developed the following strategic objectives for the 1995–1997 school years (the numbers in the second column indicate the relevant category for improvement: 1 = eliminate problems; 2 = reduce costs; and 3 = expand expectations):

Objective	Category
1. *Training/staff development.*	Improve processes to support orientation and ongoing training and education for all LISD staff. 1, 3
2. *Data analysis.*	Improve the system to provide, analyze, and use data throughout the system for informed decision making (including reducing the time needed to gather data and making more timely decisions). 2, 3
3. *Curriculum.*	Develop and improve curricula that promote intrinsic motivation to learn and achieve the graduate profile. (Much work has already been done in this area, which will enhance the aim.) 3
4. *Efficiency Issues.*	Support the district's purpose by continually improving the effective use of system resources. (Because budgets are tight, improvement will have to come from better use of existing resources.) 1, 2

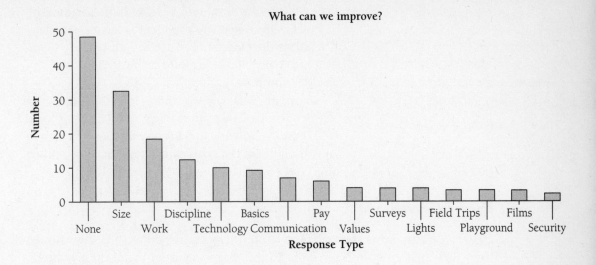

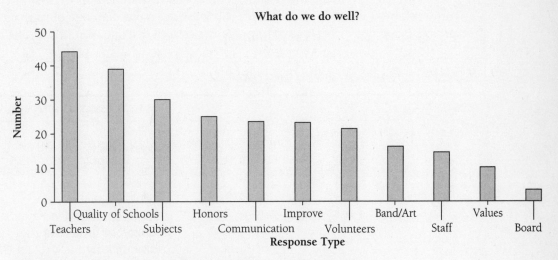

Figure 13.11. *Pareto Charts of LISD Parent Responses to Phone Survey.*

5. *Parenting/preschool.*	Partner with parents and other *partnering* agencies in developing and nurturing a learning-ready child. 3
6. *Communications.*	Develop and improve the system to communicate relevant information to parents, students, the board, staff, and community, in order to support LISD's purpose and vision. (Growth has created some short-term problems.) 1, 3

| 7. *Discipline.* | Develop a proactive system that expects and supports responsible student behavior and character development. (Rather than react to discipline problems, begin to be more proactive.) 3 |
| 8. *Facilities.* | Provide safe, secure, and comfortable facilities conducive to productivity and learning for a rapidly growing student population. (Growth of the district is a primary concern for the next two years.)   1, 3 |

Managing Improvement

LISD developed several charters to support the strategic objectives developed from their planning process. Table 13.2 presents a partial list of these charters and the objectives they support. The table makes clear that the improvement of any process, product, or service will probably impact more than one objective. LISD is focused not on trying to optimize the school district around any one

Table 13.2. *LISD's Charters and Associated Strategic Objectives.*

CHARTER	STRATEGIC OBJECTIVES SUPPORTED
Improve the process of developing school/business partnerships.	Curriculum (3) Communications (6) Parenting and Partner (5) Discipline (7) Data Analysis (2)
Develop communication links with the staff and patrons.	Communications (6) Training/Staff Development (1) Data Analysis (2)
Develop a plan to deal with increased facility usage.	Facilities (8) Efficiency Issues (4)
Develop a process and support materials to promote positive behaviors through community education children's programs.	Parenting and Partner (5) Curriculum (3) Communications (6)
Develop a benchmark system for kindergarten.	Curriculum (3) Communications (6) Data Analysis (2)
Design a process to enhance the placement of students into society upon graduation.	Curriculum (3) Communications (6) Parenting and Partner (5)

objective or specific improvement effort but on trying to *improve the district as a system*. In the process, *all* of the strategic objectives will be accomplished.

LISD's three years of work on their system of improvement culminated in the 1995–1997 plan. The immediate benefit of the planning process was to align the office of the superintendent, the staff, and the school board on a direction for the district. In the past, the board would develop annual goals for the superintendent and then conduct an annual review. During the planning process it became apparent that the accomplishment of the strategic objectives would take place over a three-year period and that the predicted improvements in the family of measures would follow in the same time frame. Understanding this delay in results created a partnership between the district staff and the board. Attention would now be paid to the specific improvements being made through the efforts of the various individuals and teams working on charters.

Alignment through the use of the planning process has also highlighted the real job of the board, which is to ensure that the purpose of the district is being achieved. Through the planning process, the board members who participated learned that the process is the forum for getting input from all district stakeholders, and that the study of these inputs is something in which a school board should be involved. In the past, single comments from parents, isolated complaints, and perceived problems would take up board meeting time. These issues would now be looked at as they related to the strategic objectives and charters functioning in the district, and they would be compared with data collected in the past.

The superintendent views participation of as many board members as possible in the 1996 planning season as important for the next planning period. (School board membership is volunteer work after regular work hours.) Steps are now being taken to ensure this participation.

Conclusion

One of the principle aims of this book has been to provide methods for developing changes that result in improvement from the viewpoint of the customer. It is important to realize that improvement efforts will not be successful over the long-term without leadership. To be leaders of change, people must make improvement a key focus of the organization while continuing to accomplish the aim of the system (such as taking care of customers, making deliveries, and providing services).

A leader must be compassionate and encouraging, but also unrelenting in the pursuit of changes that result in improvement. A key role of a leader of change is to focus the knowledge and energy of people on making improvements. These improvement efforts should be directed toward the organization or industry's important issues. Central to the leader's job, therefore, is bringing these important issues to the surface and then helping people to develop and implement relevant changes. Leaders must encourage the use of appropriate methods for making improvements to reduce the risks associated with change.

A key responsibility of a leader for change is to build a system of improvement. Why is this necessary? Because an organization is a system, and improvements of the parts (individual processes, services, and products) can lead to suboptimization of the overall organization. Leaders must manage improvements so that they lead instead to optimization of the entire organization toward its purpose, building a system for improvement by engaging in the activities discussed in this chapter. The use of these activities will accelerate the pace at which improvements are made. The structure of the five activities provides enough guidance to begin the process of building improvement into the fabric of the organization.

Appendix
A Resource Guide to Change Concepts

While all changes do not lead to improvement, all improvement requires change. The ability to develop, test, and implement changes is essential for any individual, group, or organization that wants to continuously improve. But what kinds of changes will lead to improvement? Usually, a unique, specific change is required to obtain improvement in a specific set of circumstances. Thus, there are many kinds of changes. But these specific changes are developed from a limited number of change concepts.

A *concept* is a general, abstract notion that is applied through a more specific idea. A *change concept* is *a general notion or approach to change that has been found to be useful in developing specific ideas for changes that lead to improvement.* Creatively combining these change concepts with knowledge about specific subjects can result in developing changes that lead to improvement. Many change concepts can be used to develop specific changes that do not require tradeoffs between costs and quality.

This resource guide enumerates the change concepts that have already been discussed in this book, as well as others that readers will find useful. The use of change concepts was introduced in Chapter Five, and examined more specifically in Chapters Ten, Eleven, and Twelve, in the discussion of the three categories of improvement. This resource guide organizes these ideas in one place for ease of reference and use.

The seventy change concepts listed here are organized into the following nine general groupings:

Grouping	Number of Concepts in Grouping
A. Eliminate Waste	11
B. Improve Work Flow	11
C. Optimize Inventory	4
D. Change the Work Environment	11
E. Enhance the Producer/Customer Relationship	8
F. Manage Time	5
G. Manage Variation	8
H. Design Systems to Avoid Mistakes	4
I. Focus on a Product/Service	8

A complete list of the concepts is presented first, followed by a discussion of their use. The bulk of the resource guide further describes each change concept, and presents some specific ideas and examples of how the concepts can be applied in different situations.

Complete List of Change Concepts

A. Eliminate Waste
1. Eliminate Things That Are Not Used
2. Eliminate Multiple Entry
3. Reduce or Eliminate Overkill
4. Reduce Controls on the System
5. Recycle or Reuse
6. Use Substitution
7. Reduce Classifications
8. Remove Intermediaries
9. Match the Amount to the Need
10. Use Sampling
11. Change Targets or Set Points

B. Improve Work Flow
12. Synchronize
13. Schedule into Multiple Processes
14. Minimize Handoffs
15. Move Steps in the Process Close Together
16. Find and Remove Bottlenecks
17. Use Automation
18. Smooth Work Flow
19. Do Tasks in Parallel
20. Consider People as in the Same System
21. Use Multiple Processing Units
22. Adjust to Peak Demand

C. Optimize Inventory
23. Match Inventory to Predicted Demand
24. Use Pull Systems
25. Reduce Choice of Features
26. Reduce Multiple Brands of Same Item

D. Change the Work Environment
27. Give People Access to Information
28. Use Proper Measurements
29. Take Care of Basics
30. Reduce Demotivating Aspects of Pay System
31. Conduct Training
32. Implement Cross-Training
33. Invest More Resources in Improvement
34. Focus on Core Processes and Purpose
35. Share Risks
36. Emphasize Natural and Logical Consequences
37. Develop Alliance/Cooperative Relationships

E. Enhance the Producer/Customer Relationship
38. Listen to Customers
39. Coach Customers to Use Product/Service
40. Focus on the Outcome to a Customer
41. Use a Coordinator
42. Reach Agreement on Expectations
43. Outsource for "Free"
44. Optimize Level of Inspection
45. Work with Suppliers

F. Manage Time
46. Reduce Setup or Startup Time
47. Set up Timing to Use Discounts
48. Optimize Maintenance
49. Extend Specialist's Time
50. Reduce Wait Time

G. Manage Variation
51. Standardization (Create a Formal Process)
52. Stop Tampering
53. Develop Operational Definitions
54. Improve Predictions
55. Develop Contingency Plans
56. Sort Product into Grades
57. Desensitize
58. Exploit Variation

H. Design Systems to Avoid Mistakes
59. Use Reminders
60. Use Differentiation
61. Use Constraints
62. Use Affordances

I. Focus on the Product or Service
63. Mass Customize
64. Offer Product/Service Anytime
65. Offer Product/Service Anyplace
66. Emphasize Intangibles
67. Influence or Take Advantage of Fashion Trends
68. Reduce the Number of Components
69. Disguise Defects or Problems
70. Differentiate Product Using Quality Dimensions

How to Use the Change Concepts

The change concepts presented in this resource guide are not specific enough to be applied directly to making improvements. Rather, the concept must be considered within the context of a specific situation and then turned into an idea. The idea will need to be specific enough to describe how the change can be developed, tested, and implemented in the specific situation. When describing the change concepts, we have tried to be consistent in the degree of specificity or generality of the concepts. Sometimes, a new idea seems at first to be a new change concept; but often, with further thinking, it is seen to be an application of one of the more general concepts.

We make no claim to have included all of the useful change concepts that exist. As you use this resource guide, try to develop more concepts. One way to discover concepts is to study the improvements that have recently been made in your organization:

1. What was the specific change that was made?
2. What was the idea used for the change?
3. Where (who) did the idea come from?
4. Which of the change concepts could generate that idea?
5. Can the idea be generalized for other situations?
6. Would a new concept be useful to describe this idea for change?

The primary purpose of this resource guide is to provide help to individuals and teams who are trying to answer the question, *What change can we make that will result in improvement?* The change concepts can serve to provoke a new idea for an individual or team. A team leader can choose one of the change concepts and then the team can explore some ideas for possible application of this concept to the situation of interest. The list of ideas should be recorded. After the generation of ideas is complete, the ideas can be discussed and critiqued. Any of the ideas that show promise can be further explored by the team to obtain a specific idea for a change.

Marsha's quality improvement team was trying to reduce errors made in financial documents that resulted in rework of the documents. The team developed and implemented a number of changes based on the data they had collected and on the experience of the team members. These improvements reduced the rework rate from 12 percent to 7 percent. How could the team make further reductions? They needed some more ideas to develop additional changes.

Marsha selected the change concept "reduce choice of features" and asked the team to review this concept prior to the next meeting. This concept was in the "inventory" category and did not seem relevant to most team members for preparing financial documents. At the team's next meeting, Marsha led a brainstorming session on ideas for improving the preparation of financial documents using "reduce choice of features" as the focus. The team generated more than twenty ideas for improvement. Some of the ideas seemed ridiculous at first, but in a couple of cases they helped the other team members think of more useful ideas. After a review of the list, two ideas were selected for further study. The team planned two cycles to try and develop specific changes based on each of the ideas.

At the beginning of each of the team's next five meetings, Marsha led a similar idea-generation session using one of the other change concepts. She picked concepts that were somewhat relevant, hoping to provoke ideas that the team had not previously considered. Marsha asked some of the team members to select the concept for the last two sessions. Four of the five sessions generated at least one idea that the team selected to develop into a specific change. In total, eight cycles were completed to develop change concepts from these ideas. These cycles led to four specific changes that were tested. Two of the changes were implemented in the financial document preparation process. During the next six months, these changes resulted in further reductions in the rework from 7 percent to 3 percent.

How is a particular change concept selected for focus in a session to generate ideas? The aim of the improvement effort will provide some direction. The following are some ways that have been found useful:

1. Choose a change concept that someone on the team thinks might generate some ideas that would be useful to the aim of the improvement effort.
2. Choose change concepts that have not been previously considered by the team.
3. Select one of the nine categories that is related to the aim of the improvement effort. Then randomly choose one of the change concepts in that category.
4. Randomly choose a change concept from the list of seventy.

When a concept is randomly selected, more creative ideas can be expected to come from the session because people might get further away from their usual thought processes. Conversely, it might take a long session before the relevance of ideas from a randomly selected concept is discovered. A concept, or concept category, that is obviously relevant to the aim of the improvement effort can be expected to yield a higher number of useful ideas in less time, but it may not generate a completely new approach to the activity of interest.

Some of the change concepts appear to offer conflicting advice for developing changes. For example, concept 25, "reduce choice of features" (in the Optimize Inventory category), and concept 63, "mass customize" (in the Focus on a Product/Service category) appear to be aimed in opposite directions. Change concept 4, "reduce controls on the system," and change concept 51, "standardization (create a formal process)," also suggest conflicting directions. The important consideration is the context in which the change concept is being considered.

For example, if an organization is trying to change the expectations of its satisfied customers, asking the customers to do additional tasks associated with the product or service they are purchasing might not be of interest. However, if an organization is trying to reduce costs while maintaining quality, a customer might be willing to take on some additional work that is easier done at the customer's site if that would lead to significant price reductions. It may be appropriate to increase options to a customer who values the choices (who is willing to pay a higher price), but customers who want to minimize their costs for a product or service will appreciate the efficiencies that can come from reduced choices. Standardization is appropriate for high-leverage processes, but may be overkill for processes that are not leverage points for costs, capacity, or quality. Table A.1 lists some guidelines for considering some of the change concepts that may lead in conflicting directions. When using a change concept to develop ideas for a specific change, understanding and knowledge of the particular circumstances will always be the determining factor concerning the appropriateness of the concept.

The Change Concepts

A. Eliminate Waste

In a broad sense, any activity or resource in an organization that does not add value to an external customer can be considered waste. Some examples of waste are materials that are thrown away, rework of materials and documents, movement of items from one place to another, inventories, time spent waiting in line, people working in processes that are not important to the customer, extra steps or motion in a process, repeating work that has previously been done by others, overspecification of materials and requirements, and more staff than required to match the demand for products and services.

Toyota is famous for focusing improvement on the following seven wastes:

1. Waste of overproduction
2. Waste of waiting
3. Waste of transportation
4. Waste of processing itself
5. Waste of stock (inventory)
6. Waste of motion
7. Waste of producing defective products

Table A.1. *Guidelines for Considering Specific Change Concepts.*

CHANGE CONCEPT	WHEN TO CONSIDER	WHEN NOT TO CONSIDER
3. Reduce or Eliminate Overkill	When trying to reduce costs	When trying to reduce problems in the customer's system
4. Reduce Control on the System	When trying to decrease cycle time or costs	With high-leverage processes that require adherence to standards
7. Reduce Classifications	When trying to increase efficiency and speed	When trying to meet needs of a variety of customers
9. Match the Amount to the Need	When large variations in quantity demanded	When inventory costs are low; when trying to improve production efficiencies
17. Use Automation	With a routine, quality process	With a nonstandard process with many problems
19. Do Tasks in Parallel	When cycle time reductions are important	When decisions at earlier steps affect performance of later steps
25. Reduce Choice of Features	When trying to reduce costs and cycle times; when inventory costs are high	When customers have different needs and applications of product or service
38. Listen to Customers	When trying to solve customer problems	When trying to reduce production costs
41. Use a Coordinator	When it is critical to meet customer requirements	When trying to reduce costs
44. Optimize Level of Inspection	When problems exist and before bottlenecks (increase inspection)	When trying to reduce costs or time or to increase capacity (decrease inspection)
51. Standardization (Create a Formal Process)	Leverage points in a system	When creativity, variety, or improvement in performing a task is required
55. Develop Contingency Plans	When it is critical that service be performed	When trying to minimize the standard cost of a service
63. Mass Customize	When trying to delight customers	When trying to increase value by reducing price

The following eleven change concepts are included in this category:

1. Eliminate Things That Are Not Used
2. Eliminate Multiple Entry
3. Reduce or Eliminate Overkill
4. Reduce Controls on the System
5. Recycle or Reuse
6. Use Substitution
7. Reduce Classifications
8. Remove Intermediaries
9. Match the Amount to the Need
10. Use Sampling
11. Change Targets or Set Points

1. Eliminate Things That Are Not Used Constant change in organizations results in less demand for specific resources and activities that were once important to the business. Unnecessary activities and unused resources can be identified through surveys, audits, data collection, and analysis of records. The next step is to take the obvious actions to remove the unused elements from the system.

A manufacturing company conducted an audit of the tools, equipment, and supplies in the organization. They found that almost one-half of these items were no longer useful to the organization. They sold, recycled, or scrapped the unnecessary tools and supplies. Not only did this reduce inventory costs, but it freed up space and allowed for better arrangement of stored materials.

A service organization conducted an audit of all the meetings and reports that occurred in the organization. For each meeting and report they answered the following questions: When was this meeting or report initiated? How does this meeting or report help our external customers? Are there other compelling reasons to conduct this meeting or produce this report? On the basis of an analysis of the data obtained from this audit, one-third of the meetings and 20 percent of the reports were eliminated.

The financial department of a company spent about seven hundred man-hours each quarter collecting data from the organization and updating the financial forecast for the year. At one time, these updates were used by managers in decision making and planning. But about three years ago, the managers had begun to rely on analysis of historical data to develop and update their forecasts. The quarterly input from the finance group had not been used for the past two years. After this realization, the financial manager eliminated the quarterly updates and dedicated the resources to analysis of pricing and other business decisions.

---

2. Eliminate Multiple Entry In some situations, information is recorded in a log or entered into a database more than one time, creating no added value. This practice is also called data redundancy. Changing the process to require only one entry can lead to improvement in productivity and quality (by reducing discrepancies). Recent technology developments (such as optical scanners) make it possible to enter data directly from sight or by voice. Once data is recorded, there should be no reason to reenter the same information at a later time.

Currently, the production and accounting departments enter the same data into two different computer systems. A common database (with entry only at the original source) was established, and both departments use this database for their analyses and reports. This change reduced the need for two clerical positions and one database administrator who had been reconciling the differences in the data from the two departments.

A law firm created central files so that everyone could access data and written documents, eliminating the need for the development and maintenance of individual files in each of the lawyer's offices.

The estimating department of an engineering and construction company developed detailed design specifications and estimates when they bid on the job. They had to enter all of the customer specifications into a computer system to prepare their bids, but when they won a job, this data was not used. Both the engineering design department and the construction department would go back to the customer specifications and reenter all of the information. In an effort to reduce costs, the company obtained a common computer system for all three departments. Engineering design would then use the database developed by estimation to begin their work. The construction department would access the engineering data base to develop their project schedules and budgets. The company saved about $10,000 on a typical project, reduced errors, and improved relationships among the company's departments.

---

3. Reduce or Eliminate Overkill Sometimes, a company's standard or recommended resources are designed to handle special, severe, or critical situations rather than the normal situation. Changing the standard to the appropriate amount of resources for the normal situation will reduce waste. Additional resources would be used only when the situation required it. A common reaction in many organizations to a special problem is to add more resources to the process, product, or service so that the problem will not occur if the special situation occurs again. While this can be effective in solving quality problems, the result is often overkill, amounting to higher costs and lower productivity each time the process is run, the service is conducted, or the product is produced.

The management of a hospital explored opportunities to reduce waste. First, they eliminated overuse of technologies like magnetic resonance imaging or ultrasound by making them outside the normal treatment process. Then, they eliminated automatic daily lab tests for in-patients and multiple tests that add no new information. They were able to reduce the number of blood assays required for a particular situation from twenty-three to five.

A production services company required two days to heat-treat steel parts because a thirty-six-hour processing requirement had been the practice for the past twenty-three years. The company's engineers designed a series of experiments, from which they learned that processing times of twelve to twenty hours were enough to meet customers' needs (except for a few situations that represented less than one percent of their business). By specifying target times to meet the needs of its various products, the company more than doubled its capacity and offered one-day turnaround to most of its customers.

A laboratory used highly accurate, expensive testing instruments for routine sample analysis. Much cheaper but less accurate instruments were available that would provide the required information on 90 percent of submitted samples. The laboratory changed the testing procedure so that all samples were tested using the cheaper method unless a special request was received.

---

4. Reduce Controls on the System Individuals and organizations use various types of controls to make sure a process or system does not stray too far from standards, requirements, or accepted practices. While useful for protection of the organization, these controls can increase costs, reduce productivity, and stifle improvement. Typical forms of controls include a layered management structure, approval signatures, standardized forms, and reports. A regular review of all of the organization's control procedures by everyone working in the system can result in identifying opportunities to reduce controls on the system without putting the organization at risk.

The travel department reviewed their control requirements. They currently required receipts for all charges before reimbursement. This resulted in many call-backs and delays in payment. The procedure was changed to not require receipts for charges less than $25. This eliminated about one-half of the delays in reimbursement.

An organization that was trying to reduce costs focused on the impact of controls on their system. They did a thorough review of all of the existing forms, reports, meetings, and procedures, and identified things that were being done primarily for control purposes. They then decided what minimum levels of control were required, and redesigned the activities and reports to meet these minimum levels. They were able to combine and eliminate many of the controls. From this experience they learned that many of the midlevel management functions were focused on control activities. They decided to try and eliminate one layer of management in the organization to further reduce costs.

---

5. Recycle or Reuse Once a product is created and used for its intended purpose, it is natural to discard it and the by-products created by its use. However, if other uses can be found for the discarded product or by-products, the cost of producing the product can be spread out over its use and its reuse. As concern about the effect on the environment of the disposal of materials becomes more critical, organizations will be reassessing the costs associated with throwing away materials. Many times, recycling will be found to be a cost-effective alternative. Design engineers in most manufacturing companies are learning how to "design for disassembly." New products can be designed as components or modules, with a plan for reuse. Computer programs can be developed from a set of modules of computer code that perform specific tasks such as sorting data, plotting data, and so on. Scaffolding at a construction site can be designed for easy disassembly for reuse at the next site. The ease of destruction of a product is becoming just as important as the ease of construction.

A manufacturing organization had a significant monthly cost of waste water disposal. They studied all of their processes that generated waste water. Based on this analysis, they were able to make changes in operating practices to generate 12 percent less waste water and to reuse 20 percent of the waste water in other processes.

The U.S. Federal Reserve has begun recycling worn-out currency rather than continue to add to the landfills. About 7,000 tons of bills are shredded each year. Recent changes in materials used in the currency make it possible to recycle them as ceiling tiles, particle boards, and shingles.

A camera manufacturer designed a camera in the late 1980s that could be thrown away after a roll of film was used. Hundreds of thousands of these cameras ended up in landfills. The company's engineers redesigned the camera for disassembly and component reuse. They converted the disposable camera into a recyclable camera. Eighty-seven percent of the camera (by weight) is now reused or recycled. This redesigned product became the company's fastest growing and most profitable product.

6. Use Substitution Waste can often be reduced by replacing some aspect of the product or process with a better alternative. One type of substitution is to include lower-cost components, materials, or methods that do not affect the performance of the process, service, or product (sometimes called value engineering). Another type of substitution is to switch to another process with fewer steps, less manual effort, and so on.

Timber prices doubled in the early 1990s, adding as much as $5,000 to the cost of a typical house. Environmental issues make the prospect of higher lumber prices more likely in the future. What are the alternatives to using wood to frame a house? The housing industry is looking at steel. Steel has many advantages (it resists fire, warping, rotting, termites, and so on), but only since the recent price increases in lumber has it become an attractive alternative for building a house. The biggest drawback is unfamiliarity with using steel. In 1993, one-third of builders surveyed planned to try using steel in the home-building process.

Changes in precious-metal prices were increasing the catalyst costs of a commodity chemical manufacturer. Operating costs were cut by using a substitute for the type of metals used in the manufacturing of the catalysts. Alternative formulations were developed that could be substituted for the catalysts as prices in the metals fluctuated.

7. Reduce Classifications Classifications are often developed to differentiate elements of a system or to group items with common characteristics, but these classifications can lead to system complexity that increases costs or decreases quality. Classification should be reduced when the complexity caused by the classification is worse than the benefit gained.

A commodity chemical company had developed sixty-eight "special grades" to try to differentiate its products from its competitors' products and to help market the product to new customers. These grades did not result in premium pricing, but they did require complex production schemes, excessive inventory, and late deliveries (about 15 percent). A joint production/marketing team studied the grade slate and recommended that the company produce and sell twelve grades that met the needs of all except one of their existing customers. As a result of implementing this plan, manufacturing productivity increased, inventory costs decreased, and late deliveries were reduced to less than two percent of shipments.

A concert hall sold twelve different classifications of tickets, each for a different price. Anytime someone attempted to purchase tickets, a lengthy explanation of the different classifications was required. Regular customers complained that the ticket type they wished to purchase was never available. The theater developed three classifications, which resulted in fewer hassles and fewer customer complaints.

A carpet manufacturing company reduced classifications of in-process inventory by waiting until the last steps of production to differentiate the product. This flexibility allowed them to reduce the in-process inventory and reduce delivery lead times.

---

8. Remove Intermediaries Intermediaries such as distributors, handlers, agents, and carriers may be part of a system. Consider eliminating these activities by linking production directly with the consumer. Some intermediaries add value to a process because of their specialized skills and knowledge. Often, however, eliminating these services can increase productivity without reducing value to the customer.

A manufacturer of floor coverings sold its products through a network of independent dealers/installers. Consumers buying the flooring experienced high markups and waiting times of a month or more. When large home-center chains developed as places where do-it-yourselfers could buy home-improvement products, the manufacturer established relationships directly with these retail centers to sell its products. The manufacturer provided displays of their flooring products, trained the salespeople, and managed the inventory for the home centers. Sales of their products have increased dramatically by selling directly to the retail market.

A popular restaurant chain established an in-house credit system for regular customers rather than rely on credit card companies or banks. The savings in credit fees more than offset the increased costs of billing and collections. The availability of credit was also a selling point to business customers.

For many years a chemical plant had purchased equipment and supplies from a variety of industrial distributors. As a result of several improvement efforts focused on standardization of equipment and supplies, they began to buy such items as valves, fitting, pumps, seals, pipe, and so on directly from one or two suppliers. Because of their growing knowledge of the suppliers, they did not need the level of expertise formerly required of their distributors. They eventually consolidated all of their nonstandard purchases with one industrial supplier and began purchasing the standard items directly from one other supplier. They were thus able to reduce their total equipment and supply purchasing costs by 5 percent. By working directly with the supplier, they were also able to get better service and to get the supplier involved with a joint improvement effort.

---

9. Match the Amount to the Need Rather than using traditional standard units or sizes, organizations can adjust products and services to match the amount required for a particular situation. This practice reduces waste and carryover inventory. By studying how customers use the product, more convenient package sizes can be developed.

Medical supplies came in standard packages of six units. Physicians wanted to give patients a week's supply (seven units), so they are forced to give two packages of six. Five of the units often ended up being wasted. After studying this application and other uses of the supplies, the manufacturer developed three standard package sizes of four, seven, and ten units each.

The amount of cream in creamer packages for coffee drinkers is too much for typical coffee drinkers. One supplier began offering cream in smaller sizes to match the typical use. A coffee drinker who wanted extra cream could request two packages.

A recreational facility reserved tennis courts in blocks of one hour (sixty minutes). A study of playing patterns found that most groups wanted to play for seventy-five to ninety minutes. Groups would typically reserve the courts for two hours, but for the last thirty to forty-five minutes, the court was often not used. The facility changed the reservation system to schedule in half-hour blocks. This change reduced the wasted court time and allowed more players to use the facility.

---

10. Use Sampling Reviews, checks, and measurements are made for a variety of reasons. Can these reasons be satisfied without checking or testing everything?

Many times, the standard 100 percent inspection and testing results in waste of resources and time. Formal sampling procedures are available that can often provide as good or even better information than 100 percent checking.

The hospital's infection control group used to estimate the hospital's infection rate by following up on every positive culture to see if it was an infection. The concept of sampling was used to change this process. The group began by taking a sample of twenty positive cultures each day and then estimating the infection rate from the samples. Because of the savings in number of tests and amount of data handling required, the hospital was able to eliminate one laboratory technician position.

Airlines routinely accept tickets from other airlines. The process of accounting for all of the different tickets is cumbersome and time-consuming. The airlines worked together to develop a sampling scheme to determine transfer of funds among the various entities. A sample of tickets is selected from the computer database each month, and funds are transferred based on the estimates from the sample. The cost savings are much greater than any possible error introduced by sampling.

An insurance company required prehospital screening of all patients by an HMO before allowing admission to a hospital. After review of the costs and quality hassles that resulted from this screening, the company began to sample patients and determine reasons for inappropriate hospitalization. Based on the information from this sample, they made monthly recommendations to improve the process for admitting patients.

---

11. Change Targets or Set Points Sometimes problems go on for years because some piece of equipment is not designed or set up properly. Make sure that process settings are at desirable levels. Investigate places where waste is created, and consider adjustments to targets or set points to reduce the waste.

A machine operator found that about ten percent of the parts he was cutting had excessive burrs and required a rework step in the process. After talking to some of the engineers about the causes of burrs, he adjusted the coolant and speed settings on the saw he operated. Burrs were reduced to less than two percent of the parts.

A custodian noticed that the white-paper-recycling boxes in one of the copier rooms filled up almost everyday. In other, similar rooms, the boxes were usually not full after a week.

After mentioning this to his friend Robert, one of the managers on that floor, an investigation was done. Robert found that almost everyone who made copies would throw away the first two or three copies, adjust the machine, and redo these copies. A few individuals would immediately adjust the machine before starting to copy. After talking to some of the users, Robert found that the default setting on the copier was not making the copies dark enough. He adjusted the light/dark setting on the copier to a default value more appropriate for most copies. The problem of wasted paper (and waste of people's time) went away.

Production in a manufacturing plant varied greatly from machine to machine and from shift to shift. Backlogs and downtime were common throughout the plant. The production manager held meetings with the operators and found that they had no clear direction on what speeds to run the various pieces of equipment. A production engineer developed a simulation of the plant and determined standard speed settings for each piece of equipment. The use of these settings stabilized the plant and resulted in a predictable production level. Studies were then planned to improve capacity and efficiency.

B. Improve Work Flow

Products and services are produced by processes. How does work flow in these processes? What is the plan to get work through a process? Are the various steps in the process arranged and prioritized to obtain quality outcomes at low costs? How can the work flow be changed so that the process is less reactive and more planned?

The critical-path method is one tool available to help coordinate flow in a process. Originally developed for project planning, the tool has been adapted to help synchronize work flow in complex processes in which time is a critical parameter.

The following eleven change concepts are included in this category:

12. Synchronize
13. Schedule into Multiple Processes
14. Minimize Handoffs
15. Move Steps in the Process Close Together
16. Find and Remove Bottlenecks
17. Use Automation
18. Smooth Work Flow
19. Do Tasks in Parallel
20. Consider People as in the Same System
21. Use Multiple Processing Units
22. Adjust to Peak Demand

12. Synchronize Production of products and services usually involves multiple stages. These stages operate at different times and at different speeds, resulting in an operation that is not smooth. Much time can be spent waiting for another stage to be reached. By focusing on the flow of the product (or customer) through the process, each of the stages can be brought into harmony. Some of the changes that can be developed from this concept include the use of "just-in-time" inventory practices, batching (blocking) to organize multiple activities, the linking of parallel activities during the process, and the development of timing of events to match the predicted flow of the process.

The final closing on a real estate transaction usually involves the buyer, seller, agent, broker, banker, and title company, and a lawyer. Closing day is usually very stressful for the buyer and the seller. One real estate company formed a team with a title company and financing organization to take the hassle out of the closing. The company studied typical flows of activities that led up to the closing and developed a standard synchronized system to bring all of the required activities and information together for the closing. By cooperating to support this standard process, they were able to take the stress out of closing day. Word-of-mouth references helped grow their business over the next year.

When a commercial airplane arrives at the airport gate, the ground crew assists in the docking and preparation for unloading. Most airlines wait until a plane has arrived before discharging the ground crew to assist. This results in frustrated passengers standing in the aisles after a long trip waiting for the door to open. One airline synchronized the ground crew so that the door could be opened immediately when the plane touched the gate. This resulted in a noticeable difference in waiting time for passengers, who now leave the plane in a much better mood.

---

13. Schedule into Multiple Processes A system can be redesigned to include multiple versions of the same process focused on the specific requirements of the situation. Rather than a "one-size-fits-all" large process, multiple versions of the process are available, each tuned to the different types of needs of customers or users. Priorities can be established to allocate and schedule the inputs in order to maximize the performance of the system. The specific processes can then be greatly simplified since they only address a limited range of input requirements.

The permit department of a city government redesigned its permit application to accommodate different levels of need. Previously, the same application had been used for both a small modification of an existing structure and a new development project that included many buildings. Since different documentation, studies, review, and approvals are required depending on the complexity of the project, multiple processes were designed to handle each type of application. This change cut the turnaround time in half and reduced the backlog of applications to less than one week.

An airline required twenty check-in stations at a large airport during peak hours. They developed multiple processes for passengers with different needs: baggage check-in only, buying tickets, check-in for the next flight to leave, and check-in for members of the airline's frequent flyer club. This system improved the flow of passengers through the check-in system.

A quality improvement team focused on improvement in efficiency and effectiveness in a hospital emergency center. They improved the hospital's triage system to better prioritize medical urgency. They were able to trim five thousand hours from patient stays in emergency during the first year using the new system.

---

14. Minimize Handoffs Many systems require that elements (a customer, a form, a product, and so on) be transferred to multiple people, offices, or work stations to complete the processing or service. The handoff from one stage to the next can increase time and costs and cause quality problems. The work flow can be rearranged to minimize any handoff in the process. The process can be redesigned so that any worker is only involved one time in an iteration of a process. Making changes in organization structure or position descriptions is one type of change that can be used to minimize handoffs. For example, layers of management that require multiple reviews, meetings, and approvals can be reduced; clerical jobs can be expanded to include scheduling, staffing, planning, and analysis; and workers can be cross-trained to handle many functions rather than be specialists in one specific function.

An automotive service organization had trouble with completing their work by the promised time. Cars were backed up on the lot, waiting for the next technician to do their specialty. Over a two-year period, the technicians were crossed-trained in the ten most demanded services. Now, a car can be repaired with one pass in the service center at one station rather than by shuttling it in and out of the service center. Cycle times for repairs have decreased by one half.

A custom manufacturing company expanded job descriptions to cover formerly separate jobs. Now machinists can do maintenance, inspection, calibration, setups, and so on. This change reduced waiting time in manufacturing as a job goes through the shop. Workers no longer have to hand off jobs to other workers.

A hospital redesigned its patient transfer processes to minimize handoffs of patients. For example, the emergency room can now call any of the units directly to tell them about a new patient rather than go through the bed-control department. Patients can now be admitted directly to the intensive care unit (ICU) after surgery rather than to a postanesthesia care unit and then to ICU. These and similar changes to other transfer processes have resulted in higher patient satisfaction with services and lower costs for the hospital.

---

15. Move Steps in the Process Close Together The physical location of people and facilities can affect processing time and cause communication problems. If the physical location of adjacent steps in a process are moved close together, work can be directly passed from one step to the next. This eliminates the need for communication systems (such as mail) and physical transports (such as vehicles, pipelines, and conveyor belts).

The result of moving steps closer together can be lower capital and maintenance costs, reduced inventory (especially work in process), and more frequent improvement (from better communication). If it is not possible to physically move steps in a process together, electronic hookups should be considered. For some processes, computer networks with common file structures can have an effect similar to physically moving the steps together.

Social services such as drug abuse counseling, teen pregnancy prevention, Medicaid registration, public health clinics, and unemployment services in a large city were spread throughout the city in separate buildings. The customers of these services were often the same people or from the same family. The services were reorganized into centers that provided a range of services. This allowed the city to cut the costs of these programs through reduction of overlap and through shared administrative support and equipment. It also provided the customers with more convenient access to the services.

Six organizations located in different parts of the country are involved in a large construction project. They use a common computer database and video telecommunication equipment to bring the participants in the project into the "same room" for weekly meetings.

A company that sold its products by catalogue moved the order takers and those who shipped the product into the same area. Previously, they had been on different floors. This change eliminated the time it took to walk up and down stairs when there was a need to exchange information or check on an order. It also facilitated a smoother flow of orders through the entire system.

---

16. *Find and Remove Bottlenecks* A bottleneck or constraint is anything that restricts the throughput of a system. A constraint within an organization would be any resource for which the demand is greater than its available capacity. To increase the throughput of a system, the constraints must be identified, exploited if possible, and removed if necessary. Bottlenecks occur in many parts of daily life: when exiting a concert hall, when driving in rush-hour traffic, when dealing with a telephone receptionist or the cashier in a cafeteria line. Bottlenecks can usually be found by looking where people are waiting or where work is piling up.

The state's Department of Motor Vehicles required everyone to go through a series of steps to renew a driver's license: complete a form, take an eye test, have picture taken, pay fee, and pick up new license. Citizens regularly complained about having to wait in long lines. Rather than hire additional workers, the department manager began collecting data on the length of the line at each station. She then redesigned the process at the step with the longest line to reduce the time required. After these improvements were made, she designed extra stations at each step. Then she rotated two floater employees to the current bottleneck every hour. These changes eliminated complaints about lines.

A company's reports were not getting to customers in the amount of time promised. The manager of the unit looked around to see where the work was piling up. He found that word processing was the bottleneck. He spent time with the people in word processing and discovered that more than one-half of their time was spent updating and reworking reports. He was able to remove the bottleneck by redistributing responsibility for updating the reports. The timeliness of the reports improved.

---

17. *Use Automation* The flow of many processes can be improved by the intelligent use of automation. Consider automation to improve the work flow for any process to reduce costs, reduce cycle times, eliminate human slips, reduce repetitive manual tasks, and provide measurement.

A pizza delivery store automated their customer information system. When a repeat customer called in, the system would detect the incoming phone number and immediately pull up all the information about that customer on a terminal. This cut the time to communicate the necessary information by 80 percent and helped the delivery personnel know where to go for the delivery.

A hospital developed a system to automate the completion of many of the forms required by the various departments in the hospital, the customer, and the insurance companies. They recorded patient records electronically, and then were able to generate completed forms for transfer to the interested parties.

A potato chip manufacturer had a reputation with customers for having no discolored chips in their product. Manual inspection was expensive and not perfect. The job was boring. The company developed optical inspection equipment that could be put on the production line to find and remove defective potato chips. This use of automation decreased costs and increased the quality of the product to customers.

18. Smooth Work Flow Yearly, monthly, weekly, and daily changes in demand often cause work flow to fluctuate widely. Rather than trying to staff in order to handle the peak demands, steps can often be taken to better distribute the demand. This distribution results in a smooth work flow rather than in continual peaks and valleys.

In some cities, the downtown area is overcrowded during morning and evening rush-hour periods but underutilized during the rest of the day. These cities have smoothed the traffic flow by charging a premium to use streets, bridges, and tunnels during rush-hour periods. The premium is collected daily through tolls or monthly through permit stickers that commuters can purchase.

Citizens complained that they had to wait a long time to get a safety inspection at a gas station. A study of the system found that safety inspections have a rush period during the last week of each month (when stickers expire). Rather than add capacity by licensing additional stations, the state government changed the regulations to allow for an increased charge at the end of the month, with a lesser charge during the first three weeks of the month. Each gas station could then use the fee structure to balance their inspection work demand during the month.

A landscaping company's busiest time was in the spring. They could not keep up with requested work during that time. They studied the type of work they did throughout the year. They were able to identify a number of activities (trimming of trees, fertilizing, soil preparation, preparing beds, and supporting indoor plants) that could be done at other times. They developed packages of services that would spread this work throughout the year. They were able to increase their capacity without adding new resources.

---

19. Do Tasks in Parallel Many systems are designed so that tasks are done in a series or linear sequence. The second task is not begun until the first task is completed. This is especially true when different groups in the organization are involved in the different steps of a process. Sometimes, improvements in time and costs can be gained from designing the system to do some or all tasks in parallel. For example, the work on step 5 can begin as soon as step 1 is complete rather than waiting until steps 2, 3, and 4 are done.

Customers complained about having to wait while their invoice and other paperwork were prepared. The service organization redesigned their system to begin processing the paperwork while the service was being conducted. As soon as the service technician completed the work, a release was entered in the computer system and preparation of the invoice and other paperwork was begun. The paperwork was usually ready when the customer arrived at check-out.

A restaurant developed its business concept around fast service of high quality food. The system was designed to take the customers' orders before they were seated so that work on seating, drinks, and meal preparation could all begin in parallel. By the time the customers were seated and served drinks, the meal was well on its way to being prepared.

---

20. Consider People in the Same System People in different systems are usually working toward different purposes, each trying to optimize their own system. Taking actions that help people to think of themselves as part of the same system can give them a common purpose and provide a basis for optimizing the larger system.

A company had trouble with on-time deliveries from their suppliers. After discussions and data sharing with the key suppliers, they realized that their irregular ordering patterns made planning by the suppliers very difficult. They began to share their production fore-

casts with the suppliers so that they could develop plans compatible with the manufacturing company. They tested this process with five key suppliers for one year and saw an
80 percent reduction in late deliveries.

A clinic and nearby hospital had two different identification systems for physicians. This
resulted in duplicated work and numerous coding errors. At the encouragement of the
doctors, the two units worked together to develop a common identification system. The
resulting change decreased costs, reduced error corrections, and helped communication.

---

21. Use Multiple Processing Units To gain flexibility in controlling the work flow, try to
include multiple work stations, machines, processing lines, and fillers in a system. This makes it possible to run smaller lots, serve special customers, minimize the impact of maintenance and downtime, and add flexibility to staffing.
With multiple units, the primary product or service can be handled on one line
to maximize efficiency and minimize setup time. The less-frequent products and
services can be handled by the other units.

After studying alternative designs, a soup processing plant decided to build three smaller
filler lines rather than one large one. This gave the company more flexibility in processing a variety of soups on any one day by reducing cleanup and setup times between
changeovers.

A printing shop wanted to offer faster turnaround services in order to maintain and attract
customers. The facility was redesigned to use five smaller copiers rather than two large
ones. The new system provided faster turnaround for 92 percent of the shop's jobs.

A company had one mainframe computer with terminals to do processing throughout the
service center. Whenever the mainframe was down for maintenance, delays were created throughout the center. The company redesigned the computer stations with a network of personal computers. This change added flexibility and backup systems to the
center.

---

22. Adjust to Peak Demand Sometimes it is not possible to balance the demands made
on a system. In these cases, rather than keeping a fixed amount of resources
(materials, workers, and so on), historical data can be used to predict peak
demands. Then methods can be implemented to meet the temporarily increased
demand.

The hospital staff could not keep up with the demand for drawing blood samples from patients. Rather than just add staff, the hospital studied the demand for taking blood samples. The data showed that there was a peak demand from 6:00 to 8:00 A.M. every day. This peak created a backlog that was not cleared up until the afternoon. The hospital established part-time positions for people to draw blood each morning. This eliminated the backlog.

A chemical plant experienced a large increase in demand for one of its specialty products during the winter months. The company was faced with having to add new production or storage facilities to meet this demand. Management studied the historical demand and projections for all of the company's products throughout the year. They developed a plan to dedicate all of their production capacity to the one specialty product every December and January. The demand for the other products could be satisfied by increasing production in the fall months and using existing storage facilities.

A new restaurant expected daily peak demand periods during the lunch and dinner hours. The owners designed their service jobs around these peak periods and hired people who were comfortable working just during these hours, from 11:00 A.M. to 2:00 P.M. and from 5:00 P.M. to 10:00 P.M. each day. This system of work hours eliminated potential problems from the peak demand periods. The owners had a backlog of job applications from college students and others who could benefit from being free during the morning and afternoon hours.

C. Optimize Inventory

Inventory of all types is a possible source of waste in organizations. Inventory requires capital investment, storage space, and people to handle and keep track of it. In manufacturing organizations, inventory includes raw material waiting to be processed, in-process inventory, and finished-good inventory. For service organizations, the number of skilled workers available is often the key inventory issue. Extra inventory can result in higher costs with no improvement in performance for an organization. How can the costs associated with the maintenance of inventory be reduced? An understanding of where inventory is stored in a system is the first step in finding opportunities for improvement. The use of inventory pull systems such as "just-in-time" is one philosophy of operating an organization to minimize the waste from inventory.

Four change concepts are listed in this category:

23. Match Inventory to Predicted Demand
24. Use Pull Systems
25. Reduce Choice of Features
26. Reduce Multiple Brands of Same Item

Concepts 23 and 24 seem to offer two conflicting approaches to optimizing inventory. Matching inventory to predicted demand is most appropriate when cycle times for production or assembly are long. In these situations, it is not acceptable to wait until an order is received to begin production. The use of pull systems is more appropriate when production delays are short. Often these two concepts are combined to develop an optimum inventory strategy.

23. Match Inventory to Predicted Demand Extra inventory can result in higher costs with no improvement in performance for an organization. How can the proper amount of inventory to be maintained at any given time be determined? One approach to minimizing the costs associated with inventory is to use historical data to predict the demand. Using these predictions to optimize lead times, order quantities, and so on will lead to replenishing inventory in an economical manner. This is often the best approach to optimizing inventory when the process involves lengthy production times.

An automotive dealership used the judgement of the sales staff to decide what styles of cars to order each week. Often, cars were not sold within ninety days, and cars with the colors and features the customer requested were not available. The company studied the variation in historical demands for each type and style of car. Based on this analysis, a system was developed to predict the demand for the next ninety days, and it was then used to guide ordering decisions. After six months with the new system, the company was able to cut inventory costs and to do fewer dealer trades for other cars.

An office supply warehouse had inventory problems because of long lead times on specialty items. Over the years, inventory costs had steadily increased because purchasing would automatically increase their lead time or order in larger quantities anytime a shortage occurred. An effort was made to study historical ordering patterns for the twelve product lines with the highest inventory costs. The company found some seasonal patterns as well as some special purchases in the historical data. After adjusting the data for these special orders, predictions of monthly orders were developed for each of the product lines. Orders were placed based on these predictions rather than being the same every month. These changes resulted in reduced inventory costs and fewer shortages during the next year. A plan was made to extend this process to fifty more product lines.

---

24. Use Pull Systems In a pull system of production, work at a particular step in the process is done only if the next step in the process is demanding the work. Enough product is ordered or made to replenish what was just used. This is in contrast to most traditional "push systems," in which work is done as long as inputs are available. A pull system is designed to match production quantities with a downstream need. This approach can often result in lower inventories than a schedule-based production system. Pull systems are most beneficial in processes with short cycle times and high yields. Some features of effective pull systems are small lot sizes and container quantities, fast setup times, and minimal rework and scrap.

A company introduced a system of manufacturing based on the idea that plants manufacture products as customers order them. Suppliers deliver the required components directly to the assembly line, which reduces the need to stock these component parts, and because product is shipped as ordered, there is no need for a large inventory of finished goods. Using this approach, this company reduced its inventories by more than 50 percent since 1990. By saving interest payments on supplies, the company increased its cash flow by $60 million a year.

A chain of Mexican restaurants wanted to offer a variety of food alternatives with very fast service. The traditional approach in the fast-food industry is to keep inventories of all products available for purchase. This results in a lot of waste and old products must be thrown out. This chain developed a pull system that would assemble the specific food product after the customer ordered it. To make this pull system work, the company also designed the upstream processes to minimize product assembly time. The food product components were arranged to minimize the time from order to delivery of the assembled product to the customer. Using this pull system, the restaurant chain was able to eliminate waste and still match the delivery times of their competitors.

The staffing of nurses in a hospital can be studied as an inventory problem. Each floor wants to maintain a staff of nurses to meet routine and emergency needs twenty-four hours per day. Because of the variety of skills required, overstaffing is often the result. One hospital crossed-trained its nurses to be able to work in all areas of the hospital. A hospital pool of nurses was then created on each shift. Each floor would staff to meet routine needs based on patient census. Additional help for new patients and emergencies was obtained from the nursing pool. This pull-system approach resulted in significantly reduced nursing costs.

---

25. Reduce Choice of Features Many features are added to products and services to accommodate the desires and wants of different customers and different markets. Each of these features makes sense in the context of a particular customer at a particular time, but taken as a whole, they can have tremendous impact on inventory costs. A review of current demand for each feature and consideration of grouping the features can allow a reduction in inventory without loss of customer satisfaction.

A sandwich wagon took prepackaged sandwiches to job sites and sold them to workers for lunch. The wagon had to stock a large number of sandwiches to maintain a supply of all of the varieties that customers requested. Usually about 15 percent of stock was thrown away each day. The distribution process was changed to minimize the number of varieties offered. Based on high, consistent demand, one-half of the sandwiches were prepared as before. The other half did not include condiments and extras (cheese, tomatoes, peppers, and so on). A table at the end of the lunch wagon contained these extras so that customers could customize their sandwich as desired. After two weeks with the new system, inventory waste was reduced to about 3 percent with no change in sales.

Inventory in the auto industry has been greatly reduced by packaging options into standard packages and minimizing the amount of customization. Saturn has two standard option packages for its coupe, sedan, and station wagon. These options allow the customer to "special" order their car and at the same time reduce the amount of work-in-process inventory that would normally be needed to support such customer-driven choices.

A manufacturer of personal computers wanted both to improve delivery times and reduce the inventory costs of its dealers. The company also wanted to maintain the high level of customer satisfaction it had obtained by offering customers the features they wanted. A team studied the demand for features on all of its models during the previous six months. On the basis of this analysis, they were able to design a standard model that could accommodate about 80 percent of all orders without an increase in costs. A few of the features that were rarely ordered were eliminated. Dealers were asked to only stock these standard models. An assembly system was then designed to offer two-day delivery on the expected 20 percent custom orders. These changes resulted in reduced inventory costs and reduced delivery times for about 80 percent of the company's sales.

---

26. Reduce Multiple Brands of Same Items If an organization uses more than one brand of any particular item, inventory costs will usually be higher than necessary since a backup supply of each brand must be kept. Consider ways to reduce the number of brands while still providing the required service.

A grocery store stocks eight different brands of bread. A review of customer feedback revealed that "product out of stock" was one of the biggest complaints. Because of the large number of brands, the store could only afford to stock a minimum of inventory for each brand. A quality improvement team surveyed customers and studied buying patterns for bread for three months. The team then reduced the brands offered to three and developed inventory levels for the three brands that would make the chance of being out of stock very small. The store offered an explanation and coupons to the regular customers of the brands of bread eliminated. Total inventory was down and customer complaints about bread being out of stock were greatly reduced. A few customers were disappointed in losing their favorite brands.

A service organization let its individual offices buy whatever brand of office equipment they wanted. This had not been an issue when the organization was small but a review of inventory costs indicated that office equipment was one of the larger categories. This equipment included spare parts, cartridges, special paper, bulbs, ink, toners, and so on. Multiples of each of these items were stocked to provide backup for the many different brands of equipment that were being used. The company decided to standardize on one or two brands. Over the next five years they replaced equipment with the selected brands and reduced the inventory costs in this category by a factor of three.

A chemical plant used seven different brands of pump seals in its plant. They had to maintain inventories of each size for each brand. An engineering group studied the specification process and standardized with two brands of pump seals. As maintenance was done, modifications were made, and the old seals were replaced with the appropriate one of the two selected brands. After two years, all the pump seals in the plant were one of the two types. Inventory costs for pump seals were reduced by about two-thirds.

D. Change the Work Environment

Changes to the environments in which people work, study, and live can often provide leverage for improvements in performance. Production of products and services takes place in some type of work environment. As organizations try to improve quality, reduce costs, or increase the value of their products and services, technical changes are developed, tested, and implemented. Many of these technical changes do not lead to improvement, however, because the work environment is not ready to accept or support the changes. Changing the work environment itself can be a high-leverage opportunity for making other changes more effective.

The following eleven change concepts are included in this category:

27. Give People Access to Information
28. Use Proper Measurements
29. Take Care of Basics
30. Reduce Demotivating Aspects of Pay System
31. Conduct Training
32. Implement Cross-Training
33. Invest More Resources in Improvement
34. Focus on Core Processes and Purpose
35. Share Risks
36. Emphasize Natural and Logical Consequences
37. Develop Alliances/Cooperative Relationships

27. Give People Access to Information Traditionally, organizations have carefully controlled the information available to various groups of employees. Making information available to employees relevant to their jobs allows them to suggest changes, make good decisions, and take actions that lead to improvements. The development of Cable News Network's (CNN) worldwide coverage in the 1980s is a good example of the power of information. CNN's coverage of events lets people know what is happening throughout the world in real time. This change in television reporting changed the way people think about the world. People view themselves as a part of major events rather than as passive bystanders.

A company had schedulers working in all of its manufacturing units. The scheduler used production measures and the customer order database to modify the manufacturing plan on a real-time basis to make sure that commitments for shipping would be made. The company decided to make these data available to all production personnel and to give them the responsibility for scheduling. Computer terminals at each job station were modified to allow access to real-time information on production and orders. A training session on scheduling was conducted, and the schedulers were reassigned to other jobs. For the first three months there were some problems with delayed orders, but after that, performance returned to previous levels. The company was able to reduce its staff by sixty positions.

A service organization was disappointed in its initial efforts to get employees involved in its quality improvement efforts. Many of the employee groups were working on projects that were not strategically important to the company. When this issue was raised, the managers found out that the employees did not understand the strategic issues in the company. The company began distributing a summary of its strategic and business plans each year to all employees. Quarterly updates in the plan were discussed in the employee newsletter. Employees were asked to get involved with improvement efforts related to these plans in their areas. Within six months, the results from quality improvement efforts throughout the company began to positively impact key performance measures.

---

28. Use Proper Measurements Measurement plays an important role in focusing people on particular aspects of a business. In many organizations, the things that are measured are considered important while the things not measured are considered unimportant. Developing appropriate measures, making better use of existing measures, and improving measurement systems can lead to improvement throughout the organization.

Many companies try to utilize measures that are not accurate or that are of unknown accuracy. Inaccurate measures lead people astray, resulting in tampering, ignoring problems, and so on. A study of the quality of measurement often indicates that the accuracy of many of the measures do not support the importance that managers placed on them each month. When more accurate measures are developed, everyone begins to treat the measures with more respect, and fewer changes have to be made to plans each month.

A company wanted to rely more on first-line operators, rather than engineers, for problem solving and local improvements. Many employees were reluctant to accept that role. Managers incorporated measurement, data collection, and data analysis into all jobs in order to get workers more involved with understanding the performance of their processes. This change led to increased operator involvement in testing and implementing changes.

A hospital had a cesarean section rate of greater than 40 percent. All previous efforts by the administration to reduce this rate had not been successful. The medical director began to display the C-section rate by doctor in the doctors' lounge each month. Within six months, the rate had gone down to near the national average of 25 percent.

Wrong measures motivate people to do the wrong things. A company measured their inventories on the last day of each quarter. They began holding operating managers accountable for inventories above targets. Reported inventories immediately went down, but other performance measures indicated problems. Investigations found that massive changes were being made during the last week of each quarter to redistribute the inventory where it would not be measured. The measurement system was changed to an average daily inventory. This eliminated the disruptive end-of-the-quarter activities.

---

29. Take Care of Basics There are certain fundamentals that must be done to make any organization successful. It is sometimes useful to take a fresh look at these basics to see whether the organization is still on track. If there are fundamental problems in the business, changes in other areas may not lead to improvements. Concepts like orderliness, cleanliness, discipline, and managing costs and prices are examples of fundamentals in any organization. Also, when people's basic needs are not being met, meaningful improvements cannot be expected in other areas. The "Five-S" movement, which was the beginning of quality control in Japanese workshops, got its name from the Japanese words for straighten up, put things in order, clean up, personal cleanliness, and discipline.

A quality improvement team was established to reduce errors in assembly. In their interviews with assemblers and technicians, they found that noise from equipment and radios was thought to be the number one cause of errors. The team developed a rearrangement of the floor space that would separate workers who liked to hear the radio from those who did not. Barriers were established around equipment to minimize noise, and an isolated area for equipment repairs was set up. After implementing these changes, the assembly errors dropped by 40 percent.

A leasing company found that the changes it had been making were not improving the company's competitive position. An outside group was asked to review all of the company's contracts and leases to see whether it was charging and receiving fair amounts. The outside group found that the rents the company had been collecting for the past two years were 30 percent under market value. After making significant changes to develop rates consistent with the market, the company's financial performance became very healthy. They then returned their focus to improving the operation of the business.

---

30. Reduce Demotivating Aspects of the Pay System Pay is rarely a positive motivator in an organization, but it can cause confusion and become a demotivator. Some pay systems can encourage competition rather than cooperation among employees. Another result of some pay systems is the reluctance to take risks or make changes. Review the organization's system for pay to ensure that the current system does not cause problems in the organization.

An automotive service organization was trying to reduce cycle times for activities that required customers to wait. A number of changes were developed and tested that indicated improvements in cycle time. However, when these changes were implemented, no improvements resulted. An investigation indicated that the improvements in cycle times of these processes actually decreased the workers' pay. The company changed the pay system so that it did not discourage workers from making the cycle time improvements. Management immediately started seeing improvements in their cycle time measures.

A company had a complex set of job titles with many different pay rates. Workers constantly changed jobs through a bidding system because of pay differentials. Training costs were high and experience levels in jobs were low. The management negotiated with the union to level the pay for most of the jobs. Job hopping was reduced and training costs decreased by 50 percent.

The organization's performance appraisal system was used to give merit pay increases. Employees and supervisors were constantly complaining about the inequities in the system. The company changed the pay system to one based on specific job skills and market rates. Everyone who performed successfully in a particular job received the same pay. The company then changed its appraisal system to a supervisor/worker dialogue on how to improve the organization. Pay and appraisal were no longer issues in the organization.

31. Conduct Training Training is basic to quality performance and the ability to make changes for improvement. Many changes will not be effective if people have not received the basic training required to do a job. Training should include the "why" as well as the "what" and the "how."

Every spring a new lawn-and-facilities maintenance crew would damage and destroy equipment and landscaping when they began mowing. The maintenance manager developed a half-day training sessions for all new employees on how to use the maintenance and mowing equipment. The training also covered safety issues and the types of problems that had occurred in the past. After the first session, this investment in training reduced the problems by 75 percent.

A quality improvement team at a hospital was trying to reduce medication mistakes. They developed a control chart that indicated a stable process with about fifty-five medication mistakes per month for the past three years. A study of the mistakes indicated that about

65 percent of the mistakes were connected with intravenous (IV) orders. After reviewing their findings with the nursing council, the team decided to develop a training module on IV administration. Over the next three months, the module was developed and all nurses attended the four-hour training program. The training program included a self-test. Within six months, the number of IV-related medication mistakes was reduced by 70 percent.

A supplier to the automotive industry trained all of its employees in the basics of quality improvement and statistical process control. The training included the use of such tools as flow diagrams, control charts, and basic planned experimentation. The supplier then built these concepts into the operation of the manufacturing facility. Workers were held accountable for conducting experiments and making suggestions for improvement, as well being responsible for production numbers. After everyone became experienced with the new way of operating, product quality became more predictable and improvements became a normal occurrence in the company.

---

32. Implement Cross-Training Cross-training means training people in an organization to do multiple jobs. Such training allows for flexibility and makes change easier. The investment required for the extra training will pay off in productivity, product quality, and cycle times.

A home builder was interested in offering to build a house in significantly less time than the industry average of 110 days. The standard practice was to hire separate subcontractors to build each part of a house (framing, plumbing, roofing, electrical, and so on). Each subcontractor tried to optimize its work, and often damaged the work of the other contractors. The home builder changed his approach to one based on self-managed work teams whose members were all trained to build the whole house. Each member of the team had a specialty (based on prior training and experience), but each member was also crossed-trained for all jobs. The first homes built with the teams did not show much improvement. But after they had learned to work as a team, they were able to reduce the time to build a home from an average of 110 days to 60 days.

An oil production company in Canada was looking for ways to reduce costs. The company's oil fields were spread throughout Canada. Maintenance salaries were the biggest expense, including electricians, mechanics, and hydraulic specialists. A study of these people's work showed that about 83 percent of their time was spent in traveling from one well site to the next. Often, two or three workers with different specialties were required for a maintenance work order. The company developed a two-year program to cross-train all of the maintenance personnel in all of the maintenance functions. Now only one person needs to go to each well site. Specialists can still be called in when needed. Three years after implementing cross-training, maintenance costs had decreased by 40 percent.

A study of operations in a hospital pointed out that nurses had to wait until a phlebotomist was available to draw blood from a patient. The hospital trained its nurses to draw blood rather than wait for a phlebotomist. This increased the productivity of the nursing staff and reduced waiting time for patients.

---

33. Invest More Resources in Improvement In some organizations, people spend more than a full-time job getting their required tasks completed and fighting the fires created in their work. The only changes made are reactions to problems or changes mandated outside the organization. To break out of this trap, management must learn how to start investing time in developing, testing, and implementing changes that will lead to improvements. Some methods for focusing resources on improvement include substituting improvement for non-value-added work, using full-time "SWAT" teams assigned to a process or outcome, assigning positions in research and development to process improvement, using industrial engineers in service industries, and using relief operators, temporaries, or overtime hours.

A manager in a retail operation was aware of many problems that needed to be fixed in the way the operation ran. Employees barely had time to complete their basic work (the customers kept getting in the way!) and handle the problems that cropped up, so he could not ask them to spend time developing and making improvements. He decided to hire temporary workers to free experienced workers from routine and support tasks that did not interact with customers. He established quality improvement teams to invest the workers freed-up time. These teams were able to develop and implement changes that eliminated many of the recurring problems in the stores. With fewer problems, employees were able to assume all of their previous duties and still have over five percent of their time to invest in making improvements.

The president of a distribution company was frustrated about his company's lack of progress in integrating ongoing improvements into the business. His review sessions with each manager revealed that they needed time to work on improvement. The management team developed a plan for each manager to ask his or her internal customers the reason for each report, meeting, and review currently produced. On the basis of the results of this survey, the managers eliminated the activities that did not directly support the purpose of the organization or that were not viewed as high priority by the customers. They were able to free about 12 percent of the management team's time requirements. This time was then invested in efforts aimed at integrating continuous improvement into their business activities. Three years later, the company was recognized as one of the top distributors in the industry.

---

34. Focus on Core Processes and Purpose Why are people doing all of the activities that go on in the organization? Which activities are directly related to the purpose of the organization? These are the core processes. Core processes can also be characterized as those activities that provide value directly to external customers. To reduce costs, consider reducing activities that are not part of the core processes.

A service company needed to reduce its overhead costs to stay competitive in its routine work areas. Each department manager asked everyone to review their work by asking the question, *How does this activity add value to our external customer?* To answer this question, the path of each person's work was followed until the connection was made to an external customer. Each department manager then developed a list of activities for which there was not a positive answer to the question and worked to phase out those activities.

A health care organization used an expensive home monitor to test for preterm labor, but when the condition was diagnosed, they had no treatment for it. The use of the monitor was eliminated until a productive use could be found for the test results.

An airline was involved in making travel arrangements for its customers, including hotel reservations, ground transportation accommodations, food service reservations, and entertainment plans. At one time, this service had been considered an important and profitable part of the business, but the cost of keeping up-to-date on hotels, rental cars, and so on had become greater than the revenue received from the service. The company ran some tests to see if eliminating the service would affect the core business. After finding no effect, this noncore activity was eliminated, and the company became a low-cost, no-frills airline.

---

35. Share Risks Every business is faced with taking risks, and their accompanying potential rewards or losses. Many people become more interested in the performance of their organization when they can clearly see how their future is tied to the long-term performance of the organization. Developing systems that allow all employees to share in the risks can lead to an increased interest in performance. Types of plans for sharing risks and gains include profit sharing, gain sharing, bonuses, and pay for knowledge. Care must be taken with these types of programs. Companies can undermine workers' job satisfaction and creativity by placing too much emphasis on extrinsic motivation from incentives. Systems must be carefully designed to keep everyone focused on the purpose of the organization and not just on the potential short-term gains.

A construction company had trouble convincing potential clients to allow the company to use new, unproved technologies and methods in their engineering/construction work. To obtain new business, the company offered to share the risks and rewards with their clients. They agreed to accept half of the downside costs of failures in return for a percentage of savings from the successes. The company was thus able to get commitment for new business that met its revenue requirements, and to create win-win situations for the company and its clients.

A service company with a cyclical business wanted to reduce costs when business was down without laying off workers. The employees agreed to tie 25 percent of their current compensation to the company's net earnings each quarter. Their pay would depend on quarterly performance relative to the previous year's average quarterly revenue. When business was good, they received more than their previous salaries. During a nine-month recession, when the company was not making money, they received significantly less pay than they had previously. The employees consequently became much more interested in the business and the markets in which they worked.

---

36. Emphasize Natural and Logical Consequences An alternative approach to traditional reward-and-punishment systems in organizations is to focus on "natural and logical consequences." Natural consequences follow from the natural order of the physical world (for example, not eating leads to hunger), while logical consequences follow from the reality of the business or social world (for example, if you are late for a meeting, you will not have a chance to have input on some of the issues discussed). The idea of emphasizing natural and logical consequences is to get everyone to be responsible for their own behavior rather than to use power, judge others, and force submission. Rather than demanding conformance, the use of natural and logical consequences permits choice.

Joe was having problems with truck drivers arriving at the terminal late in the morning. When this happened, he had to repeat announcements a number of times and shift delivery assignments. He would regularly complain to certain drivers about showing up late, but this did not help the problem. Joe decided to quit complaining and reworking the load assignments; instead, he emphasized the logical consequences of the drivers' late arrival. He made it clear that beginning the following week, any driver who did not arrive in time for the 6:00 A.M. meeting would not receive any delivery assignment that day and would therefore not be paid for deliveries. After a few weeks (during which some drivers had to work overtime to cover loads missed), the late arrivals were eliminated.

Car manufacturers in Europe have begun to design their products to facilitate eventual recycling of materials. A concept that has been proposed by some environmental advocates is that the producer of any product should also be responsible for its ultimate disposal. When the consumer is finished with a product, they should return it to the producer. The producer can than reuse or recycle the product. This will require producers to consider recycling potential in the design of products and packaging.

37. Develop Alliances/Cooperative Relationships During recent years, many industries have gone through a period of consolidation, acquisition, and merger. Often the result is fewer and larger organizations in an industry, but not much effort to integrate the pieces into an overall system. Consequently, there is no increase in value to the industry's customers. Various types of alliances based on the principle of cooperation to optimize the interactions between the parts of the system offer a better approach for integration of organizations.

During the period from 1992 to 1994, a frenzy of mergers, acquisitions, and alliances were carried out in the health care industry. While many different organizations fell under common ownership, few initially became integrated systems. The same problems and barriers that existed prior to the mergers were incorporated into the new organization structures. However, a few organizations formed alliances with the objective to create a truly integrated health care system. These organizations first developed a statement of their common purpose. Then they set out to optimize the interactions among the various parts of the system by predicting demand for services, standardizing leverage points, smoothing the work flow between parts, and integrating the customer into the system.

Acquisitions brought three companies with competing product lines into the same corporation. The chairman brought the heads of each of the companies together and asked them to merge product lines and begin to use common systems. After struggling for a year, performance for each of the companies and the corporation was worse than prior to the acquisition. The chairman then took a different approach to integrating the companies. He held a joint meeting with the management staff of each company. Together they developed a statement of purpose with a strong customer focus. Then they formed intercompany teams to integrate the product lines and systems, with each team's aim being to optimize the overall organization toward the common purpose. In less than a year, the performance had turned around and the expected synergies had begun to be realized.

The demand for school services in a community had decreased significantly as the population became older. The public and private schools in the community had begun competing for students. The result of the competitive efforts was increasing costs for all of the schools. This resulted in higher tuitions, losses in revenue, and higher tax rates. The chamber of commerce formed an alliance of all of the schools in the community based on cooperation rather than competition. The alliance developed a purpose: to optimize the interactions between the various schools toward the education of the children in the community. During the next five years, the community made the transition to being a smaller system with lower costs and improved measures of learning for its students.

E. Enhance the Producer/Customer Relationship

To benefit from improvements in quality of products and services, the customer must recognize and appreciate the improvements. Many ideas for improvement can come directly from a supplier or from the producer's customers. Many problems in organizations occur because the producer does not understand the customer's needs, or because customers are not clear about their expectations of suppliers. The interface between the producer/provider and its customers provides opportunities to learn and develop changes that will lead to improvement.

The following eight change concepts are included in this category:

38. Listen to Customers
39. Coach Customers to Use the Product/Service
40. Focus on the Outcome to a Customer
41. Use a Coordinator
42. Reach Agreement on Expectations
43. Outsource for "Free"
44. Optimize Level of Inspection
45. Work with Suppliers

38. Listen to Customers It is easy for people to get caught up in the internal functioning of the organization and forget why they are in business: to serve their customers. Time should be invested on a regular basis in processes that "listen" to the customers. Sometimes, it is important to figure out how to communicate with customers further down the supply chain, or even with the final consumer of the product or service. Talk to customers about their experiences in using your products. Learn about improvement opportunities.

After spending time with patients (the consumer), a medical supply company learned that needles packaged with a drug the company sold caused pain to the patients. The patients were buying their own needles and throwing the ones in the package away. The hospitals and clinics that the company supplied had never given them this feedback.

The owner of a hardware supply company wanted to differentiate his company from competitors based on customer service. He developed a system to get his sales managers involved in learning from the customers. Once each quarter, each sales manager would identify his or her five largest accounts. Each manager would follow an order from each of these customers from call-in to delivery at the customer's site. The sales representative would talk to someone at the customer site while the delivery was being unloaded and listen for opportunities to make it easier to use the products being received. This practice established this organization as the premier supply chain in the company's market.

---

39. Coach Customers to Use the Product/Service Customers often encounter quality problems and actually increase their costs because they do not understand all of the intricacies of the product or service. Companies can increase the value of their products and services by developing ways to coach customers and consumers on how to use them.

A car rental company analyzed accident data for their rental fleets every year. The top three to five types or causes of accidents were identified. Various methods were then used to make renters aware of the situation when these causes were present. The format of this coaching was changed every three to six months to keep it from becoming routine. For example, a list of airport-related potential hazards was placed on the steering wheel, from which it had to be removed before driving the car.

Airlines have a difficult time getting passengers to listen to flight instructions and safety messages. One airline added some humor to these messages to get people to pay attention. More passengers now listen carefully to the coaching so that they do not miss the punch line.

A supplier of expensive laboratory equipment was able to differentiate its products by assigning a technician to work in a laboratory that purchased the equipment. The technician would coach the laboratory personnel for one day a week for the first three months after purchase.

---

40. Focus on the Outcome to a Customer Make the outcome (product or service) produced by your organization the focus of all activities. First, clearly understand the outcomes that customers expect from your organization. Then, to focus improvement efforts on a particular work activity, answer the question, *How does this activity support the outcome to the customer?* Make improvements in the quality, costs, efficiencies, cycle times, and so on of that activity. Organize people, departments, and processes in a way that best serves the customer, paying particular attention to the producer/customer interfaces. This change concept could also be described as "begin with the end in mind."

A law firm that specialized in government regulation began to focus its work on the outcome of its services. After discussions with clients, the firm determined that the important outcome was "approval by regulators as quickly as possible." All of the firm's services that focused on this outcome were studied, as were data from past cases, to determine what affected this outcome. Changes were made in the standard pricing method to emphasize quick results. Members of the law team were encouraged to bring in experts from outside the firm who had knowledge of particular regulations. Resources were increased on activities that had been bottlenecks in past cases. The result of these effort was that the firm became the place to go to get quick regulatory approval.

A health services organization was overwhelmed with the advances in technology in the health care industry. The organization had spent more than six million dollars during the previous two years on new medical equipment. Consequently, its costs were higher, but there was no evidence of improvement in the quality of its services. The organization decided to focus future decisions to purchase new types of equipment on the outcome of the organization's services—the diagnosis and treatment of patients. New equipment would be purchased only if the organization could conduct tests that showed how the equipment would improve their medical diagnoses or the treatment of the patient. They found that their purchase of new equipment declined during the next year, but the equipment that was purchased was being used by all of the staff.

How can public education systems be improved? Outcome-based education is based on what educators want students to do or be able to do. This approach to education involves a process that allows school districts to clarify what all stakeholders in their respective communities want as a result of schooling for their students. Personnel, facilities, equipment, and budget are then organized to accomplish the desired results. The school district managers hold themselves accountable for achieving these outcomes. A number of school districts throughout the United States have used this approach and achieved higher student scores on standardized tests, lower dropout rates, and advanced placement in schools at the next level.

---

41. Use a Coordinator A coordinator's primary job is to manage producer/customer linkages. For example, an expeditor is someone who focuses on ensuring adequate supplies of materials and equipment or who coordinates the flow of materials in an organization. Having someone coordinate the flow of materials, tools, parts, and processed goods for critical processes can help prevent problems and downtime. A coordinator can also be used to work with customers to provide extra services. One example of a coordinator is a *case manager,* who acts as a buffer between a complex process and the customer. The case manager must have the authority to get things done when the customer's needs are not being met.

A trucking company wanted to differentiate its delivery and hauling services by providing additional value to customers who used these services. A position was developed at each delivery terminal to focus on minimizing the impact of problems on the customer. Some of the services and activities performed by the person in this position were calling truckers to find out status of deliveries, sending help or calling the customer when a delivery was going to be late, and providing tips to customers to make it easier for them to use their services on a day-to-day basis. Customers began to depend on this service and were willing to pay a premium for it on their deliveries.

To manage patient flow, a clinic created a new position of "nurse coordinator." The responsibility of this position included minimizing the number of visits a patient must make. Nurse coordinators looked for situations where the handoff between departments in the clinic was not smooth. This new position also created a career track for nurses interested in moving into administration.

People do not like to spend time in lines. An airline found that one of its most frequent customer complaints was that they had to wait so long in lines for ticketing and checking baggage. The airlines began to use a coordinator at busy times to walk the line and help passengers with their needs. The coordinator listened to problems, moved customers to faster lines, helped the customers get prepared for their transaction, took care of special needs, and offered cheery interactions for the customers who had to wait. Instead of complaints about waiting, a number of comments were received on how friendly the service was at the affected terminals.

---

42. Reach Agreement on Expectations Many times customer dissatisfaction occurs because the customers feel that they have not received the products or services they were taught to expect as a result of advertising, special promotions, and promises by the sales group. Marketing processes should be coordinated with production capabilities. Clear expectations should be established before the product is produced or the service is delivered to the customer.

A phone service company advertised "friendly service," but had no hiring, development, or training process to deliver special services. After numerous customers dropped their business because of lack of friendly service, the company changed its approach to marketing. It learned not to advertise until it had a system in place that could really deliver friendly service.

A study by a quality improvement team in a construction company found that fewer than 15 percent of their jobs were completed within the original schedule. The company tried to handle customer complaints by showing the customer that most of the delays were in areas beyond their control (weather, financing, customer changes, and so on). This often infuriated the customers, and they responded negatively in satisfaction surveys. The team recommended that a written schedule showing the key stages of construction be used to determined how long each stage normally took. This schedule was reviewed with the customer prior to signing a contract. The customer was notified about the cause of any significant delays immediately when they occurred. These changes in clarifying expectations resulted in better management of job schedules and an increase in customer satisfaction ratings.

43. Outsource for "Free" Sometimes it is possible to get suppliers to perform additional functions for the customer with little or no increase in the price to the customer. A task that is a major inconvenience or cost for the customer can be performed inexpensively and efficiently by the supplier. The supplier might be willing to do this task for "free" in order to secure ongoing business with the customer.

A distribution company offered to order and stock supplies for a chemical plant's warehouse. The chemical company could thus eliminate six full-time positions currently used to stock the supplies delivered by the distributor. By performing the stocking, the distributor could obtain better lead times for deliveries and learn about other supply needs of the customer. The savings in inventory more than offset the labor costs incurred by the distributor. After six months performing this service, the distributor made a series of recommendations on layout and ordering patterns that further reduced the chemical company's cost of materials.

By observing customers, a computer distributor found that the biggest hassle in the purchase of a new computer was loading all the desired software on the system. The distributor began advertising that it would load all standard commercial software "for free" when the computer was ordered. The company also developed agreements with software suppliers to purchase the software at discounts and load it onto all the computers it sold. This free service became a profitable component of the business.

---

44. Optimize level of inspection What level of inspection is appropriate for a process? All products will eventually receive some type of inspection (possibly by the user). Options for inspection at any given place in the supply chain are: no inspection, 100 percent inspection, or reduction or increases to the current level of inspection. A study of the level of inspection can potentially lead to changes that increase quality of outcomes to the customers and/or decrease costs.

W. Edward Deming developed a method for making an economic decision on the amount of inspection that should be done at various stages of manufacturing and assembly. A manufacturing company used this economic analysis to decide if any 100 percent inspection should be done for each type of product. The company was able to reduce the number of defects going to customers, and to decrease their total cost of inspection.

A chemical producer had a series of expensive settlements due to contaminated products. One of the potential sources of contamination was the rail car into which the product was loaded. The company started doing railroad car inspections prior to loading. Records were kept on how often problems were found during these inspections. After one year, the company shared the data with its customers and decided to eliminate the inspections. By conducting the inspections and sharing the data, the company was able to develop fair and cost-effective practices.

A military organization decided to have selected maintenance workers fly on the test flight of an aircraft after major maintenance activities. This heightened the level of focus of the maintenance crews on the inspection work.

45. Work with Suppliers Inputs to a process sometimes control the costs and quality of performance of a process. Working with suppliers to use their technical knowledge can often reduce the cost of using their products or services. Suppliers will even have some ideas on how to make changes in a company's process that will surprise its customers.

A food company requires its suppliers of processing equipment to participate on improvement teams focused on customizing their equipment. The objective of the teams is to optimize the food product. Planned experiments are conducted regularly in the plant to improve the various types of processing equipment. In one series of studies, the company was able to practically eliminate bone chips from a processed meat product.

A large oil company asked its liquid storage tank supplier how the company could reduce the total cost of tank construction and maintenance. Based on the oil company's recommendations, the supplier took over the inspection responsibility of the constructed products. This approach has reduced the number of previously redundant inspections and has reduced typical project costs by two percent.

F. Manage Time

"Time is money." This age-old concept provides an opportunity to make time a focal point for improving any organization. An organization can gain a competitive advantage by reducing the time to develop new products, waiting times for services, lead times for orders and deliveries, and cycle times for all functions in the organization. Many organizations have estimated that less than five percent of the time needed to manufacture and deliver a product to a customer is actually dedicated to producing the product. The rest of the time is spent starting up or waiting.

There are five change concepts in this category:

46. Reduce Setup or Startup Time
47. Set up Timing to Use Discounts
48. Optimize Maintenance
49. Extend Specialists' Time
50. Reduce Wait Time

46. Reduce Setup or Startup Time Time can be lost and costs increased while getting ready to produce a product or service. Setup times can often be cut in half just by getting organized for the setup. Minimizing setup or startup time allows the organization to maintain lower levels of inventory and get more productivity out of its assets. One approach to reducing setup time incorporates four steps:

1. Define time internal to the setup and time external.
2. Do all of the external work ahead of time.
3. Convert additional internal time to external.
4. Improve the processes affecting the internal time.

A consulting organization received inquiries about its services from all over the world. Consultants in the organization communicated with potential clients over the phone and then wrote a letter describing the conversation and actions to be taken later. After a while, someone noted that this process involved several "standard" letters. These letters were reviewed and three types of letters were developed into a template that the consultant could use for 90 percent of the inquiries. This reduced the need to setup a new letter of response for each inquiry. It also enabled the consultant to spend a little more time making sure that the letter addressed the particular concerns of the potential client. Overall, the amount of time crafting letters declined, resulting in more timely responses to potential clients, and more useful communication.

When patients come out of by-pass surgery in a hospital, they need to be immediately placed on monitors. This is a very risky time for a patient. The first step in hooking up the monitors is to remove some of the intravenous lines put in during surgery. To reduce this setup time, the hospital changed the process for removing the surgical intravenous lines. Personnel in the recovery room began removing the lines before sending the patient to be placed on the monitors. This change in the process reduced the setup time during this risky period by one-third.

---

47. Set up Timing to Use Discounts The planning and timing of many activities can be coordinated to take advantage of savings and discounts that are available. Designing a process to take advantage of available discounts can save money and reduce operating costs. An organization must have a system in place to take advantage of such opportunities. For example, taking advantage of available discounts on invoices offered by suppliers for paying bills within ten days of the invoice date requires a system that can process an invoice and cut a check within the discount period. Opportunities to apply this concept require a flexible process and knowledge of the opportunity to take advantage of the timing.

Airlines set their rates so as to take advantage of the traveler who cannot plan ahead. Business people often end up paying two to four times the ticket price of someone who has a Saturday night stay over and who purchased the ticket weeks in advance. One company decided to turn this situation into a possible perk for their employees. They offered employees who were willing to travel early or stay over through Saturday two-thirds of the savings in ticket price. This savings could be applied to hotel, restaurant, and entertainment during their weekend stay. The company saved money, and many employees were delighted to take advantage of this perk.

Large groups can be set up in an organization or industry to take advantage of volume discounts. Thirty pharmacies in a hospital system coordinated their purchase of drugs. Together they were large enough to negotiate directly with the drug manufacturers for timing and volume discounts. This coordination of purchases reduced costs by fifteen percent.

---

48. Optimize Maintenance Time is lost and quality often deteriorates when production and service equipment breaks down. A preventive maintenance strategy attempts to keep people and machines in good condition instead of waiting until there is a breakdown. Through proper design and the study of historical data, an efficient maintenance program can be designed to keep equipment in production with a minimum of downtime for maintenance. Learning to observe and listen to equipment before it breaks down is also an important component of any plan to optimize maintenance.

A large corporation wanted to decrease its costs for medical insurance. It structured its medical package to encourage employees to invest in prevention of health care problems through regular checkups and by eliminating behaviors potentially detrimental to their health. The company provided regular education in their newsletters about health tips and healthy eating habits. After focusing on these preventive health maintenance methods for two years, health care costs were down, and the company started receiving discounts in their insurance premiums.

A power plant could not afford to have one of its large turbines break down. The plant was designed with enough capacity to keep one turbine off-line at any time for maintenance. This strategy worked until demand increased beyond the planned capacity. To reduce off-line time for maintenance, the company developed vibration-monitoring equipment to "listen" to the turbines. Measurements were plotted and studied to decide when to perform preventive maintenance on a turbine. Using this strategy to optimize maintenance, they reduced downtime of the "extra" turbine by 80 percent and were able to meet the greater capacity demands.

49. Extend Specialists' Time Organizations employ specialists who have specific skills or knowledge, but not all of their work duties use these skills or knowledge. Try to remove assignments and job requirements that do not use the specialists' skills. Find ways to let specialists have a broader impact on the organization, especially when the specialist is a constraint to throughput in the organization.

The principal of a school wanted the teachers to spend more of their time developing new teaching methods. They negotiated with the local university to provide more "practice teachers" to the school. The practice teachers were assigned routine teaching assignments to free up the experienced teachers to work on curriculum development.

In rural communities there is always a shortage of medical specialists. It is not practical to have specialists available for all possible medical conditions in sparsely populated areas. One hospital system has used information technology to extend the availability of all of its medical specialists to primary care doctors in these communities. The results of X-rays, electrocardiograms, and other tests are transferred electronically to the specialist. The specialist reviews the test results and then communicates back to the primary care physician.

50. Reduce Wait Time Nobody likes to wait. Reduction in wait time can lead to improvements in many types of services. Ideas for change that can reduce the time that customers have to wait are especially useful. This applies not only to the time to perform a service for the customer, but the time it takes the customer to use or maintain a product.

A chemical supplies manufacturer studied its customers' systems to find ways to differentiate the manufacturer's products from the products of other companies. The manufacturer learned that wait time from order to receipt was the most important measure of quality on which to work. It changed its inventory practices, contracted with an overnight delivery company, and began offering overnight delivery on about 90 percent of its chemicals (with about a 20 percent increase in price). This change differentiated the company's products from those of its competitors and helped the company to double its sales within two years. Customers gladly paid the 20 percent premium to not have to wait.

In the 1980s, travelers were used to waiting in lines to sign forms before obtaining a rental car. Rental car companies have changed their systems so that regular customers will not have to wait in any lines or sign any forms to receive their car. At first this practice differentiated the services of a few of the major companies, but now it has become a customer expectation.

G. Manage Variation

Everything varies! But how does knowing this help to develop changes that will lead to improvement? Many quality and cost problems in a process or product are due to variation. The same process that produces 95 percent on-time delivery or good product is the same process that produces the other 5 percent of late deliveries or bad product. Reduction of variation will improve the predictability of outcomes (and may actually exceed customer expectations) and will help to reduce the frequency of poor results. Many procedures and activities are designed to deal with variation in systems. Consideration of Shewhart's concept of common and special causes opens up opportunities to improve these procedures. By focusing on the variation issues, some ideas for changes can be developed.

Three basic approaches can be taken to deal with variation:

1. Reduce the variation
2. Compensate (deal with the variation)
3. Exploit the variation

The benefits of reducing variation have been well-documented. For example:

A manufacturer of heat exchangers was having problems sealing tubes in their exchanger. Variation in the air pressure system contributed to most leaking tubes. The air pressure system was updated and the stability of 80 psi maintained. This resulted in a dramatic decrease in the number of leaking tubes. This problem had previously been viewed as the fault of workers assembling the heat exchangers.

An automotive company has learned to manufacture engine and transmission parts with minimum variation. The superb fit of the parts has allowed them to reduce the normal lubrication and servicing required for most cars. They also expect to have better engine reliability and lower repair and replacement warranty costs.

This category includes eight change concepts:

51. Standardization (Create a Formal Process)
52. Stop Tampering (Use Statistical Process Control)
53. Develop Operational Definitions
54. Improve Predictions
55. Develop Contingency Plans
56. Sort Product into Grades
57. Desensitize
58. Exploit Variation

The first four concepts deal with ways to reduce the variation. Concepts 55, 56, and 57 provide ways to deal with existing variation. Concept 58 deals explicitly with exploiting variation.

51. Standardization (Create a Formal Process) The use of standards, or standardization, has a negative and bureaucratic connotation to many people. However, an appropriate amount of standardization can provide a foundation upon which improvement in quality and costs can be built. Standardization is one of the primary methods for reducing variation in a system. The use of standardization, or creating a more formal process, should be considered for the parts of a system that have big effects on the outcomes (that is, the leverage points).

In the early 1980s, one of the largest industrial companies in the United States had thirty-four different payroll systems. They required a large number of employees to support these different systems. The systems were standardized and one common system was developed. This reduced the number of financial processing centers from five to one and allowed the corporation to cut finance operations payroll by 40 percent over ten years.

A hospital's records showed much variation among patients in recovery time from knee operations. Average costs for this particular operation were higher than other health systems. The hospital worked with a team of doctors and therapists to develop a standard process for patients who had a knee joint replaced. After implementing the standard process, recovery times became more consistent and the hospitals costs were in line with other systems.

In the United States, school curriculums vary from district to district and from state to state. This variation causes problems when students transfer to other districts. In Japan, the elementary school curriculums have been standardized throughout the country. This allows teachers to focus their energies on teaching technique rather than content. The quality of classroom teaching is high. Also, when students transfer to a new school, there are no gaps or duplication.

---

52. Stop Tampering Tampering is defined as interfering so as to weaken or change for the worse. In many situations, changes are made on the basis of the last result observed or measured. Often these changes actually increase the variation in a process or product. The methods of statistical process control can be used to decide when it is appropriate to make changes based on recent results. Adjustments to a stable process based on the previous result will usually make performance worse, but when special causes are present, adjustments can be useful.

A project-focused engineering company demanded a written report for any project whose estimate was not within 10 percent of the final cost. Explanations were written for eight projects during a one-year period. When a review of these reports was done at the end of the year, only one of the reports was found to contain information that was useful for future projects. The others were just reiterations of the events that transpired during the project. The company changed its focus to study common aspects of all projects and only do special investigations if there are indications that a project was affected by special causes.

Laboratory procedures required that a certain gauge be recalibrated to a standard after each inspection. The laboratory manager conducted a test to study potential tampering.

She found that the gauge variation was reduced by continuing to check the gauge against the standard after each inspection but only recalibrating the gauge when the difference from standard was outside control limits established for the calculated actual standard. She changed the procedure to reflect this new learning.

---

53. Develop Operational Definitions Reduction of variation can begin with a common understanding of concepts commonly used in the transaction of business. The meaning of a concept is ultimately found in how that concept is applied. Simple concepts such as on-time, clean, noisy, and secure, need operational definitions in order to reduce variation in communications and measurement. An operational definition will usually have two parts: (1) a measurement procedure, and (2) criteria for judgment.

An automotive service dealership found that "noise not fixed" was one of the biggest reasons customers brought their cars back complaining that they were not fixed. The company developed a checklist with operational definitions of words like *whine, click, hum, knock, hiss,* and *growl.* The use of these definitions by both customers, service advisors, and technicians helped reduce the number of cars that were returned to be fixed again.

A trucking company and a major chemical producer needed a common definition of "on-time." What is meant by the requirement that the delivery should be on-time? Whose time? By what measure? Where? Will it be considered on-time if it is fifteen minutes early? What about fifteen minutes late? Both the supplier and the customer agreed that the delivery would be considered on-time if it arrived at the receiving dock no more than fifteen minutes earlier or later than scheduled, using the time clock at the dock. All parties were then able to collect consistent data and focus on improvements in timeliness.

A hotel regularly received complaints from guests that their rooms were not clean. The records from the maids showed that all of the rooms that received complaints were marked "clean." A team of the maids was given the assignment of developing an operational definition of a clean room. They developed a one-page checklist that incorporated all of the issues in the guests complaints, as well as some other important issues the maids identified. After implementing the use of this operational definition of a clean room and the check sheet, guest complaints about clean rooms almost disappeared.

---

54. Improve Predictions Plans, forecasts, and budgets are based on predictions. For many situations, predictions are built from the ground up each time a prediction is required, and historical data is not used. The study of variation from past predictions can lead to alternative ways to improve the predictions. There are six basic approaches to develop predictions:

1. Base them on research when results cannot be seen for a long time (for example, school curriculums).
2. Use leading indicators (for example, use housing starts to predict demand for flooring material).
3. Develop time series models to take advantage of autocorrelation in historical data.
4. Make real-time updates of predictions as new information becomes available.
5. Use simple averages of historical data.
6. Anticipate special causes (for example, airlines change cutoffs for loads when a large group books a flight).

A company that distributed heating oil found itself responding to many panic calls from customers whose furnaces had stopped running because they had run out of oil. The company designed a new service that allowed it to deliver oil on a periodic basis without the customer having to call. The frequency was established using predictions developed from historical data on the customer's patterns of use.

A big problem for chemical companies is the management of their rail fleet. They want to always have cars available when a shipment is due, but they also want to minimize the number of cars in the fleet. One company developed a simulation model based on historical data to predict the number of cars required in the fleet in order to meet shipment demands. The model considered variation in customer orders, fleet maintenance issues, and variation in transit. The model was run annually to make decisions on purchasing or releasing cars. It was also run quarterly with updated data to make decisions on short-term leasing of cars. The use of the model allowed the company to control the number of late shipments from their plants.

---

55. Develop Contingency Plans Variation in everyday life often creates problems. Reducing the variation might eventually eliminate the problems, but how do people survive in the meantime? One way is to prepare backup plans, or contingencies, to deal with the unexpected problems. When the variation is due to a special cause that can be identified, then contingency plans can be ready when these special causes of variation occur.

The staff of the doctor's office knew that waiting time to see the doctor was very important to their patients. They continually worked to develop a schedule that would minimize wait time and allow the doctor to see all patients. However, when the doctor was called to the emergency room at the hospital, people usually had to wait a long time. The office developed a contingency plan for times when the doctor was called out to the emergency room. The receptionist would immediately notify all patients in the waiting room and offer to reschedule. She then would call the patients scheduled to come in for the next appointments and offer to reschedule, or she would let them wait at home until she called back. The patients were very appreciative of this plan. They would tell their friends how well they were treated.

Why do people lose their car keys? Whenever it happens, a lengthy explanation of the special circumstances is usually offered. But losing car keys or locking the key in the car can be traumatic. One automotive manufacturer provides a "credit card key" to be carried in the wallet or purse in case you lock yourself out of the car. This card provides a back up and some peace of mind for customers. It also conveys the message that the company has its customers well-being in mind, which is the focus of their marketing strategy.

---

56. Sort Product into Grades Creative ways can be developed to take advantage of naturally occurring variation in products. Ways of sorting the product or service into different grades can be designed to minimize the variation within a grade and maximizing the variation among grades. The different grades can then be marketed to different customer needs.

Food products have natural patterns of variation determined by growing and weather conditions. Since this variation will not go away, the U.S. Department of Agriculture develops grades based on variation in quality-characteristics of a product. The different grades are sold for different end uses. For example, USDA grades of poultry and beef allow consumers to buy the quality of meat they need for baking, frying, or grilling.

A company that manufactures cardboard drums had problems in the appearance (color, grain, texture, and so on) of the drum. This appearance was important to some customers, but did not matter to others. No economical solutions were found to eliminate the appearance problem, which was primarily due to raw material variability. The company established a grading scheme and sorted the drums into grade A (no appearance problems), grade B (standard), and grade C (appearance problems). They charged a premium price for the grade A drum to offset the discount offered for grade C drums. Customers were able to get the quality of drum to meet their needs.

Because of variation in demand and the introduction of new computer models, it is very difficult to predict demand for new products. One computer manufacturer makes some minor adjustments to machines and then sells off excess inventory as "reconditioned." In fact, these machines represent slow-moving inventory. The price is lowered and guarantees are reduced. This allows for the reduction of inventory without compromising the value of the "new" machines of the same type. The customer who is interested in price is satisfied, and the one who wants a "new" machine is happy.

---

57. Desensitize It is impossible to control some types of variation: between students in a class, among the ways customers try to use a product, in the physical condition of patients who enter the hospital. How can the impact on the outcome (education, function and health) be minimized when this variation is present? It can be done by desensitizing or causing a nonreaction to some stimulus. This change concept focuses on desensitizing the effect of variation rather than reducing the incidence of variation. Examples of this concept include desensitizing the customer to variation in a product or service, desensitizing a process to variation of incoming parts, and desensitizing a product to variation from the perspective of different users.

Disney uses flowers, music and Disney characters throughout their theme parks to create an environment that is clean, pleasant, and communicates a "good day" to the theme park customer. On normal days everyone is pleased with the environment. On days in which the lines are long, this environment acts to desensitize the customer to the longer waiting times. They hum "zip-a-dee-doo-dah" and watch their children play with Disney characters as they wait in line.

A chemical company had decided to differentiate its batch products from those of its competitors by minimizing batch-to-batch variation. Over a two-year period, many of the sources of variation had been eliminated. The current biggest contributor to variation was the ambient weather (temperature, humidity, and barometric pressure) while a batch was being produced. Since they could not eliminate this source of variation, they ran a series of experiments to desensitize the chemical process to the variation in weather. Operating conditions were found that minimized the impact of weather changes on the process. These experiments led to an additional 30 percent reduction in the variation of the key quality-characteristics of the product.

---

58. Exploit Variation It sometimes is not obvious how variation can be reduced or eliminated. Rather than just accepting or "dealing with" the variation, ways can be developed to exploit it. This change concept deals with some ways to turn the negative variation into a positive method to differentiate products or services.

A tennis camp has learned to differentiate its services by exploiting variation in the way that people learn. It is well known that people have different preferred learning styles. Some people learn by reading and studying. Some learn by listening, others by watching, and still others by doing. Previously, the camp's solution for dealing with this variation was to offer a variety of teaching styles to all students so that eventually they get to experience their preferred style. A few seasons ago, the approach was changed to exploit this variation and thus differentiate the services of the camp from those of other camps. At the beginning of a visit to the camp, each athlete was given a series of tests designed to identify his or her preferred learning style. The athletes were then organized into groups on the basis of the preferred style. The instruction for each group was then designed to optimize the use of that learning style. This approach has led to delighted customers.

Diversity in the workplace is a major issue in the 1990s. Diversity among people is a form of variation that can be exploited. An organization that produced consumer products found that its products often were not purchased by women and many ethnic groups. The company began to emphasize diversity in their hiring and development of product design engineers. The design of their products received inputs from engineers with a great range of backgrounds. The result was new products that were acceptable in a much broader market.

H. Design Systems to Avoid Mistakes

Mistakes (also called errors or slips) occur when actions do not agree with intentions, even though one is capable of carrying out the task. Often a person has to act quickly in a given situation, or he or she is required to accomplish a number of tasks sequentially or even simultaneously. Making slips is part of being human. People might do such things as

- Forget to enter information or enter it incorrectly

- Leave out a step in a process or do them in the wrong sequence

- Include the wrong merchandise in a shipment

- Try to use something in the wrong way

- Put something together incorrectly

Although these mistakes are the result of human actions, they occur because of the interaction of people with a system. Some systems are more prone to mistakes than others. Mistakes can be reduced by redesigning the system to make their occurrence less likely. This type of system design or redesign is called mistake or error proofing.

The frequency of mistakes is a function of the number of opportunities to make mistakes and the probability of making a mistake given the opportunity. For example, if the same information is entered into a computer on three separate occasions, three times more errors would be expected than if the information were only entered once.

Companies should always be looking for ways to reduce the number of steps in a process or the number of parts in a product. This will reduce the opportunity for mistakes. Mistake proofing is then used to reduce the probability of making an error for a given opportunity. Mistake proofing can be done by using technology (such as by adding equipment to automate repetitive tasks), by using methods to make it more difficult to do something wrong, or by integrating these methods with technology. Methods for mistake proofing are not directed at changing people's behavior, but rather at changing the system to prevent slips. They aim to reduce mistakes from actions that are done almost subconsciously when performing a process or using a product.

One way to mistake proof a system is to make information necessary to perform a task available in the external world and not just in one's memory. This can be done by writing it down or by actually making it inherent in the product or process. This leads to four important change concepts for mistake proofing:

59. Use Reminders
60. Use Differentiation
61. Use Constraints
62. Use Affordances

59. Use Reminders Many mistakes are made by forgetting to do something. Reminders are aids for remembering. They can come in many different forms. A reminder can be a written notice or a phone call, a checklist of things to accomplish, an alarm such as on a clock, a standard form, or the documented steps to follow for a process. Reminders are simple to develop, but they are probably the least effective way to mistake proof. Although they do make information available in the external world, reminders can still be overlooked or ignored. For example, a standard process can be defined, but people may have trouble breaking old habits, or they might chose not to refer to the flow diagram or other documentation.

A number of people were missing or arriving late for their dental appointments. This caused disruption in the dentist's schedule, which had an effect on other patients. The dentist asked the receptionist to call and remind each patient the day before their appointment. This resulted in a reduction in the number of late arrivals and cancellations.

Laboratory experiments had determined that a critical characteristic of a final product was affected by the temperature at a particular stage in the chemical process. If the temperature was above or below a certain level at this stage, the quality of the final product was affected. Because the operators were so busy, they sometimes forgot to check the temperature readout and make the appropriate adjustment. They therefore decided to install an alarm that would signal when the temperature was outside the acceptable region.

A consultant was constantly forgetting documents and other items when she took trips. This happened even though she spent a couple of hours getting things prepared for each trip. She developed a checklist for travel that included all of the types of documents and items she might take on a trip. Using this checklist, she did not have to rethink everything required for each trip. Her time to prepare for a trip was reduced, and she no longer forgot items.

60. Use Differentiation Mistakes can occur when people are dealing with things that look similar. A person may copy a wrong number or grab a wrong part because of similarity or close proximity to other numbers or parts. Mistakes can also occur when actions are similar. A person may end up in the wrong place or use a piece of equipment in the wrong way because the right directions or procedures are similar to others they might have used in a different situation. For example, a person might drive to work on Sunday morning instead of to the bakery. A person's mind will at times associate the required object or action with similar but inappropriate ones. Familiarity that results from experience can actually increase the chance of committing mistakes of association. To reduce mistakes, steps should be taken to break patterns. This can be done by, for example, color coding, sizing, using different symbols, or separating similar things.

An eight-digit number (such as 31469518) was used by an order processing group to identify a specific product. Each two columns represented a specific bit of information that was necessary for inventory and shipping purposes. Mistakes were so frequent in the use of these numbers that 100 percent inspection was used. Even then, not all of the mistakes were found and corrected. The group suggested that a mix of numbers and letters (for example, 31DF95AH) be alternated for each of the two columns. This made it easier for them to distinguish the different columns and reduced the number of mistakes.

A mail order company offered different types of clothing, each in different sizes, styles, and colors. The orders were picked and shipped from one central location. The numbering of an item followed a rational approach: similar items had similar numbers. This resulted in gloves being in one section, socks in another, and so forth. The people who filled the orders often made mistakes by picking the wrong type of gloves or the wrong type of socks from the many different types that were available in each section. Mistakes were greatly reduced when random stock numbers were used and similar types of clothing were no longer in close proximity.

---

61. Use Constraints A constraint restricts the performance of certain actions. A door that blocks passage into an unsafe area is a constraint. Constraints are an important method for mistake proofing because they can limit the actions that result in mistakes. They do not just make information available in the external world, they also make it available within the product or system itself. To be effective, constraints should be visible and easy to understand. Constraints can be built into a process so that accidental stopping or an unwanted action that will result in a mistake can be prevented. Constraints can also be used to make sure that the steps performed in a process or when using a product are accomplished in the correct sequence.

Many customers of a bank were leaving their cards behind after using the automatic teller machine (ATM). At this bank, if a person was making a withdrawal from the ATM, their money would come out first and then their card. The result was that once people had received their money, they often forgot to wait for their card. The bank changed the procedure so that the money would come out only after the card was removed.

Certain types of medication cannot be taken at the same time without harmful side effects. Many pharmacies keep a computerized record of the medication that people are presently taking. If a new medicine that is prescribed should not be taken at the same time as one presently being taken, the computer will signal that the prescription should not be filled.

The operators of a certain machine were experiencing some hand injuries. To reduce the injuries, dual palm buttons were installed to operate the machine. This kept both of the operators hands busy and out of the way of the machine. Hand injuries were reduced by 37 percent during the next year.

---

62. Use Affordances An affordance provides insight, without the need for explanation, into how something should be used. In contrast to a constraint, which limits the actions possible, an affordance provides visual (or other sensory) prompting for the actions that should be performed. Once a person sees the fixtures on a door, he or she should be able to determine whether it opens in, opens out, or slides. There should not be a need to refer to labels or to use a trial-and-error approach. If a process or product can be designed to lead the user to perform the correct actions, fewer mistakes will occur.

An organization had started a recycling program in its cafeteria. The intention was to separate cans, bottles, plastic utensils, and paper plates and cups. Bins were used to collect the items and each one was identified by a sign. At the end of the day, the workers in the cafeteria still had to spend more than an hour separating the items that had been placed in the wrong bin. They decided to put a top on each bin with an opening in the shape of the appropriate item to be recycled. After this change, the workers in the cafeteria spent little or no time separating misplaced items.

When visitors to a hotel entered their room, they were met with a horizontal array of eight switches. The switches turned on and off the lights that were situated in various areas of the room. Guests would get very frustrated trying to figure out which switch affected which lights. To make it easier to determine which switch turned on which light, the hotel arranged the switches on a diagram of the room. This diagram was visible as soon as the door to the room was opened. Complaints about light switches went to zero.

An amusement park had signs posted throughout that directed visitors to other rides and activities in the park. Many people did not find these signs that were "up in the air with an arrow pointing out in space" very useful. Park employees were constantly being stopped and asked for directions when they were trying to perform their work. The park tried painting directions on the walkways throughout the park. The arrow that the directions were printed on pointed to the path required to get there. During the test, the number of visitors that asked for directions dropped to almost half of that prior to using this affordance.

I. Focus on the Product or Service

Most of the change concepts in the other categories address the way that a process is performed. However, as the examples of applying the ideas show, many of the concepts also apply to improvements to a product or service. This section contains eight other change concepts that are particularly useful for developing changes to a product or service that do not naturally fit into any of the other groupings.

There are eight change concepts in this grouping:

63. Mass Customize
64. Offer Product/Service Anytime
65. Offer Product/Service Anyplace
66. Emphasize Intangibles
67. Influence or Take Advantage of Fashion Trends
68. Reduce the Number of Component Parts
69. Disguise Defects or Problems
70. Differentiate Product Using Quality Dimensions

Since customers define quality in different ways, concept 63 refers to customizing products in a cost-effective way to meet various definitions of quality. Concepts 64 and 65 refer to aspects of convenience. Concept 66 refers to the intangible aspects of a product or service. Concept 67 pertains to a particular type of intangible: fashion. Concept 68 is concerned with simplification of a product by reduction of the number of its component parts. Concept 69 discusses changes associated with mitigation of the effects of defects or problems. The last concept uses the dimensions of quality to develop specific changes that will differentiate a product or service.

63. Mass Customize Most consumers of products and services would agree that quality increases as the product or service is customized to the customer's unique circumstances. Most consumers would also expect to pay more or wait longer for these customized offerings than for a mass-produced version. To mass customize means combining the uniqueness of customized products with the efficiency of mass production.

New technology may contribute to the ability to mass customize-genetically engineered drugs would be an example. Another method of mass customization is differentiation of the product or service at the last moment, perhaps even by the customer himself. Learning to design and use modules is another way to apply this concept. Mass customization can be done after building knowledge to predict the most likely choices of customers or to understand the causes of desired outcomes. For example, knowledge of which fertilizer will work best under different conditions can lead to a product customized for particular customers.

A telephone company has developed more than two hundred options for local telephone service. Rather than offer all of these potential options to any one customer, the company analyzed historical use and then sent each customer a customized letter that offered the services that would actually save that customer money. The letter also offered some new services that analysis indicated might interest the customer.

A publishing company serving the college market found a way to customize textbooks to the course being taught. Rather than have authors write a complete textbook, the company commissioned specific modules. Professors were then given the opportunity to choose from a number of different modules to assemble the text for the course. Besides the increase in quality from customization, this approach reduced the cost and time of publishing subsequent additions.

---

64. Offer the Product or Service Anytime Many products and services are available only at certain times. The movie will be shown at 7:00 P.M. and 9:30 P.M. The Motor Vehicle Bureau is open from 9:00 A.M. to 5:00 P.M. The doctor's office hours are 1:00 P.M. to 5:00 P.M. Monday through Friday. The bank is open from 9:00 A.M. to 3:00 P.M. Your new car will be available in two weeks. These constraints almost always detract from the quality of the product or service. How can these constraints be removed? In some cases a technology breakthrough such as the ATM is needed. In other cases, prediction plays an important role—for example, predicting what type of cars customers will order. However, in many situations the constraint is created because it is more convenient for the provider of the service than for the customer. Would most people prefer the bank to be opened from 9 A.M. to 3 P.M. or from 3 P.M. to 9 P.M.? Offering the product or service anytime is different from just reducing wait time. To achieve this goal often takes a totally new conceptualization of the product or service. For this reason, "anytime" is an important concept for expanding the expectations of customers.

An HMO and a private specialty practice cooperated to design a system that allowed patients who needed to see a specialist virtually as soon as the health problem was recognized. Previously, patients who needed to see the specialist had to wait two-weeks before an appointment with the specialist was available. By analyzing the historical rates of referral from the HMO to the specialty practice, the HMO and the doctor's office were able to predict the number of appointments that were needed each week. The specialty practice reserved an appropriate number of appointments, allowing the HMO's members almost daily access to them.

In cooperation with a bank, a local gas station designed a system so that customers could use their ATM card to buy gas at anytime of day regardless of whether the station was open or not. Customers could pay for the gas using the bank account of their choice. This allowed the station to reduce cost by staying open fewer hours while greatly increasing sales.

A law firm received frequent complaints from its clients that they could not contact their lawyers when they needed them. The law firm realized that access to information anytime, not access to the lawyer, was the issue. A system was designed that included digital pagers, confidential computer bulletin boards, and knowledgeable backups for each attorney, and the quality problem was eliminated.

---

65. Offer the Product or Service Anyplace An important dimension of quality for most products and services is convenience. To make a product or service more convenient, free it from the constraints of space. Make it available anyplace. For products, the constraint of space is often related to the size of the product. Making a product smaller or lighter without adversely affecting any of its other attributes almost always improves the quality of the product. One of the most striking examples is the miniaturization of the computer to the point that it can now be carried in a briefcase and used virtually anyplace.

Miniaturization is often the result of technology breakthroughs. However, technology is not the only means by which to obtain "anyplace" attributes. A product or service that the customer must obtain by coming to the provider's facility can be made available in the customer's space, and thus expand the customer's expectations.

A county education system was interested in offering a diverse curriculum delivered by teachers with special knowledge. The ten high schools in the county were electronically hooked together to allow classes such as Chinese language and highly advanced mathematics to be offered to the thirty or so students in the county high schools who desired them. The students remained in their home schools and participated in the class through the audio and video link.

A company that specialized in the repair of glass such as car windshields and windows wanted to increase its business. The current system required the customer to come to the company. This was the norm in the industry. To change this expectation, several vans were equipped to repair windows and windshields anyplace that the customer needed them. Customers were not even required to be present. They simply had to tell the company what needed to be repaired and where it was located. This resulted not only in more business, but also in higher profits. Customers were willing to pay more for the service, and the increased price more than offset the increased cost of providing the service.

---

66. Emphasize Intangibles The tangible aspects of a product or service are those aspects that can be readily perceived, especially by the sense of touch. Tangible aspects are associated with mass or matter—for example, the shape of the table or the roominess of the interior of the airplane. Although services have matter associated with them, such as equipment, services are usually less tangible than products.

Opportunities for improvement can be found by embellishing the product with intangible aspects. Three ways to accomplish this are by miniaturizing, by providing information (electronically or otherwise), and by developing producer-customer relationships. For mature products, this may be the primary way to change customer expectations. For many years the tangible aspects of computers, such as their size, were the focus of improvements in quality. Today, clones of all types are available at low prices. The intangible aspects of the software that runs on the computers have become more important.

One of the negative experiences, or intangibles, of being in the hospital is the loss of privacy. One cause of this loss is the variety of strangers who come to take temperatures, draw blood, bring food, and move the patient from place to place. One hospital reorganized the services that were provided so that most of the people involved in satisfying the patient's needs were resident on the unit. Teams of nurses and other workers were assigned to specific patients, enabling them to establish a better working relationship with the patients. This resulted in a two-thirds reduction in the number of people who came into the patient's room, and a substantial increase in the satisfaction of the experience of care as measured by interviews.

A local hardware store found itself competing with a new store that was a part of a national chain whose economies of scale allowed it to charge low prices. To keep its customers, the local store focused on the intangible of "advice." First, it developed education programs for its employees that were offered at night and at slow times during work to increase the employees' knowledge level about home repair. They also changed hiring processes to make knowledge of home repair an important criterion. The tangible hardware could be bought at either store, but the intangible advice was available only at the local store. Initial worries that customers would buy their products at the new store but get advice from the local one disappeared during a test of the new service.

---

67. Influence or Take Advantage of Fashion Trends The word "fashion" evokes images of French dress designers presenting their new collections of expensive women's clothes in Paris. However, for many products such as everyday clothes, automobiles, furniture, dishes, and floor coverings, quality is defined as much by aesthetics as by utility. Often the utility of the product is assumed and the aesthetics are what change the expectations of customers.

Trends in public opinion have an aspect of fashion to them and as such are also a source of ideas for new or redesigned products. Health, safety, or security concerns may dominate public discourse. The economic environment will influence whether people prefer luxury or frugality in the products they buy.

A food products manufacturer predicted trends in consumer preferences by keeping up-to-date with the latest in medical research relating to nutrition. For example, the connection between cholesterol and heart disease provided opportunities for redesigning some of the company's products. Before the results of the research were published and made known to the general public, it had to go through a lengthy process of peer review. By keeping up with the research as it was being done, the company was able to design products consistent with the findings and the resulting public opinion.

An automotive manufacturer found that colors and styles that customers wanted in automobiles could be predicted by the popular colors and styles for less-expensive consumer items purchased in the previous year. By keeping track of these fashion trends in other consumer items, the manufacturer was able to offer aesthetics in its cars that were at the leading edge of the trends.

---

68. Reduce the Number of Components Reducing handoffs was one of the change concepts for simplifying a process. Similarly, reducing the number of component parts is a way to simplify a product. Benefits accrue to the manufacturer, to the customer, and to the those who repair or maintain the product. Components in this context can mean component parts, ingredients, or multiple types of the same component.

Reduction in the number of components can be achieved in different ways. One way is through design of the product so that one component performs the functions previously performed by more than one. Another method is to standardize the size, shape, or brand of similar components. A third method is to package components into modules.

A company that sold gas barbecue grills received numerous complaints from customers about how difficult it was to assemble the grills. The company redesigned the product so that it could be shipped in six modules. The company arranged for each component to be produced by one supplier to promote efficiency of assembly. Assembly time for the customer was reduced from hours to about twenty minutes, and complaints dropped 90 percent.

A pharmaceutical manufacturer realized that people were often using more than one of their products at the same time because they had more than one ailment. This necessitated multiple purchases and some "bookkeeping" to take the correct pills at the correct time. In interviews with doctors, pharmacists, and patients, the manufacturer determined some of the most frequent combinations of drugs taken. The company then developed pills that contained the multiple medications. This was particularly helpful for the elderly, who often had trouble keeping track of the multiple medications they needed.

---

69. Disguise Defects and Problems "Buy the darker color; it will hide the dirt." One can easily imagine this bit of advice being provided to a couple with two young children who are purchasing a rug for their living room. The darker color will hide the defect (the dirt), although it will not remove it. The couple could try to remove the defect by not allowing the children in the living room, but this change would cause more problems than it would solve.

The basic idea behind this change concept is that in some instances, especially in the short term, it may be better to hide the defect in a product or service than to remove it. However, the longer-term strategy is to remove the defect. Also included in this category are actions taken to make the defect more palatable to the customer. This change concept does not include false advertising, in which claims about the product are made that are not true. Also excluded are defects that are hidden at the time of sale only to emerge in later use of the product.

A manufacturer of vinyl floor tiles was testing a new flat white pattern. The pattern was very attractive to customers who wanted the look of a ceramic tile floor but at a cheaper price. This was the first time that this type of pattern had been produced. During the manufacturing tests it was discovered that small black specs were evident in some of the tiles. The flat white surface of the tiles made them particularly conspicuous. This was not a problem for the other patterns and colors the company made. Rather than install an expensive air filtration system to the plant, the designers added some small black specs to the pattern that essentially camouflaged the dirt specs.

To compensate for people who do not show up for their flights, an airline frequently booked more passengers for a plane than there were seats available. Every once in a while, more people would show up for the flight than could fit in the plane. The airlines gave the available seats to passengers on a first come, first served basis. Those who were not able to get on the flight were furious. The airline changed its approach and asked for volunteers to take the next available flight to the destination. In addition, the volunteers would get a coupon that could be redeemed for a free flight anywhere in the country at some later date. This virtually eliminated complaints about overbooking and allowed the airline to continue a cost-effective policy of overbooking.

---

70. Differentiate Product Using Quality Dimensions Quality is improved as the match between products and services and the needs they are designed to satisfy is improved. The degree of matching is determined using the definition of quality. Customer research can provide an understanding of how customers define quality and how this definition differs among different groups of customers. The dimensions of quality provide a model to help categorize various measures of quality. The measures of quality for a specific product do not have to contain all of the dimensions. Two completely different products can be considered "high quality" because different dimensions of quality are considered important for the two products. To compete on quality, an organization must determine what dimensions are important to the group of customers (segment of the market) on which the organization is focusing.

A manufacturer of electronic equipment focused its business strategy on service. It was close to the industry average on most of the other dimensions of quality, but it was number one on service. It maintained about a 12 percent market share, and was consistently more profitable than its competitors.

A new restaurant opened up in an already crowded lunchtime market. It differentiated its service by offering high-quality food and fast service. It attracted businesspeople who expected food to be well-prepared and well-presented, but who also did not want to waste time waiting to be served. The restaurant was full within a month, consistently taking about five percent of the market.

An overnight package delivery company learned that "personal interface" was an important dimension of quality to many of its customers as well as to its employees. Many of the company's current procedures emphasized on-time delivery, productivity, and efficiency in drivers' interface with customers. Internal procedures were changed to encourage each driver to spend a half-hour per day strengthening ties with customers. The revenue increases obtained from this change were many times the cost of the drivers' time.

Notes

Introduction

p. xxiii   For more on Deming's system of profound knowledge see Deming, W. E. *The New Economics*. Cambridge: Massachusetts Institute of Technology, Center for Advanced Engineering Study, 1994.

p. xxiv   "One need not be eminent . . ." is from p. 93 of *The New Economics*.

p. xxiv   Deming, W. E. *Out of the Crisis*. Cambridge: Massachusetts Institute of Technology, Center for Advanced Engineering Study, 1986.

p. xxiv   Ishikawa, K. *Guide to Quality Control*. New York: Unipub, 1976.

p. xxiv   Juran, J. M., and Gryna, F. M. (Eds.). *Quality Control Handbook*. New York: McGraw-Hill, 1979.

p. xxv   To read more about people's propensity to make changes to avoid losses rather than to obtain gains see Hogarth, R. *Judgment and Choice* (2nd ed.). New York: Wiley, 1987, Chapter Five.

Chapter One

pp. 3–7   The ideas of a fundamental approach to improvement, the structure of the three questions, and the PDSA cycle were derived mainly from the work of Deming, Shewhart, and Lewis:

Deming, W. E. *The New Economics for Industry, Government, Education*. Cambridge: Massachusetts Institute of Technology, Center for Advanced Engineering Study, 1993.

Lewis, C. I. *Mind and the World Order*. New York: Dover, 1929.

Shewhart, W. A. *Economic Control of Quality of Manufactured Product*. Milwaukee, Minn.: American Society for Quality Control, 1980. (Originally published 1931.)

Shewhart, W. A. *Statistical Method From the Viewpoint of Quality Control* (edited by W. E. Deming). Washington, D.C.: The Graduate School, The Department of Agriculture, 1939.

Chapter Two

pp. 13–24   All of the skills introduced in Chapter Two are explored in more detail later in the book. The references attached to those later chapters will therefore be more thorough. However, two influences on Chapter Two need to be mentioned here: Walter Shewhart, for his ideas on data and variation, and Edward DeBono, for his methods on generating creativity.

DeBono, E. *Six Thinking Hats*. New York: Little, Brown and ICCT, 1986.

Shewhart, W. A. 1980. *Economic Control of Quality of Manufactured Product*. Milwaukee, Minn.: American Society for Quality Control, 1980. (Originally published 1931.)

Shewhart, W. A. 1939. *Statistical Method From the Viewpoint of Quality Control* (edited by W. E. Deming). Washington, D.C.: The Graduate School, The Department of Agriculture, 1939.

Chapter Three

p. 44   The example of improving the teaching of biology is based on the work of LaVonne Betalden at Volunteer State Community College.

Chapter Four

p. 52   The example of a concept design is based on work by the medication systems team at the Children's Hospital in Boston.

p. 59   The example of a cycle to evaluate the participation of suppliers in early concept design is based on the work of a natural business team at Supelco Inc. in Bellefonte, Pennsylvania.

p. 72   Shewhart, W. A. *Economic Control of Manufactured Product*. New York: Van Nostrand, 1931. (Reprinted by the American Society for Quality Control, 1980)

For more information on variation and use of the concept in actual situations in business, industry, and government, see Nolan, T. W., and Provost, L. P. "Understanding Variation." *Quality Progress*, May 1990, pp. 70–78.

Wheeler, D. J., and Chambers, D. S. *Understanding Statistical Process Control*. Knoxville, Tennessee: Statistical Process Controls, 1986. A good technical reference for the development and use of control charts.

Chapter Five

p. 76   Watzlawick, P., Weakland, J., and Fisch, R. *Change*. New York: W. W. Norton, 1974. A key source for concepts of first- and second-order change and the utopia syndrome.

p. 78   Hammer, M., and Champy, J. *Reengineering the Corporation*. New York: HarperCollins, 1993.

p. 82   Henkoff, R. "Smartest and Dumbest Managerial Moves of 1994." *Fortune Magazine,* January 16, 1995, page 94.

p. 84   For further discussion of the concepts of common and special causes, see Nolan, T. W., and Provost, L. P. "Understanding Variation." *Quality Progress,* May 1990, pp. 70–78.

p. 85   de Bono, E. *Serious Creativity.* New York: HarperCollins, 1992. De Bono's ideas on creative thinking are the basis of our approach to innovation and methods of creativity.

p. 89   Deming, W. E. *The New Economics.* Cambridge: Massachusetts Institute of Technology, 1993.

Chapter Six

p. 98–100   For more information on different types of studies see Judd, C. M., Smith, E. R., and Kidder, L. H. *Research Methods in Social Relations* (6th ed.). Troy, Mo.: Holt, Rinehart, & Winston, 1991.

Kerlinger, F. N. *Foundations of Behavioral Research.* New York: Holt, 1964.

p. 100   Example based on work of the Brickman Group, Laurel, Md.

p. 104   For further study of factorial experiments see the following:

Box, G., Hunter, W., and Hunter, J. S. *Statistics for Experimenters.* New York: Wiley, 1978, Chapter 7.

Moen, R. M., Nolan, T. W., and Provost, L. P. *Improving Quality Through Planned Experimentation.* New York: McGraw-Hill, 1991.

Chapter Seven

p. 118–119   The authors would like to thank Donald Berwick, CEO of the Institute for Healthcare Improvement, for his insight on the role of replication versus expansion of implementing change.

p. 122   More information on how individuals react to change can be found in the following two sources:

Myers, D. G. *Social Psychology* (3rd ed.). New York: McGraw-Hill, 1990.

Kreitner, R., and Kinicki, A. *Organizational Behavior* (2nd ed.). Homewood, Ill: Irwin, 1978.

p. 128   The zoo story is taken from Priest, G. "Zoo Story." *Inc.,* October 1994, pp. 27–28.

p. 135, 138   Information on the history of the metric system in the United States can be found in documents published by the National Institute of Standards and Technology, available from the U.S. Government Printing Office in Washington, D.C. The following two sources provide good summaries:

Judson, L. V. *Weights and Measures Standards of the United States: A Brief History.* NBS Special Publication 447. Washington, D.C.: U.S. Department of Commerce, March 1976.

"The United States and the Metric System, A Capsule History" (NIST LC 1136). Washington, D.C.: U.S. Department of Commerce Technology Administration, May 1992.

p. 136   The authors wish to recognize the contribution of Jane Norman for work on Exhibit 7.2.

Chapter Eight

p. 139   Thanks to Bob Cole for his input into the case study, "Improving the Process of Collecting Blood Plasma."

p. 146   The authors would also like to thank Ross Carn, Dave Jones, Steve Knott, Wayne Hunson, and Jim Derby for their review of and help on the reengineering case study.

Chapter Nine

p. 166   Deming, W. E. *The New Economics for Industry, Government, Education.* Cambridge: Massachusetts Institute of Technology, Center for Advanced Engineering Study, 1994. See references to price and cost to use.

A good summary of the strategic issues in pricing is contained in Dolan, R. J. "How Do You Know When the Price Is Right?" *Harvard Business Review,* Sept.–Oct. 1995, pp. 174–183; and Marn, M. V., and Rosiello, R. L. "Managing Price, Gaining Profit." *Harvard Business Review,* Sept.–Oct. 1992, pp. 84–94.

p. 167   The chain reaction from improving value is adapted from Figure 1 in Deming, W. E. *Out of the Crisis.* Cambridge: Massachusetts Institute of Technology, Center for Advanced Engineering Study, 1986.

p. 168   The chain reaction for a government organization was suggested to us by A. Keith Smith.

p. 170   The three categories of improvement were adapted both from discussions with Noriaki Kano and from Kano, N. *Quality in the Year 2000: Downsize Through Reengineering and Up Size Through Attractive Quality Creation.* Paper presented at American Society for Quality Control Conference, Las Vegas, Nevada, May 24, 1994. p. 000   The importance of discussing the different ways that people are affected by improvement activities in each of the three categories was pointed out to us by A. Keith Smith.

p. 172   Klein, J. L. "The Human Costs of Manufacturing Reform." *Harvard Business Review,* Mar.–Apr. 1989, pp. 174–183.

Chapter Ten

p. 179   Deming, W. E. *Out of the Crisis.* Cambridge: Massachusetts Institute of Technology, Center for Advanced Engineering Study, 1986.

p. 182   The example of a complaint system is based on a system developed at Supelco Inc. in Bellefonte, Pennsylvania.

p. 185   Technical Assistance Research Programs Institute (TARP) for the United States Office of Consumer Affairs. *Consumer Complaint Handling in America: An Update Study.* Arlington, VA.: TARP, 1986. TARP can be reached at (703) 524–1456. This study is an update of the original study conducted in 1979.

p. 191–193 Norman, D. A. *The Psychology of Everyday Things.* New York: HarperCollins, 1988.

Chapter Eleven

p. 217   For further study of bottlenecks and constraints, see Goldratt, E. M., and Cox, J. *The Goal.* Croton-on-Hudson, N.Y.: North River Press, 1984.

p. 221   Productivity is defined throughout business, industry and government as output divided by input. More on this topic can be obtained from the American Quality and Productivity Center in Houston, Texas. Charles T. Horngren gives a cost-accounting view of efficiency in *Cost Accounting: A Managerial Emphasis* (5th ed.). Englewood Cliffs, N.J.: Prentice-Hall, 1980.

Chapter Twelve

p. 223   Kano refers to improvements in Category 3 as "attractive quality creation." The three categories of improvement were adapted from discussions with Noriaki Kano and from Kano, N. *Quality in the Year 2000: Downsize Through Reengineering and Up Size Through Attractive Quality Creation.* Paper presented at the American Society for Quality Control conference, Las Vegas, Nevada, May 24, 1994.

p. 227   Feigenbaum, A. V. *Total Quality Control: Engineering and Management.* New York: McGraw-Hill, 1961. Feigenbaum discussed the different characteristics that form the composite concept of quality. The original list of dimensions of quality was proposed by David Garvin in an article entitled "Competing on the Eight Dimensions of Quality." *Harvard Business Review,* November 1987, pp. 101–109. The list of fifteen dimensions is based on the work of Garvin and others.

p. 231   Magnet, M. "Let's Go for Growth." *Fortune,* Mar. 7, 1994, pp. 60–72.

p. 232   Gouillart, F., and Sturdivant, F. "Spend a Day in the Life of Your Customer." *Harvard Business Review,* Sept.–Oct., 1995, pp. 174–183.

p. 237   Urban, G. L., and Von Hippel, E. "Lead User Analyses for the Development of New Industrial Products." *Management Science,* 1988, 34(5), pp. 00–00.

p. 238   Lawton, W. H., "Design, Marketing, and Quality Management: Parts of a Whole." *Chemical and Process Industries Division News.* Milwaukee, Minn.: American Society for Quality Control, Spring 1992.

Urban, G. L., and Hauser, J. R. *Design and Marketing of New Products.* New York: Prentice-Hall, 1980.

p. 239   Kano, N. "Attractive Quality Creation." Paper presented at Convergence Conference, Dearborn, Michigan, October 17, 1994.

Center for Quality Management. "A Special Issue on Kano's Methods for Understanding Customer-Defined Quality." *The Center for Quality Management Journal,* 1993, 2(4).

Kano, N. "Quality in the Year 2000: Downsizing Through Reengineering and Upsizing Through Attractive Quality Creation." Paper presented at American Society for Quality Control conference, Las Vegas, Nevada, May 24, 1994.

Shiba, S., Graham, A., and Walden, D. *A New American TQM: Four Practical Revolutions in Management.* Portland, Oreg.: Productivity Press, 1993.

p. 240   Rick Rush was instrumental in providing test opportunities to develop this example of the Kano survey methodology.

p. 242   Martin, J. "Ignore Your Customer." *Fortune,* May 1, 1995, pp. 121–126.

p. 242–243 For more on change concepts such as offering the product "any time" or "any place" see Davis, S. M. *Future Perfect.* Reading, Mass.: Addison-Wesley, 1987.

p. 245–246 Methods for creativity can be found in books by Edward de Bono, including *The Six Thinking Hats* (Boston: Little, Brown, 1985) and *Serious Creativity* New York: HarperCollins, 1992.

Chapter Thirteen

p. 256   Deming, W. E. *The New Economics.* Cambridge: Massachusetts Institute of Technology, 1993. For more on attributes of a leader. pp. 116–120.

p. 256   Deming, W. E. *Out of the Crisis.* Cambridge: Massachusetts Institute of Technology, Center for Advanced Engineering Study, 1986. For more on creating an environment conducive to improvement, see Chapter Two.

p. 256   Deming, W. E. *The New Economics.* Cambridge: Massachusetts Institute of Technology, 1993. A discussion of the leader's use of the three sources of power is found on p. 129.

p. 260–291 The information in the section "Building a System of Improvement" is taken from material developed over the past eight years by Associates in Process Improvement (API). The book *Quality as a Business Strategy* (Austin, Texas: API, in press) describes the philosophy and methods for making improvement the focus of an organization's business strategy. The elements of the strategy evolved from Deming's "Production as System," first presented by him in 1950. In the API system, five activities are to be led by the top management of the organization to provide the structure to begin working on making quality a business strategy. These activities center around the purpose of the organization, viewing the organization as a system, obtaining information to improve, planning, and managing improvement. The five activities formed a system for the leaders of an organization to focus their learning, planning, and actions.

The authors' experience with quality as a business strategy has been that it accelerates the pace at which organizations improve, and it reduces the chance that improvement will be a short-lived experience. The structure of the strategy, centered around the five activities, provides enough guidance to begin the process of building improvement into the fabric of the organization.

p. 265   Figure 13.2 is a modification of Deming's "Production Viewed as a System," from Deming, W. E. *Out of the Crisis.* Cambridge: Massachusetts Institute of Technology, Center for Advanced Engineering Study, 1986, p. 4.

p. 270   Handscombe, R. S., and Norman, P. A. *Strategic Leadership: The Missing Links.* London: McGraw-Hill, 1989.

Appendix: A Resource Guide to Change Concepts

p. 293   The information in this resource guide came from hundreds of sources collected by the authors over the last twenty years. Many of the examples come directly from experiences with clients we have helped with improvement efforts during the last fifteen years. Many came from newspaper and magazine articles. Some of the examples are stories related to us by friends and colleagues. Many of the change concepts have been presented individually in books on quality, marketing, industrial engineering, and social psychology. The importance of concepts became clear to us from studying Edward de Bono's work. The following are some references that have been useful in our research on change concepts.

Davis, S. M. *Future Perfect.* Reading, Mass: Addison-Wesley, 1987.

de Bono, E. *Serious Creativity.* New York: HarperCollins, 1992.

de Bono, E. *Sur/Petition.* New York: HarperCollins, 1992.

Deming, W. E. *Out of the Crisis.* Cambridge: Massachussetts Institute of Technology, Center for Advanced Engineering Study, 1982.

Hall, R. W. *Attaining Manufacturing Excellence.* Irwin, Ill.: Dow Jones, 1987.

Hammer, M., and Champy, J. *Reengineering the Corporation.* New York: HarperCollins, 1993.

Imai, M. *Kaizen: The Keys to Japan's Competitive Success.* New York: Random House, 1986.

Joiner, B. L. *Fourth Generation Management.* New York: McGraw-Hill, 1994.

Juran, J. M. (Ed.). *Quality Control Handbook* (3rd Ed.). New York: McGraw-Hill, 1979.

Norman, D. A. *Psychology of Everyday Things.* New York: HarperCollins, 1988.

Schonberger, R. J. *World Class Manufacturing.* New York: Free Press, 1986.

Shingo, *Zero Quality Control: Source Inspection and the Poka-yoka System.* Portland, OR.: Productivity Press, 1986.

Index